ON-LINE SYSTEMS DESIGN AND IMPLEMENTATION (Using COBOL and Command Level CICS)

Charles J. Kacmar

RESTON PUBLISHING COMPANY, INC
Reston, Virginia
A Prentice-Hall Company

Library of Congress Cataloging in Publication Data

Kacmar, Charles J.
  On-line systems design and implementation.

  Bibliography: p.
  Includes index.
  1. On-line data processing. 2. System design.
3. COBOL (Computer program language) 4. CICS/VS (Computer
system)   I. Title
QA76.55.K33 1984   001.64'404   84-4752
ISBN 0-8359-5231-2

Copyright © 1984 by
Reston Publishing Company, Inc
A Prentice-Hall Company
Reston, Virginia 22090

10 9 8 7 6 5 4 3 2 1

PRINTED IN THE UNITED STATES OF AMERICA

CONTENTS

PART II: IMPLEMENTING ON-LINE APPLICATIONS (USING COBOL AND CICS)   127

PREFACE

Welcome to the exciting world of on-line processing! This area of data processing is becoming increasingly important as the need for timely information and user friendly systems continues to grow.

The approach to this topic here is somewhat different from earlier approaches, which have been based on the belief that a technical background is necessary for an understanding of on-line development. Most authors therefore place design topics *after* the more technical aspects of on-line processing. Several years of experience with on-line systems development in both universities and industry have taught me that a number of factors are critical to the successful development of an on-line project. These include: understanding the role of on-line systems within a user environment: interfacing on-line systems with existing systems; understanding how on-line systems work and what they provide; integrating the on-line system into the user's business flow; and finding solutions that are maintainable and performance conscious. As a result, the first half of this text is devoted to a detailed study of on-line processing that includes design, user interfacing, performance considerations, and sample applications and their implementation (down to the pseudocode level). The final solutions are presented in several ways to give the reader an idea of the many possible approaches that might be available to solve an on-line processing problem.

The second half of the text is devoted to the more technical aspects of on-line development, particularly to implementing the application by means of the COBOL programming language and IBM's on-line software monitor, CICS. Here, you'll learn about the various components of the CICS system and how to use these components in on-line development. Many examples are provided to enhance your understanding of these concepts.

Therefore, the goals of this text are twofold: first, to help you understand various on-line design strategies by giving you an opportunity to work through a complete system design; second, to help you develop an appreciation and understanding of on-line system implementation using the CICS software monitor. This unique combination of topics, which brings together at least three or four vendor-offered classes in this area, and the personal experiences offered throughout the text provide one of the most thorough discussions of on-line processing available. The thought questions at the end of each chapter warrant serious consideration as they reflect on key issues that are common stumbling blocks in the on-line development process.

At this point I want to thank all of my students and business contacts for their patience and the experiences that they have provided me with in this area by allowing me to try out my ideas on them over the course of several years. I also want to thank you for your interest in this text. I hope that you will achieve the same level of success that my students have had when implementing their systems in class projects or for the companies that they have worked for, or now work for. Good luck, and enjoy your study of this exciting area.

Charles J. Kacmar

I

OVERVIEW OF ON-LINE
SYSTEMS: DESIGN, USE,
AND PACKAGING

1

THE ON-LINE CONCEPT

On-line processing has been defined in many ways, but in this text it means quite simply the ability to access information immediately. I'm sure that many of you "heavyweights" might object to such a simplistic summarization. But let's face it, on-line processing is simply the need to access information as soon as possible, or *right now!*

Let's suppose, for example, that you were going shopping and you wanted to know which store offered the lowest price on an item. If all the stores and you were connected in an on-line system (assuming you have a terminal in your home), you could enter your request and obtain the reply immediately. Further, if the store was out of stock at that time, you could place an order with the store and save an unnecessary trip. Now, consider a situation involving a political election. If every home were able to enter candidate choices during an election, the results could be derived in a matter of seconds with a large-scale computer system. A computer system might also be used to control a machine in a production environment that is able to analyze parts and identify defects in those parts, or to monitor a home security system. Upon detecting an intruder, the latter system could call the police, turn on the lights, photograph the intruder, and so on.

Although each of the situations above could be regarded as immediate processing, there is a difference between them. The last two systems, those that detect defects or protect homes, employ the computer to control other machines. In the first examples presented, people interact with a computer. This distinction between people-to-computer and computer-to-machine systems distinguishes on-line systems from real-time systems, which constitute the two primary types of interactive computer systems.

In this chapter, we look at on-line processing and introduce some basic terminology that will be used throughout the book. Real-time processing will be saved for other authors and other texts.

ON-LINE SYSTEMS

The term *on-line,* like many other terms used in data processing, may have a number of meanings. In this text, on-line refers to a system that provides immediate access to data, while controlling that access from various system management perspectives. But what does this really mean? Well, in order to understand on-line processing, let's compare it with perhaps a more familiar concept—batch—and see how the two differ.

BATCH VERSUS ON-LINE SYSTEM PROCESSING

Batch processing means that the data used can be gathered in many ways. They can be typed onto data cards, placed onto a tape by using a key-to-tape machine, entered on a floppy disk, or fed directly into the computer (by means of an on-line system) to be stored in a file for later batch system processing. The programs designed to process the data are then fed into the computer and associated with the data to be processed (using control languages such as JCL) so that processing can result.

If processing is to take place, however, the programs designed to process the data must be in a form that the computer can understand. This form is usually called *machine language,* which is the result of transforming a PL/1, COBOL, or other higher level language during a *compilation* process. If the programs are already defined to the system in a load module form (stored in a load module library), then the programs can simply be initiated by the operating system to process the data supplied. On the other hand, if the programs are not in executable form, then they might need to be compiled prior to execution. In either case, the end result is processing of the data. Following execution, the results of the program processing can be printed, if the system printers are not in use at that time. If they are in use, then another scheduling operation must be performed so that the output from the processing phase can be printed as soon as possible.

In each step of the processing cycle—data collection, scheduling for execution, execution, print scheduling, and printing—the time from submission until you have your output in hand may vary from a few seconds to a few days, depending on computer load. As already pointed out, it may also be necessary to compile that program before it can be executed, although in most batch production environments, the batch programs are already compiled and reside in a system library in an executable form so that ordinarily compilation is not required. In any case, each of these processing phases takes time, and with the nature of batch job scheduling, you may or may not get your output from the computer fast enough.

THE NEED FOR AN ON-LINE SYSTEM

In an on-line processing environment, processing occurs somewhat differently. Any request for information will be answered by the system immediately. In other words, if you wanted to know how a company's stock is doing right now, you wouldn't use a batch system to give you this information. Further, if you were going to use that information in a stock-purchase decision, then you would turn to an on-line system for this answer because a batch system might not provide the answers soon enough. Therefore, in an on-line environment, programs *must* be in a load module form (since compilation is not productive) to provide the fastest possible response to the terminal user. Also, since each initiation of an on-line program involves just one set of related data records, program control functions and processing can be streamlined to provide the fastest possible path through the code to try to maximize performance.

Don't be misled, however, into thinking that scheduling does not occur in an on-line environment; on the contrary, on-line program scheduling does occur, but, since the volume of data handled by each program is much smaller and the number of functions performed by the program is fewer, processing generally takes less time. Hence, although input and output are sent to and from user terminals, the actual amount of processing between request and response activities is generally smaller, and thus the user tends to think that on-line systems run faster. This ability to respond to requests quickly is what makes the on-line system so promising for the future (although it is in use right now!).

In environments that have both batch and on-line systems, batch processing is usually done outside of normal business hours so that prime time (on-line) users can be given adequate turnaround time. Since most users and management do not work outside of prime time, management and users must understand that batch systems necessitate delays in their processing requests. Users who are supported by on-line systems achieve their results during prime time only because they are supported by on-line system processing.

Although users and management may be equally satisfied with the tools that they have to support their business activities, some of them may be using batch systems and others may be using on-line systems. In this environment the group using on-line systems may have a somewhat higher status than the batch system users because they have access to the computer during prime time. As a result, the batch group may begin to develop on-line needs to achieve the same level of stature that the other group has. Although some of these needs *may not* necessitate immediate response, a delay of twelve or twenty-four hours isn't satisfactory either. It is easy to see why a batch group might even go to the lengths of developing an on-line system that duplicates the current batch system. Another solution to the problem of prime time usage might be to handle a limited number of priority batch requests during prime time to minimize the batch turnaround delay as much as possible.

To be simplistic again, we can say that the primary difference between on-line and batch systems is in the length of time that users can get a response to their requests. If the user *must* have results in a matter of seconds and overnight turnarounds won't do, an on-line system is needed. Note, however, that the use of a system as a status symbol should not be a factor in deciding whether to use on-line or batch processing.

CHARACTERISTICS OF ON-LINE SYSTEMS

On-line processing is designed to answer questions and provide services over very short units of time. Processes normally completed over intervals of a minute or an hour are done in seconds with an on-line system. This is not to imply that on-line programs run faster than batch programs: rather, these programs are substantially different in design and function. Suppose, for example, that an apartment owner wants a list of all outstanding problems that have been reported by tenants, the names of those who are to correct them, and the scheduled times for the work. With this information, the apartment owner can review staff assignments and, it is hoped, reduce the interval between the time a tenant reports a problem and the time that the problem is corrected, while keeping staff to a minimum. If the data were in a machine-readable form, this information could be provided in a few minutes or hours. How important is it for this apartment owner to have this information in the next few seconds? A few hours would probably be soon enough—unless an irate tenant is on the phone wanting to know when the problem is going to be taken care of. A quick response by the apartment owner may mean the difference between a happy and an unhappy tenant.

DATA-TRANSACTION-PROGRAM RELATIONSHIPS

Obviously, two different situations are described in the preceding paragraph. They differ not in the information reported, but rather, in the *time* in which the information is needed. This distinction should help you see the difference between batch system processing and on-line system processing. You should also have noticed that the amount of data is different in the two situations above. In the first case, many problem summaries may be reported, whereas in the irate tenant situation only one (we hope) problem has to be reviewed. These distinctions—timeliness of response, quantity of data being processed, and functions performed by the program—are three of the primary differences between batch system and on-line system processing.

Yet another distinction lies in the relationship between the transaction data and the program. In a batch environment, data must be collected before a batch of data can be fed into the computer for processing. When an on-line system is initiated, on the other hand, the *user* is the one who initiates the system and instructs it how to process a request at that time. During batch system processing, the program reads or acquires a data record and the program determines what processing is to be done on that set of data. Understanding the relationship between data, program initiation, and control is a key factor in recognizing the difference between on-line and batch program design and implementation.

By now you should be able to understand the basic differences between on-line and batch systems. As you progress through this text, you'll encounter many more terms that are associated with on-line processing. Keep in mind that a software package or a set of programs is not the only factor that determines whether an application is on-line, batch, real-time, distributed, or whatever; rather, the *design* and *usage* of that *application* determine whether people are using a system in an on-line mode or whether they are abusing the on-line environment with batch system processing. The next chapter turns to the processes involved in developing on-line software and raises several issues related to the various activities that take place during the development life cycle.

THOUGHT QUESTIONS

1. *What does the term* on-line *mean to you?*
2. *How do on-line and batch systems differ? What are some criteria for determining whether or not a new application should be on-line or batch oriented?*
3. *Describe three other applications that warrant on-line processing. Explain why they do so.*
4. *Describe an application that does not require on-line processing.*
5. *What techniques can be used to evaluate batch system performance? Can these same techniques or criteria be applied to on-line processing systems?*

2
STEPS IN ON-LINE
APPLICATION DESIGN

In the development of on-line applications, the user, analyst, designer, and programmer must carefully design the system in order to ensure a complete, cost-effective and high-performance system. In this chapter we touch on some basic components of on-line systems design. We also establish some standards for on-line application performance to get you thinking about standards and performance *early* in the on-line design process.

In the design of on-line systems, several steps are particularly important: user work-flow analysis, documentation, screen layout design, program-to-program relationship and design, file design, user-application dialogue and performance. You're probably saying that you follow these steps in batch designing as well as on-line designing. You're right! But, in the development of an on-line process, these activities take on a slightly different meaning and emphasis than they do in batch system design. In fact, many may not even be considered steps in the design process. Here, however, we want to give them the attention that they merit during on-line applications design.

Probably the most important design components to the user are work-flow analysis, user-application dialogue, and system documentation. Here, the data processing group and user group work together to describe the flow of data and user activities in their working environment. This procedure helps the user understand his duties and arrive at ideas and designs for automating his tasks. For example, if a user must continually refer to documentation for a system that has too many options or too many coded fields, then possibly the developer failed to communicate with the user during the design processes. Further, if the screen displays and event sequencing within a transaction are such that the system doesn't flow smoothly, then lack of communication may again be at fault. If a component of the user's routine procedure has been omitted, then possibly the user's work activities and habits have not been analyzed properly or the dialogue between the user and other parts of the system has been omitted because of an oversight on the part of the user or the development staff. The blame may not lie entirely with the data processing staff either. Many users still operate in the "tell me what I want" mode rather than communicating their needs to the developers and thus helping them to arrive at a smooth and workable system.

Designing a user-application dialogue is a difficult task, especially if there are several users for a system. Each user may have his own ideas as to how the system should flow and what it should do. Nonetheless, designers should try to reach an acceptable compromise, one that satisfies the needs of all users and yet can be implemented by the data processing staff. Incidentally, that is an important point—the designer must be aware of implementation restrictions during design so that a proposed system does not become bogged down during implementation as a result of an oversight or lack of knowledge about system capabilities.

Effective on-line application development depends on communication between the user and the designers, the designers and the programmers, and so on. Studying and analyzing the user's activities and the data employed by the user are a critical step in the design process. Cooperation between all user groups is imperative if a workable systems solution is to be achieved. Get the users involved! Encourage them to assist in the design cycle and begin working together *early* to ensure a smooth working relationship in your design process.

TAILORING A SYSTEM TO A USER

When a user-application dialogue is being formulated, it may be beneficial to watch the user's interactions, gestures, and behavioral patterns. A user who appears disorganized or who jumps from topic to topic may have no problem with a system designed in pieces, each of which forms a discrete unit. On the other hand, a user who is well organized and moves from topic to topic with ease may require a comparable design in the system. In other words, a system designer may want to be aware of these tendencies in the user so that the system can be tailored to that user. On the other hand, a system designed in this way may *not* be flexible enough for all the users who may *eventually* use the system *after* implementation.

During the development of this diaglogue flow, documentation can become a very important tool. Rough screen layouts and projected system activities or system models help the user gain a better understanding of the system. You may also want to consider terminal operating procedures and an operation's guides during this phase of your development. Finally, hands-on training sessions with the user can help that first-time user become acquainted with a computer system or lend confidence to a veteran user as to the abilities of the data processing staff.

CONVERSATION FLOW DIAGRAMS

One of the most effective forms of documentation during the design phase is what I call a conversation flow or on-line tutorial. Here, a user is given a picture of a screen, a description of the processing that occurs with that screen, and the resultant screen display or response from the system. For example, in our irate tenant situation, we might explain the inquiry component of the system by using a conversation-flow design tool like this one:

INQUIRY FUNCTION:

On the next screen, you'll see the system menu. On that menu you'll see a select option that allows you to request information about a reported problem. Select that item and press the enter key to continue.

You can easily tell if you have made a mistake and selected the wrong item by looking at the second line of the display screen, where you should see INQUIRY FUNCTION. If you don't, then you know that you have selected the wrong item. If you don't see INQUIRY FUNCTION and the system menu is still displayed, look at the bottom of the screen for another message describing some other type of error that may have been made.

```
┌─────────────────────────────────────────────────────────┐
│           LANDLORD MANAGEMENT ON-LINE SYSTEM             │
│                      SYSTEM MENU                         │
│                                                          │
│  SELECT THE NUMBER THAT CORRESPONDS TO THE FUNCTION      │
│  THAT YOU WOULD LIKE TO PERFORM. ENTER YOUR SELECTION    │
│  HERE ------?                                            │
│                                                          │
│      1. INQUIRE ABOUT PROBLEM INFORMATION                │
│      2. REPORT A NEW PROBLEM FROM A TENANT               │
│      3. UPDATE INFORMATION ABOUT A REPORTED PROBLEM      │
│      4. DELETE INFORMATION ABOUT A PROBLEM THAT HAS      │
│         BEEN FIXED AND IS OVER SIX MONTHS OLD            │
│                                                          │
│                                                          │
│                                                          │
│                                                          │
│                                                          │
│                                                          │
│                                                          │
│                                                          │
│  PRESS CLEAR TO EXIT THE SYSTEM                          │
└─────────────────────────────────────────────────────────┘
```

In the menu screen above note the question mark after the dashed line. In this example and the ones that follow, the question mark indicates where the user is to enter data or his response to a question or topic. Underscoring may be used as well, or the user may prefer not to mark the point of input at all. The desired position of input fields and their definition on the screen also have to be established during the on-line development process.

After you press the *enter* key, you should see the screen that follows. Again, if you don't, look at the message at the bottom of the system menu, which should tell you what error you have made. Make sure that you entered only a number and that the number was the proper selection for an inquiry function.

The next screen is what you'll see if you selected the proper item on the menu to perform an inquiry function. This screen has an area in which to enter the problem number associated with this report from a tenant. If the tenant doesn't know the problem number, then you'll have to use the printed copy of all outstanding reports in order to find information on the problem in question.

Once you find the problem number, simply enter the number in the area shown and press the *enter* key.

If the problem number that you enter is not on file, a message will appear at the bottom of the screen informing you of this situation. If the problem is on file, then the information about that problem will be displayed for you immediately.

LANDLORD MANAGEMENT ON-LINE SYSTEM
INQUIRY FUNCTION

ENTER THE PROBLEM NUMBER FOR THE PROBLEM YOU WOULD
LIKE INFORMATION ON. ENTER THE NUMBER IN THE AREA
BELOW.

---- ???? ----

AFTER ENTERING THE PROBLEM NUMBER, PRESS ENTER TO
CONTINUE PROCESSING THIS REQUEST.

PRESS CLEAR TO EXIT THE SYSTEM

   In the screen above the user is entering the problem number given to him by
the tenant. In reality, this may not be an appropriate design for this system
because it's a little unreasonable to expect the tenant to remember a four-digit
number concerning a reported problem. If the tenant forgets the number, some
other method of recovering the problem number must be available, such as
looking it up on a printout. Obviously, it would be more helpful to store the
problem under the tenant's name or the tenant's apartment number. This would
be more meaningful to the terminal operator and would relate the problem to the
tenant reporting the problem. Although this may not be the best design, let's
simply assume that the landlord wanted the system to operate this way. Since the
landlord was paying the bill for development, he can have it any way he wants.
Recording the problem number as shown, by the tenant's name or apartment
number, is implemented in relatively the same way. Hence, this design will not
affect later discussions of implementation in this text.

At this point you should have entered the number of the problem that you want to view. For example, suppose that the tenant tells you that his problem number is thirteen (13). You can enter the problem number 13 in either of the following ways:

```
---- 13?? ----
---- 0013 ----
```

After entering this number, press the *enter* key. Information about this problem will now be displayed.

When you have viewed the information about the problem that you just inquired about, simply press the *enter* key. You will be returned to the system menu so that you can perform another function if you so desire.

Now, let's suppose that problem number 13 did exist in the system. When you enter the problem number and press *enter,* you will see the following screen.

```
    LANDLORD MANAGEMENT ON-LINE SYSTEM
              INQUIRY DISPLAY

PROBLEM REQUESTED ----- 0013
DATE REPORTED ----------- 01/24/77
REPORTED BY -------------- BILL SMITH
APARTMENT NUMBER ------ 101
URGENCY OF PROBLEM ----- NOT URGENT
TIME REQUIRED TO FIX ------ 3 HOURS

PROBLEM CATEGORY ------- PLUMBING

DESCRIPTION: ---- THE BATHROOM FAUCET DRIPS AND
             ---- SEEMS TO NEED NEW WASHERS
             ----

SCHEDULED TO BE FIXED ON ---- 01/28/77
SCHEDULED TO BE FIXED BY ---- RALPH




MSG: PRESS ENTER TO RETURN TO MENU,
     CLEAR TO EXIT THE SYSTEM
```

When the inquiry display screen is shown, you will have all of the information about the problem that you requested.

Remember, you cannot change any of the information on this screen because you are in inquiry mode and not update mode. If an update is required on some of the information for this problem, press the *enter* key and return to the system menu. Then, select the update function. Continue with the update function as described in this manual under the section entitled "UPDATING PROBLEM RECORDS."

After viewing the problem, press the *enter* key to return to the system menu, or press the *clear* key to terminate your processing needs.

Notice the English language format in this documentation form. It clearly tells the user what is happening and what processing the system is going to do for each screen in this component of the application. In addition, this format can be used to train beginners, or it can be used as a reference should an error occur while the system is in operation. In general, any form of documentation that suits the needs of the user and the data processing staff can be considered effective if it does the job now, and still does it in the future when that system is ready for enhancement or modification.

FUNCTIONALITY VERSUS MODULARITY— TRADE-OFF DECISIONS

Many designers emphasize functionality and modularity. To a great degree, a modular system does service itself in the long run, but a system that is too modular can also be detrimental to an on-line system, much more so than to a batch system. For example, suppose that a modular system performs many program calls in order to accomplish some given function, and that as module size decreases, program calling increases. If your system is designed in this way, you may be wasting a substantial amount of computer time linking from program to program. In fact, some modular systems are so modular that more than 50 percent of the computer time used by an on-line transaction can amount to system overhead caused by program calls. Hence, an on-line system designer must be especially aware of these traps in on-line application processing.

A modular system may actually be more inefficient than a monolithic system, but as machine speed continues to increase, this factor becomes less important to a systems developer. Hence, easier maintenance and easier and faster problem resolution become more important considerations in the design cycle than performance. This trade-off between functionality and performance creates problems for those who design, those who implement, and those who use on-line systems.

PERFORMANCE STANDARDS

One way of solving these problems is to establish standards for good system design and performance. Clearly, such standards are hard to define and even harder to enforce, but without them, you can expect many disagreements within your on-line development groups. If you are considering establishing acceptable performance standards or even if you've tried to do so already, here are some steps that you should consider:

- Divide large systems by functional boundaries to minimize program size and limit program functions.
- Limit program-to-program and program-to-system calls.
- Establish acceptable response time requirements during design, and meet those standards after the system has been implemented.
- Limit I/Os for each transaction or system component.
- Minimize the number of resources that must be shared by several concurrent users, especially if those resources can only be used by one user at a time.
- Before design and implementation are completed, try to measure the impact of adding your application to the current system configuration.
- Set a total CPU time limit on a transaction.
- Try to avoid transactions that hold on to resources when the transaction is not performing useful work.
- Enforce the standards that are set down.

Clearly, the last guideline is the hardest to follow because if you are six months behind schedule and $50,000 over your budget, but the system is completed, most people will not want to see it again, let alone rewrite parts of it, if it doesn't meet performance standards. Instead, they'll go out and spend $300,000 to upgrade their CPU or other hardware because transactions implemented at the same time without regard for standards affect response time to such an extent that additional hardware may be necessary. Sometimes I wonder whether common sense is ever used in data processing.

ON-LINE SYSTEM PACKAGING

Measuring the impact of a new transaction on an environment is a difficult task. Modeling packages assist greatly in this endeavor, but so do existing systems. If current system statistics accurately reflect application activities, the impact of a new system can be "guess-timated" by comparing the system with existing systems. Obviously, the closer the old and new systems, the more accurate are your predictions concerning resource requirements. In general, however, any reasonable estimate of system impact is better than no estimate at all. Installing a new system without any idea of its impact on existing processing can lead to serious problems.

Finally, it may be a great idea to modify a batch system to run on-line or to mimic a batch system that is performing well in the hope that it will run as well on-line. I'm not sure where your systems stand in this regard, but, remember, on-line program design *is* different from batch design in terms of the amount of data being processed and in the functionality of the user requests. Timeliness of data and response times are your goals, whereas a converted batch system is probably not designed with those goals in mind. In any case, program design is a critical factor that is largely determined by the overall design of the system. A system that is designed well all the way down through the program level will no doubt perform well and stand up over time.

File design is yet another crucial area in the design of an on-line system. In many installations, a single file may be shared by several users within a computer system. If that file was held in exclusive control by one user for some time, transaction response for all transactions also needing access to that file would be greatly affected. Hence, in the design of files for an on-line system, several "common sense" considerations require attention:

- Type of access
- Current file size
- Anticipated growth
- Amount of activity

- Number of concurrent users
- Type of access to the file
- Type of file access method used
- Frequency of reorganization
- File-type limitations imposed on the designer by the on-line software monitor
- Coordination of file use with batch systems

You're probably already familiar with each of these points and you've no doubt made file management decisions before. Many of you may also have had to consider data base processing at this point in your systems design, and, as you may have discovered, many of the same considerations apply to both. The last two points, file limitations and batch coordination, may need a little more explanation.

Some on-line software packages may restrict the types of file organizations that you can use. If this is the case, then the designers must be made aware of such limitations so they won't design a system that requires a file organization not supported by your on-line software package. Further, some software packages "own" all files used under them, and concurrent access to those files by a batch system is not permitted even if the access is for read-only processing. Hence, if a design calls for concurrent batch and on-line processing, the designers may be in for a great surprise when in the testing phase they realize it can't be done. If you get to this point and you are the designer, you have several options: quit, redesign the system, or (and this is what is most commonly done) report it as a bug in the software package or a bug in the operating system.

In general, taking file design lightly during the development of an on-line system may prove to be disastrous later in the development process or after implementation. A design staff that does not understand the capabilities of an on-line system may also ruin the application being developed, not to mention already existing applications.

BUILDING FRIENDLINESS INTO A SYSTEM

The last point to consider under on-line system design is how to design and lay out a user display screen. This point is particularly important to a user, who is the one most exposed to the screen.

Many people become confused when it comes to the question of how to design screens; yet, they may have volume after volume of standards for designing batch reports and file formats. If this situation applies to you, then you probably don't realize that an on-line screen display is simply a report that is printed at a terminal instead of on a piece of paper. Good screen design consists of simple techniques and is governed mainly by common sense. Some general guidelines follow.

First, the user should be involved in the on-line screen design process, even to the point of being allowed to design the screen layout completely, under your supervision. Let the user select field color, highlighting, intensity, positioning, and so on, but *you* must maintain screens according to company standards. You must also remember to be consistent and make sure that the user's design is acceptable to the user and to the company. Each screen should have a system title and a screen name (or id number). This referent is valuable if an error occurs in the system and the user must call you about the problem.

Allow for messages to be displayed on the screen. Some screen generator packages may perform this function for you automatically, but if they do not, choose a message format and location consistent with other on-line applications at your installation and consistent with the screen design standards at your site.

Arrange data in a meaningful manner, placing important data at the top of the screen and grouping related data items together. If the user is entering data at the terminal from a printed form, arrange the material on the screen to correspond with the printed form. These details help improve screen readability and user concentration.

Don't cram data onto a screen when two or three screens might be used to better advantage. On the other hand, too many screens can interfere with user concentration. When determining the number of screens to use in a dialogue, a designer must be aware of implementation details. The reason is that in some on-line systems it may not be easy to enter data, store them temporarily, enter more data, add to the stored data, then enter still more data in order to collect one set of data. In this case, it may be easier to cram the data on a screen. Nonetheless, some trade-off decision must be made. Here we might be sacrificing user understanding because of an implementation constraint, or we might be making the overall performance of the transaction change in some way. In other words, in some situations the designers and the users must agree on what emphasis is to be placed on readability, function, implementation, and performance. These trade-offs must be considered early in the design process if later system alterations are to be kept to a minimum.

Design the flow of all screens in the system to match the flow of work performed by the user. For example, if the user's job requires him to fill out form A before filling out form B, then the on-line system should flow from screen display A to B to correspond with the paper forms A and B. Matching user activities to screen sequencing can have a significant effect on user productivity and the user's interest in the system that you develop.

Another screen design consideration is how to compose a terminal display. In some on-line systems, a logical screen display to the user may consist of one, two, three or more physical displays. That is, if information is to be displayed on a screen composed of, say, 24 lines and 80 columns, it can be displayed in many ways. The program could send 24 lines of output to the terminal (each one sent one at a time) to compose one display, or the program could send one set of lines

(24 lines of data) to the screen to compose one display. In other words, what the user sees at the terminal is what we'll call a logical display. *How* the program constructs this logical display is the physical display. In the first case, the program constructed 24 physical displays to form one logical display. In the second case, the program constructed one physical display to form one logical display. The end result to the user looks the same after all physical messages have been transmitted.

If your screens are constructed from several physical displays, some considerations should be given to the order in which these physical displays are to occur, where they are to be placed, and how they are to be processed by the application. It may be a trivial task to construct a terminal display from several physical displays, but it may be a difficult task to process that display after the transaction is initiated by the user. In general, a simple philosophy of "one logical display is composed of one and only one physical display" may be the easiest way to implement screens and avoid problems during implementation, especially for the beginner. Let me give an example of this situation just to make sure that you understand the difference between logical and physical displays.

Let's use our tenant problem reporting application again and let's look at a menu screen for this application. To the user, the menu may look like this:

```
          LANDLORD MANAGEMENT ON-LINE SYSTEM
                     SYSTEM MENU

 PLEASE SELECT THE MENU OPTION THAT IDENTIFIES WHAT
 YOU WOULD LIKE TO DO ------?

    1. INQUIRE ABOUT A PROBLEM RECORD
    2. REPORT A PROBLEM
    3. UPDATE PROBLEM INFORMATION
    4. DELETE A PROBLEM RECORD




 MSG: xxxxxxxxxxxxxxxxxxxxxxxxxxxxxxxxxxxxxxxxx
```

But to the application program, the menu could actually be defined as three separate screen displays, as follows:

Display 1

LANDLORD MANAGEMENT ON-LINE SYSTEM

Display 2

```
                         SYSTEM MENU




PLEASE SELECT THE MENU OPTION THAT IDENTIFIES WHAT
YOU WOULD LIKE TO DO ------?

    1. INQUIRE ABOUT A PROBLEM RECORD
    2. REPORT A PROBLEM
    3. UPDATE PROBLEM INFORMATION
    4. DELETE A PROBLEM RECORD
```

Display 3

MSG: xxxxxxxxxxxxxxxxxxxxxxxxxxxxxxxxxxxxxxxxxx

If this approach is taken, then some of its advantages and disadvantages should be pointed out.

ADVANTAGES: The system title needs to be "coded" only once, and since it probably appears on all screen displays in this system, one-time coding eliminates duplicate coding.

The subtitle and body are unique to the processing being performed and hence the screen can be considered functionally built.

A common message area can be used in the application and needs to be coded only once, making the message area consistent within the system, as was the case with the system title.

DISADVANTAGES: It may be hard to implement such a composition.

Three terminal I/Os are required for each screen display; thus the amount of line traffic and system interaction could be increased. This may also increase response time.

Depending on how the terminal I/O requests are handled at the terminal, the user may actually see three different displays arrive at the terminal in a very short time period. This may be confusing to the user and may not be user friendly.

As you see, there *is* some difference in the format of screens and in the way they can be displayed at the terminal. The screen design and construction process is a primary consideration in the construction of the user/application dialogue.

Now that we've seen how screens can be built, let's say that each screen display is one and only one logical–physical composition. This makes screen processing easier to understand and reduces the implementation requirements for the on-line software package that we use for on-line implementation later in this text. One last point to note is that when the term *map* appears in this text, it refers both to physical display and—since we've adopted a 1-to-1 policy—to logical display. This term is commonly used by others to refer to screen displays. Remember, though, throughout this text a map means a logical entity *as well as* a physical entity. Since the term may be used differently in other discussions about on-line screen construction, make sure you know how it is being used. In fact, you should seek clarification of any terms that you are unsure of.

APPROACHES TO MENU SCREEN DESIGN

To further enhance your understanding of screen displays, let's look at a few menu screen layouts and discuss the differences between each screen design.

Design 1

> ### LANDLORD MANAGEMENT ON-LINE SYSTEM
> ### SYSTEM MENU
>
> CHOOSE ONE OF THE NUMBERED OPTIONS BELOW AND ENTER
> YOUR SELECTION HERE ------?
>
>   1. INQUIRE ABOUT A REPORTED PROBLEM
>   2. REPORT A NEW PROBLEM
>   3. UPDATE PROBLEM INFORMATION
>   4. DELETE AN OLD PROBLEM THAT HAS BEEN FIXED
>
>
>
>
>
>
>
>
> PRESS CLEAR TO EXIT THE SYSTEM

On the screen above, the user has only one field in which to enter data. From an applications programming or editing point of view, several possible edits can be done on this field. First, the field can be edited for the presence of any data. That is, if the user doesn't make a selection, then this may constitute an error and a message might have to be displayed to request that the user make a selection on the menu. For example, this screen may show the following message:

```
LANDLORD MANAGEMENT ON-LINE SYSTEM
              SYSTEM MENU

CHOOSE ONE OF THE NUMBERED OPTIONS BELOW AND ENTER
YOUR SELECTION HERE ------?

    1. INQUIRE ABOUT A REPORTED PROBLEM
    2. REPORT A NEW PROBLEM
    3. UPDATE PROBLEM INFORMATION
    4. DELETE AN OLD PROBLEM THAT HAS BEEN FIXED




            PRESS CLEAR TO EXIT THE SYSTEM




ERROR: PLEASE CHOOSE 1, 2, 3, OR 4 FROM THE LIST ABOVE
```

Incidentally, the placement, wording, and characteristics of each error message should be carefully planned during the design process. The standards in some shops may dictate where messages should be placed and how they should appear at the user's terminal. The point is that there should be no question in anyone's mind as to what the system has done and what is to be done by the user when a message is sent out to the terminal.

The next edit that can be done is to determine whether or not the user entered a number and, if so, whether the number is a valid choice on the menu display. For example, the user can select only items 1, 2, 3, or 4 on the menu screen. Any other selection (0,A,B,5,8, . . .) will be considered an invalid selection and, of course, an appropriate error message should be displayed in this case.

Design 2

Another possible menu might be the following screen:

```
        LANDLORD MANAGEMENT ON-LINE SYSTEM
                   SYSTEM MENU

PLACE AN X BESIDE THE OPTION THAT YOU WOULD LIKE TO
PERFORM.

   ? INQUIRE ABOUT A REPORTED PROBLEM
   ? REPORT A NEW PROBLEM
   ? UPDATE PROBLEM INFORMATION
   ? DELETE AN OLD PROBLEM THAT HAS BEEN FIXED




    PRESS CLEAR TO EXIT THE SYSTEM
```

In the screen above, you'll notice the user can enter data in several fields. Further, the instructions state that the letter X is to be placed alongside the option that the user wishes to select. This screen serves the same function as the previous screen, but, from an implementation point of view, more editing is required on this screen than on the previous screen. The fields would have to be edited for presence of data, of course, just as in the previous screen. In addition, however, the fields would have to be edited to ensure that no more than one selection was made by the user, who could in fact select more than one option (this was not possible on the previous menu). Next, the field selected would have to be edited to ensure that an X was used to select the menu item. If this last edit was eliminated and any character could select a menu item, the directions and processing would be inconsistent; such inconsistency could confuse a new user.

Finally, consider what would happen if the user entered a selection in the following way:

LANDLORD MANAGEMENT ON-LINE SYSTEM
SYSTEM MENU

PLACE AN **X** BESIDE THE OPTION THAT YOU WOULD LIKE TO PERFORM.

Ø INQUIRE ABOUT A REPORT PROBLEM
X REPORT A NEW PROBLEM
Y UPDATE PROBLEM INFORMATION
? DELETE AN OLD PROBLEM THAT HAS BEEN FIXED

PRESS CLEAR TO EXIT THE SYSTEM

According to the directions, only one X has been placed on the screen, even though other selections have been made. Such decisions about selection design may have to be made by both the user and developers so that no confusion arises during user interaction with the system.

At this point you may have decided not to use this type of menu selection design, although in another situation this format might be appropriate, especially if a light pen could be used to select the item. In other words, when considering a screen layout, you should examine several options and carefully analyze them in terms of user opinions, processing requirements, and resources available. To throw out a screen design because it didn't work in a previous system dialogue design may be a mistake.

Design 3

Yet another menu design might require the use of program-function keys, as follows:

```
LANDLORD MANAGEMENT ON-LINE SYSTEM
           SYSTEM MENU

PRESS THE PF KEY AS INDICATED ALONGSIDE THE OPTIONS
LISTED BELOW.

  PFK-1 INQUIRE ABOUT A REPORTED PROBLEM
  PFK-2 REPORT A NEW PROBLEM
  PFK-3 UPDATE PROBLEM INFORMATION
  PFK-4 DELETE AN OLD PROBLEM THAT HAS BEEN FIXED




PRESS CLEAR TO EXIT THE SYSTEM
```

In this menu design, no screen fields have to be edited, unless you consider a PF key to be a field. If your on-line software package considers a PF key a field, then this type of screen design becomes the same as that shown under Design 1. If your on-line monitor considers the PF key a process-initiator, then your application program must be able to handle the situation when the user presses a key that is not PF1, PF2, PF3, or PF4 to initiate the application. Logically, the field-initiation editing is almost the same as it is for Design 2. In other words, did the user press PF1, PF2, PF3, or PF4 in the selection process? Design 3 offers a feature that no other design can match—namely, minimal keystrokes to initiate the application. Clearly, if the user makes the correct choice, this PF-key-driven design requires the fewest number of keystrokes of the designs presented here.

Note, however, that this design requires a special type of terminal for implementation. If your terminal is not equipped with PF keys, such a design cannot be used.

Design 4

This menu design is similar to Design 1, except that from a user's point of view, there may be less chance of selecting the wrong item. Let's see what you think.

```
 _____
/                                                                \
|             LANDLORD MANAGEMENT ON-LINE SYSTEM                  |
|                       SYSTEM MENU                              |
|                                                                |
|   ENTER THE KEYWORD THAT DESCRIBES THE OPTION THAT YOU         |
|   WOULD LIKE TO PERFORM ------???                             |
|                                                                |
|                                                                |
|                                                                |
|     KEYWORD              OPTION TO BE PERFORMED                 |
|   _____         _____            |
|       INQ          INQUIRE ABOUT A REPORTED PROBLEM           |
|       RPT          REPORT A NEW PROBLEM                        |
|       UPD          UPDATE PROBLEM INFORMATION                  |
|       DEL          DELETE A FIXED PROBLEM RECORD               |
|                                                                |
|                                                                |
|                                                                |
|                                                                |
|   PRESS CLEAR TO EXIT THE SYSTEM                              |
_____/
```

Here, the user must type in a "word" to indicate what he would like to do. Although the editing is similar to the editing proposed on screen Design 1, with Design 4 the user might be less apt to request a function that he didn't want. For example, in Design 1, it would be easy for a user to make the mistake of striking a 2 or a 3 instead of a 1 for the selection wanted. Here, however, the keywords require more unique keystrokes and thus help to decrease the chances of selecting an unwanted function. Still another advantage to this screen is that the keywords are descriptive in that they are an abbreviation of the word denoting the function being performed. In Design 1, the numbers 1, 2, and 3 have no bearing on the functions to be performed.

Design 5

Although Design 4 requires more keystrokes than do other designs, it may be less susceptible to user error. On the other hand, the 1, 2, 3, and 4 selection codes, if slightly modified, might be the best design for this particular application:

```
        LANDLORD MANAGEMENT ON-LINE SYSTEM
                   SYSTEM MENU

   CHOOSE ONE OF THE LETTERS BELOW THAT IS ASSOCIATED
   WITH THE OPTION THAT YOU WOULD LIKE TO PERFORM
                      ------?


      I---INQUIRE ABOUT A REPORTED PROBLEM
      R---REPORT A NEW PROBLEM
      U---UPDATE PROBLEM INFORMATION
      D---DELETE AN OLD PROBLEM THAT HAS BEEN FIXED
```

Here, the letters I, R, D, and U relate directly to the functions of *I*nquiry, *R*eport, *D*elete, and *U*pdate.

As you can see, even in a simple screen such as a menu, many screen layouts are possible and many factors have to be considered. The point to be made is that when you're involved in screen design, you must carefully consider the many options available to you as long as they are supported on your system. Further, you'll find that many of these screen guidelines or techniques can be applied to report layouts used in batch systems. In any case, in the screen design process you must review each step of the design with the users, the programmers, and the management. If you do not, you may find yourself in trouble when implementation of proposed designs meets with resistance from your staff or from the system.

In this chapter we have briefly discussed several basic aspects of on-line systems design: user work-flow analysis, documentation, user-application interaction, performance, program design, file design, and screen layouts. It is hoped that in developing your on-line system, you will apply some standards and evaluative techniques to enhance the systems you create. In the next chapter we look at an on-line software monitor system and the services it provides. This system is the software tool by which the on-line applications presented in this text are implemented. As you read about the facilities and services provided, try to determine where design and implementation should be considered in on-line application development and the services they relate to in that software package.

THOUGHT QUESTIONS

1. *What are the advantages of designing and implementing a system that has a small number of large programs? What are the advantages of designing and implementing a system that has a large number of small programs and many calls between the components of this system?*

2. *What types of file structures are particularly suited to on-line applications?*

3. *Discuss the role that sequential files could or should play in an on-line environment.*

4. *Consider a system that you have designed in the past and evaluate its modularity versus its performance.*

5. *Contact your systems programming staff or your software vendor and find out how many instructions are required to perform a program link within your on-line system.*

6. *What are the guidelines that your company uses for evaluating application design? What areas are lacking in this structure? How can the current guidelines be improved? Who administers the current guidelines? How well are they followed? If they are not adhered to, why not?*

3

AN ON-LINE
MONITOR—CICS

This chapter may seem out of place in a discussion about application design, and maybe you're justified in thinking so. On the other hand, the design of an on-line system, or for that matter any system, can well depend on how it will be implemented and what constraints that design will be subject to. For this reason, the IBM Customer Information Control System (CICS) software monitor is briefly reviewed here so that you will be aware of its services, capabilities, and behaviors. Since the application presented will be implemented under CICS control, you should have some general understanding of how CICS works and what it will do for you.

On-line processing is a difficult task unless you have some type of support to make your job easier. For example, instead of writing in machine language, you could write in an assembly language, or instead of writing in assembly language you could write in a code such as PL/1, COBOL, PASCAL, and so on. This chapter offers a higher-level introduction to the CICS processing system and gives a brief outline of the advantages of on-line software packages before looking at the IBM software monitor called CICS.

BASIC COMMUNICATIONS STRUCTURE

A typical basic on-line system may look like this:

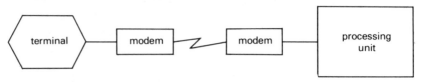

This diagram shows a terminal, a CPU, and some medium over which messages can be sent from the terminal to the CPU and back again. If the terminal above is truly on-line, then the application programs in the computer must be able to communicate with that terminal as well as allow immediate access to data within the system. These tasks cannot be performed unless the programmer writes commands to carry them out. Further, the commands that the programmer must learn are syntactically different and operate differently from the commands necessary to read cards and write print lines. As a result, the programmer may have to learn how to "talk" to a terminal in a new language; that is, the programmer must know how to send data or obtain data from a terminal from within an application program.

Let's look at still another problem that could arise in this processing environment. Suppose that four users need to be on-line at the same time and that each of them requires access to a common file. As one user is updating the file, some protection must be built into each of those systems to prevent simultaneous updates or uncoordinated updates to the file. Similarly, add requests and delete requests must also be coordinated.

You might argue that these problems are actually easy to solve and that in fact reasonable solutions exist. Unless these management tasks are automatically done for you, however, they must be designed into the system during its development. Further, every time an on-line system is developed, a series of modules to communicate with the terminals must be incorporated into your system or a module(s) set will have to be developed to manage file access. Tailoring each of these modules in such a way as to fit into current systems and to allow flexibility for future systems is a difficult task and could take a great deal of work.

If this seems to be a never-ending series of tasks or turns you away from on-line software monitors, just relax. The software packages on the market handle all of these problems for you, and more. Many software packages on the market provide a more comfortable design and implementation environment for application development. Rather than consider every software package of this nature on the market, we're going to concentrate on just one: CICS. With a package such as CICS, the two problems just described disappear—or, I should say, the first one does. Although the second problem, file access, is also solved by the CICS file management components, if proper design is not exercised in the development of a system, file availability can still be a problem across application boundaries when it comes to performance.

CICS OPERATION AND COMPONENTS

The CICS processing system operates in the same way that any other set of programs in the computer might, but possibly gives better service to on-line users over batch users. CICS contains all the components necessary to communicate with terminals, control file access, execute application programs, manage storage, and so on. Each of these services is handled by a separate component or series of components within CICS called "control programs." That is, CICS is much like an operating system with its memory management component, job scheduler, access method components, and so on.

There are many control programs within CICS, but we concentrate on just a few—those necessary for basic on-line application implementation and those that the applications programmer needs to use most. For more information about the workings of CICS and its other management components, the reader should consult the IBM manuals *IBM CICS/VS System Application Design Guide* and *IBM CICS/VS Application Programmer's Reference: Command Level,* available through your local IBM representative.

As we look at the basic elements of CICS, we see that this system five *primary* components, each of which plays a key role in the execution of applications:

TASK CONTROL:	Controls the execution of applications within the CICS operating environment
PROGRAM CONTROL:	Fetches programs from libraries and monitor their use by applications.
STORAGE CONTROL:	Controls CICS storage areas for use by applications and by other components of the CICS system.
FILE CONTROL:	Monitors file usage by applications for the various access methods supported.
TERMINAL CONTROL:	Provides support for communications between the application and the terminal.

Each of these components is designed to service your application. In other words, the amount of work required to implement an application is greatly reduced owing to the services provided by these components. Further, these components free the designers and programmers from having to attend to intricate technical details about processing, because they can now be taken for granted. For example, suppose that our irate tenant is on the phone and we want to find out the status of his problem. For the sake of simplicity, let's assume that a special identification number is assigned to each problem reported, and that the tenant always refers to a problem by this special number.

Let's also assume that the problem id number is 1234 and that it was given to us by the tenant. If the problem exists in the file with that number, all we have to do is display the information about that problem on the user's terminal in the staff office and, we hope, we'll obtain the correct information that satisfies or pleases the tenant. If we assume that this was done and the problem information was displayed, we can say that the on-line system performed an inquiry operation. The question is, what allowed this to occur and how was CICS involved in satisfying this request? Let's reiterate the processing and describe the services that CICS provides as well as its contribution to application execution.

Note that we are primarily interested in knowing *how* CICS services the application and not in explaining the application itself. Hence, we refer mainly to the components of CICS and mention little about the application logic or coding within the application used to carry out the inquiry request.

Suppose that the tenant is on the phone and has just given us the problem id number of 1234. We turn to our terminal and type in a four-character code called a *transaction identification* (let's say the transaction id is INQR). The four-character code will inform CICS management components which application program is to be run for this terminal operator's request. We can also assume that a table inside CICS memory contains the following data:

four-character code	program to run
ABCD	PAYROLL
CALC	CALCULTR
INQR	FINDPROB
TEXT	TEXTMGMT
TXT2	TEXTMGMT

This table contains several transaction ids (tranids) and the programs to be executed by CICS when these transaction ids are received by CICS from a terminal. In the case of our tranid INQR, CICS will execute the program FINDPROB to perform our inquiry function. You'll also notice that the program TEXTMGMT can be invoked through two different transaction ids. This step may become necessary in a situation where one program can service two groups of users, each of which can perform only a certain set of functions. Although the same program will be initiated, it can be designed to determine which transaction id initiated the program and process accordingly. (This type of functional grouping and the possibility of using the same program from many different transaction ids will be discussed in a later chapter.)

CICS CONTROL AREAS AND TABLES

Now, let's assume that the user types in a four-digit problem id number immediately after the transaction id on the terminal screen. Hence, the data on the terminal screen would look like this:

INQR1234

When the *enter* key is pressed, the TERMINAL CONTROL component of CICS will be invoked to retrieve the data from the terminal and present it to the application program FINDPROB. To do this, TERMINAL CONTROL will request storage from STORAGE CONTROL so that the data from the terminal can be stored in a "buffer" and made available to the application. When storage is obtained, the data on the terminal are "read" from the screen and placed into this terminal buffer by TERMINAL CONTROL; this terminal buffer area is called a Terminal Input/Output Area (TIOA). In other words, the TIOA holds information coming in from a terminal and destined for an application, or holds data going from an application on the way to a terminal. All of these TIOA areas are processed by the CICS management component called TERMINAL CONTROL.

TERMINAL CONTROL now notifies TASK CONTROL that there is work to be done at this terminal, and TASK CONTROL uses the first four characters from the terminal screen, I-N-Q-R, to determine what program is to be executed. It does so by looking up the tranid in a table (similar to the one you've already seen) called the PROGRAM CONTROL TABLE (PCT). If the tranid is found in the PCT, TASK CONTROL sets up processing control blocks for this application so as to control the execution of the application. It does so by retrieving other information from the PCT and other CICS tables to build the necessary control blocks. (The PCT will be discussed in more detail in later chapters.)

TRANSACTION VERSUS TASK— TERMINOLOGY

Once that control block is initialized, TASK CONTROL recognizes the request for work at our terminal, and at this point our transaction becomes a measurable unit of work within CICS, normally called a *task*. This unit is the means by which CICS will "recognize" the work at *our* terminal from now until the program fulfills our request and our information is displayed at the terminal.

TASK CONTROL now calls on PROGRAM CONTROL to start executing the program called FINDPROB. To do this, PROGRAM CONTROL looks in a table called the PROCESSING PROGRAM TABLE (PPT) to find the memory address of the FINDPROB program, or to find the library address (TTR) of the program out on disk. Without going into the PPT here, let's simply see how a PPT might be organized:

program name	memory address	disk address
PAYROLL	000000	0AC
CALCULTR	0D10C0	014
FINDPROB	000000	0B6
TEXTMGMT	000000	000

In the table above, you'll notice that the program TEXTMGMT is not in memory, nor is it in the library. Hence, when the transaction id TEXT is entered at the terminal, an error will occur because no program is available for the TEXT transaction id. Notice, too, that program FINDPROB is in the library but is not in memory. For this reason, PROGRAM CONTROL must call upon a subcomponent of itself to load the FINDPROB program into memory. To do so, it must call STORAGE CONTROL to obtain storage in which our program can be placed. Let's assume that storage has been obtained and that our program has been loaded into memory. Now, the PPT is updated to show the current memory address of the program so that if the program is referenced in the future, loading the program from disk will not be necessary.

APPLICATION EXECUTION

At this point the program can be executed. To do this, PROGRAM CONTROL simply branches to the address of the loaded program and execution begins. In other words, our application program behaves as if it were a subroutine to the CICS system, which can thus simply call upon our subroutine to handle a request at a user's terminal.

Program execution now begins and continues until the program terminates, abends, or voluntarily gives up control. CICS will not interrupt an executing program in the same manner that an operating system would to time-slice among other users in the system. As a result, if a program should even go into a loop, it could place the entire CICS system in a loop indefinitely.

Now that our program is being executed, its first task is to obtain the data from the terminal and determine what problem is to be inquired about. To obtain data from the terminal, the application program FINDPROB issues a RECEIVE command requesting that TERMINAL CONTROL make the terminal data available to the application by providing addressability to the TIOA. TERMINAL CONTROL does so, allowing the application to get the problem number 1234 from the TIOA. After obtaining this problem number, a simple edit is done, and the data (problem number) is found to be valid. The application then builds a record key to access the problem file associated with the application. Once the key is constructed, the program issues a file request to read the associated record from the problem file. This file request is handled by FILE CONTROL. At this point, the program is suspended to wait for I/O completion.

FILE CONTROL searches a table called the FILE CONTROL TABLE (FCT) for the name of the file (ddname) that we want to read. (We pass this to FILE CONTROL as a parameter along with the key of the record that we want to access.) If our file name is found in the FCT, then FILE CONTROL carries out our request by obtaining storage from STORAGE CONTROL in which to place the record. Once this storage area—let's call it a file work area (FWA)—is created, FILE CONTROL is given the address of the record buffer area. FILE CONTROL then passes the request on to the operating system access methods. FILE CONTROL also notifies TASK CONTROL that this task is waiting for a file completion so that in the meantime other on-line applications can be executed. (FCT is discussed in a later chapter along with file-processing commands.)

Through event sequencing and notification, TASK CONTROL notes that the file request has been processed and returns control to FILE CONTROL to verify that the proper record has been retrieved. If the proper record has been retrieved, FILE CONTROL returns to the application program and processing continues. The application moves the data from the record buffer area into a fresh TIOA (by requesting one from STORAGE CONTROL) so that the requested information can be displayed at the terminal free of any system or application-dependent information. Incidentally, if the input TIOA is large enough, the application program could choose to reuse the input TIOA rather than obtain a fresh TIOA from STORAGE CONTROL. Such a saving could help improve transaction performance when a substantial amount of terminal I/O is present within application processing.

The application then issues a terminal request to SEND the data to the terminal. At this point the TERMINAL CONTROL component is called upon to send the information to the terminal by the operating system terminal access methods. After the transfer of data, program control returns to the application, which notes that the data were sent to the terminal as requested and terminates execution. The inquiry task at our terminal is now completed.

Although the application has finished execution at this point, CICS has not. All control areas associated with this task, as well as the TIOA areas and file areas used in accessing the record from the problem file, are returned to STORAGE CONTROL. Following this clean-up operation, CICS removes any trace of our task from the system by removing the execution control blocks for our task from within the TASK CONTROL task chains. Now we have finished execution and the user has the data displayed at the terminal.

As you can see, the various components of CICS *service* the application. That is to say, many functions normally designed, controlled, and programmed by the applications programmer or analyst are already a part of the CICS system and hence there is no need to program those services. As a result, this book looks upon CICS as a tool that simplifies the job of an on-line applications programmer or analyst. Because of these advantages provided by CICS, on-line application problems can be solved at the design level, where they should be handled, and not at the implementation level.

Our discussion of CICS will not go much further than this because we want to treat CICS as a service tool and not have to worry about its intricate details. I hope that you're not disappointed with this approach, but if you are, let me refer you again to the CICS manuals mentioned earlier. These and other CICS manuals can provide the necessary details to fill the void that we are leaving here.

Let's briefly review our discussion of CICS.

To the operating system, CICS is a standard program but possibly has higher priority. CICS has five primary components: TASK CONTROL, which manages the initiation and control of applications (tasks) running within the CICS environment; PROGRAM CONTROL, which manages program usage and program location for application execution; STORAGE CONTROL, which services not only the application but also other CICS management components in providing buffers and other storage areas for execution; FILE CONTROL, which provides an interface between the application and the CICS environment and the operating system access methods to control the accessing and availability of files to CICS applications; and TERMINAL CONTROL, which provides terminal communications between the application and the user. Each of these components provides services to the applications programmer that simplify the job of programming.

Various tables within CICS assist in the management of CICS resources and application resources during CICS application execution. The primary tables of concern to data processing staff are the PROGRAM CONTROL TABLE (PCT), PROCESSING PROGRAM TABLE (PPT), and the FILE CONTROL TABLE (FCT).

A transaction identification (tranid) is required to initiate execution in a CICS environment. Further, this transaction id (defined in the PCT) is related to one application program (defined in the PCT and PPT) which can then call other application programs (defined in the PPT) to perform one or more functions.

Each unit of work within CICS requires the presence of a task. A task exists within a transaction and is unique to a given terminal. This unit, the task, is what CICS uses to maintain control and provide management to each terminal using your transaction. Further, each terminal operator using your transaction is kept separate from all others using your transaction since each has a unique task in the CICS environment. (The relationship between transaction and task is discussed in later chapters.)

If an application is to run under CICS control, it must adhere to CICS programming rules to ensure that proper communication is maintained between CICS and the application program, and that a given application does not jeopardize the integrity of any other applications running within that CICS environment.

MAINTAINING CICS TABLES

Many CICS control tables must be preloaded with entries to define the application and resources needed by that application. Generally, these tables are maintained by a systems programming group or on-line administration staff within a company. The application programmers convey their requests to these staff members to have necessary entries defined and available for usage. If your shop does not have a special group to assist you in defining your table entries, you should consult the *CICS/VS Systems Programmer's Reference Manual* for CICS version 1.5, and the *CICS/VS Resource Definition Guide* for CICS 1.6.

On-line processing must be coordinated with other on-line users as well as batch users so that conflicts between file sharing and file access can be kept to a minimum.

Some of the points we have just discussed are design related and others are implementation related. You must carefully weight the merits of each of these at the appropriate time during on-line application development, whether you are using CICS or some other software monitoring system. Remember, too, that we have only discussed five of the many components of CICS. Briefly, some of the other components of CICS that you're likely to use are:

TRACE   Maintains and records information about task execution
CONTROL: and chronological event occurrences during the life of a

CICS system. This component is useful in debugging and in gathering statistics about task and transaction processing.

JOURNAL
CONTROL:

Records images on journal files in the event that a system failure should occur. Allows file recovery and backsout a file if such a failure does occur for an application or the entire system

TEMPORARY
STORAGE
CONTROL:

Provides a "scratch pad" for applications or an area to pass information between one or more applications.

Before we go on to the next chapter, we should take a moment to clear up a few things about the running of CICS. Since CICS is organized as a series of components, each of these components is, of course, composed of one or more programs. Each of these programs must have been compiled and link-edited into a library prior to the actual execution of CICS. Installing or doing a "gen" on CICS is much the same as getting a large batch system ready to process. Hence, each CICS component can be considered a series of programs that have been assembled (compiled) and link-edited into a system library. The main CICS library shown below is called CICS.PROGRAMS. (It may not have the same name in your installation.) The application programs to support on-line users are stored in the library called APPL.PROGRAMS. To execute CICS, you simply provide the following IBM system control language (JCL):

```
//    EXEC PGM=CICS
//STEPLIB  DD  DSN=CICS.PROGRAMS,DISP=SHR
//DFHRPL  DD  DSN=APPL.PROGRAMS,DISP=SHR
```

When the initialization module of CICS is loaded into memory, it simply "bootstraps" the other CICS components into storage and then prepares the system for execution. Ultimate control of CICS execution is handled by TASK CONTROL.

Clearly, this isn't the only JCL needed to run CICS. Each CICS file and application file must be defined as would normally be done in running a batch program. It should be pointed out, however, that this is an oversimplification. In later releases of CICS and IBM's MVS operating system, dynamic file allocation can be used with CICS processing and components of CICS are integrated into the operating system. In any case, let's suppose that additional JCL is needed, as is shown below:

```
//T001    DD  UNIT=301
//T002    DD  UNIT=302
//T003    DD  UNIT=303
//AP001  DD  DSN=APPLICA.TION.FILE.ONE,DISP=SHR
//AP002  DD  DSN=APPLICA.TION.FILE.TWO,DISP=SHR
```

Here we see five application files. What is actually shown above is the allocation of three terminals (T001, T002, and T003) to CICS for on-line processing and two application data files (AP001 and AP002) that hold user data to be used in application processing. The labels T001, T002, T003, AP001, and AP002 are called *file names,* or *ddnames* in the IBM environment. These labels are the primary ties between the outside world and the application's internal processing. Let's assume that this is all of the JCL needed to execute our system.

If a user at terminal T001 enters a transaction, TERMINAL CONTROL is notified that a request is waiting to be processed. This notification takes place via table called the TERMINAL CONTROL TABLE (TCT) that is defined to the CICS system. This table contains entry T001. Characteristics about the unit 301 are specified so that TERMINAL CONTROL will know the type of terminal and hence the format of the data coming in from the terminal. In MVS systems using the Virtual Telecommunications Access Method (VTAM), the applications are even less dependent on the type of device they are communicating with since such device dependent responsibilities are handled by the operating system and the VTAM access method.

If we assume that TERMINAL CONTROL now calls TASK CONTROL to begin transaction execution, the PCT is scanned to validate the transaction id. Once found, the program associated with the transaction id is cross referenced into the PPT. If we continue to assume that no errors in entry search have occurred, PROGRAM CONTROL will now attempt to execute the program. If FINDPROB is *not* in memory, the CICS loader is invoked to load the member FINDPROB from the libraries identified on the DFHRPL JCL statement shown earlier. The data set that contains the member FINDPROB is the library called APPL.PROGRAMS.

At this point the program FINDPROB really becomes a subroutine to CICS and CICS's PROGRAM CONTROL is now responsible for application execution. Many programs (even many CICS modules) are considered to be subroutines to the CICS environment. However, since our application program (FINDPROB) was not an *integral part* of the CICS components, it can be loaded *when needed* rather than being forced into memory as it would be if FINDPROB was "hard" link-edited to the CICS system (as is usually the case with batch systems.) Hence, by using the PPT to locate and reference the FINDPROB program, we can consider this program to be "soft" link-edited to CICS.

If this program did not exist in the application library, CICS could still operate on other applications even though the application supported by FINDPROB could not be run, whereas a reference to a nonexistent program in a batch system usually results in an abend. This type of "soft" attachment to CICS also provides more storage for applications since programs can be loaded when needed and deleted when no terminal users are invoking the transactions supported by those application programs. This ability of CICS to dynamically attach modules to itself when execution is needed and to properly handle situations for which programs cannot be found is a powerful feature of the CICS processing component called PROGRAM CONTROL.

Now let's assume that FINDPROB issues an I/O request to the file AP002. This request is given to FILE CONTROL, which associates FINDPROB's request with the application file defined on the AP002 JCL statement. FILE CONTROL verifies that AP002 is a legitimate file name (by looking in the FCT) and then passes the request on to the operating system access methods. The I/O then takes place as described earlier. However, if other users were accessing the same record for update purposes, FILE CONTROL would queue FINDPROB's request so that unsynchronized updating would not occur. (Other features of FILE CONTROL are discussed in a later chapter.)

The main point to be made here is that CICS runs in the same way that any other program in the system does and in many respects resembles a very large batch program. CICS provides many services to the application program and handles situations that would normally turn out to be a disastrous error for any other batch system. Although you could perform many of the services provided by CICS if you wanted to, rather than spend the time developing your own terminal communications component or file management component for every on-line application, you can simply call upon CICS to provide these services instead.

In the next chapter we begin concentrating on applications, treating CICS almost as if it didn't exist. Further, with the CICS programming approach that is being used in this book, CICS itself is of little concern becauses the sophistication of the CICS package and the services that IBM has designed into this package make on-line programming an easy task. I hope that you, too, will agree with this statement by the time you finish this text. The next few chapters will reinforce this stance by developing an application in its entirety with the intent of implementing that application under a CICS environment. As you progress through these chapters, you too will see that the services needed by an application under the CICS software monitoring system are conceptually simple, easily identified, and easily implemented.

THOUGHT QUESTIONS

1. *What is the difference between a transaction and a task?*
2. *How many terminals can share the same transaction?*
3. *How many terminals can share the same task?*
4. *What other information do you think might be found in the PCT, PPT, and FCT?*

5. *Other than the CICS service components described in this chapter, what services might an application need to support execution in an on-line environment? Hint: what if the program should abend?*

6. *What do you think would happen if a transaction id entered at a terminal were not found in the PCT during initiation of a task?*

7. *What problems in file management could occur if several on-line applications had to share a common set of files? Describe in more detail than was done in this chapter.*

8. *Should on-line files be sharable with batch systems? Why or why not? When would sharing be acceptable? When would such sharing not be acceptable?*

4
A SIMPLE ON-LINE APPLICATION

The remainder of this book concentrates on application programs, first their design and then their implementation. We begin in this chapter with an application that you have already seen in this book. By relating this application to the functions and needs of your processing environment, you too will be able to develop CICS applications in no time at all. Later chapters focus on the implementation and coding necessary for program execution under CICS, but, for now, let's look at a simple CICS application.

Recall the irate tenant on the phone and the need to provide this tenant with information quickly. Let's expand on this application and provide a complete on-line system for a landlord or apartment owner.

In general, computer systems allow the user to: inquire or obtain information about some data; report or add information to a data file; remove or delete information from a file; and change or update information. In the on-line application presented here, the apartment owner or staff will have an on-line system that will allow them to:

- Record problems reported by a tenant that require fixing or work by the staff in the apartment complex.

- Display those reported problems to the user (apartment staff) at a display terminal.

- Delete or remove "old" information from the file.

- Update information about a problem report or indicate the status of a problem.

Further, all of these functions will be done on-line. We could get into a heated discussion about whether or not some of these functions should be in an on-line or a batch mode, or whether such a system will serve the needs of the user. For our purposes, however, let's just assume that there is a need, that the user wants such a system, and that the user is paying for it. The last point alone is enough justification!

What is important here is not so much the application but rather the type of processing that can be supported under CICS. In our application, we are exhibiting file management services performed by a system for a given user. These services include add, change, delete, and inquiry of data records against a single file. This simple application contains the most basic functions commonly desired by users when an on-line system is proposed. Other functions such as graphing, statistical reporting, and multifile structuring are purposely omitted as these are no more than extensions of the basic features. Without further discussion, let's look at the application.

COMPLETE SYSTEM FLOW

The Landlord Management On-line System, as we will call it, consists of four basic functions, all of which will be implemented in an on-line environment. You already know what these four basic functions are, so we need not repeat them here. To use this system, we'll assume that the apartment owner has the proper hardware and software to support our application. With this in mind, recall that every application under CICS must have at least one transaction id associated with it. For our application, let's say that we have one and only one transaction id for our system and that this transaction id is LAMS (Landlord Management System). Since this system has only one transaction id, the apartment owner has to remember only one, simple four-letter "word" to use this system. What could be easier from a user's point of view? Therefore, to initiate this on-line system, the apartment owner would type in the letters L-A-M-S as shown on the screen below.

LAMS

Report Function

When the *enter* key is pressed, the first screen (map) to be displayed will be the system menu. Let's not worry about how the program knew to display this menu; let's just follow the application as the user would see it.

```
LANDLORD MANAGEMENT ON-LINE SYSTEM
              SYSTEM MENU

PLEASE SELECT ONE OF THE OPTIONS BELOW TO BE PER-
FORMED. ENTER ONE OF THE LETTERS (R, I, U, OR D) IN THE
AREA THAT FOLLOWS ------?

  OPTION LETTER                 FUNCTION TO DO

       R                  REPORT A NEW PROBLEM
       I                  INQUIRE ON PROBLEM INFORMATION
       U                  CHANGE PROBLEM INFORMATION
       D                  DELETE A PROBLEM'S DATA
```

```
PRESS CLEAR TO EXIT THE SYSTEM
```

Here, the user is allowed to select the desired function. Suppose that R is entered as the selection in order to report a problem. Upon receiving this request, the system will display a screen that will allow the user to enter the information about a tenant's problem into the system. This display screen might look like the following one:

```
 ┌─────────────────────────────────────────────────────────┐
            LANDLORD MANAGEMENT ON-LINE SYSTEM
                    REPORT A PROBLEM

 PROBLEM NUMBER ----------------------- xxxx
 REPORTED ON (DATE PROBLEM OCCURRED) - xx / xx / xx

 REPORTED BY (TENANT'S NAME) ----------- xxxxxxxxxxxxxxx
 APARTMENT NUMBER HAVING THE
    PROBLEM ----------------------------- xxx

 DESCRIPTION OF THE PROBLEM:
    ---- xxxxxxxxxxxxxxxxxxxxxxxxxxxxxxxxxxxxxxxxxxxxxxx
    ---- xxxxxxxxxxxxxxxxxxxxxxxxxxxxxxxxxxxxxxxxxxxxxxx

 REPAIR INFORMATION: FIXED ON --------- xx / xx / xx
                     FIXED BY --------- xxxxxxxxxxxxxxx
                     TIME REQD. ------- xx (IN HOURS)
                     QUALITY ---------- x  (E,G,A,P,T)




 PRESS ENTER TO RECORD THIS PROBLEM
 └─────────────────────────────────────────────────────────┘
```

Note that this screen has a field called a problem number. This number will be assigned by the system software when the terminal operator chooses the "report-a-problem" function on the system menu. In other words, the application program associated with this system will maintain a control record in the file that keeps track of the next problem number to be used when a problem is to be reported. For this reason, the user need not keep track of used or unused problem numbers; that job is automatically done by the system. Also, since the current date is obtained from the system, the user doesn't have to enter this information either. These convenience features make this on-line system more friendly in that they reduce the amount of data that the user needs to enter to report a problem from a tenant.

After the user enters the necessary information on the screen, the system can carry out the R function by storing the reported information into the landlord management file. Should the user make an error in entering the data, the system would respond with an appropriate message related to the error(s) made. If the data were entered correctly, the user would be informed of this action after the information was stored by the following display message:

```
                  LANDLORD MANAGEMENT ON-LINE SYSTEM
                            REPORT A PROBLEM

   PROBLEM NUMBER ----------------------- xxxx
   REPORTED ON (DATE PROBLEM OCCURRED) - xx / xx / xx

   REPORTED BY (TENANT'S NAME) ----------- xxxxxxxxxxxxxx
   APARTMENT NUMBER HAVING THE
      PROBLEM ---------------------------- xxx

   DESCRIPTION OF THE PROBLEM:
      - - - - xxxxxxxxxxxxxxxxxxxxxxxxxxxxxxxxxxxxxxxxxxxxxxx
      - - - - xxxxxxxxxxxxxxxxxxxxxxxxxxxxxxxxxxxxxxxxxxxxxxx

   REPAIR INFORMATION: FIXED ON --------- xx / xx / xx
                       FIXED BY -------- xxxxxxxxxxxxxx
                       TIME REQD. ------- xx (IN HOURS)
                       QUALITY --------- x  (E,G,A,P,T)




   MSG: PROBLEM RECORDED, PRESS ENTER TO RETURN TO
        SYSTEM MENU
```

Note that the message at the bottom of the screen indicates the status of the request and also tells the user what to do next. Clearly, not all systems need to be designed in this way, but, as we noted earlier, the more attention that you pay to the user-application dialogue, the more usable and friendly your system will be to a user.

Inquiry Function

Now let's suppose that the user selected item I on the system menu in order to look at previously recorded information on a problem. After the I option is selected and the *enter* key pressed, some further information has to be entered into the system before the information about a problem can be displayed at the terminal. That information, of course, is the problem number. Hence, the user must enter the problem number to be inquired about on a screen, as shown below:

```
 _____
/                                                    \
|           LANDLORD MANAGEMENT ON-LINE SYSTEM        |
|               INQUIRE ON PROBLEM DATA               |
|                                                     |
| IN THE AREA SHOWN BELOW, ENTER THE NUMBER OF THE    |
| PROBLEM THAT YOU WANT TO LOOK AT.                   |
|                                                     |
|              ------- ???? -------                   |
|                                                     |
| AFTER YOU HAVE ENTERED THE PROBLEM NUMBER, PRESS    |
| THE ENTER KEY TO HAVE THIS INFORMATION DISPLAYED AT |
| YOUR TERMINAL OR PRESS CLEAR TO EXIT THE SYSTEM.    |
|                                                     |
|                                                     |
|                                                     |
|                                                     |
|                                                     |
|                                                     |
|                                                     |
|                                                     |
|                                                     |
_____/
```

It should be noted that this sequence could have been streamlined by allowing the user to enter the problem number on the system menu so as to avoid having to develop the screen above and the coding necessary to communicate with the user.

After the user enters this number, the system will retrieve the record from the file keyed to this problem number. The format and display at the terminal will be similar to those for the report function, for example:

```
 _____
/                                                                \
|            LANDLORD MANAGEMENT ON-LINE SYSTEM                   |
|                 INQUIRE ON PROBLEM DATA                         |
|                                                                 |
|   PROBLEM NUMBER --------------------------- 0226               |
|   REPORTED ON (DATE PROBLEM OCCURRED) ---- 12/25/82             |
|                                                                 |
|   REPORTED BY (TENANT'S NAME) -------------- JOHN SMITH         |
|   APARTMENT NUMBER HAVING THE PROBLEM -- 432                    |
|                                                                 |
|   DESCRIPTION OF THE PROBLEM:                                   |
|     ---- CHRISTMAS TREE FELL OVER AND CAUSED A SHORT IN         |
|     ---- THE LIGHTS, BURNING OUT AN ELECTRICAL OUTLET           |
|                                                                 |
|   REPAIR INFORMATION: FIXED ON -------- 00/00/00                |
|                       FIXED BY --------                         |
|                       TIME REQD. ------ 01 (IN HOURS)           |
|                       QUALITY ---------     (E,G,A,P,T)         |
|                                                                 |
|                                                                 |
|                                                                 |
|                                                                 |
|   MSG: PRESS ENTER TO RETURN TO SYSTEM MENU                     |
_____/
```

Update Function

Note that some information is missing from the screen just presented. Additional fields at the bottom of the screen are not yet filled in. The reason here is that the repair job has not been assigned to anyone yet and so no staff member's name, date to be fixed, or quality has been supplied for this problem. Since the REPAIR information may not be known at the time the problem is reported, at some later time this problem record must be updated so that a staff member assignment can be entered. This may necessitate the use of a batch reporting system to give the apartment owner a list of all of the problems to be dealt with by the staff during the upcoming week; a batch system may already exist for scheduling problem repairs according to staff qualifications and experience. In any case, the information about when and who is going to handle each problem reported by tenants must be entered into the system. This may be done using the U or update component of the system. Let's recall the system menu:

```
╭─────────────────────────────────────────────────────────╮
│          LANDLORD MANAGEMENT ON-LINE SYSTEM              │
│                     SYSTEM MENU                          │
│  PLEASE SELECT ONE OF THE OPTIONS BELOW TO BE PER-       │
│  FORMED. ENTER ONE OF THE LETTERS (R, I, U, OR D) IN THE │
│  AREA THAT FOLLOWS ------?                               │
│     OPTION LETTER              FUNCTION TO DO            │
│          R            REPORT A NEW PROBLEM               │
│          I            INQUIRE ON PROBLEM INFORMATION     │
│          U            CHANGE PROBLEM INFORMATION         │
│          D            DELETE A PROBLEM'S DATA            │
│                                                         │
│                                                         │
│                                                         │
│                                                         │
│                                                         │
│                                                         │
│                                                         │
│  PRESS CLEAR TO EXIT THE SYSTEM                          │
╰─────────────────────────────────────────────────────────╯
```

By choosing the U or update function, the user is informing the system that there is a problem record for which information must be changed. To do this, the user could enter the problem number on a screen similar to the one used in the inquiry, as shown below:

```
┌─────────────────────────────────────────────────────┐
│                                                       │
│         LANDLORD MANAGEMENT ON-LINE SYSTEM            │
│              UPDATE PROBLEM DATA                       │
│                                                       │
│   IN THE AREA SHOWN BELOW, ENTER THE NUMBER OF THE    │
│   PROBLEM THAT YOU WANT TO UPDATE OR CHANGE.          │
│                                                       │
│               ------- ???? -------                    │
│                                                       │
│   AFTER YOU HAVE ENTERED THE PROBLEM NUMBER, PRESS    │
│   THE ENTER KEY TO HAVE THIS INFORMATION DISPLAYED AT │
│   YOUR TERMINAL OR PRESS CLEAR TO EXIT THE SYSTEM.    │
│                                                       │
│                                                       │
│                                                       │
│                                                       │
│                                                       │
│                                                       │
│                                                       │
└─────────────────────────────────────────────────────┘
```

After the user enters the problem number to be updated and presses the *enter* key, the information about that problem is displayed on the terminal in much the same way as it was done during the inquiry function. However, at this time the user is able to change the information about that problem description by simply typing over the current information displayed. When the *enter* key is pressed, the overtyping is reflected in the permanent record associated with the displayed problem, the record is retrieved from the file, the changes are applied, and the rewritten record with its new data is submitted to the file. This will complete the update process for any of the records to be updated by the user.

An additional item of note is that during the update process the user may not be able to change all of the fields on the display screen. That is, some fields may be protected or may be nonchangable during the update function. Such fields might be the problem number, date of reporting, owner's name, and apartment number. This protection can be easily applied to screen fields from the application program supporting this system. (You'll hear more about this in a later chapter.)

After the record is updated, a response back to the user similar to the screen below might be appropriate to assure the user that the changes were applied as requested:

```
           LANDLORD MANAGEMENT ON-LINE SYSTEM
                  UPDATE PROBLEM DATA

PROBLEM NUMBER ----------------------------- 0226
REPORTED ON (DATE PROBLEM OCCURRED) ---- 12 / 25 / 82

REPORTED BY (TENANT'S NAME) --------------- JOHN SMITH
APARTMENT NUMBER HAVING THE PROBLEM -- 432

DESCRIPTION OF THE PROBLEM:
   ---- CHRISTMAS TREE FELL OVER AND CAUSED A SHORT IN
   ---- THE LIGHTS, BURNING OUT AN ELECTRICAL OUTLET.

REPAIR INFORMATION: FIXED ON ------ 12 / 26 / 82
                    FIXED BY ------ BILL
                    TIME REQD. ---- 01 (IN HOURS)
                    QUALITY ------- E  (E,G,A,P,T)




MSG: RECORD  UPDATED  AS  SHOWN,  PRESS  ENTER  FOR
     SYSTEM MENU
```

Finally, note again that, as in all previous functions, control returns back to the system menu. This may not be desirable for the design of your applications but in this system, it was decided to return to the system menu after the completion of every function.

Delete Function

The last function that the user can select is to delete a record from the system. When the user selects function D on the system menu in order to delete a record from the file, the following (familiar) screen will be displayed:

LANDLORD MANAGEMENT ON-LINE SYSTEM
DELETE A RECORD FROM THE SYSTEM

IN THE AREA SHOWN BELOW, ENTER THE NUMBER OF THE PROBLEM THAT YOU WANT TO DELETE.

------- ???? -------

AFTER YOU HAVE ENTERED THE PROBLEM NUMBER, PRESS THE ENTER KEY TO VERIFY THAT THIS IS THE RECORD THAT YOU REALLY WANT TO DELETE, OR PRESS CLEAR TO ABORT THIS REQUEST.

After the user enters the problem number and presses the *enter* key, the system will retrieve the record from the file and display it, as was done in the inquiry and update functions. The user will thus be able to verify that this is the record that he wants to delete from the system file. Further, the user must verify that this is the correct record by entering "YES" in the field at the bottom of the screen as shown:

```
╭─────────────────────────────────────────────────────────────╮
        LANDLORD MANAGEMENT ON-LINE SYSTEM
              DELETE A PROBLEM RECORD

    PROBLEM NUMBER --------------------------- 0226
    REPORTED ON (DATE PROBLEM OCCURRED) ---- 12/25/82

    REPORTED BY (TENANT'S NAME) -------------- JOHN SMITH
    APARTMENT NUMBER HAVING THE PROBLEM -- 432

    DESCRIPTION OF THE PROBLEM:
      ---- CHRISTMAS TREE FELL OVER AND CAUSED A SHORT IN
      ---- THE LIGHTS, BURNING OUT AN ELECTRICAL OUTLET.

    REPAIR INFORMATION: FIXED ON ------ 12/26/82
                        FIXED BY ------ BILL
                        TIME REQD. ---- 01 (IN HOURS)
                        QUALITY ------- E  (E,G,A,P,T)

       VERIFY -- ???




    MSG: ENTER "YES" TO COMPLETE THE DELETE OF THIS RECORD
╰─────────────────────────────────────────────────────────────╯
```

Note that this verify field did not appear on any of the previous screens because it wasn't needed for any other function except the delete. This verify field is called a "hidden" field because it has been hidden on the screen until now, when it is needed. To hide a field one simply changes the attributes or characteristics of the field (as is discussed in a later chapter). If the user enters "YES" in the verify field, the record displayed will be deleted from the system file.

If the user attempts to delete a record from the system in which the problem has not been fixed or is not "older" than a certain date, the system could respond as follows:

```
LANDLORD MANAGEMENT ON-LINE SYSTEM
            DELETE A PROBLEM RECORD
PROBLEM NUMBER --------------------------- 0334
REPORTED ON (DATE PROBLEM OCCURRED) --- 12/10/82

REPORTED BY (TENANT'S NAME) -------------- MARY JONES
APARTMENT NUMBER HAVING THE PROBLEM -  124

DESCRIPTION OF THE PROBLEM:
  ---- DOOR ON KITCHEN CABINET FELL OFF THE HINGES.
  ----

REPAIR INFORMATION: FIXED ON ------ 00/00/00
                    FIXED BY ------
                    TIME REQD. ---- 01 (IN HOURS)
                    QUALITY -------    (E,G,A,P,T)




MSG: RECORD CANNOT BE DELETED, PROBLEM NOT FIXED
```

As you can see, fail-safe or protection methods can be easily built into the design of a system to help protect users from their own errors or help them maintain the integrity of a system.

Although this completes our discussion of the Landlord Management On-line System, a few closing comments are in order. First, no mention was made of field editing or error handling, which are both important topics. Next, other than the first initiation of the transaction, there didn't seem to be a need for the transaction id LAMS. Finally, you might well ask whether all CICS applications have to operate in this fashion. These are valid considerations that need to be dealt with. However, the purpose of this chapter was merely to present an application, as we have done.

Now that you've seen a simple on-line application and have a feeling for CICS services, we can talk somewhat more generally about on-line application design and the problems just mentioned. We also want to look more closely at transactions and transaction flows in the next few chapters to complete the overall picture of CICS application system design and CICS application program design. Take some time to think about these questions now. Then, after you read the next few chapters, compare your answers with the directions taken in this text.

THOUGHT QUESTIONS

1. *Describe the types of errors that could occur during processing for the application just presented.*

2. *What edits would you make on the fields within each reported problem record?*

3. *Instead of returning the user to the system menu each time, what other alternatives might be better?*

4. *How else can you protect a user from accidentally deleting records from a file other than by using the verify approach that you've just seen?*

5. *Only one hidden field was used in this application. Can you justify the use of hidden fields for any of the other fields or screens presented to you?*

6. *Instead of using a batch system that reports all outstanding problems on file to the apartment owner, what could be done on-line to provide this information?*

7. *Instead of having the apartment owner assign staff members to individual problems or having a batch system do the same thing, could this function be built into the reporting component of this system? Why or why not?*

5
PROGRAM DESIGN AND PACKAGING

This chapter is concerned with several topics: the distinction between various types of on-line designs; user-application dialogue structure; reasonable actions that can be taken to handle an exceptional condition (error situation); and the meaning of a few more key terms.

In the last chapter we described a processing environment for a Landlord Management System that supported four basic functions that a user could select: add, change, delete, and inquiry. The user progressed through a series of screens to carry out each function and return to the system menu. The system flowed smoothly and predictably since the user only had to respond to the screen display and press the *enter* key. No other user action was required. We can compare the general processing dialogue between the user and the application system to a conversation between two people whose names are U and S. The user-application dialogue for a small part of our system might be as follows:

U: Initiate the system by typing in the tranid.
S: Display the menu screen.

U: Select a menu option.
S: Display the next screen in sequence with respect to the option selected.

U: Fill in the necessary information to continue procesing this request.
S: Carry out the function to be done. Inform U of the results of the processing.

U: Review the results and approve the results by continuing; or change the results by redoing the function being processed.
S: Display the menu to request the next function to be done by U.

You will notice, however, that no errors or exceptional conditions arose during our processing. In other words, the user always entered only valid data, and during every inquiry, delete, or update the requested record was always found in the file. Since this may not always be the case in your processing environment, some attention must be given to processing when one of these conditions occurs. Now let's consider this entire system a second time and see where exceptional condition processing might be needed.

ERROR HANDLING

The general structure of the system might be described as follows:

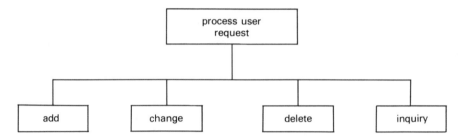

However, this simple hierarchical diagram does not show where exception handling fits into the system. By refining our diagram, we might picture the system as a collection of components, one component, for example, being the inquiry. As shown in the diagram below, the inquiry function *does* involve processing not previously discussed.

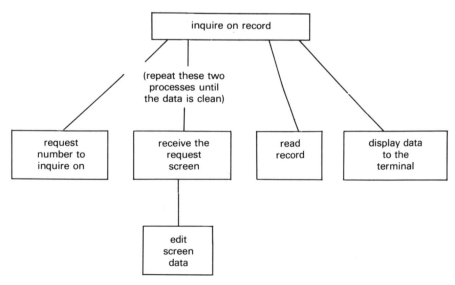

Note that a loop exists in the system until the user enters a valid number on the enter-a-problem-number display screen. But what constitutes a valid problem number? In this case, the editing performed simply ensures that all characters entered by the user are digits and that the proper number of digits has been entered so that a READ can be issued against the problem file. If the data entered by the user are not valid, the system will probably display a message on the screen informing the user of such an error. For example, a screen like the one shown below might appear at the user's terminal:

LANDLORD MANAGEMENT ON-LINE SYSTEM
INQUIRE ON PROBLEM DATA

IN THE AREA BELOW ENTER THE PROBLEM NUMBER THAT YOU WOULD LIKE TO LOOK AT.

- - - - - 02%5 - - - - -

AFTER YOU ENTER THE NUMBER IN THE AREA ABOVE, PRESS THE ENTER KEY TO HAVE THE INFORMATION ABOUT THIS PROBLEM DISPLAYED AT YOUR TERMINAL

MSG: INVALID CHARACTERS ENTERED: CORRECT AND REENTER

This situation is what we call an exceptional condition since it would not have occurred if the user had entered the data properly. An exceptional condition can thus be defined as any situation that may cause processing to deviate from a normal or valid path through the system. As you can see, this failure of the data to pass editing required the system to interrupt the normal flow of processing so that the user could reenter or correct the error in order to complete the inquiry function.

Another exceptional condition that needs to be discussed within the inquiry function is the one that arises when the user requests record number 1234, for example, and there is no record by that number in the file. This situation would also require some exceptional processing; the user might even have to enter the problem number a second time or might be returned to the system menu instead. In either case, when the system asks a file for a record that is not there, an exceptional condition occurs. Therefore, the complete diagram for the inquiry component of our system might be illustrated as follows:

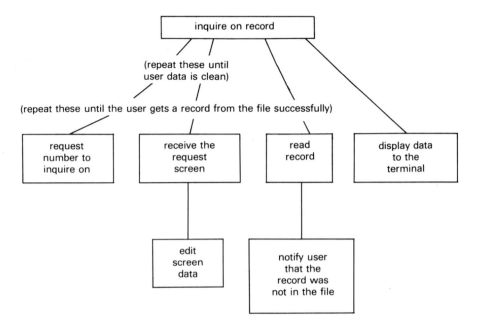

Two loops are present in this diagram—one connected with editing, the other with record existence. Although the diagram itself may not be the method you would use to represent this situation and the processes described may not be the ones you would have placed in each component, the point is that in a simple inquiry, the designers must take into account whatever exceptional conditions might occur. Without regard for the action to be taken as a result of the exceptional condition, you must design your system so that these conditions are handled; if you don't, your transaction is sure to abend or your system may even abend if the error is of a critical nature.

Now that we have a general design for the inquiry function, let's define a complete user-application dialogue for this component of the application previously presented.

U: Selects I on the system menu and presses the *enter* key.

S: Edits the selection and, since I is a valid choice, displays the screen by which the user can specify the problem number to be inquired about. If the user selected a choice not defined to the system, the system would display the menu and the user's choice that was entered, along with a message stating that an invalid selection was selected and that a valid selection should be chosen.

U: Enters the number of the reported problem that is to be viewed; then presses the *enter* key.

S: Edits the user input data and if invalid, displays a message stating that the data are not valid and that the user should correct them and try again.

U: Corrects the input entered (if there was an error) and reenters the data.

S: Again, verifies that the data are valid and if so, reads the record with this problem number from the problem file. If the record is not found, a message is displayed on the terminal informing the user that the record with the number entered was not in the file. This will allow the user to correct the data and reenter the request.

U: Reenters the correct problem number and presses the *enter* key, or aborts the transaction by pressing the *clear* key. This might be done if the terminal operator was sure that he or she entered the correct problem number but there just wasn't a problem record in the file with that key.

S: Verifies that the data are valid and attempts to read the requested record from the file. If found, a display screen is formatted and the requested information is displayed at the user's terminal.

U: Reviews the data at the terminal and when finished, presses the *enter* key or the *clear* key to end the transaction.

S: If the *enter* key was pressed, the system recognizes that a display screen was at the user terminal and that there are no data to be processed and so the system menu is displayed.

Obviously this is a rather detailed and lengthy dialogue. Although you might construct a shorter one, you must at least handle this minimal processing to guard against transaction failures. When constructing the user dialogue, you should identify where editing and error-handling techniques are to be used so that these can be incorporated into the program coding during implementation.

You have seen just one component of an on-line transaction, and that was a very simple component to implement. Each of the other components would have to be developed by you in the same manner for your applications. For the sake of brevity, we'll skip over the dialogues for the add, delete, and update components of this application. Instead, you'll be presented a pseudolanguage format of the general processing flows with respect to each of the components as well as the inquiry a second time. The pseudolanguage for the inquiry transaction is probably the logical point of departure here, so here it is:

1. Send out the request a number screen.
2. Receive the request a number screen.

3. If the problem number on that screen is not valid, then display a message on the request a number screen telling the user that the data are invalid. Go back to step 2.

4. Build a record key from the user's data.

5. Read the record from the file.

6. If the record was not found in the file, then display a message on the terminal. Go to step 2.

7. Build a display screen for the request record's information.

8. Send out the display screen with information about the problem the user wanted to see.

9. Receive the request to continue after waiting for them to view the screen data.

10. Send out the system menu.

Many extremely important points need to be discussed here, and all of them are controversial. Let's handle each one separately.

First, the logical code as shown would not work in a CICS operating environment. The problem lies not in the use of the GO TO statement or in the design of the algorithm, but in the *way* that CICS will process the various commands. In fact, the GO TO cannot be replaced with a DO WHILE or DO UNTIL, or some other logical construct, because of the way in which commands are processed by the CICS service components. For this reason, we'll have to rewrite the code into a *workable* format.

Now, just what is the problem with this code? The problem lies in steps 5 and 6, where the READ is issued. The problem is that under CICS you must issue step 6 before step 5. I hope you now see why we spent some time discussing CICS before finishing the design component. This may sound ridiculous to you, but just be patient; it's really not such a bad situation after all. For example, we can replace steps 5 and 6 of the code shown with the following code:

5. If the next READ request results in the record not being found in the file then go to 15

6. READ the requested record from the file

.   .   .

.   .   .

.   .   .

15. Display a message on the request a number screen that the record could not be found.

16. Go to step 2.

I bet you're really confused now! Let me try to straighten things out. First, in a CICS implementation environment, all exceptional conditions (other than editing) must be issued *before* the code that could actually raise that exceptional condition. Second, when such an exceptional condition occurs—for example, a record may not be in a file—*control is transferred* to a "subparagraph" within the application program structure. Note that the subparagraph is not performed in the sense of a PERFORM statement in COBOL; rather, control is transferred to the paragraph by CICS as in the sense of a GO TO statement. Hence, the only way to get out of the subparagraph (in our example, steps 15 and 16) is to issue a GO TO statement, as shown in step 16. Although the resulting program *is* "workable" under CICS, it still does not constitute good programming style for an on-line environment. To some of you, it may not constitute good programming style in any environment! This brings us to the second major problem in this code—program resource control.

You'll notice in our example that every time a display is sent out to the user terminal, the next action is a "receive" of the terminal data. The time between the completion of the previous SEND and the RECEIVE varies in length, depending on how fast the user responds and what information has to be looked at. If the user chooses to take a coffee break during one of the SEND-RECEIVE groups, the application program remains idle, but yet is being executed in the CICS system. That is, CICS still retains this transaction as a potentially executable task and maintains all the control information about this task, but the task associated with the inquiry transaction is not doing any productive work while waiting for a terminal operator response. This idle and yet active time can create severe problems for other applications under CICS. Let me explain.

Suppose that all applications are written in this way within your CICS system and suppose that the average program and working-storage requirements are 20K. If we assume that your CICS environment has 150K of usable storage that must be shared by all applications, then clearly, about seven or eight transactions could be running simultaneously.

Now, let's suppose that six users are currently using one of these transactions and that all have paused at one of the SEND-RECEIVE pairs. If all users go out for a meeting, to the rest room, or a coffee break for half an hour or so, during that time CICS will be able to run only about two or three other transactions from all of the other terminals in your company. Why, you may ask. The answer is quite simple and stems from the fact that the six idle transactions are holding on to about 120K of storage so that they can remain active. This leaves 30K of storage available to *all* other CICS users. Since the average transaction takes 20K (as we said earlier), then probably two to three transactions would be the maximum number that could run while the six transactions remained idle, holding on to resources that they are not actively using and resources that are valuable to other users. For this reason, it is advantageous to minimize if not eliminate these SEND-RECEIVE pairs within an on-line application under CICS.

CONVERSATIONAL PROGRAMMING STYLE

Despite the technical appearance of this discussion, what we're really describing is a common situation in on-line development, except that we're using CICS as an example. Many on-line systems operate in this same way. What you'll soon see is that we are describing a way of implementing and designing on-line application programs that is commonly used in the on-line software being developed in industry. A little later you'll see a different way of implementing the same application that eliminates many of the drawbacks here.

Not only must a manager of data processing know about such situations if he or she is to maintain a highly effective and performing system, but the applications programmer or analyst must also be aware of them if such traps or bottlenecks are to be avoided. How can they be avoided and how can the logic of an application program be changed so as to minimize or eliminate this implementation technique? Actually, it can be done rather simply.

The method involved can be called conversational, as opposed to nonconversational, on-line program design. A conversational transaction is a transaction that performs the functions as requested by the user, but that holds on to resources for varying lengths of time when those resources are not being *effectively* used by the task because the task may be inactive while waiting for a user response. You'll recall that earlier the term *task* was identified as a component of a transaction. Hence, a transaction in which the task fluctuates between idle, inactive, or suspended states and active states is what we'll call a conversational transaction. But wait a minute, what is a *transaction*? This term has been appearing more and more often here but it has not yet been defined.

CLASSIFYING AND PACKAGING ON-LINE TRANSACTIONS

A transaction can be defined as the activities of a system from initiation by the user until termination by that user. Hence, when the user types in the transaction id and initiates the application, all processing conducted by the system, for that application, up to the time that the user clears the screen and initiates another application (by typing in a different transaction id), is considered a transaction. Transactions are also defined as the processing that occurs from the time that the user initiates a transaction to the time that the user receives a response from the application in the form of a screen display or message. Yet another definition is—a transaction is as a component of an application or even an entire application. For example, the Landlord

Management System could be considered a transaction, *or* each of the components (add, delete, update, and inquiry) could be regarded as transactions.

The point is that many definitions of *transaction* exist, but these are the primary ways of defining the term. Yet another factor must be mentioned, however. Applications are defined to CICS as the designers and developers see fit. An application could be defined as one entity to the CICS system or could be defined as many entities. For example, the Landlord Management System could be defined as one application or it could be defined as four applications (add, delete, update, and inquiry). It all depends on the way the system is packaged by the designers and developers. Each "application" definition has a *unique* "transaction identification" assigned to it. When this transaction identification is defined, a transaction has just been defined to CICS. Note that CICS is not able to determine whether this transaction is an entire application or a component of an application. In fact, it doesn't matter.

Hence, if an application is packaged in such a way that its functions are processed by a set of programs (each set being initiated by its own transaction id), then the application could be considered to be composed of several transactions. On the other hand, if one *common* transaction id is used to drive a common set of programs such that *the programs* determine what functions are to be done, then the terms *application* and *transaction* become synonymous. In other words, the two terms differ in meaning whenever application functions are divided. If the transaction ids are assigned on the basis of function, then the application is composed of more than one transaction. If one transaction id drives the entire application, then the *programs* must define functional boundaries.

CLASSIFYING TRANSACTIONS BY RESOURCE UTILIZATION

In an on-line environment, an application may be developed in several ways. First, the application can be divided by function, and each function can be driven by a unique transaction definition (tranid) within the system. On the other hand, the application can be divided by function at the program level; this method requires a more extensive decisionmaking code on the part of the application programs.

Next, the application programs can be written in either a conversational mode, a nonconversational mode, or a mixture of both. The way in which an application is defined to the on-line environment does not necessarily have any bearing on the way in which the application programs are written. However, if the application programs are written in a conversational mode, then transaction definitions tend to be composed of more than one function within an application, rather than having each function divided at the transaction level. For this reason, and because of the fact that conversational transactions hold on to resources during idle times whereas a nonconversational transaction does not, it is suggested that all on-line applications be written in a nonconversational mode of programming when the CICS on-line monitor is being used.

If you look back at the inquiry component pseudocode presented earlier, you'll note that this code is written in a conversational mode. Also, it's not clear whether this component has been divided at the functional level or at the program level. Let's suppose that it has been divided at the functional level.

For each function, then, there must be defined to the on-line system a unique transaction id that will cause the programs associated with that function to be executed by the on-line monitor. This "definition" is carried out by placing an entry in the PROGRAM CONTROL TABLE (PCT) for each function within the application. For example, let's suppose that our entries are:

transaction id	program to be executed
LAMS	LAMENU
LAMI	LAMINQ
LAMD	LAMDEL
LAMA	LAMADD
LAMU	LAMUPD

Hence, for each function in this system, including the user's primary menu selection, we have defined a unique transaction id and application-transaction functional component to our on-line monitor. The discussion now has to become more technical because the organization and definition of the application to an on-line monitor directly affect program coding, logic, and design structure. Further, the definition of such information to your on-line monitor should be done *after* the final module specifications and packaging of your system have been completed, but prior to the testing of your system.

According to this definition, when the user types the transaction id LAMS, the program LAMENU will be executed; if the user types LAMI, LAMINQ will be executed, and so on. However, the user does not have to know about the transactions LAMI, LAMD, LAMA, or LAMU because each of the application programs can initiate each of the other functions, all of which will be transparent to the user. Hence, the user only has to know the one transaction id, LAMS, and all other functional divisions will be handled by the application code within the programs. Although it appears that the programs are making the functional divisions, the programs are just telling the on-line monitor which function is to be executed next, and thus are not really performing that function themselves. That is, the responsibility for actual execution of each functional component rests with the on-line monitor and not the application programs.

Before we concentrate on the application program logic to implement a nonconversational code, we have to address one last thing. Recall that in the pseudolanguage code presented for the inquiry function each SEND was followed immediately by a RECEIVE. Between the SEND and RECEIVE the system held the application program(s) in a suspended state until the user reinitiated the execution of the transaction. Recall, too, that this implementation approach is the one that is used in conversational programming. In a nonconversational programming mode, a much different programming style must be used. Now, recall the dialogue for the inquiry application:

U: Selects I on the system menu and presses the *enter* key.

S: Edits the selection and since I is a valid choice, displays the screen by which the user can specify the problem number to be inquired about. If the user selected a choice not defined to the system, the system would display the menu and the user's choice entered, along with a message stating that an invalid selection was selected and that a valid selection should be chosen.

U: Enters the number of the reported problem that is to be viewed; then presses the *enter* key.

S: Edits the user input data and if invalid, displays a message to the effect that the data are not valid and that the user should correct them and try again.

U: Corrects the input entered (if there was an error) and reenters the data.

S: Again, verifies that the data are valid and if so, reads the record with this problem number from the problem file. If the record is not found, a message is displayed on the terminal informing the user that the record with the number entered was not in the file. This will allow the user to correct the data and reenter the request.

U: Reenters the correct problem number and presses the *enter* key or aborts the transaction by pressing the *clear* key. This might be done if the terminal operator were sure the correct problem number had been entered but there just wasn't a problem record in the file with that key.

S: Verifies that the data are valid and attempts to read the requested record from the file. If found, a display screen is formatted and the requested information is displayed at the user's terminal.

U: Reviews the data at the terminal and when finished, presses the *enter* key or the *clear* key to end the transaction.

S: If the *enter* key was pressed, the system recognizes that a display screen was at the user terminal and that there are no data to be processed and so the system menu is displayed.

SESSION, APPLICATION, TRANSACTION, AND TASK ENTITIES

In this dialogue, you can see that after every S action is completed, the task performing work within the transaction initiated by the user becomes suspended; that is, it is placed in a wait state while awaiting U's answer. The inquiry transaction can therefore be described as a series of active and suspended sessions in which a session is defined as a U- and S-activity interaction. Further, within a session, only half of the session requires computer processing, namely, the half performed by person S. Let's call this half-session of activity a *task*. Therefore, a task will mean a measureable unit of work performed for a transaction, and during a session, by one or more application programs within the computer. If these terms seem confusing, maybe the following diagram will help:

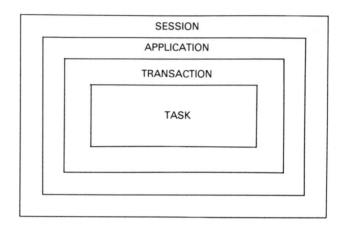

TRANSACTION DIVISIONS
AND RELATIONSHIP TO TASKS

But where does conversational or nonconversational program design come into the picture? The answer is: if an application is developed in a conversational mode, then, as far as the on-line monitor is concerned, a transaction is composed of *one, long* running task. If an application is developed in a nonconversational programming style, then the on-line monitor measures the transaction as a *series* of *small, short* running tasks. Note that the word *task* is plural in the nonconversational approach but not in the conversational approach.

With this subdivision, we can now see that if a task division is to occur in a nonconversational mode of implementation, a program must *give up control, abend,* or *end.* For this reason, it is necessary for an application program to remember (with the aid of the on-line monitor) where it was when it stopped during its last active session. Let me explain this concept further.

Suppose that whenever a transaction is initiated from a terminal, a special area that we'll refer to as memory is initialized to blanks. Further, assume that *each* terminal has a memory and so it's really not the application that must acquire or manage that memory area, but let's just assume that it's always available, and that it is provided to us by the on-line monitor. Then, as a transaction executes, the monitor can place information into the memory to help it remember what to do next. Hence, while the user goes for coffee, to a meeting, or to the rest room, the system is not required to manage or maintain *anything* associated with that user's task. Now you might argue that the system must keep track of the memory value. Although this is true in one sense, in another, the area of memory that we are going to use to help transactions remember requires no management of resources by the on-line monitor at all. This nonconversational programming approach is the most efficient method of programming under CICS and provides for the most accurate measurement of transaction resource utilization. With this understanding of tasks, sessions, transactions, applications, functional divisions, and conversational versus nonconversational programming style, we can now formulate the application program logic for our Landlord Management System. Remember, the logic that follows is for a nonconversational implementation of this system.

SAMPLE APPLICATION PSEUDOCODE

The first part of the menu program could be coded as follows:

```
If "memory" = 'Ø' then
    do
        send out the menu screen
        set memory = 'M'
        end the program with "next" tranid = "LAMS"
    end do
```

Note that the program ends, but before doing so, it places a value in memory so that the program knows that the menu screen has been sent out. The value placed in memory is the value M. Also, since the program didn't switch transactions before it ended, the next time the user presses the *enter* key, this *same* program will be executed *from the beginning of the program* as if it had never been executed before. As you should begin to see, since the memory has been given a value, it will not be blank the next time the program is initiated, and so it will not redisplay the menu. This is a very important concept in programming under CICS because this memory controls the logic of the application program, while the transaction id determines which program is to be executed the next time the user presses the *enter* key.

Also notice that before the program ends, it tells the on-line monitor what transaction id will be initiated next from that user's terminal. As a result, it is guaranteed that this same set of application programs will have control to complete the user's request on the next initiation of this system (when the user presses the *enter* key).

Continuing with the menu program, we have:

```
Receive the menu screen
If menu selection is not valid then
    do
        send out the menu screen with an
            appropriate error message
        set memory = 'M'
        end the program with tranid = "LAMS"
    end do
If menu selection = 'I' then
    transfer control to program LAMINQ
else
    If menu selection = 'R' then
        transfer control to program LAMADD
    else
        If menu selection = 'D' then
            transfer control to program LAMDEL
        else
            transfer control to program LAMUPD
```

The menu processor or driver program, as we'll call it, is structurally simple, but must use the memory to remember what to do on the next initiation of this program. Notice that the value that this program stores in memory could be something other than a blank or an M since the program only uses the memory to determine whether this is the first time or a subsequent time that the program is being initiated. However, in the other programs within this system, notice how the memory is used *as well as how* the application programs are initiated and *who* initiates them.

Did you also notice that this program *transfers* control to the other functional programs in this system? In other words, once a menu selection is made, the menu driver program is really no longer needed to complete that function. Therefore, rather than calling a functional program, the program transfers control to that module. Hence, when the target functional program terminates, control returns to the on-line monitor and not to the menu driver program.

INVOKING PROGRAMS IN A SYSTEM

Let's think ahead for a minute. After this driver module transfers control to one of the functional modules, what will that module do? Clearly, the next set of modules in this system will probably display a screen to allow the user to enter a problem number (in the case of the inquiry, update, and delete), or display a blank screen to be filled in by the user when a problem is to be reported to the system. Since displaying a screen is *so easy to do,* why not have the driver module display the next screen associated with the next function to be performed, *rather than* transferring control *of the same function* to that module? In this way, the driver module will not have to depend on any other modules and can be implemented and tested separately. Although this *set-up* requires that the driver module know the identifications of the screen displays to be used for each of the functions, this requirement isn't much different from having to know the names of the modules to transfer control to. Hence, instead of what you've just seen, the code for the driver module could be as follows:

```
If "memory" = 'ø' then
   do
      send out the menu screen
      set memory = 'M'
      end the program with "next" tranid = "LAMS"
   end do
Receive the menu screen
If menu selection is not valid then
   do
      send out the menu screen with an
         appropriate error message
      set memory = 'M'
      end the program with tranid = "LAMS"
   end do
If menu selection = 'I' then
   display the "enter a problem to
      inquire on" screen
else
   If menu selection = 'R' then
      display the "report a problem" screen
   else
      If menu selection = 'D' then
         display the "enter a problem to
            delete" screen
      else
         display the "enter a problem to
            be updated" screen
```

How does this look to you? It may look like a good alternative, but that depends on your system. There is still another slight problem with this logic—did you find it?

Recall that when this application was presented in an earlier chapter, it was to automatically supply a key for a new problem being reported by a tenant. That is, when a problem was being reported, the logic supporting the add function would assign a problem number for the user that was based on a field in a special control record in our problem file. This helped ensure that no two problems would ever have the same number. Yet, in the logic above, we don't see any access to this control record, nor do we see that a problem number has been assigned to this report.

A few options are available to solve this problem. We could put the necessary code to assign a problem number to a newly reported problem here, before the "report a problem" screen is displayed. However, since the *real* ADD LOGIC *will* require this code, then we'll have the same code in two places. This arrangement may not be desirable in terms of the future maintenance it will require. Another option might be to ask the ADD LOGIC to supply a number for us, but then we'd be back to the first logic presented. Still another possibility would be to delay the assignment of a problem number until the user has entered all the data for a new problem report and those data are ready to be added to the master file. Since the actual processing of the data on this screen must be done by the ADD LOGIC, this may be our best solution. In the final analysis, you yourself will have to decide how to handle the implementation of the driver module. (The last solution will be demonstrated later when the ADD LOGIC is described so that you can review its structure and see how it can be used with a driver module that does not transfer control or call subordinate functional modules but instead displays next-level screens associated with those functional modules.)

The inquiry program can now be written in a nonconversational way, as shown below. Remember that this program is usually initiated by the transaction id LAMI as defined to the on-line monitor. However, since it is possible for the menu driver program to invoke this program, the program must accommodate this situation, as shown in the first few lines of this program logic. Notice that a similar section of program logic appears in each of the programs that can be invoked from the menu program.

```
If initiating tranid not equal 'LAMI' or current screen is
    unformatted then
    do
        send out the "request a problem number screen"
        set memory to '1'
        end the program and set the next transaction
            id to LAMI
    end do
If memory = '1' then
    do
        receive the "request a problem number screen"
```

```
if problem number is not valid then
  do
    send out the "request a problem number screen"
      with an appropriate error message
    set memory to '1'
    end the program and set the next tranid
      initiator to LAMI
  end do
else
  do
    build master record key from the screen data
    if the read that follows fails then
      go to subparagraph A
    read the associated master record from the
      proper file
    build the screen to display the information
      on this master record
    send out the display screen
    set memory to '2'
    end the program and set the next tranid
      initiator to LAMI
      end do
  end do
else
  do
    send out the menu screen
    set memory to 'M'
    end the program and set the next tranid
      initiator to LAMS
  end do
subparagraph A.
  send out the "request a problem number screen" and
    a message that the record requested was not
    in the file
  set memory to '1'
  end the program and set the next tranid initiator
    to LAMI
```

This logic has several important features. First, every time a program ends, it first places a value in memory and then ends by informing the on-line monitor which transaction id is to be executed next at the terminal currently executing this active transaction. This step ensures that this program logic *will* be restarted. Second, the exceptional condition logic is established just *before* the READ is issued against the file. Do you remember why the logic here must be carried out in this way? (Hint: Look back at Chapter 4.) Third, the use of the subparagraph is mandatory because of the way in which the on-line monitor processes an application that raises an exceptional condition. Also, once control is transferred into this subparagraph or exceptional condition paragraph, the logic simply writes an error message, which is displayed on the screen at the terminal; then the program logic ends. *It is not possible* for control to return to the point at which the exceptional condition is raised, as is normally done in higher-level programs, *unless* a GO TO command is issued from subparagraph A to an earlier point in the program. That "earlier" point in the program is, of course, the point at which the READ failed.

It is important to remember that if an exceptional condition occurs within a CICS on-line program, one of two things can occur. If an exceptional condition paragraph has *not* been established for this condition, the execution of that logic is terminated *abnormally;* in other words, the task is abended. If a special paragraph *has* been established for that exceptional condition, control is transferred to that paragraph, at which point the program can issue a message to the terminal and end or return to another point in the program through the use of a GO TO command.

In the above discussion the term *paragraph* is taken directly from the COBOL programming language. Appropriate terminology for other programming languages could be applied in every usage so that this inquiry logic could be used in another implementation language.

Finally, notice that after the master record is displayed and the user presses the *enter* key, *this program logic* is reinitiated and sends out the menu, switches transaction ids for next initiation, and then ends. This switch occurs so that the menu or driver module is executed as the next task initiation is done by the terminal operator. This transaction switch is transparent to the user and allows him or her to cross functional or transaction boundaries within the system.

CONTRASTING PROGRAM DESIGN STRUCTURES

Clearly, another structure could be used for this program logic, possibly one that adds some performed sections of logic or even calls up some subroutines. In any case, this logic would have to remain generally the same across the paragraph or subprogram boundaries. The important point to remember if you *do* organize your code into subroutines or paragraphs is this: you must take care to specify and handle exceptional conditions at the appropriate time. If an exceptional condition paragraph has been defined in a program and if a performed section of code that is being processed raises that exceptional condition, then the perform command is no longer in effect since *all* control has now been transferred to the exceptional condition subparagraph. As a result, PERFORM-THRU logic, in which the exceptional condition paragraphs are "housed" within the boundaries of the performed logic, may now have to be used. Take some time and make sure that you understand how this logic operates and how errors must be handled.

One alternative solution might be to isolate I/O in externally called modules in which control values indicating the success or failure of an I/O request are passed back and forth. Another solution might be to GO TO an earlier section of code in the program—namely, the statement following the READ, as shown here—*after* setting a "flag" in the exceptional condition subparagraph. In any of the solutions, carefully evaluate your implementation approach in terms of functionality, maintainability, and performance. Many people will sacrifice performance in this area in favor of good program design, especially since this is only a noniterative calling structure to a lower-level module performing the requested I/O.

The following code is an example of program logic that would *not* be able to handle exceptional conditions in a program:

```
            .      .      .
            .      .      .
            .      .      .


    build master record key
    READ master record from file with
        key specified
    If record is not found then


            .      .      .
            .      .      .
            .      .      .
```

However, a simple alteration to this code might produce satisfactory results as long as the paragraph XYZ is *not* being performed from some other point in this program—unless, of course, the code from XYZ to XYZ-PARAGRAPH-END is being PERFORMED-THRU.

```
    XYZ.
            .      .      .
            .      .      .
            .      .      .


    build master record key
    move 'found' to record-read-indicator
    If the next READ fails then
        go to subparagraph NOTFOUND
    READ master record from file with
        key specified
```

CONTINUE-PROCESSING.
If record-read-indicator = 'notfound' then

.   .   .

.   .   .

.   .   .

go to XYZ-PARAGRAPH-END

NOTFOUND.
move 'notfound' to record-read-indicator
go to CONTINUE-PROCESSING

XYZ-PARAGRAPH-END.

Logic for the delete component of this application could be described in the following:

If initiating tranid not equal LAMD or current screen
  is not a formatted screen then
  do
    send out the "request a problem number to delete" screen
    set memory to 1
    set next tranid to LAMD
    end execution
  end do
If memory = 1 then
  do
    receive the "request a problem to delete" screen
    if the problem number is not valid then
      do
        send out the "request a problem to delete" screen
          and an error message
        set memory to 1
        set next tranid to LAMD
        end execution
      end do
    else
      do
        build master record key from screen data
        if the read that follows fails then
          go to subparagraph A
        READ the master record from the file
        build the screen to display this master record
          so that the user is sure that this is the
          record to be deleted

```
            send out this record display
            set memory to 2
            set next tranid to LAMD
            end execution
         end do
      end do
   else
      do
         receive the problem information display
         if user really wants this record deleted by
            responding YES to the "are you sure" question
            then
            do
               build master record key from screen data
               if the delete that follows fails then
                  go to subparagraph B
               DELETE the associated master record
               send out the menu screen with a message
                  that says record xxx was deleted
               set memory to M
               set next tranid to LAMS
                  end execution
            end do
         else
            do
               send out the menu screen with a message
                  that the delete request was aborted
               set memory to M
               set next tranid to LAMS
               end execution
            end do
      end do
   subparagraph A.
      send out the "request a problem to delete" screen and
         a message that the record was not on file
      set memory to 1
      set next tranid to LAMD
      end execution
   subparagraph B.
      send out the "request a problem to delete" screen
         with a message that the problem record has been
         deleted underneath user's request or that an
         error has occurred in the system
      set memory to 1
```

set next tranid to LAMD
end execution

In the delete logic, pay particular attention to the need for subparagraph B, which is used in the same way as subparagraph A but at a different time in the delete processing. In other words, for every possible occurrence of an exceptional condition, you should define a separate exceptional condition paragraph to handle that specific request. If a paragraph for another exception *will* also explain why this particular request was not completed or whatever, paragraph sharing can be used to reduce the coding efforts of your programming staff. In terms of the design structure, however, sharing paragraphs may create maintenance problems since a change to one section of code necessitates a change in the exceptional subparagraph, and thus affects the use of that shared paragraph by some other point in that module. Hence, a separate paragraph may be more desirable for *each* exceptional condition that may be raised.

Take another close look at subparagraph B. In this case, we are telling the user exactly what happened in the delete processing. In fact, the record has been deleted from underneath this particular user. Do you have any suggestions as to how to prevent this file design situation? An alternative might have been to define separate subparagraphs for this single event to explain the various reasons that the delete could not have been carried out. For example, we could have raised an I/O error, the record may not have been found, the file could have been closed between the last read and our delete, and so on. In other words, paragraphs and logic should handle as many situations as are likely to occur so that a transaction *does not* abend and leave the user "holding the bag." Planning for exceptional conditions is an important part of the design of a system and should not be left to implementation as these conditions do affect user-system dialogue, especially user confidence in the system.

In reviewing the logic for the update process that follows, you'll notice it is quite similar to some of the previous logic that has been presented. Note, however, that this logic has two READ commands within the same process. If you look carefully, you'll see that the first READ is a read without the intent to update. This means that when this read is issued, the system will not enqueue on this record while the user is reviewing it at the terminal. This situation could cause dual-update problems from another terminal user. Therefore some other method may be more desirable for instances in which several users might be updating the same record. If this is not a problem, then while the record is being displayed, the program is not operational, that is, not executing. When the user has finished updating the data fields on the screen and reinitiates the transaction by pressing *enter,* you'll notice the second READ, a READ *with* the intent to update. At this point the system enqueues on the record so that another user cannot access this record during this time. The record is updated and rewritten to the file to complete the update processing.

By now this logic should be clear since you should understand the use of memory and the use of tranid values to restart the transaction execution.

```
If initiating tranid not equal LAMU or current screen
  is an unformatted screen then
do
  send out the "request a problem number to update" screen
  set memory to 1
  set next tranid to LAMU
  end execution
end do
If memory = 1 then
do
  receive the "request a problem to update" screen
  if the problem number is not valid then
    do
      send out the "request a problem to update" screen
        and an error message
      set memory to 1
      set next tranid to LAMU
      end execution
    end do
  else
    do
      build master record key from screen data
      if the read that follows fails then
        go to subparagraph A
      READ the master record from the file
      build the screen to display this master record
        so that the user is sure that this is the
        record to be updated
      send out this record display
      set memory to 2
      set next tranid to LAMU
      end execution
    end do
  end do
else
  do
    receive the problem information display
    if any of the fields have been modified then
      do
        edit each of the modified fields
        if any fields do not pass edit then
          do
            send out the "update display" screen and
              all of its data with a message about
```

```
                    the bad fields
                set memory to 2
                set next tranid to LAMU
                end execution
            end do
        else
            do
                build master record key from screen data
                if the update that follows fails then
                    go to subparagraph B
                READ FOR UPDATE the associated master record
                move changed fields from screen
                    to master record
                REWRITE the master record
                send out the menu screen with a message
                    that says record xxx was updated
                set memory to M
                set next tranid to LAMS
                end execution
            end do
        end do
    else
        do
            send out the menu screen with a message
                that the update request was aborted
            set memory to M
            set next tranid to LAMS
            end execution
        end do
    end do
subparagraph A.
    send out the "request a problem to update" screen and
        a message that the record was not on file
    set memory to 1
    set next tranid to LAMU
    end execution
subparagraph B.
    send out the "request a problem to update" screen
        with a message that the problem record has been
        deleted underneath your request or that an
        error has occurred in the system
    set memory to 1
    set next tranid to LAMU
    end execution
```

Another interesting feature here concerns the decision as to whether or not any fields have been modified on the update screen. Later you'll learn that it *is* possible to determine whether or not a field has been changed by the user when it is sent out to a terminal for updating. Hence, by checking all fields in this way to see if any have been modified, a rather important section of code that reads for update, updates, and rewrites can be avoided if no updating is really necessary. Although this may seem a rather trivial process, it really is not—it *is* difficult to determine whether fields have been modified on the update screen. Many designers and implementers of on-line systems opt to perform the update anyway, making no changes to any of the data fields in the records involved. Although this step wastes time, it may save a substantial amount of coding and maintenance in the future should modifications be made to the screen displays involved in the updating process.

The final section of logic presented below is for the add process. Although it is simple, this logic, too, demonstrates a new usage of the exceptional condition paragraph. Several common versions of the add logic are presented for your review. You can decide which ones, if any, are to your liking.

```
If initiating tranid not equal LAMA or current screen
   is unformatted then
   do
      move 'CTRL' to control-key
      if next read fails then
         go to subparagraph READ-BAD-PROBLEM
      READ FOR UPDATE master file for 'CTRL'
      move next-key-value to problem-number-on-screen
      add 1 to next-key-value
      REWRITE 'CTRL' record to master file
      move built-in-date-in-system to screen-date
      display "report a problem screen" with problem number
         and date just obtained
      set memory to 1
      set next tranid to LAMA
      end execution
   end do
If memory = 1 then
   do
      receive the "request a problem to report on" screen
      if any field fails editing then
         do
            send out the "request a problem to report on" screen
               with all data and appropriate error messages
            set memory to 1
            set next tranid to LAMA
```

```
            end execution
         end do
      else
         do
            build master record from screen data
            if the WRITE that follows fails then
               go to subparagraph A
            WRITE the new master record to the file
            send out the "report a problem screen" with a
               message that the record was added to the file
            set memory to 2
            set next tranid to LAMA
            end execution
         end do
   end do
   else
      do
         send out the menu screen
         set memory to M
         set next tranid to LAMS
         end execution
      end do

subparagraph A.
   send out the "request a problem to report on" screen and
      a message that the record was already on file and
      that there is a rather severe error in the system
   set memory to 1
   set next tranid to LAMA
   end execution

subparagraph REAL-BAD-PROBLEM.
   send out the system menu screen with a message that the
      main control record for determining problem numbers
      has been destroyed and that the user should call the
      analyst immediately.
   set memory to M
   set next tranid to LAMS
   end execution
```

In the add logic that you've just seen, notice the special control record in the master file that indicates the "next" problem number to be assigned in this system. (We hinted at this feature in earlier chapters and in this chapter when we were discussing how to implement the driver module.) This feature keeps the number assignment in ascending sequential order and thus prevents duplicates from appearing. Because this record requires updating and exceptional condition handling, the REAL-BAD-PROBLEM paragraph must be introduced to handle situations when the control record is not in the file. You can see that if the control record was not in the system somewhere, as it was supposed to be, you would certainly have a "real bad problem."

Let me also call your attention to the way that the record is added to the file. Because it is assumed in this logic that the record will not be in the file, the WRITE is issued without any preceding READ. You may object to this type of program design. If so, consider the second solution that follows—it incorporates a different ADD logic to READ before the WRITE is actually issued.

```
If initiating tranid not equal LAMA or current screen
   is unformatted then
   do
      move 'CTRL' to control-key
      if next read fails then
         go to subparagraph REAL-BAD-PROBLEM
      READ FOR UPDATE master file for 'CTRL'
      move next-key-value to problem-number-on-screen
      add 1 to next-key-value
      REWRITE 'CTRL' record to master file
      move built-in-date-in-system to screen-date
      display "report a problem screen" with problem number
         and date just obtained
      set memory to 1
      set next tranid to LAMA
      end execution
   end do
If memory = 1 then
   do
      receive the "request a problem to report on" screen
      if any field fails editing then
         do
            send out the "request a problem to report on" screen
               with all data and appropriate error messages
            set memory to 1
            set next tranid to LAMA
            end execution
         end do
```

```
    else
      do
        build master record from screen data
        If next read fails then
          go to subparagraph A
        READ master file for record with this key
        if the WRITE that follows fails then
          go to subparagraph A
        WRITE the new master record to the file
        send out the "report a problem screen" with a
          message that the record was added to the file
        set memory to 2
        set next tranid to LAMA
        end execution
      end do
    end do
else
  do
    send out the menu screen
    set memory to M
    set next tranid to LAMS
    end execution
  end do
subparagraph A.
  send out the "request a problem to report on" screen and
    a message that the record was already on file and
    that there is a rather severe error in the system
  set memory to 1
  set next tranid to LAMA
  end execution
subparagraph REAL-BAD-PROBLEM.
  send out the system menu screen with a message that the
    main control record for determining problem numbers
    has been destroyed and that the user should call
    the analyst immediately.
  set memory to M
  set next tranid to LAMS
  end execution
```

You might argue that obviously the READ should not be issued immediately before the WRITE. Note, however, that the same exceptional condition paragraph is used in both the READ and WRITE commands. Hence, the READ is not really necessary at all. On the other hand, it does point out that exceptional condition paragraphs can be shared by more than one I/O or any request as long as the actions in that paragraph are appropriate for the situation that has occurred. In this case, they are.

In a situation in which the user assigns his or her own key value to the records, a READ in the upper portion of this module (where the CTRL record processing occurs) would indeed be appropriate to determine if a record with this value was added to the file at some earlier time. The CTRL record would not be necessary if the user assigned his or her own key to every record added to the file. If this is done, however, you must also coordinate the use of screens with this logic so that information about the key of the record to be added can be checked before you make the terminal user go through the process of entering all the data for a record, only to find that the record already exists.

The final version of the ADD LOGIC is different in that the problem number is assigned *after* the user completes the data entry for the problem to be reported. This version, like the ones presented earlier, has certain advantages and disadvantages. Before we discuss them, let's look at this logic:

```
If initiating tranid not equal LAMA or current screen
   is unformatted then
   do
      display "report a problem screen" for the user
         to enter in the problem data
      set memory to 1
      set next tranid to LAMA
      end execution
   end do
If memory = 1 then
   do
      receive the "request a problem to report on" screen
      if any field fails editing then
         do
            send out the "request a problem to report on" screen
               with all data and appropriate error messages
            set memory to 1
            set next tranid to LAMA
            end execution
         end do
      else
         do
            move 'CTRL' to control-key
            if next read fails then
               go to subparagraph REAL-BAD-PROBLEM
            READ FOR UPDATE master file for 'CTRL'
            move next-key-value to problem-number-for-record
```

```
            add 1 to next-key-value
            REWRITE 'CTRL' record to master file
            move built-in-date-in-system to master-rec-date
            build master record from screen data
            if the WRITE that follows fails then
                go to subparagraph A
            WRITE the new master record to the file
            send out the "report a problem screen" with a
                message that the problem just reported was
                assigned a problem number of xxxx and was
                successfully added to the file
            set memory to 2
            set next tranid to LAMA
            end execution
         end do
      end do
   else
      do
         send out the menu screen
         set memory to M
         set next tranid to LAMS
         end execution
      end do
   subparagraph A.
      send out the "request a problem to report on" screen and
         a message that the record was already on file and
         that there is a rather severe error in the system
      set memory to 1
      set next tranid to LAMA
      end execution
   subparagraph REAL-BAD-PROBLEM.
      send out the system menu screen with a message that the
         main control record for determining problem numbers
         has been destroyed and that the user should call
         the analyst immediately.
      set memory to M
      set next tranid to LAMS
      end execution
```

As you can see, the CTRL record is obtained, updated, and rewritten just before the problem record is stored in the master file. This procedure appears to have a potential problem, but it's really not a problem at all. Notice that control is given to the paragraph REAL-BAD-PROBLEM if there is a problem in accessing the CTRL record. Since the user will have filled out a complete screen before this problem is discovered, the user may become frustrated when the screen is rejected because of a system problem. On the other hand, since accessing CTRL should *never* be a problem, the user should rarely if ever have his or her screen rejected.

This brings us to the WRITE statement. If the program fails here, control goes to subparagraph A, which is where control would reside in any of the versions presented. Hence, there is really no disadvantage or advantage here.

Finally, we come to an important trade-off. Let's suppose that while the terminal operator is typing in the problem information, the tenant decides to cancel the report for some reason. The terminal operator is now looking at a partly filled screen. To terminate this problem-reporting session, the terminal operator presses the *clear* key. If the logic in the two earlier versions had been implemented, a problem number will have been wasted since the CTRL record would have been updated before the reported problem information was stored in the file. In this version, however, if the terminal operator aborts the request, no numbers are lost because the CTRL record has not yet been accessed. Remember, in this last version, the CTRL record is only accessed when a problem record *is* stored in the file. This may save a substantial number of wasted numbers in such an implementation.

At this point you might ask: If the terminal operator cancels a request by pressing the *clear* key, why not access the CTRL record a second time to change the incremental key to its original value? This is a good idea if only one terminal operator is using the system. However, since most systems have more than one concurrent user, a serious problem could arise if we tried to "undo" this add request. Let me describe such a processing situation.

Suppose that the next-problem-key value in the CTRL record is the value 15. Suppose that two terminal operators are using the system at the same time and we've implemented an undo-a-problem-number scheme. Processing might be as follows:

T1: Accesses the CTRL record, obtains the number 15, updates this value to 16, and rewrites the CTRL record to the file with the value 16. The tenant that T1 is servicing is therefore assigned the problem number 15.

T2: Accesses the CTRL record in the same way that T1 just did. Hence, the "next key" value now in the CTRL record will be 17 after this record is rewritten to the file. T2's tenant is assigned problem number 16.

T1: The tenant being serviced by T1 decides to cancel the report. T1 presses the CLEAR key. The system accesses the CTRL record, changes the "next key" value to 16 (17 minus 1), and places this value in the file.

T2: Finishes the request and record 16 is stored in the file.

Now, according to the value now contained in the CTRL record, the next problem number to be assigned is the value 16. But record 16 has already been stored in the master file! Clearly, the next problem report request will fail because a duplicate key error has been made. As you can see, the use of a control record as described in this application must be carefully planned so as to avoid application errors and to maintain a dependable system. These three approaches to the same problem are all feasible, but each has its own problems. A situation involving this type or processing should be analyzed to avoid as many problems as possible and to tell users exactly what is to be done if an error should occur.

A less complicated solution to this sequential number problem may have been to use the current time and date as a key to the record so as to avoid any need for a record similar to the CTRL record used here. On the other hand, a time and date may be harder to remember than a four-digit number like the one defined for this application. The tenant's name, or even the tenant's apartment number combined with a sequence number, could be used as the key. It would then be possible to obtain a list of all problems reported by a given tenant or all problems within a certain apartment. Finally, we might ask: Since there are only four digits to hold a problem number, what will happen when the CTRL record "next key" reaches a value of 9999? I'll let you think about this situation.

Obviously, many different considerations must be taken into account in the design of a system. We've adopted one design that may not be the most flexible design for such a system. However, it has allowed us to point out design flaws and raise issues concerning system usability that may not have been possible had the system been designed "perfectly" in the first place.

It is difficult to summarize in one or two short paragraphs all the information presented in this chapter. Many important concepts about program logic appear here alongside key terms such as *transaction, task, session,* and *conversation.* The use of special reserved memory and transaction id restart values are two topics of particular interest. Because a considerable amount of material has been covered here, you may want to study the logic presented a second time. If you do, see whether you can modify the logic to fit the standards of your company, or see whether the proposed logic will work within your on-line software monitor system. We continue the discussion of transaction-program design in the next chapter by studying the conversational approach to transaction implementation. We also look at another way of implementing a nonconversational transaction so that it will carry out the same activities described in this chapter, but under a single transaction. This will round out our brief study of the design of on-line transactions and programs for use in a software monitor system similar to IBM's CICS. This background should be more than sufficient to enable you to make reasonable decisions about transaction design and implementation for on-line applications within your environment.

THOUGHT QUESTIONS

> *1. Can you alter the nonconversational logic presented so that the application functions in a conversational mode?*

2. *How will module decomposition affect the use of exceptional condition processing? That is, how would design and use of exceptional conditions be affected if your paragraphs were physically implemented as separate callable modules?*

3. *What restrictions does the software monitor that you are using impose on the design of your transactions or programs?*

4. *If it is possible for two terminal operators to update or delete a record at the same time, how can you protect your system from problems if your code has been implemented in a nonconversational programming style?*

5. *The logic presented in this chapter offered a way of implementing a simulated-sequential-file-processing mode of operation. In your environment, is sequential file processing available? If so, what impact does sequential file processing have on performance? Do any of your access methods require an interruption in processing to carry out that file request?*

6

ALTERNATIVE DESIGN AND PACKAGING STYLES

The analyst, designer, and programmer of today may be aware of several feasible approaches to the development of an on-line system. One approach taken in the last chapter was to functionally decompose the application so that each function became a unique definition to the on-line operating environment; further, the application programs were implemented in a nonconversational rather than conversational programming style. In this chapter, other implementation styles and their benefits and disadvantages will be presented. As was argued earlier, the nonconversational implementation approach should be used at the lowest level of implementation, regardless of how the system is functionally organized. In this chapter, you'll see both conversational implementation and nonconversational implementation solutions to the same application presented in the earlier chapters.

The putting together of the individual pieces of a system to form paragraphs or modules or programs is what we call packaging. Many terms can be used to define a piece of a system and the various methodologies by which you can be guided along in your packaging tasks. In an on-line environment, however, the packaging of a system should be done with functionality, maintainability, and flexibility as well as performance in mind. Many of the packaging techniques applied to batch systems do not work well for on-line systems because those who package the system tend to forget that there is another level of software that must be communicated with—namely, the on-line monitor. For this reason, many a system runs poorly after it is packaged and ready to go because of system overhead. So the blame is put on the software monitor such as CICS, IMS, or TSO, and not on the packaging of the application, where the blame might very well lie. This chapter presents several approaches to packaging that may not agree with your philosophy. However, if we agree that packaging is an important design issue, then we'll be on the same track singing the same song.

In Chapter 5, we decomposed the on-line system along functional boundaries to arrive at five transaction definitions. Five definitions may be just right according to your standards; five may be too few; or five may be too many. Also, the activities of the programs may have been too many; thus, some of the activities or functions within each program may have been handled better by a subroutine or subprogram. Finally, maybe the total number of lines of code per program exceeded some arbitrary limit so that each program now needs to be divided to make its size acceptable to your standards.

Although the points above dictate the packaging guidelines, each guideline has certain drawbacks and benefits that the packagers must be aware of.

TRADE-OFFS IN SYSTEM PACKAGING DESIGNS

First, as the number of transaction definitions increases, the functionality of an application generally becomes more divided, with the result that the system is better understood and maintained. Further, as the number of transaction definitions increases, program size tends to decrease, as does the number of activities performed by each program. In some on-line monitors, however, an application consisting of a large number of transactions may increase system overhead because table searches are required for transaction initiation. Note that in this instance the *software monitor* may be influencing your system packaging decisions. To maintain this delicate balance the systems programming staff or on-line administration group must carefully monitor and communicate with the application areas so that system control tables do not become a bottleneck within the on-line operating environment. This effort may require that table entries be regularly reorganized on the basis of usage and user demand for the applications.

Under CICS, for example, each time that a transaction is initiated, CICS service components search the PCT to associate the transaction id with the first program to be initiated and to verify that the transaction id entered by the user is legitimate. Generally, the searching of the PCT (as defined by the systems programming staff) can be done in one of two ways, linear or binary. If a linear searching technique is selected for this table, and it then starts at the first entry in the table and analyzes each entry until a match is found, these service components may take a considerable amount of time, especially if the table is large. If your entry resides three-fourths of the way down a lengthy table and if your application is used heavily, a substantial amount of computer time may be used by the on-line monitor merely in searching the PCT for your transaction id. A simple reordering of this table that places your entry closer to the top could substantially improve your average transaction response time. In one instance, a reordering of several large control tables (including the PCT and PPT) improved transaction performance between 10 and 35 percent! As you see, establishing transaction definitions does have an impact on transaction performance in an on-line environment.

The definition and placement of table entries must be well planned by developers and system staffs if overall system availability is to be maintained and functionality, maintainability, or system flexibility not sacrificed. Clearly, this goal is difficult to achieve.

Now let's consider the activities within a program module. Refer back to the nonconversational program logic in Chapter 5. You'll notice that each program performs some similar processing. For example, the first half of the update and delete is just like the inquiry process. In each of these functions, the record is read from the file and displayed on the screen prior to actual delete or update processing. Why not modularize this component, then, so that this activity can be contained in one module and invoked when needed? This seems like a good idea, but, wait a minute, a few things might have to be considered before we jump to this conclusion.

First, when the problem information is displayed during the update process, fields can be changed to reflect the needs of the user. Further, it may be the case that not *all* of the fields on the update screen can be modified by the user; that is, some fields might be marked "protected" or "nonmodifiable." Since the user cannot change *any* of the data field values on the inquiry screen, maybe *all* of the fields are protected in this case.

If a proposed system structure includes a module to display the problem information as described, then some control indicator may need to be passed to that module so that the appropriate fields are *protected* before the data are displayed to the screen, depending on the function to be performed. This flag or indicator may not agree with your design standards for module coupling or cohesion. Hence, we've reached another point where a trade-off decision has to be made during the design process.

Still another related problem may be that each time a program calls another program within an on-line environment, an intervening call may have to be made to the software monitor to request that program control be changed to another module. This call to the on-line monitor clearly costs time in terms of application performance, possibly as much as two to three thousand machine instructions or more. If you take a large, highly modular system in which transactions might issue twenty-five or more program calls, the on-line monitor could easily spend one, two, or more seconds of computer time in changing module processing because of application calls or transfers. Hence, as an on-line system is being developed, you must remain aware of the number of program invocations within each transaction so that you can predict how much time will be needed by the software monitor to support that transaction. You will then be able to determine the average response time for that transaction, and thus will have a basis for evaluating transaction performance. Overmodularity could cost you a substantial amount of response time once the system is implemented. Investigate these costs early in the development process.

IMPACT OF DESIGN ON TESTING
AND IMPLEMENTATION

Design also has a substantial impact on implementation and testing. For example, in the design presented in Chapter 5, each module was a stand-alone unit and could have been implemented and tested independently of any other module. In the example that you are about to see, you'll notice that since the logic for all the functions is packaged into a single module, much more coordination and communication are needed between the members implementing these approaches. A poor team member can pull down the development of all functions, not just his own, if the system is packaged in fewer modules. Again, we see that packaging related to functional boundaries within the system requires close attention during the design phase.

The modularity of a system is an especially difficult and controversial topic for on-line system designers to deal with, yet it is critical to the performance of a transaction, user satisfaction, and even performance of other transactions within the on-line environment. In general, I think that the applications and systems programming staffs should carefully measure existing systems to determine the percentage of system overhead within a transaction structure. The results can be used to establish guidelines on program size, number of program calls per transaction, and transaction structure so as to safeguard against developing a system that will perform poorly or degrade other applications using the computer.

If you find that your transactions are too modular and that performance is suffering because of system overhead (owing to the design of the application), then it might be reasonable to subdivide a transaction into two or more smaller transactions. The transactions will accomplish the same functions and minimize the impact of a long-running and large transaction on the operating environment. Further, measuring the impact of a transaction on a system is an extremely complex task and may require analysis of the results produced by your hardware and software performance monitors to derive accurate statistics about program performance. Also, keep in mind that hardware is getting faster and faster. If your installation is planning a hardware upgrade in the future, then an extensive reworking of a system could be postponed or eliminated by acquiring faster hardware. On the other hand, you could be delaying the inevitable.

Let's now look at three other on-line programming styles to implement the Landlord Management System that you saw in the previous chapters. Remember that in the last chapter we looked at a multitransaction nonconversational design of this application. Here we look at a *single*-transaction nonconversational approach, then at a multitransaction conversational implementation, and, finally, at a single-transaction conversational implementation.

SINGLE-TRANSACTION
NONCONVERSATIONAL DESIGN

In the implementation of this application, all application programs are initiated by defining *one* transaction to the system. Hence, the functional divisions of the application must be made within the application program or programs. This approach is actually not much different from the one presented in Chapter 5, as you'll see. Also, notice in the logic that follows how the memory area is again used to remember what was done by the application during the last execution or initiation of the application's programs.

Driver Logic

```
If "memory"(1) = 'b' or screen is unformatted then
   do
      send out the menu screen
      set memory(1) = 'M'
      set memory(2) = ' '
      end the program with "next" tranid = "LAMS"
   end do
Receive the menu screen
If memory(1) = 'M' then
   If menu selection is not valid then
      do
         send out the menu screen with an
            appropriate error message
         set memory(1) = 'M'
         end the program with tranid = "LAMS"
      end do
If menu selection = 'I' or memory(1) = 'I' then
   go to INQUIRY LOGIC
else
   If menu selection = 'R' or memory(1) = 'R' then
      go to ADD LOGIC
   else
      If menu selection = 'D' or memory(1) = 'D' then
         go to DELETE LOGIC
      else
         go to UPDATE LOGIC
```

Inquiry Logic

```
set memory(1) = 'I'
If memory(2) = ' ' then
  do
     send out the "request a problem number screen"
     set memory(2) to '1'
     end the program and set the next transaction
        id to LAMS
  end do
If memory(2) = '1' then
  do
     receive the "request a problem number screen"
     if problem number is not valid then
        do
           send out the "request a problem number screen"
              with an appropriate error message
           set memory(2) to '1'
           end the program and set the next tranid
              initiator to LAMS
        end do
     else
        do
           build master record key from the screen data
           if the read that follows fails then
              go to subparagraph IA
           read the associated master record from the
              proper file
           build the screen to display the information
              on this master record
           send out the display screen
           set memory(2) to '2'
           end the program and set the next tranid
              initiator to LAMS
        end do
  end do
else
  do
     send out the menu screen
     set memory(1) to 'M'
     set memory(2) to ' '
     end the program and set the next tranid
        initiator to LAMS
  end do
```

subparagraph IA.
  send out the "request a problem number screen" and
    a message that the record requested was not
    in the file
  set memory(2) to '1'
  end the program and set the next tranid initiator
    to LAMS

Delete Logic

set memory(1) = 'D'
If memory(2) = ' ' then
  do
    send out the "request a problem number to delete" screen
    set memory(2) to 1
    set next tranid to LAMS
    end execution
  end do
If memory(2) = 1 then
  do
    receive the "request a problem to delete" screen
    if the problem number is not valid then
      do
        send out the "request a problem to delete" screen
          and an error message
        set memory(2) to 1
        set next tranid to LAMS
        end execution
      end do
    else
      do
        build master record key from screen data
        if the read that follows fails then
          go to subparagraph DA
        READ the master record from the file
        build the screen to display this master record
          so that the user is sure that this is the
          record to be deleted
        send out this record display
        set memory(2) to 2
        set next tranid to LAMS
        end execution
      end do
  end do

```
        else
          do
            receive the problem information display
            if user really wants this record deleted by
                responding YES to the "are you sure" question
                then
              do
                  build master record key from screen data
                  if the delete that follows fails then
                    go to subparagraph DB
                  DELETE the associated master record
                  send out the menu screen with a message
                    that says record xxx was deleted
                  set memory(1) to M
                  set memory(2) to ' '
                  set next tranid to LAMS
                    end execution
              end do
            else
              do
                send out the menu screen with a message
                  that the delete request was aborted
                set memory(1) to M
                set memory(2) to ' '
                set next tranid to LAMS
                end execution
              end do
          end do
    subparagraph DA.
      send out the "request a problem to delete" screen and
      a message that the record was not on file
      set memory(2) to 1
      set next tranid to LAMS
      end execution

    subparagraph DB.
      send out the "request a problem to delete" screen
        with a message that the problem record has been
        deleted underneath your request or that an
        error has occurred in the system
      set memory(2) to 1
      set next tranid to LAMS
      end execution
```

Update Logic

```
set memory(1) to 'U'
If memory(2) = ' ' then
   do
      send out the "request a problem number to update" screen
      set memory(2) to 1
      set next tranid to LAMS
      end execution
   end do
If memory(2) = 1 then
   do
      receive the "request a problem to update" screen
      if the problem number is not valid then
         do
            send out the "request a problem to update" screen
               and an error message
            set memory(2) to 1
            set next tranid to LAMS
            end execution
         end do
      else
         do
            build master record key from screen data
            if the read that follows fails then
               go to subparagraph UA
            READ the master record from the file
            build the screen to display this master record
               so that the user is sure that this is the
               record to be updated
            send out this record display
            set memory(2) to 2
            set next tranid to LAMS
            end execution
         end do
   end do
else
   do
      receive the problem information display
      if any of the fields have been modified then
         do
            edit each of the modified fields
```

```
                    if any fields do not pass edit then
                      do
                        send out the "update display" screen and
                          all of its data with a message about
                          the bad fields
                        set memory(2) to 2
                        set next tranid to LAMS
                        end execution
                      end do
                    else
                      do
                        build master record key from screen data
                        if the update that follows fails then
                          go to subparagraph UB
                        READ FOR UPDATE the associated master record
                        move changed fields from screen to master record
                        REWRITE the master record
                        send out the menu screen with a message
                          that says record xxx was updated
                        set memory(1) to M
                        set memory(2) to ' '
                        set next tranid to LAMS
                        end execution
                      end do
                  end do
                else
                  do
                    send out the menu screen with a message
                      that the update request was aborted
                    set memory(1) to M
                    set memory(2) to ' '
                    set next tranid to LAMS
                    end execution
                  end do
              end do
            subparagraph UA.
              send out the "request a problem to update" screen and
                a message that the record was not on file
              set memory(2) to 1
              set next tranid to LAMS
              end execution

            subparagraph UB.
              send out the "request a problem to update" screen
                with a message that the problem record has been
```

deleted underneath your request or that an
error has occurred in the system
set memory(2) to 1
set next tranid to LAMS
end execution

Add Logic

set memory(1) to 'R'

If memory(2) = ' ' then
   do
      move 'CTRL' to control-key
      if next read fails then
         go to subparagraph REAL-BAD-PROBLEM
      READ FOR UPDATE master file for 'CTRL'
      move next-key-value to problem-number-on-screen
      add 1 to next-key-value
      REWRITE 'CTRL' record to master file
      move built-in-date-in-system to screen-date
      display "report a problem screen" with problem number
        and date just obtained
      set memory(2) to 1
      set next tranid to LAMS
      end execution
   end do

If memory(2) = 1 then
   do
      receive the "request a problem to report on" screen
      if any field fails editing then
         do
            send out the "request a problem to report on" screen
              with all data and appropriate error messages
            set memory(2) to 1
            set next tranid to LAMS
            end execution
         end do
      else
         do
            build master record from screen data
            if the WRITE that follows fails then
               go to subparagraph AA
            WRITE the new master record to the file
            send out the "report a problem screen" with a
              message that the record was added to the file

```
            set memory(2) to 2
            set next tranid to LAMS
            end execution
          end do
      end do
  else
    do
       send out the menu screen
       set memory(1) to M
       set memory(2) to ' '
       set next tranid to LAMS
       end execution
    end do
subparagraph AA.
    send out the "request a problem to report on" screen and
       a message that the record was already on file and
       that there is a rather severe error in the system
    set memory(2) to 1
    set next tranid to LAMS
    end execution
subparagraph REAL-BAD-PROBLEM.
    send out the system menu screen with a message that the
       main control record for determining problem numbers
       has been destroyed and that the user should call
       the analyst immediately.
    set memory(1) to M
    set memory(2) to ' '
    set next tranid to LAMS
    end execution
```

Did you notice how the functions are divided within this logic? Can you identify components that could be modularized? Did you notice any difference between this logic and that presented in Chapter 5? Finally, do you understand how the different memory values dictate the processing to be done on the next initiation of the program for this transaction?

You should be able to answer each of the questions above easily, and you should be able to understand how the logic flows from one task to another under the auspices of a single transaction definition to the on-line environment. You should also be able to see that the value in memory at the time that this logic is invoked determines which function is to be performed and which activity within that function is to occur. Since this is a nonconversational implementation style, you should have noticed that there are many return points or exit points within the logic. If this arrangement does not agree with your style, it can easily be changed so that there is a single exit point from within this system. Lastly, notice the many exceptional conditions being used with each function having its own set of such paragraphs. This is similar to the logic presented earlier.

This logic is, of course, an implementation having all functions within a single program that is driven by one transaction id. It would not be difficult to modularize this system (as we noted in Chapter 5) so that each function is a different module but still drives this system under a single transaction id. Let's spend just a little time comparing the nonconversational style here with the one in Chapter 5.

What has changed in the approach here? It should be obvious that the driver module has changed, since it has become the focal point of all reinitiation of this application. In the multitransaction version, each function could be initiated by the system independently, since each function was related to a transaction definition to the on-line environment. Here, however, all initiation occurs at the same point and so values are assigned to memory to aid the driver component in determining the function to be invoked. Further, all users must go through the menu to get to a particular function. In this version, then, all users enter the application at a common point, whereas in the earlier version users could enter the system from any of five different points. This may be yet another important aspect to consider in your design approach.

Now let's look at the logic within each function. If you carefully compare the two styles, you'll notice little difference in the functional logic except for *where* the logical code is physically placed and who invokes it. That is, in the multitransaction version presented in Chapter 5 the code for each function was in its own module, invoked by the on-line monitor through the transaction id. In this style, the same functional logic is made up of a set of paragraphs, and a single section of code within this logic gives control to the various functions. In other words, the packaging of these two implementation styles is different.

Now let's think about the differences in the implementation of the two approaches. In Chapter 5, more on-line control table entries would be required because the approach there necessitates more transaction definitions and more programs. Here, only one transaction definition is needed, and only one program definition. Rather than four or five small programs, we'll have one *big* program running in the system to support the various functions. As a result, you may favor the earlier approach, which tends to use storage resources more efficiently than the approach just presented, especially if one or two of the functions are rarely used.

Still another trade-off between these styles has to do with security. What!? Yes, the design of these systems may seriously affect security in your environment. Let me explain. In the multitransaction version presented in Chapter 5, each function had its own unique transaction id. Hence, if several users wanted to use this system, you could tell each user which specific transaction ids he could use. If you didn't want certain users to know about the delete function, you wouldn't tell them about the transaction id for invoking the delete program(s), or you'd make sure that they were not cleared to use this transaction under their sign-on. On the other hand, since the system menu displays all of the functions, such a menu may not be desirable when multiple users are involved and when you want to restrict certain users to a particular number of functions.

In the single-transaction approach, the situation is different. Since there is only one transaction definition to the system and since system security is usually done at the transaction level and not at the program level, all users could do any of the functions within this system. Where does the security burden lie in this implementation? You guessed it—within the application programs. More specifically, it lies within the driver component or subprogram invoked from within the driver logic. This situation leads to problems when a communication line or terminal goes down and you want to swap coaxial cables or lines for a user, or when a user is allowed access to another function. No change can be made without modifying the application program; that constraint is not desirable for large, multiuser application systems.

Both approaches will work, however, from a user's point of view, and both will perform about the same. The first approach may be somewhat faster and the second may be packaged a little tighter, but both do the job. Thus, these two nonconversational approaches offer the user roughly the same response time and they use about the same amount of resources (that is, if we forget about table entry placement for the time being). The packaging decision is left up to you. However, *both* approaches are much better than the next two implementation styles that you'll see.

MULTITRANSACTION CONVERSATIONAL DESIGN

In the multitransaction conversational approach to implementation, functions are defined to the on-line environment as individual, unique transactions, just as they were in Chapter 5. Hence, the multitransaction nonconversational design and the multitransaction conversational design do not differ on the functional level, but rather on the coding or implementational level, as you'll soon see.

If you recall, a transaction is composed of one or more tasks, and a task is a measurable amount of work being performed by the program(s) within a transaction definition. In a conversational implementation, each transaction is usually composed of only *one* task. However, that task fluctuates between active and suspended states during the course of transaction processing. In other words, when a conversational transaction is initiated by the user, its resources always have to be managed by the on-line monitor. Recall that in the nonconversational approach, as soon as an activity is completed by the program, the program returns control back to the software monitor, thus ending its execution. This action marks the end of a task entity; more generally, each logical function is composed of several task entities to be managed by the online monitor. This is not the case in conversational transactions.

Again, let's look at a simple example. Suppose that the user initiates the transaction and that the menu for the system is displayed. At this point, the application program must wait for the user's response. If the software monitor does *not* have to keep track of the fact that the program is waiting, then the program's resources do not require managing. This can only occur if the transaction-task-program is *not* in the system—in other words, if it is not executing.

On the other hand, if the program simply pauses and is sitting in an idle state *waiting* for the user's response, then that task *does* require services from the on-line monitor to keep track of storage assignments, program status, task priority, and so on. As a result, this program has not ended execution but is said to be in a "wait" or "suspended" state since it is waiting to resume processing. If the user chooses to go out to lunch at this time, waiting continues indefinitely, as does the needless use of system resources by this task. There is a great difference between the execution of these systems and application implementations.

In the logic that follows, you'll see the points where the program pauses to wait for an operator response. Each pause occurs as a result of a communication with the terminal. Hence, a conversational transaction differs from a nonconversational transaction primarily in how that transaction communicates with the terminal and what the transaction does while waiting for a user's response. A simple change in your style of terminal-to-application communication can help improve the performance of your system, as well as help the performance of other users in the system who are competing with you for task resources. Let's now turn to the *two* conversational implementation styles; the first to be discussed is the multitransaction implementation style, the second, a single-transaction implementation.

Driver Module

```
If "memory" = 'b̸' then
   do
      set memory to 'M'
      send out the menu screen
   end do
Receive the menu screen
Do while menu selection is not valid and user has
   not pressed the CLEAR key
   send out the menu screen with an appropriate
      error message
```

```
    receive the menu screen
end do while
If CLEAR key was pressed then
    end execution
If menu selection = 'I' then
    transfer control to program LAMINQ
else
    If menu selection = 'R' then
        transfer control to program LAMADD
    else
        If menu selection = 'D' then
            transfer control to program LAMDEL
        else
            transfer control to program LAMUPD
```

Inquiry Logic

```
If initiating tranid = 'LAMI' or current screen
    is unformatted then
    do
        send out the "request a problem number" screen
        set memory to 1
    end do
RESTART-THE-INQUIRY
Receive the "request a problem number" screen
Do while memory not equal ' ' and CLEAR key is not pressed
    If problem number is not valid then
        do
            send out the "request a problem number"
                screen with an appropriate error message
            set memory to 1
            receive the "request a problem number"
                screen
        end do
    else
        do
            build master record key from screen data
            if the READ that follows fails, then
                go to subparagraph IA
            READ the associated master record
            build the "display screen" associated with
                this master record
```

```
        send out the "display screen"
        set memory to ' '
        receive the "display screen"
     end do
  end do while
If CLEAR key was pressed then
  end execution
else
  If initiating tranid not equal 'LAMI' then
     do
        set memory to ' '
        transfer control to LAMENU
     end do
  else
     do
        send out the "request a problem number"
          screen
        set memory to 1
        go to RESTART-THE-INQUIRY
     end do
subparagraph IA.
  send out the "request a problem number screen"
     with a message that the record requested
     was not on file
  set memory to 1
  go to RESTART-THE-INQUIRY
```

Delete Logic

```
If initiating tranid not equal LAMD or current screen
  is unformatted then
  do
     send out the "request a problem to delete" screen
     set memory to 1
  end do
RESTART-THE-DELETE
Receive the "request a problem to delete" screen
Do while memory not equal ' ' and CLEAR key not pressed
  if problem number is not valid then
     do
        send out the "request a problem to delete"
          screen with an appropriate error message
```

```
            set memory to 1
            receive the "request a problem to delete" screen
        end do
        else
            do
                build master key from screen data
                if the READ that follows fails then
                    go to subparagraph DA
                READ master record with this key
                build the "delete display" for this master record
                send out the "delete display" screen
                receive the "delete display" screen
                if the user really wanted this record deleted then
                    do
                        if the DELETE that follows fails then
                            go to subparagraph DB
                        DELETE the master record having this key
                        send out the "delete display" with a
                            message that this record has been
                            deleted from the file
                        set memory to ' '
                        receive the "delete display" screen
                    end do
                else
                    do
                        send out the "delete display" with a
                            message that the record was not
                            deleted as requested
                        set memory to ' '
                        receive the "delete display" screen
                    end do
            end do
    end do while

    if the CLEAR key was pressed then
        end execution
    else
        if initiating tranid not equal LAMD then
            do
                set memory to ' '
                transfer control to LAMENU
            end do
        else
            do
                send out the "request a problem to delete"
```

```
         screen
      set memory to 1
      go to RESTART-THE-DELETE
   end do
subparagraph DA.
   send out the "request a problem to delete"
      screen and a message that the record was
      not on file
   set memory to 1
   go to RESTART-THE-DELETE
subparagraph DB.
   send out the "request a problem to delete"
      screen with a message that the problem
      record was deleted from underneath
      the delete request and so it has been
      deleted from the file
   set memory to 1
   go to RESTART-THE-DELETE
```

Update Logic

```
If initiating tranid not equal LAMU or current screen is
   unformatted then
   do
      send out the "request a problem to update"
         screen
      set memory to 1
   end do
RESTART-THE-UPDATE
Receive the "request to update" screen
Do while memory not equal ' ' and CLEAR key not pressed
   If problem number is not valid then
      do
         send out the "request to update" screen
            with an appropriate error message
         set memory to 1
         receive the "request to update" screen
      end do
   else
      do
         build master key from screen data
```

if the READ that follows fails then
    go to subparagraph UA
READ FOR UPDATE this master record
build the "update display" screen from
    this record's information
display the "update display" screen
receive the "update display" screen
if any fields have been modified then
    do
        do while any fields fail editing and
            CLEAR key is not pressed
            send out the "update display" with
                a message describing the fields
                in error
            receive the "update display" screen
        end do while
        if CLEAR key has not been pressed then
            do
                move changed fields to master record
                REWRITE master record
                send out "update display" with a
                    message that master record has
                    been updated
                set memory to ' '
                receive the "update display" screen
            end do
        else
            unlock file from update mode for this
                master record key
        end do
    else
        unlock file from update mode for this
            master record key
    end do
end do while
If CLEAR key was pressed then
    end execution
else
    if initiation tranid not equal LAMU then
        do
            set memory to ' '
            transfer control to LAMENU
        end do
    else

```
        do
            send out the "request a problem to update"
              screen
            set memory to 1
            go to RESTART-THE-UPDATE
        end do
```

subparagraph UA.

```
    send out the "request a problem to update"
      screen and a message that the record was
      not on file
    set memory to 1
    go to RESTART-THE-UPDATE
```

subparagraph UB.

```
    send out the "request a problem to update" screen
      with a message that the problem record has
      been deleted underneath your request or that
      an error has occurred in the system
    set memory to 1
    go to RESTART-THE-UPDATE
```

Add Logic

```
If initiating tranid not equal LAMA or current screen
    if unformatted then
    do
        if the next READ fails then
            go to subparagraph REAL-BAD-PROBLEM
        READ FOR UPDATE the CTRL record
        move next-key-value to problem-number-on-screen
        add 1 to next-key-value
        REWRITE CTRL record to master file
        move built-in-date-in-system to screen-date
        display "report a problem" screen with
            problem number and date just obtained
        set memory to 1
    end do
RESTART-THE-ADD
Receive the "report a problem" screen
Do while memory not equal ' ' and CLEAR key not pressed
    If any field fails editing then
        do
```

```
            send out the "report a problem" screen
               with an appropriate error message
            set memory to 1
         end do
      else
         do
            build master record from this screen data
            if the WRITE that follows fails then
               go to subparagraph AA
            WRITE the master record to the file
            send out a blank "report a problem" screen
               with a message that the record has been
               successfully added to the file
            set memory to ' '
         end do
      Receive the "report a problem" screen
   end do while
If CLEAR key was pressed then
   end execution
else
   if initiating tranid not equal LAMA then
      do
         set memory to ' '
         transfer control to LAMENU
      end do
   else
      do
         if the next READ fails then
            go to subparagraph REAL-BAD-PROBLEM
         READ FOR UPDATE the CTRL record
         move next-key-value to problem-number-on-screen
         add 1 to next-key-value
         REWRITE CTRL record to master file
         move built-in-date-in-system to screen-date
         display "report a problem" screen with
            problem number and date just obtained
         set memory to 1
         go to RESTART-THE-ADD
      end do
subparagraph AA.
   send out the "report a problem" screen
      with a message that the record was
      already on file and that there is a
```

rather severe error in the system
set memory to M
set next tranid to LAMS
end execution

subparagraph REAL-BAD-PROBLEM.

send out the system menu with a message that
the main control record for this system
has been destroyed and that the user should
call for help immediately
set memory to M
set next tranid to LAMS
end execution

Several important points need to be mentioned about the logic above:

1. Modules transfer control to one another and calling between modules is not needed.

2. The code is iterative in that each function continues doing the same processes until it is terminated by the user when the *clear* key is pressed.

3. The only exit from the system is that provided by the *clear* key. Any other key continues task execution.

4. If a module was *not* initiated through its *own* transaction id—that is, it was initiated from the menu driver module—then the module performing the function returns control back to the menu driver to await further processing. On the other hand, when functional modules *are* initiated by their own transaction id, they *repeat* the same function until the user discontinues that function by pressing the *clear* key.

5. Note that in the UPDATE logic, it may be possible for a record to be held in the UPDATE mode for a substantial amount of time, especially if the user is a poor typist. Only after all errors are corrected and the record rewritten is the record available for access by another user. This may not seem to be a serious problem, but if your file access structure is VSAM oriented, you may be locking several users out of your file since VSAM enqueues at the control interval level and not at the individual record level. Lack of understanding here could cause serious response time problems for many users sharing a single or set of files.

6. Did you notice that after a screen was displayed it was "received" soon afterwards? As pointed out earlier, this time factor is the primary difference between conversational and nonconversational programming and it is the major reason why conversational transactions hold on to resources during their idle periods.

SINGLE TRANSACTION CONVERSATIONAL DESIGN

The last logic discussed here applies to single-transaction conversational programming implementation. Since it will appear familiar, you should have no trouble understanding its operation.

Driver Module

```
If "memory" = 'b' then
  do
    set memory to 'M'
    send out the menu screen
  end do
Receive the menu screen
Do while menu selection is not valid and user has
  not pressed the CLEAR key
    send out the menu screen with an appropriate
      error message
    receive the menu screen
end do while
If CLEAR key was pressed then
  end execution
If menu selection = 'I' then
  go to INQUIRY LOGIC
else
  If menu selection = 'R' then
    go to ADD LOGIC
  else
    If menu selection = 'D' then
      go to DELETE LOGIC
    else
      go to UPDATE LOGIC
```

Inquiry Logic

```
If current screen is unformatted then
  do
    send out the "request a problem number" screen
    set memory to 1
  end do
```

RESTART-THE-INQUIRY

Receive the "request a problem number" screen

Do while memory not equal ' ' and CLEAR key is not pressed

    If problem number is not valid then

        do

            send out the "request a problem number"

                screen with an appropriate error message

            set memory to 1

            receive the "request a problem number"

                screen

        end do

      else

        do

            build master record key from screen data

            if the READ that follows fails, then

                go to subparagraph IA

            READ the associated master record

            build the "display screen" associated with

                this master record

            send out the "display screen"

            set memory to ' '

            receive the "display screen"

        end do

end do while

If CLEAR key was pressed then

    end execution

else

    do

        set memory to ' '

        go to DRIVER MODULE

    end do

subparagraph IA.

    send out the "request a problem number screen"

        with a message that the record requested

        was not on file

    set memory to 1

    go to RESTART-THE-INQUIRY

Delete Logic

If current screen is unformatted then

    do

        send out the "request a problem to delete" screen

```
        set memory to 1
    end do
RESTART-THE-DELETE
Receive the "request a problem to delete" screen
Do while memory not equal ' ' and CLEAR key not pressed
    if problem number is not valid then
        do
            send out the "request a problem to delete"
                screen with an appropriate error message
            set memory to 1
            receive the "request a problem to delete" screen
        end do
    else
        do
            build master key from screen data
            if the READ that follows fails then
                go to subparagraph DA
            READ master record with this key
            build the "delete display" for this master record
            send out the "delete display" screen
            receive the "delete display" screen
            if the user really wanted this record deleted then
                do
                    if the DELETE that follows fails then
                        go to subparagraph DB
                    DELETE the master record having this key
                    send out the "delete display" with a
                        message that this record has been
                        deleted from the file
                    set memory to ' '
                    receive the "delete display" screen
                end do
            else
                do
                    send out the "delete display" with a
                        message that the record was not
                        deleted as requested
                    set memory to ' '
                    receive the "delete display" screen
                end do
        end do
end do while
```

```
if the CLEAR key was pressed then
   end execution
else
   do
      set memory to ' '
      go to DRIVER MODULE
   end do
subparagraph DA.
   send out the "request a problem to delete"
      screen and a message that the record was
      not on file
   set memory to 1
   go to RESTART-THE-DELETE
subparagraph DB.
   send out the "request a problem to delete"
      screen with a message that the problem
      record was deleted from underneath
      the delete request and so it has been
      deleted from the file
   set memory to 1
   go to RESTART-THE-DELETE
```

Update Logic

```
If current screen is unformatted then
   do
      send out the "request a problem to update"
         screen
      set memory to 1
   end do
RESTART-THE-UPDATE
Receive the "request to update" screen
Do while memory not equal ' ' and CLEAR key not pressed
   If problem number is not valid then
      do
         send out the "request to update" screen
            with an appropriate error message
         set memory to 1
         receive the "request to update" screen
      end do
   else
```

```
do
    build master key from screen data
    if the READ that follows fails then
        go to subparagraph UA
    READ FOR UPDATE this master record
    build the "update display" screen from
        this record's information
    display the "update display" screen
    receive the "update display" screen
    if any fields have been modified then
        do
            do while any fields fail editing and
                CLEAR key is not pressed
                send out the "update display" with
                    a message describing the fields
                    in error
                receive the "update display" screen
            end do while

            if CLEAR key has not been pressed then
                do
                    move changed fields to master record
                    REWRITE master record
                    send out "update display" with a
                        message that master record has
                        been updated
                    set memory to ' '
                    receive the "update display" screen
                end do
            else
                unlock file from update mode for this
                    master record key
        end do
    else
        unlock file from update mode for this
            master record key
    end do
end do while
If CLEAR key was pressed then
    end execution
else
    do
        set memory to ' '
        go to DRIVER MODULE
    end do
```

subparagraph UA.

    send out the "request a problem to update"
       screen and a message that the record was
       not on file
    set memory to 1
    go to RESTART-THE-UPDATE

subparagraph UB.

    send out the "request a problem to update" screen
       with a message that the problem record has
       been deleted underneath your request or that
       an error has occurred in the system
    set memory to 1
    go to RESTART-THE-UPDATE

Add Logic

If current screen is unformatted then
    do
        if the next READ fails then
          go to subparagraph REAL-BAD-PROBLEM
        READ FOR UPDATE the CTRL record
        move next-key-value to problem-number-on-screen
        add 1 to next-key-value
        REWRITE CTRL record to master file
        move built-in-date-in-system to screen-date
        display "report a problem" screen with
          problem number and date just obtained
        set memory to 1
    end do

RESTART-THE-ADD

Receive the "report a problem" screen

Do while memory not equal ' ' and CLEAR key not pressed

    If any field fails editing then
        do
          send out the "report a problem" screen
            with an appropriate error message
          set memory to 1
        end do
    else
        do
          build master record from this screen data
          if the WRITE that follows fails then

```
            go to subparagraph AA
            WRITE the master record to the file
            send out a blank "report a problem" screen
                with a message that the record has been
                successfully added to the file
            set memory to ' '
        end do
    Receive the "report a problem" screen
end do while
If CLEAR key was pressed then
    end execution
else
    do
        set memory to ' '
        go to DRIVER MODULE
    end do
subparagraph AA.
    send out the "report a problem" screen
        with a message that the record was
        already on file and that there is a
        rather severe error in the system
    set memory to ' '
    go to DRIVER MODULE
subparagraph REAL-BAD-PROBLEM.
    send out the system menu with a message that
        the main control record for this system
        has been destroyed and that the user should
        call for help immediately
    set memory to ' '
    go to DRIVER MODULE
```

These two approaches differ in the same ways that the nonconversational implementations did. Hence, the same trade-offs could be made between these approaches.

Now that most of the major points have been brought out about the four approaches, we should note that many other variations of this logic are possible, and that another design may be more efficient or structurally better than the methods presented. I'm leaving it up to you to analyze what has been presented here and to derive a design that is acceptable for implementation in your environment.

You have seen several different approaches to implementing a solution to the same problem. You have also been exposed to some advantages and disadvantages that need to be considered when you are choosing an implementation strategy. The overall discussion of the approaches and the trade-offs should improve your understanding of on-line development, design, and packaging approaches available. Now we can move from on-line design (but not forget it!) to the more technical aspects of on-line implementation. Hence, the remaining chapters of this text concentrate on activities such as screen coding, program coding, and on-line commands. With your understanding of the on-line application structure, you should find the implementation rather simple. In the next chapter, we begin the implementation of our Landlord Management System by first developing our screen displays. Next, we study each area of the IBM CICS Command-Level programming structure so that we can implement our application using this software tool. We'll conclude our implementation with workable programs in which you'll see reflected the pseudologic just presented. You will be surprised to find how easy it is to implement a CICS on-line application. Without further discussion, let's implement our well-designed application.

THOUGHT QUESTIONS

1. *For each design style presented in this chapter and in Chapter 5, "modularize" those styles into separate programs and discuss the impact of that modularization in terms of functionality, maintainability, security, and performance.*

2. *Is communicating with a file the same as communicating with a terminal as far as conversational versus nonconversational implementation goes? Explain.*

3. *What external restrictions are placed on the design of your on-line systems from management, systems programming, the software monitor, or other areas within your environment? Can any be changed?*

4. *In terms of security, how can you design a menu so that each user could begin the system through a menu rather than by having to know several different transactions for each function that he or she wants to perform? How would you implement this menu on the screen and how would you operate or process this menu from the application program?*

5. *Do you have large single-transaction driven on-line applications? How did they come about? Are they necessary? What alternative designs might improve the overall performance and design of such transactions and maybe even make them more user friendly?*

II

IMPLEMENTING
ON-LINE APPLICATIONS
(USING COBOL
AND CICS)

7
COMMAND-LEVEL PROGRAMMING

In Part I we concentrated strictly on the analysis, structure, and design of an on-line application. We are now ready to implement our solutions using the CICS software monitor as our implementation instrument. Before we do so, however, we should note that, in addition to being a subroutine to the CICS system, our application program involves another level of software called *execute interface*. Since this level provides the communication between CICS and our application, it makes the commands in our programs simple and easy to understand. Hence, before we examine the commands used to implement our display screens and our programs, we must understand the interfaces and the various roles of the software components in our application processing. Execute interface is the primary level of software between our application program and the CICS management components.

EXECUTE INTERFACE PROGRAM

The execute interface program (EIP) is a system that fits between our application program and the CICS components. Each time that we want to send a display to the terminal, read a record from a file, enqueue on a resource, or whatever, our requests first go through EIP before being passed on to the CICS system. In other words, our application program can be thought of as a subroutine to EIP in the communications hierarchy, as shown below:

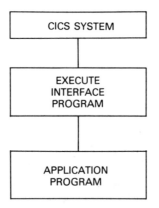

TRANSFERRING INFORMATION
BETWEEN ON-LINE COMPONENTS

In the communications chain, we communicate our requests to EIP through a special control block called the *execute interface block* (EIB). This control block is automatically placed into your applications program by a special batch component of the CICS system called the *command-level translator*. The EIB is simply an argument-parameter list between your application program and the service modules within CICS. When your application issues a CICS command, the code generated by that command will automatically place the proper information into the EIB and pass control to the execute interface program (EIP) to have your request processed. Hence, the application programmer does not have to know what is contained in the EIB, since the CICS commands automatically manage the EIB for the programmer. For example, fields in the EIB will inform CICS that your application wants to read the file MASTR for the record having the key ABC. If the record is found, return control to the next command; otherwise, return control to the paragraph name "xxxxxxxx."

When our request is passed to EIP, EIP translates the information we have stored in the EIB into a form that the CICS modules understand. The communication between EIP and CICS is the primary control block for our task, which is called the *task control area* (TCA). Our application program does not have to know the format of the TCA (which is a rather large control block) thus providing more integrity to the system; instead, CICS relies on EIP to place the proper information into the TCA before calling the appropriate CICS component to carry out our request. If we managed the TCA directly, we could easily enter the wrong information into this area and thus cause CICS to perform the wrong function or to abend our application. With EIP as a go-between, our communications are made easier and the results become more predictable.

After the CICS component performs our request, control returns to EIP to analyze the results. If the request is successful, EIP returns control to our program at the point where we left off, and we can continue with our processing. If the request is not successful, EIP will give control to the paragraph specified in the EIB as established by the applications programmer. Through the facilities of EIP, our program can "trap" exceptional conditions and take actions to correct them without having a forced abend occur. Further, minimal coding will allow our requests to be communicated through CICS so that we can perform whatever processing is needed. Finally, EIP assists in the debugging of our on-line application program by interfacing with another component of CICS called *execution diagnostic facility* (EDF). Through EIP and EDF, we can debug our programs on-line by "stepping" through the code and carefully looking at our logic, storage areas, and requests in order to obtain the fastest and one of the most reliable forms of on-line debugging available.

COMMAND-LEVEL COMMAND FORMAT

Communication with the execute interface program takes place through a series of commands called *command-level commands*. These special instructions are coded in our COBOL (PLI, RPG, or ASM) programs that communicate our requests to EIP. These commands are not standard COBOL instructions and will *not* compile normally without the use of a command-level language translator. In other words, when we are ready to define our application programs to the CICS system, our source code must be processed several times, as illustrated on following page:

First, our source code must be processed by the command-level translator, which converts our command-level code into COBOL code. Then the resulting COBOL code is directed into the COBOL compiler, which then compiles our program to produce an object module. Finally, the resulting object module is link-edited into a CICS load module library, and thus the loading of the program to the CICS system is completed. Of course, if any errors are detected along the way, processing terminates so that such errors can be corrected by the programmers.

COMMAND-LEVEL TRANSLATOR

The command-level translator simplifies the commands that we programmers must know, keeps to a minimum the knowledge that we must have about CICS processing, and thus enables us to place more emphasis on application design rather than on programming. Hence, the command-level statements that we code will generate a series of COBOL instructions from the

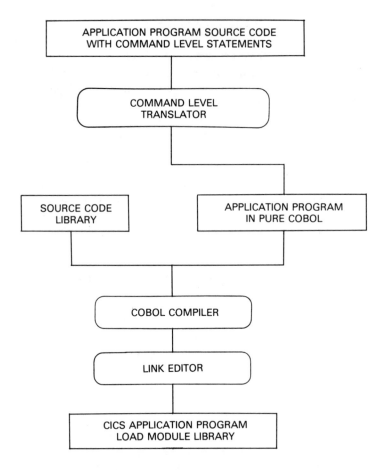

operands and values that we supply for our statements. These values will be placed into the execute interface block, a call will be issued to the execute interface program, and our request will be processed by the proper CICS component. Each of these processes occurs when only one command-level statement is coded. Hence, the command-level commands operate much like assembler language macrostatements in that these commands are expanded within our COBOL program into many COBOL instructions, which generate the communication needed between our program and CICS to carry out our requests.

Further, notice that after the translation phase of our source code into COBOL commands, the resulting application program is sent into a compile phase so that the COBOL compiler can produce a resulting executable module. Since two translation phases occur when command-level commands are used, two levels of diagnostic messages can be produced. In other words, the command-level translator provides syntax checking and other diagnostics for our program code during the translation phase and then another more detailed level of diagnostics is obtained from the COBOL compiler. With these two levels of diagnostics, programmers can easily detect errors in coding and resolve these errors, whether they are due to command-level coding or to other COBOL statements.

The fact that the application program is loaded into the load module library does *not* mean, however, that this module has been defined to the CICS system. Remember that in order to define a program to the CICS system, two things must occur: the name of the program must be placed into the PPT (processing program table) prior to being used within the CICS system, *and* the program must reside in one of the CICS load module libraries. Hence, we've completed only one of the steps in defining the program to CICS.

Defining the program in the PPT is *not* a component of command-level or execute interface; the program must be defined for any type of module to be used under CICS, regardless of the fact that it is a command-level program. Usually, program definition in the PPT is handled by an on-line administration group or by the systems programming staff at your installation. In either case, the definition of the program in the PPT and the loading of the program into a CICS load module library must be done carefully to ensure that the program does not fail when execution begins.

Following this procedure, the program is ready to use under the CICS system. But wait a minute, what does the program really look like from a programmer's point of view?

SAMPLE PROGRAM FORMAT

A command-level CICS program (COBOL) looks quite different from a batch program because of the services provided by CICS. Here's a skeleton command-level on-line program, the contents of which we are about to analyze:

```
IDENTIFICATION DIVISION.
  PROGRAM-ID.    MAINPGM.
  DATE-WRITTEN.  DECEMBER 25, 1900.

ENVIRONMENT DIVISION.

DATA DIVISION.

WORKING-STORAGE SECTION.
01 TIOALEN                     PIC S9(4) COMP VALUE +1920.
01 COPY MYMAPS.

PROCEDURE DIVISION.
```

Notice that the file section of the program has been omitted. In fact, *you should not* code a file section in any CICS program, whether it be written in COBOL, PL/1, RPG, or assembler language. Because file requests are handled by the file management component of CICS, no file definitions are needed within your program—the files have already been defined to CICS. Don't forget that since your program is a subroutine to CICS, having the files defined to CICS is equivalent to having the files defined to *your* program. Also, your program should not issue any OPEN or CLOSE commands for the files needed by your application program. These functions are also taken care of by FILE CONTROL. If you should issue an OPEN or CLOSE for a file defined in your program, you're likely to cause a complete CICS system failure.

Next, notice the absence of a report section—that is, there appears to be no way of printing the results from your program. (Actually, this isn't true at all.) The copy statement (COPY MYMAPS.) in the working storage section of the program will copy in the necessary screen definitions to allow our program to communicate with the terminal through the execute interface program and CICS's TERMINAL CONTROL component. These screen definitions will be copied from the "source code library," as shown in the above diagram. (How they got into this library in the first place is covered in the next chapter, which deals with the creation of screen displays.)

You may be surprised at the simplicity of this program. With the files removed and the reports removed, there's not much left in the upper part of the COBOL program. Instead of having these elements in the program, we're going to communicate these requests through EIP by using special commands called command-level programming statements. These statements will allow us to do almost anything that a typical application program might want. You'll find that programming in command-level is easy since the commands are simple and easy to code.

To carry out your on-line processing, you will place your COBOL commands *and* command-level commands after the PROCEDURE DIVISION statement. In later chapters, we study each of the various command-level commands that can be coded to carry out your on-line processing. At this point, we only need to run through these commands.

COMMAND-LEVEL STATEMENT FORMAT

The command-level command has three parts: the command-level keyword; the functional operands; and the end-of-command indicator. In all languages, the command-level keyword is the word EXEC CICS or EXECUTE CICS. Most installations use the abbreviated form simply to save coding time.

The functional operands are keywords and values that are unique to the function that you want to perform. For example, if you were performing a file request, then one of the keywords that you might use would be READ or WRITE or DELETE. If you wanted to send some information out to a terminal, you might code the operand SEND. Each of these functional operands provides (through your execute interface block) EIP with the information that CICS management components need to perform your request properly.

Finally, the end-of-command indicator defines to the command-level translator where the end of your statement occurs. This end-of-command indicator varies from language to language, but for COBOL, the end-of-command indicator is the character string END-EXEC; in PLI the end-of-command indicator is the semicolon. Within a COBOL program the typical command-level statement looks like this:

EXEC CICS   [functional operands]   END-EXEC

A period might follow the END-EXEC delimeter if it marks the end of that particular "sentence." On the other hand, if this command-level statement is embedded within an IF-THEN-ELSE construct, a period may not appear at the end of this command. The command-level commands adhere to normal coding rules for COBOL and are treated just as any other statement in the COBOL language is treated. After you become more familiar with the functional operands, you'll see that command-level coding is one of the easiest forms of on-line implementation available in IBM systems.

For example, the following command will read a record from the file called MASTR. The key of the record to be read is ABC. When the record is read, it will be placed in the 01-level area defined in WORKING-STORAGE called MASTER-REC. For the time being, let's assume that no error is made when this command is issued:

EXEC CICS READ DATASET ('MASTR') RIDFLD ('ABC')
INTO (MASTER-REC) END-EXEC.

The format of the command is simple. Well, when do you need to use command-level statements? The answer, too, is simple. Whenever you want to communicate with or obtain data from anything outside of the bounds of your program, you should use a command-level command. In short, command-level commands are used to communicate with a terminal, perform file operations, obtain or release storage areas, test the completion of operations, call or transfer control to other modules, edit data fields, and reserve resources for exclusive control. These are just a few of the functions provided through command-level programming that you should use as a command-level programmer under CICS. If you want to perform any of the functions above, you should perform that function by issuing a command-level command; if you fail to do so, you may severely jeopardize the integrity and reliability of your entire on-line system.

USING THE EXECUTE INTERFACE BLOCK

The execute interface block is simply a parameter list between *your program and EIP*. In another sense, however, it's a parameter list between *you and CICS,* since EIP is simply a go-between in application execution. Hence, EIP can provide your program with meaningful information from CICS through the EIP.

Depending on the version of CICS that you are running (1.6 was used for the examples in this text), your set of fields in the EIB may differ from the ones that we are looking at in this text. However, the fields that I'm about to describe have been around quite a while and should not make one version incompatible with another. To be sure about the contents of your EIB, consult the *CICS/VS Application Programmer's Reference Manual* listed in the bibliography.

Probably the most important group of fields to your application program are those that provide information on the success of an operation. These fields are "status code" fields and provide information on what you tried to do, how you tried to do it, and what happened when you did it. These fields are discussed in more detail in a later chapter concerned with application debugging and error handling. For now, let me simply tell you the names of those fields: EIBDS, EIBRSRCE, EIBFN, and EIBRCODE.

The two easiest fields to use are EIBTIME and EIBDATE. Both are defined as PIC S9(7)COMP-3 in the execute interface block. They can provide the time and date that your task was initiated. The EIBTIME field has a format of 0HHMMSSs, where the last position is the sign of the packed decimal field, always positive. Hence, if you regularly forget your watch, you can develop an on-line CICS transaction to tell you the time.

The EIBDATE field is based on the *Julian calendar*. The date appears in the form 00YYDDDs. Although users may find no need to do so, it might be good experience to write a conversion routine to convert forms from the Julian calendar to the Gregorian. I prefer to simply move CURRENT-DATE to whatever data area I need and obtain the date from the COBOL subroutine in the form mm/dd/yy. This method seems to provide more information to users than the conversion method. These fields enable a user to record the time an activity was done; thus, auditing or tracing of such information can be provided through your on-line application.

For a user to initiate your application, he or she must type in a transaction id. The transaction id that caused your transaction to be initiated is stored in an X(4) field called EIBTRNID. You can do many things with this information. For example, let's suppose that your application program can be initiated from five different transaction ids, as defined to CICS in the PCT. Each user who needs to use your application has been assigned a different transaction id. Hence, when user A enters transaction id AAAA, your program knows that user A is on the terminal and that he is allowed to do only certain functions. On the other hand, when user B enters transaction BBBB, he is allowed to update as well as inquire about records in the files accessed through your application. As a result, the application can service many users simply by restricting what a user can do by knowing the transaction id associated with each authorization. Many CICS users rely on EIBTRNID, which is a rather inexpensive way of making your on-line environment a little more secure.

A field called EIBTRMID can be used in much the same way that the EIBTRNID is used. This X(4) field will supply your program with the terminal address that initiated your application. Hence, if a user at terminal XXXX is *not* authorized to use your transaction, you can simply return a message stating that this user cannot use your transaction. If you combine the EIBTRNID and EIBTRMID fields, you can derive a table that your program could access to determine which users could use which terminals to run your application from. Hence, by checking both terminal and transaction id, you can prevent most users from abusing your on-line applications. You could expand on this idea by forming a complex security package for restricting CICS usage by means of the terminal, user, or transaction id, and probably sell it for a small profit.

When a transaction is initiated under CICS, we know that the resulting execution requires the creation of a task. This task is the primary method by which CICS distinguishes one executing CICS application from another. The task is identified by a number assigned to the application when it is initiated. The first task initiated for a day is assigned task number 1, the one-hundredth task initiated is assigned a task number of 100, and so on. Your task number is available to you in a PIC S9(7) COMP-3 field called EIBTASKN if you need it for anything. Although this number is useful in the event that your application abends, I haven't found anyone using this field other than for debugging or tracing transaction flows.

When a user presses the *clear, enter,* PF, or PA keys or uses a light pen to initiate a transaction, a code associated with the key used to initiate that transaction is provided to the application (EIBAID). The position of the cursor on the screen at the time of transaction initiation is also made available to the application program (EIBCPOSN). Hence, the program could interrogate these fields to determine whether the user wanted to continue applications processing, stop processing, or even switch functions. Further, the program could use the cursor position to determine which field the user was looking at or to determine what menu the user selected. This type of processing is user friendly and requires a minimum amount of work on the part of the user. Further, processing and decisionmaking can occur with little data transmission to and from the terminal, especially if the application is supporting information retrieval activities.

The fields in the EIB that support this type of processing are EIBAID and EIBCPOSN. The EIBAID field is a X(1) field holding a value that indicates the key that was pressed to initiate your application. This field can be tested against a list of probable values, predefined to CICS through a data structure called DFHAID, which can be copied into your program. Hence, by using a simple decision structure, your program can determine whether the *clear* key

(DFHCLEAR), the PF1 key (DFHPF1), or the *enter* key was pressed (DFHENTER) to initiate your application. (The possible field values are discussed in a later chapter.)

The EIBCPOSN field is defined as a S9(4) COMP field and holds the relative position of the cursor on the screen. Hence, if the cursor is in the uppermost corner of the screen, the value of EIBCPOSN will be zero. If the cursor is on row 4 and column 27 when the user presses the *enter* key, then the value of EIBCPOSN will be 266 (assuming that the terminal screen size is 24 by 80).

This is just a brief overview of the data in the execute interface block; only the most commonly used fields have been presented. For more information on the EIB, you should refer to the *CICS/VS Application Programmer's Reference Manual,* which provides a detailed description of each EIB field.

Although this has been a rather brief introduction to the CICS command-level programming environment, it should give you a basic idea of implementing applications in a CICS command-level mode. As we progress through the second half of this text, we'll provide more details about CICS on-line programming so that by the end of the book you will be familiar enough with CICS to carry out most of your on-line application implementations.

THOUGHT QUESTIONS

1. *If a file section is not needed in our on-line programs, briefly describe how a file request might be processed through EIP to FILE CONTROL by using the EIP and the TCA.*

2. *What might "life" be like without EIP? How would you communicate your requests to the various CICS components?*

3. *Suppose that your program requires one or more subroutines to carry out the processing for your application. How do you communicate your requests to your subordinate programs in a batch mode? Relate this communication chain to the chain between EIP and your application program.*

4. *We mentioned in passing that an application can be accessed through several different transaction ids if the proper entries have been placed into the PCT to accomplish this type of definition. Describe situations in which this type of funneling of transaction ids into a common application program would be beneficial to a system. Describe cases where such a relationship would not be desirable for applications processing.*

8
CREATING SCREEN DISPLAYS

Now that we have developed a workable pseudocode to solve our application problem (that is, the Landlord Management System), we are ready to carry out the implementation. We code our application with the aid of the COBOL programming language and IBM's CICS software monitor.

In Chapter 7, we pointed out that an on-line system has several components, one of which is the terminal display needed to provide communication between the on-line program and the terminal operator. This is the element of implementation that we concentrate on in this chapter. By the end of the chapter, you should be able to construct CICS screen displays using the support language called BMS (basic mapping support). Further, you should understand the structure of the communication between application program and screen definition and the role of the screen processing component of CICS. In most on-line applications implemented under CICS, each element of terminal communications must be fully understood if the communications between the programs and the terminal operator are to be accurate and reliable.

The first step in our coding phase is to implement our screen displays in a format usable under CICS. First we have to learn a new language that is unique to CICS—basic mapping support (BMS).

Although BMS is easy to use, screen coding becomes a tedious keypunching task and takes time. Usually, one to two hours are required to code a simple screen display using the BMS language. The BMS language and CICS have been criticized by non-CICS users who point out that many other on-line environments have screen manipulation languages and techniques that are much easier to use. On the other hand, a number of on-line and batch packages on the market today can provide assistance in this aspect of CICS application implementation. Such packages are called screen generators or map-generator systems; some of these are on-line and others are batch oriented. (They are discussed later in this chapter.)

Here we concentrate on the more common operands and uses of this coding language, leaving the fancier components for a later chapter. Hence, the format of our BMS code consists of just three simple instructions, which are used over and over to generate the necessary requirements for terminal-to-program communications. However, before we go into the details of the commands, let's make sure that you understand screen usage under CICS.

MAP-TO-PROGRAM RELATIONSHIP

A screen display in any on-line system is simply a report displayed at a terminal. However, the report is used not only to communicate information *from* the program to the user, but also to *receive* information—from the user—that is to be processed by the program. Hence, screen communication is a two-way process that allows users to converse with the application programs. For this reason, some screens must be designed to accept input from the terminal operator or to display information to the terminal operator; still other screens can be used to do both. The way in which a screen is used is, of course, determined by the coding within the application program. Hence, when you define your screens to CICS, you must specify how your screens are going to be used in communicating with the user. Here we use our screens in both ways, sending data out to a terminal and receiving data from a terminal.

Earlier we pointed out that a logical display to the user could actually be composed of one or more physical displays. However, we will restrict ourselves, as we did earlier, to a one-to-one correspondence between physical and logical screens. Each screen to and from the user will consist of only one transmission operation; thus we can minimize our terminal I/O, screen display coordination, and program coding. With this in mind, we can now discuss the format of a screen definition under CICS.

To simplify matters, let's say a screen display under CICS consists of one or more fields. Of course, some fields are "header" or "information-only" fields, while other fields allow data to be entered, changed, or erased either by the terminal operator or by the application program. For example, the screen below has many header fields but only two data fields, the data fields being the area in which the user enters the menu selection *and* the error message line (manipulated by the program) at the bottom of the screen.

```
┌─────────────────────────────────────────────────────────────┐
│              LANDLORD MANAGEMENT ON-LINE SYSTEM               │
│                         SYSTEM MENU                           │
│                                                               │
│   CHOOSE ONE OF THE LETTERS BELOW THAT IS ASSOCIATED          │
│   WITH THE OPTION THAT YOU WOULD LIKE TO PERFORM.             │
│   ENTER YOUR SELECTION HERE, ------?                          │
│                                                               │
│       I  --  INQUIRE ABOUT A PROBLEM REPORT                   │
│       R  --  REPORT A NEW PROBLEM                             │
│       U  --  UPDATE PROBLEM INFORMATION                       │
│       D  --  DELETE AN OLD PROBLEM THAT HAS BEEN FIXED        │
│                                                               │
│                                                               │
│                                                               │
│                                                               │
│                                                               │
│                                                               │
│                                                               │
│                                                               │
│   MSG: xxxxxxxxxxxxxxxxxxxxxxxxxxxxxxxxxxxxxxxxxxxxxxxxx       │
└─────────────────────────────────────────────────────────────┘
```

Although these fields appear different to the terminal user, who may or may not be able to type into a field, the actual definition or coding of these fields using BMS is practically identical. (We'll see how close they really are when we get to screen coding.)

MAPPING TERMINOLOGY:
MAPSET, MAP, FIELD

We now need to change the terminology that we've been using to discuss screen displays. Instead of referring to a display at the terminal as a screen display, we're going to call this a *map*. Hence, a map can be considered a collection of logically related fields used in creating a *single* (our restriction) screen display for terminal communications. This term is more in line with the terminology IBM uses to discuss screen communications when using BMS.

Earlier you saw several map displays for the landlord system application. A typical on-line application usually has several map definitions to support the program-to-user communications. If we think of all of these maps together, we can say that we have a set of maps for the landlord application. Hence, rather than defining each map as a separate or unique entry in CICS—by placing such an entry in the processing program table (PPT)—we can simply define each map as a member of the set of maps associated with the landlord system. This set of maps can be called a *mapset*. Therefore, a field on a map will be just one of many fields, within many maps, within a mapset. The mapset is the entity used by CICS basic mapping support to assist the program in communicating with the terminal.

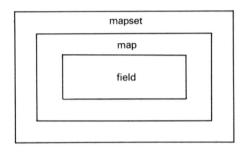

Yet another way of representing this relationship between field, map, and mapset is as follows:

MAPSET

    -- MAP
        -- field
        -- field
        -- field
        -- field

    -- MAP
        -- field
        -- field

    -- MAP
        -- field
        -- field
        -- field

MAPSET END

The mapset is the definition of all maps to CICS that are to be used in support of an on-line application. Therefore, when an on-line system is being developed, designers and programmers must organize maps into mapsets, and they must define each mapset in the PPT so that BMS can provide the necessary assistance to the application program to communicate with the terminal. But wait a minute. A PPT entry is the definition of a *program* to the CICS system (we learned this in an earlier chapter). Why, then, is our mapset considered a program to the CICS system? The answer is rather complicated, but we must be able to understand this concept before we can fully understand BMS services.

To repeat: a field is an element of a map that can be used to display information to a terminal or obtain data from a terminal; a map is an element of a mapset that consists of a set of logically related fields, generally associated with a function (or component of a function) within an application; and a mapset is the collection of all maps for an application (or subset of that application) that allows BMS to keep track of map usage and to assist programs in their terminal communications.

PHYSICAL VERSUS SYMBOLIC MAPS

When a mapset is defined to the CICS system, we know that an entry has to be placed in the PPT. Here's the reason behind this. BMS code is written in IBM assembler language using macros. When this code is assembled, the BMS statements that you code generate five or more assembler language statements. Hence, as your code is expanded into a usable form, the resulting printout of your assembly process will be much larger than you expected and may be rather difficult to decipher. (A technique for reducing this expansion and aiding readability is discussed later.) In any event, two results are achieved. The first entity is called a *symbolic mapset,* the second a *physical mapset.* The following diagram might help you understand what is happening in this situation and where each of these entities comes from.

Here you see that the symbolic mapset becomes a member of a copy library and that the physical mapset becomes a member of a load module library. Hence, the symbolic mapset can be thought of as an FD or data structure for referencing fields within each map. When the symbolic mapset is copied into the application program during COBOL compilation, it becomes just that—a description of the field layout for each map used by the application. Hence, the symbolic mapset is *COBOL code* produced by the assembly process to be used later in the application program's compilation. This code will allow the application program to refer to the fields on a map in a meaningful way, by data name or variable name. (We'll look at a symbolic mapset later in this chapter.)

The physical mapset, on the other hand, is link-edited into a load module library. When an executing application refers to a map within this mapset, the physical mapset is loaded into CICS memory from this load module library to be used by BMS to construct the transmission data stream to send data out to a terminal, or to decode a data stream coming in from a terminal so that the terminal data is in a format consistent with the symbolic mapset. The BMS programs

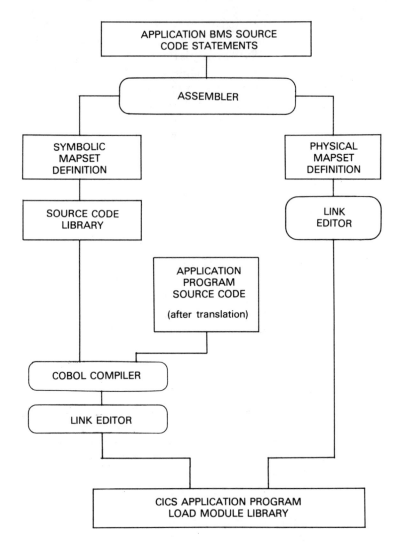

within CICS (a component of TERMINAL CONTROL), use the physical mapset as a rule book for arranging the data fields given to BMS by the application program in the proper format in the output terminal input-output area (TIOA) to be sent to the terminal over communication lines. Also, the physical mapset is used to arrange data coming *from* a terminal to an application program (through an input TIOA) so that the application program can reference the fields in the proper way by using the symbolic mapset. Notice that in both cases, BMS operates on TIOA storage areas. In other words, the TIOA serves as a buffer between the application program and the terminal, which is managed by

BMS, to convert data to a form usable by the application program or displayable by the terminal hardware. Let me give you an example.

Suppose that for a given application, records are stored on a disk in a compressed format to save space on that disk drive. When an application program wants a record *from* a file, it calls a routine to retrieve the record, expand it, and make the record available to the requesting program in the format specified by that application program. When a record is to be stored, the reverse happens; the expanded data structure is passed to a routine, which compresses the data and stores the record onto the disk. Clearly, the routine(s) to expand or compress the data must follow a certain set of rules that will enable the application program to obtain or store data on disk properly.

This process is analogous to the symbolic and physical mapsets used by BMS to improve terminal communications in your program. BMS is the expansion and compression program, and it uses the TIOA as a work area to perform its operations. The physical mapset contains the rules that BMS uses in its compression-expansion algorithm. Finally, the symbolic mapset is the structure of the data as it appears to the application program.

We can draw several other conclusions from this discussion. BMS attempts to optimize data transmission by minimizing the amount of unnecessary data being transmitted to and from the terminal. Although BMS does this effectively, a great deal depends on what data the application program wants transmitted and what rules must be followed. In other words, BMS does not alter the data in the true sense of our compression and expansion routine, but it does format the data into a structure that is compatible with the data structure defined in the application program (symbolic mapset) and compatible with the terminal involved in communicating with the application program. Hence, when an application program wants to send data to a terminal or receive data from a terminal, the application issues a request to BMS to provide this service. This request is called a mapping operation. Therefore, BMS is simply another service component of CICS that relieves application programs of the worry about the hardware dependencies in data transmission. By using your physical mapset, BMS and TERMINAL CONTROL allow your application program to communicate with almost any terminal device supported by CICS without having to worry about data transmission message formats or communication protocol.

If a mapset can consist of several maps, is there any limit to the number of maps per mapset? The answer is not really, but some trade-offs have to be made with respect to map packaging. When an application program is using a map in a mapset, *all* the information necessary to process that map must be in memory for BMS. However, since *that* map is in memory, then *all* other maps within that mapset must also be in memory inasmuch as they are all packaged under the same mapset, and the mapset itself is the smallest unit known to the CICS system (the mapset must be defined in the PPT; the maps cannot). If only a few maps are being used from a large mapset, a substantial amount of valuable CICS memory may be wasted.

On the other hand, it is possible to package each map within *its own* mapset. Hence, when that map is being used, only that map's information need be in memory for BMS and application usage. However, each mapset requires a PPT entry, so that as mapset definitions (one for each map in this case) increase, the number of PPT entries increases, and thus PPT search time increases, as we have already noted. What's the solution? Well, it all depends on how you want to package your maps into mapsets. You can package by application, function within application, program usage, number of times used, and number of fields per map. I'll let you decide how to package your maps.

DEVICES SUPPORTED BY CICS

In the CICS environment, we concentrate strictly on communicating with IBM 3270 compatible devices. Hence, in our discussion of screen coding, map sizes and processing characteristics apply only to these terminal types. Contact your systems programming staff or data communications staff for details on how to communicate with other devices supported by CICS. Further, we are going to take a *simple* approach to BMS coding, utilizing the basic facilities of BMS and omitting many of the more complex features. If this approach seems inadequate, let me assure you that our discussion *will* provide you with the background you need to implement most standard on-line applications.

CODING A MAPSET DEFINITION STATEMENT

Coding a mapset definition statement is a simple procedure and requires knowledge of just a few items. Once you do it, you can merely copy from mapsets that you've developed in the past, as most people do. First you must decide on a name for your mapset. The mapset name can be any group of one to eight characters as long as the first character is a letter (A-Z) and all other letters are of the set (A,B,...,Z,0,1,2,...,9,@,$,#). You should avoid using the special characters as they may not be valid in some programming languages. In addition, use your transaction id as part of the mapset name. For example, if your tranid is LAMS, then an appropriate mapset name might be LAMSM (the final letter M standing for "mapset," of course). This name reflects the association between tranid and mapset, should you ever need to be reminded of it.

Once you pick a name for your mapset, the rest is easy. In fact, let me code the complete mapset definition statement that we'll use in defining the landlord management mapset to the CICS system. Column numbers are given to aid in picturing how to code BMS commands.

```
0          1          1                                    7
1          0          7                                    2

LAMSM      DFHMSD     TYPE=DSECT,MODE=INOUT,               X
                      LANG=COBOL,TIOAPFX=YES,              X
                      STORAGE=AUTO,CTRL=FREEKB
```

The first thing to notice in this statement is the keyword (also called macroname) DFHMSD. It could be said to mean map-set-definition. This must be the first statement in the code for this mapset (other than comments or print control statements) and it informs the assembler that this mapset generation really begins here. This is generally coded in column 10, although you could start it in column 9. If you begin coding in column 9 rather than column 10, the operands for your DFHMSD statement line up better in column 16 when operands must be continued from line to line. Hence, column 9 is suggested for your macroname (DFHMSD) to improve the consistency of your BMS coding; in using this column, however, you also restrict the length of your mapname to less than or equal to seven characters (which in most instances causes no problems and is a requirement in COBOL).

In other words, we can say that there is a *specific format* for coding these BMS macrostatements. All mapset, map, and field names must begin in column 1. The macroname (DFHMSD) begins two columns to the right of the last character of the name field (leaving one space between the field name and the macroname) or, the macroname begins in column 9 or 10 for coding consistency.

The operands begin two positions to the right of the macroname (again leaving one blank column) or in column 16 (if possible), whichever you prefer. If all operands do not fit on one line, then you must end the line with a complete operand and its value followed by a comma, or type the operands through column 71. Next, place some character (A-Z) in column 72 to indicate continuation and then start the remaining portion of your operands on the next line, *starting in column 16*. You *must* leave columns 1-15 blank on a continued statement, and you *must* begin in column 16.

All macronames can be coded beginning in column 9 and all operands can be coded to begin in column 16. Below are different ways of achieving successful code generation.

```
0          01         11                                   7
1          90         67                                   2

LAMMAPS    DFHMSD     TYPE=DSECT,MODE=INOUT,               X
                      LANG=COBOL,STORAGE=AUTO,             X
                      TIOAPFX=YES,                         X
                      CTRL=FREEKB
```

```
        LAMMAPS   DFHMSD   TYPE=DSECT,                                    X
                           MODE=INOUT,                                    X
                           LANG=COBOL,                                    X
                           STORAGE=AUTO,                                  X
                           TIOAPFX=YES,                                   X
                           CTRL=FREEKB


        LAMMAPS   DFHMSD   TYPE=DSECT,MODE=INOUT,LANG=COBOL,X
                           CTRL=FREEKB,STORAGE=AUTO,TIOAPFX=YX
                           ES
```

Below are examples of how *not* to code your BMS statements.

```
0              01        11                              7
1              90        67                              2

LAMMAPS    DFHMSD    TYPE=DSECT,
                     MODE=INOUT,
                     LANG=COBOL,
                     STORAGE=AUTO,
                     TIOAPFX=YES,
                     CTRL=FREEKB


    [forgot the continuation characters in column 72]


LAMMAPS       DFHMSD    TYPE=DSECT,MODE=INOUT,      X
                        LANG=COBOL,CTRL=FREEKB,     X
                        STORAGE=AUTO,TIOAPFX=YES


    [operands are continued on subsequent lines beginning
     in column 17 and not column 16 as required]


LAMMAPS       DFHMSD    TYPE=DSECT,MODE=INOUT,LANG=
                        COBOL,CTRL=FREEKB,STORAGE=AX
                        UTO,TIOAPFX=YES
```

[the equal sign of the LANG=COBOL operand is absorbed
as the continuation character in column 72 on the
first line]

```
LAMMAPS    DFHMSD   TYPE=DSECT,MODE=INOUT,      X
                    LANG=COBOL,CTRL=FREEKB,      X
                    STORAGE=AUTO,  TIOAPFX=YES
```

[the mapset name does not begin in column 1 of the
coded statement; there's a blank space between
the STORAGE and TIOAPFX operands]

Before we look at each of the operands and the other BMS statements that follow, you may want to know about a few non-BMS statements that can enhance readability and reduce the assembly costs for generating your maps.

You can place comments within the lines of your mapset by entering an asterisk ('*') in column 1 of any line. Then, you can type any information that you desire in columns 2-71 of that line. You *can* continue a comment line, but that's not recommended.

You can reduce the costs and time involved to assemble your maps by placing the statement

```
          0      1
  1       9      6
          PRINT  NOGEN
```

before the DFHMSD statement. This procedure eliminates a substantial amount of printed output normally produced by a mapset generation process. On the other hand, if you really want to see the resulting code from the assembly, omit this statement, even if it is expensive to do so.

You see several operands in the DFHMSD statement. The first one that should be rather straightforward is the LANG=COBOL operand. PLI, COBOL, RPG, and ASM are the languages that may be used to implement your CICS applications. Whatever language is used here, you *must* generate your mapset under the same language format. Hence, if your programs are written in COBOL and your mapset generated under the LANG=PLI operand value, you'll probably have trouble communicating with the terminal through the various components of CICS to support terminal communications.

The TYPE=DSECT operand tells the assembler to produce both a symbolic and a physical mapset definition. If you change any map within a mapset, then the usual procedure is to reassemble the entire mapset. However, this may not be necessary. For example, suppose that a field is now displayed in the color green and the user wants it displayed in blue. Since this type of change does not affect field location or field length, a total reassembly of the mapset is a waste of time. Instead, you could change the TYPE=DSECT operand to TYPE=MAP to alter this field's color (and other fields if desired), reassemble this mapset, and hence replace only the physical mapset definition to CICS, without having to regenerate the symbolic mapset. This method could save considerable time in processing such a trivial change.

Now let's suppose that a field changes its location or length within a map. In this case, *both* the physical and symbolic mapset definitions must be entirely regenerated. Further, since the symbolic mapset definition has changed, *all* application programs using this mapset must also be recompiled so that they now know the new format of the fields on the various maps. Clearly, in such a relationship between map and application program, it becomes cumbersome as well as expensive to change a field. This is another reason why BMS is criticized by users of other on-line software packages.

The operand MODE=INOUT, as discussed earlier, informs BMS that maps within this mapset are used for input and output operations, some in both modes. Although one could code MODE=IN or MODE=OUT to exclusively restrict maps to input or output operations only, MODE=INOUT should probably be coded since certain restrictions in processing apply when the other forms are used. This code also avoids problems when a map constructed as an output map but is placed within a mapset specified for input-only processing.

The TIOAPFX=YES operand may look strange but its use and specification are important to the execution of your application program. Every terminal input and output area (TIOA) allocated to an on-line application has a control field 12 bytes long in front of it that is used by the CICS service components. If you are using command-level commands, you should code TIOAPFX=YES for your mapset definitions. If you are coding in the macrolevel command language then it might be feasible for you to code TIOAPFX=NO if you want to build and manipulate your own TIOA prefix area. When you use command-level commands, the TIOA prefix area is managed for you automatically by the execute interface program and the CICS service components. Hence, it is not necessary for you to access this area on your own. Since all of our examples use command level for implementation, we'll code TIOAPFX=YES for all of our mapset definitions. Again, with the aid of the execute interface program (EIP), we will be accessing or placing data into this TIOA prefix storage area *through* EIP; therefore we do not need to access it on our own and we can specify TIOAPFX=YES for all of our mapset definitions and use EIP to accomplish the same results—with less effort.

I've emphasized the coding of this command several times because this operand can cause serious problems during processing if it is not specified correctly. If the mapset is generated with TIOAPFX=NO (or TIOAPFX=YES) and the symbolic map in the application program has the opposite TIOAPFX definition, all communications with the terminal will be off by twelve bytes. Hence, field data will be processed incorrectly by the application programs, and maps sent out by the program with field data will be distorted by a total of twelve bytes. Depending on the data to be transmitted, this distortion may not only cause abends, but may cause a terminal error.

The next operand, STORAGE=AUTO, informs the assembler that each map is to be assigned its own storage area during execution. In other words, if the mapset was to be processed in the WORKING-STORAGE section of your program, then each map will be treated as if it has a separate data name. Obviously, this will increase the size of your WORKING-STORAGE section, but, it will allow the program to reference fields on two different maps at the same time.

Alternatively, STORAGE=AUTO need not be coded at all. Instead, each map redefines each other map, and this method, of course, saves storage. It is generally used when maps are to be processed in the LINKAGE SECTION of the program (as would be the case if locate-mode processing was being used) or when two maps are not used simultaneously in the application. However, if data on one map needs to be copied to fields on another map, you'd first have to move the data to WORKING-STORAGE (or some other holding area accessible by your program), reinitialize the shared map storage area, then move the data from the holding area to the new map area. The trade-offs are rather obvious here; storage versus processing. Careful consideration must be given to selecting (or not selecting) the STORAGE=AUTO operand because this operand can affect your transaction performance, especially if your mapset is large. In either case, both implementations will work; I'll let you decide which method to use. (We'll discuss this operand in a later chapter, where we will show some examples of the different ways that it can be used and discuss its impact on application processing.)

If you omit the STORAGE=AUTO operand so that each map shares a common storage area, then you must inform the assembler of the name of the data area in your application program that is to be the target of the redefined maps within that mapset. To do this, you must code the operand BASE= dataname, where "dataname" is the data name on the storage area (usually defined as 1,920 bytes for a 24-line by 80-column screen) within your application program. Hence, in a sample COBOL program, you'd have a code situation similar (not exactly) to the one shown below if BASE=SHAREMAP was coded on the DFHMSD statement.

```
      01  SHAREMAP           PIC X(1920).

      01  COPY MYMAPS.

   C  01  MAP1   REDEFINES SHAREMAP.
   C        . . .
   C        . . .
```

```
C           . . .
C  01  MAP2  REDEFINES SHAREMAP.
C           . . .
C           . . .
C  01  MAP3  REDEFINES SHAREMAP.
C           . . .
C           . . .
```

On the other hand, if you omit the BASE= operand and code the STORAGE=AUTO value, then your maps would appear somewhat similar to the following code:

```
01  MAP1.
        . . .
        . . .
01  MAP2.
        . . .
        . . .
01  MAP3.
        . . .
        . . .
```

You can see that in the first example, when BASE=SHAREMAP is coded, each map redefines each other map within the mapset. In the second example, however, each map has its own storage area and does not redefine any of the other maps in the mapset. Hence, if a map shares a storage area with another map, then only *one* map may be used at a time, but less memory is required to contain all of the maps within that mapset. In the second example, however, any of the maps can hold data simultaneously without disturbing the data stored in any of the other maps; on the other hand, much more storage is required to hold these maps than is the case when all maps share the same storage area. Depending on the processing that you need to do, you should select the appropriate map definition by coding either the STORAGE or the BASE operands on the DFHMSD statement.

The last operand, CTRL=FREEKB, is used to increase the friendliness of your on-line system. This informs BMS to free the keyboard every time that a map is sent *to* the terminal. If you did not code this operand, then the user would have to press the *reset* key before he or she could begin typing information into the screen fields. This step might be desirable if you *wanted* to make it difficult for someone to use your system, or if you wanted to control the keyboard usage from your application program (this topic is discussed in a later chapter). By freeing the keyboard, you eliminate some unnecessary keystrokes and avoid frustrating the terminal operator who is trying to enter data quickly. Some other options may be coded when the CTRL operand is being used, but they are not applicable to our mode of on-line processing.

Of course, many other operands on the DFHMSD statement might be suited to your environment or your application. The operands that we've discussed are the basic ones under which most of your applications could probably be completed. In a later chapter we discuss enhanced mapping features as well as additional operands for the DFHMSD statement, but the operands that we've just discussed are sufficient to generate the necessary symbolic and physical mapset definitions for our on-line application.

ENDING A MAPSET DEFINITION

After all mapset, map, and field definition statements are completed, a mapset must be ended. This procedure requires an alternate form of the DFHMSD statement, which simply indicates to the system that the end of the mapset has arrived. This statement, which is quite simple since it has only one operand, is coded as follows:

```
        0       1
  1     9       6
        DFHMSD TYPE=FINAL
        END
```

Wait a minute! Two statements are coded above. The DFHMSD statement actually ends the definition of the mapset, and, as far as you're concerned, the mapset definition has been completed. However, the assembler does not stop processing until an END statement is reached. Hence, you could assemble more than one mapset at a time, but in most cases, you should code only one mapset definition per assembly to prevent one mapset from affecting the success or failure of another mapset generation.

MAP DEFINITION STATEMENT

The next control statement to be used under BMS will define a map to the system and to your application. As you know, a map is a group of fields that are to be displayed or received from a terminal. Although the statement is simple, you must remember that *every* map requires a map definition statement, whereas a mapset has just one DFHMSD (mapset definition) statement (not counting the mapset END statement).

You must give every map in your mapset a name. This name must be unique (not the same as the mapset name or any other map or field within this mapset), and it must be less than or equal to *seven* characters long. Further, the characters used in this name follow the same rules used in selecting a mapset name.

After choosing a name for your map, you must determine how large your map will be. Here we are assuming that every logical map consists of only one physical map definition; thus, for a terminal having 24 lines and 80 columns, our map would be 24 $\times$ 80, which is written as (24,80) on the map definition statement. You could have a one-line, two-line, up to twenty-four-line map, but in our case, all maps will be the same size. Also, since our maps fill or define the entire screen, we'll position them so that they start on line one and column one of the screen (the upper left corner). Hence, for all maps in our mapset, the map definition control statements will be identical except for the name of that particular map.

The macroname for a map definition control statement is DFHMDI and so the map definition statement for a map called MENU would be:

```
            0     1
 1          9     6
MENU     DFHMDI SIZE=(24,80),LINE=1,COLUMN=1
```

Again, other operands could be coded on the DFHMDI statement, but they are generally not needed for basic terminal-to-program communications.

Remember that in an earlier chapter we defined a separate map for the title, body, and message area of a terminal display. In this case, each of these maps would physically account for only a part of the complete terminal display. However, the map definition statements for each of those three maps might be as follows:

```
TITLE    DFHMDI  SIZE=(1,80),LINE=1,COLUMN=1

BODY     DFHMDI  SIZE=(22,80),LINE=2,COLUMN=1

MSGMAP   DFHMDI  SIZE=(1,80),LINE=24,COLUMN=1
```

Obviously, the SIZE, LINE, and COLUMN operands inform BMS where to position that map on the screen when the map is sent out by the application program.

That's all there is to defining a map to CICS (except for the fields within the map). Before we find out how to code a field definition statement, however, let me point out a problem that first-time BMS coders sometimes run into. If you recall, a mapset ended with a mapset-end statement. A map *does not* have such a statement form. Hence *do not* code a DFHMDI TYPE=FINAL statement because you'll get an error. The assembler will know that a map ends when it encounters another map definition statement or the mapset-final statement.

FIELD DEFINITION STATEMENT

At the last level of coding required to define a map to CICS, each field within your map is defined. Although the field definition statement has more operands than the last statement we looked at, it is still easy to code. The only problem with BMS coding lies in the number of field definition statements that one must code to define a map. A screen with many fields may take *days* to code because of the amount of keypunching required to properly specify the characteristics of each field within your map.

In coding the field definition statement (DFHMDF), you should remember to code fields from upper left to lower right on the screen. That is, in some versions of CICS, the field definition statements must follow this order or an error will occur. Although later releases of CICS-BMS allow for unordered field positioning, the cost in processing time for each terminal request is quite high. Even though you may have the version of CICS that allows field definitions in any order, *do* order them to make your terminal communications faster. Further, by using a terminal display layout sheet to develop your maps, you can transfer your diagram to BMS commands in a smooth and orderly fashion and will have a hard copy of the document to show the user what the screen(s) will look like.

Fields within a map are defined to CICS in much the same format as a map within a mapset. In column one, you can place a name for that field, which must be unique within the *entire mapset*. This means that no two maps can have the same name when both maps reside in the same mapset. Field names must be less than or equal to seven characters in length and must adhere to the same guidelines discussed for mapset and map names. The name that you choose for a field is important because it is the name (with a slight alteration) that your COBOL program must use when referencing this field. Hence, by naming a field, you are actually defining the variables to be used in your COBOL program during on-line processing.

You place the macroname DFHMDF in column 9 or 10 (depending on the coding style that you've selected). Beginning two columns to the right of this keyword (leaving one space between the keyword and the first operand), you start your operands, continuing them in column 16 on the next line after placing a character in column 72. This is, of course, the same format we discussed a little earlier.

The operands for the field definition statement are easy to use and learn. You will recall that these operands tell the system where to place the field on the screen, how long the field is, what to initialize the field to, and what characteristics (attributes) are to be assigned to that field. A typical field definition statement might be:

```
APT   DFHMDF  POS=(10,5),LENGTH=3,ATTRB=(NUM)
```

Here we've instructed the system to position the field on line 10 *within the map to which this field belongs,* beginning in column 5. This field will be three positions long and will hold only numeric data. Hence, if the terminal operator tries to type in the letter X, for example, the keyboard will lock, and the terminal operator will have to press the *reset* key in order to continue typing in data.

The position operand (POS) is simple and specifies the row and column of where to place that field on the screen within that map. You should understand that the POS operand indicates where that field is positioned on the screen *within that map.* If you recall, a map can be positioned at a line and column other than the upper left corner of the screen. For example, if the menu map was defined as follows, with the APT field as shown, the APT field would actually appear on line 14 of the user display screen.

```
MENU   DFHMDI   SIZE=(10,80),LINE=5,COLUMN=1
  .        .         .
  .        .         .
  .        .         .
APT    DFHMDF   POS=(10,5),....
  .        .         .
  .        .         .
  .        .         .
```

However, if you position your maps at line 1 and column 1, then the relative field position specified in the POS operand *will* match the actual positioning of the field at the terminal.

The LENGTH=n operand must be coded to specify the length of field in terms of number of bytes. The largest field is 256 and the smallest is 1. The number specified is a little distorted, however, since the field actually occupies $n+1$ bytes. Since *every* field on a screen in which mapping is used to display information or obtain information from a screen *requires* an attribute byte character, field length is really n-bytes for the data area and 1-byte for the attribute byte (which precedes the data field on the screen). Hence, the total number of bytes for a field is $n+1$ on the terminal display, even though you've specified LENGTH=n in its definition.

The attribute byte field is one position long and holds the characteristics of that field. These characteristics inform the *terminal hardware:* whether or not the user can type into that field; whether the hardware will accept only numeric characters in that field when they are typed in by the terminal operator; how the field should be displayed to the terminal operator (dark, normal, or bright); and whether or not the field has been changed or modified either by the terminal operator or the application program.

ASSIGNING ATTRIBUTES TO A FIELD

The attribute byte *precedes* the field on the screen. Hence, when APT is defined with a position of (10,5), the attribute byte is actually placed at this position and the data field begins in (10,6). You must be aware of this factor, especially in the case of fields that are to appear at the far right or left of the terminal screen.

To specify the attributes for a field, you must code the ATTRB operand. The values for this operand are specified by abbreviations enclosed in parentheses and separated by commas. Hence, to define a numeric field (NUM) that is to appear bright (BRT) at the terminal, and to allow the terminal operator to type into that field (UNPROT), you would code the following attribute specification:

ATTRB=(BRT,NUM,UNPROT)

You could have also coded the attribute specification as

ATTRB=(NUM,BRT,UNPROT)

or any number of other versions. In other words, the order of the operands within the attribute list is not significant for the DFHMDF statement.

Below is a description of each of the attributes and their impact on a field when displayed. Defaulted ATTRB field values are underlined.

ASKIP   is used to specify that a field cannot be typed into by the terminal operator. Also, if the terminal operator is tabbing forward on the screen, the cursor will *not* stop at this field as it is encountered.

BRT   is used to highlight a field and make it stand out on the screen. Highlighting all fields on a screen, however, merely gives the user a severe headache.

DRK   is used to "hide" a field so that the terminal operator can't see the data in that field. This is especially helpful for codeword or security-oriented fields within an application.

FSET   indicates that the data in that field are to appear to the applications program as if they were typed in by the terminal operator. For example, suppose that a field can be defaulted. Rather than having the user enter the default value, the field can be marked FSET and given a value by the applications program before that screen is displayed. When the user presses the *enter* key (even if he or she doesn't type anything into that field), the default data displayed on the screen will be processed by the application program as if they were entered by the terminal operator.

IC   is used to position the cursor on the screen when the screen is sent to the terminal. This operand can be over-ridden by a cursor-positioning operand within the application program.

NORM specifies that when this field is displayed at the terminal its intensity is not to be DRK (dark) or BRT (bright). Rather, the field is to be displayed with normal intensity. If you do not want a field to be DRK or BRT, it is not necessary to code NORM since it is the default. Most displays utilize normal (NORM) field intensity and use BRT to highlight, or DRK to secure applicable fields.

NUM allows the terminal hardware to control the type of characters that a user may type into a field. With this operand, the user can type only a numeric character (0,1,2,...,9,.,–). Any field defined with this specification will be automatically right-justified by BMS before being available to your application. Any field not defined with this attribute will be left-justified.

PROT controls the typing of a data into this field by the terminal operator. The terminal operator is *not* allowed to type any data into this field. The cursor will not skip past (or over) this field when the terminal operator is tabbing forward. Hence, when the cursor reaches this field, the terminal operator must tab forward a second time to bypass this field. If the operator tries to type data into the field, the keyboard will lock and he will have to press the *reset* key before he can continue.

UNPROT specifies that the user can type data into this field and that the cursor is to stop at this field when a *tab-forward* or *tab-backward* key is pressed.

Below is a list of the attribute specifications that are mutually exclusive; that is, they should not be specified together.

BRT – DRK – NORM

ASKIP – PROT – UNPROT

Clearly, attributes are important to a field as they control the information that can be placed into that field by the terminal operator. Attributes can also be used to control *how much* data can be placed in a field. For example, assume that several fields are adjacent to each other on a line, as shown below:

ENTER YOUR MENU SELECTION HERE ------?

The two fields are

"ENTER YOUR MENU SELECTION HERE ------" and "?".

Each of these fields has attribute bytes associated with them. Let me indicate where the attribute bytes would be located *if* we could see them on the screen (the character + will be used to indicate their position).

+ENTER YOUR MENU SELECTION HERE - - - - - -+?

Now you should clearly see the two fields. But why didn't we use just one field instead? If we did that, the user could type over our header information and might not even type over the question mark (as we wanted him to do). So, if the user enters a menu selection of 1, it may or may not be in the correct position on the screen for our program to process the request.

+1NTER YOUR MENU SELECTION HERE - - - - - -?

If we position the cursor properly, the field typed in by the user should appear as we want it to:

+ENTER YOUR MENU SELECTION HERE - - - - - - 1

In other words, we're playing a guessing game as to where the user will type in the data. Clearly, we can't protect the entire field, or the user wouldn't be able to type in *any* data. On the other hand, if we don't protect any of the "header" information, we're still not sure the data will be typed in the proper location on the screen. Remember, the user can type anywhere in the field between the attribute byte and the next attribute byte on the screen (which we can't see in our example above).

Clearly, we have a problem. Let's take the easy way out and look at another situation instead of trying to solve this problem. Consider your social security number (SSN). You could think of it in several ways: as a nine-digit number; a nine-digit number with dashes at various points within the nine digits; or a combination of three-, two- and four-digit number fields, which, when joined together, form a social security number. You could even think of it as a three-digit field, a dash, a two-digit field, a dash, and a four-digit field. Each of these possibilities represents the same social security number but requires different amounts of user typing and program processing to form whatever configuration is required for processing.

If you define SSN as an eleven-digit field, then the user must type in the dashes to separate the digits. Your program may have to perform much more extensive editing on this field when it comes into your program from the terminal screen. This takes extra processing time.

If you defined the field SSN as only a nine-digit field, then you could specify NUM to help in field editing. But wait a minute, the dash is a legitimate character since it could be used to indicate negative numbers. Oh well! A social security number could be defined without dashes, but that might appear awkward to the user (you could always tell him that the "computer" requires it to be this way).

If you defined the social security number as three separate fields that you could then put together in your application program, you could still specify the NUM attribute for every field as well as display the dashes between the various parts. Again, if we use the plus sign to denote attribute-byte positioning, your field definitions might appear as follows:

$$+ddd+-+dd+-+dddd$$

with attributes appropriate to the content of the field. Hence, the dashed fields could be set ASKIP so that the user couldn't type into them and so that the user could automatically skip over them to enter the next set of digits. In this case, then, the terminal operator will need only nine keystrokes to enter the social security number, given the specifications above.

This definition still has a problem, though—the last four digits of the social security number have not been ended. Hence, the terminal operator could type in the last four digits and could continue typing until the *next* screen field's attribute byte is encountered. In other words, we have not placed a boundary on our last field in this example (we had the same problem in the menu selection example). Note that this was not a problem in the first two segments of the social security number since they *were* bounded by the dashed field definitions, and their associated attribute bytes marked ASKIP. That is, the range of a field extends from *its* attribute byte to the *next* attribute byte on the screen.

This problem can be easily solved by placing a one-character "null" field at the end of the last social security number segment, as follows:

$$+ddd+-+dd+-+dddd+$$

Hence, when the user accidently types in the tenth digit, he will either automatically skip to the next unprotected data field on the screen (if the attribute byte for the "null" field is ASKIP), or he will halt at the null field when he types in the tenth character (if the attribute byte for the null field is PROT).

Whether the user halts at this point or skips to the next field depends on the value of the attribute byte that has been set by you. The point is that if you want to restrict the amount of data that a user can type into a field, then *you* must define either a null field or define another header field immediately after the user-enterable field (unprotected) on the screen. Finally, this adjacent field can either halt the user's typing progress to make the user aware that he has tried to type data after the end of the field, or you can skip that user to the next unprotected screen field so that he can continue typing. Incidentally, if the user is halted at the null field, he must press the *reset* and *tab-forward* keys to begin typing into the next data field on the display screen.

Also keep in mind that with attribute bytes, your application program is *not* performing the NUM editing or askipping or halting; rather, the terminal hardware is doing this work for you. Your application will only begin to execute when the user stops entering data and actually presses the *enter* key or some other execution-initiation key (such as a PF key) on the terminal keyboard.

The next operand on the DFHMDF statement is the INITIAL operand, which allows you to give a field a default value. This value will be stored in the physical mapset and will be displayed at the terminal when you send out this map, unless, of course, you override the default value from your application program.

If a field is to be referenced or manipulated by the application program, then the field *must* be given a field name. If a field is not going to be referenced or changed either by the terminal operator or by the application program (such as a title on a screen), then there is no need to assign a name to that field because it merely makes your symbolic map for this screen longer. Hence, although the INITIAL operand can place data into a field, the application program can change this data value if necessary by simply referring to the name of this field within the application program.

For example, the map title field for the Landlord Management On-line System might be shown as follows:

LANDLORD MANAGEMENT ON-LINE SYSTEM

and the menu selection line might appear as:

ENTER YOUR MENU SELECTION HERE ------?

Clearly, the only difference between the two is that the terminal operator should not be able to change the title or the menu selection header field; but rather, only the question mark field. Since the only field that needs to be modified for the lines shown is the question mark area, then the two lines could be defined with the following associated DFHMDF statements:

Landlord Management On-line System

```
0           1           1                        7
1           0           6                        2

      DFHMDF      POS=(1,28),LENGTH=34,    X
                  ATTRB=(ASKIP,BRT),       X
                  INITIAL='LANDLORD MANAGEX
                  MENT ON-LINE SYSTEM'
```

```
      ENTER  YOUR  MENU  SELECTION  HERE  ----- ?
```

```
              DFHMDF        POS=(10,5),LENGTH=35,    X
                            ATTRB=(ASKIP,NORM),      X
                            INITIAL='ENTER YOUR SELEX
                            CTION HERE ----- '
CHOICE        DFHMDF        POS=(46,1),LENGTH=1,     X
                            ATTRB=(UNPROT,NUM),      X
                            INITIAL='?'
              DFHMDF        POS=(48,1),LENGTH=1,     X
                            ATTRB=ASKIP
```

Carefully review the code presented and notice that a null field is defined after the menu choice. With the format of the coding presented, the DFH' statements clearly begin in column 10 instead of column 9 on each of the 80-column line images.

The operands POS, LENGTH, ATTRB, and INITIAL are the basic operands to be used in specifying a field to BMS. Two other operands that may be used are the PICIN and PICOUT operands (not shown above), which allow you to specify a PICTURE clause for your data fields so that they can be processed as such by the application program. These operands are only valid for fields that have been assigned field names, since such fields are the only ones that can be referenced by the application program. Normally, all fields will be defined as alpha numeric fields with the PIC X(nnnn) operand specification. If you expect dollar and cent values or other such specifications to be used in a field, then you might want to code a PICIN or PICOUT clause for your data field.

For example, suppose that a three-digit field is to be displayed from the program to the terminal with leading zeros suppressed. This can be done by moving the data to an intermediate variable in WORKING-STORAGE defined as ZZ9, and then moving this variable to our output screen field defined as PIC X(3). This process can be simplified by simply coding PICOUT='ZZ9' on the DFHMDF statement for that screen field. This places the specification of ZZ9 on the definition for this field rather than PIC X(3).

Now, suppose that this same field is to be defined as PIC 999 on input to your program. If you don't specify a PICIN clause, then the input storage area for this field will have a defaulted PICTURE clause of X(3). Again, this can be changed by specifying PICIN=999 on the DFHMDF statement for this field. However, you must be careful here. If the same field has a PICOUT clause of ZZ9 and a PICIN clause of 999, you might abend your program with a data exception abend if your program both sends out and then receives that same field. In other words, if the value 7 is sent to the terminal, it will be sent out as ƀƀ7. If that value comes into your program for processing, then the first two characters of this field are *not* valid 0-9 digits, as required by the 9's specification in the PICIN clause resulting in a data exception abend. You must carefully consider the coordination of your PICIN and PICOUT clauses when they are used in field definition.

We've been discussing field processing within each map in terms of positioning the field on the screen, defining its length, specifying attributes, initializing the field, and processing the field. We have seen that a field can have an input as well as an output field specification. Clearly, a data name in COBOL can have only *one* PICTURE clause, but in our example, we identified an input and an output specification that were not the same. This is possible in CICS screen processing since a map really has two definitions—one definition for input processing, and one for output processing. The symbolic mapset has two entities for each map within that mapset. One entity defines the data as they would be used *from* the terminal to the application program; the other defines the data as they would be used from the application program *to* the terminal.

To summarize all of the concepts involved in screen processing and to help you understand screen development, let's analyze a simple on-line application and the screen required to carry out its processing. This will provide a firm basis for the discussion in the next chapter, where we describe how to write the on-line application program for this system. We will also discuss a couple of screen definitions for this application (as a result of changing some of the DFHMSD operands), along with the complete physical and symbolic mapsets for this application. After that, you should be able to undertake screen development and definition for a CICS application.

SCREEN REQUIREMENTS FOR
A SIMPLE ON-LINE APPLICATION

Suppose that we want to write an application that will allow us to add, subtract, multiply, or divide two numbers. This application requires no file I/O as it communicates directly with the terminal. The user enters the two numbers and selects the type of operation to be performed (add, subtract, multiply, or divide), and the program performs the calculation, displaying the results to the terminal screen.

To implement this application, we'll need one screen for program input (to bring in the user values) and output (to present the results of the computation to the user). Since every application's maps must be part of a mapset, then we'll have only one map within one mapset for this application. The map for this application might appear as follows:

```
CALC        EXPENSIVE ON-LINE CALCULATOR

ENTER YOUR FIRST OPERAND HERE ------

ENTER YOUR SECOND OPERAND HERE ------

WHAT OPERATION WOULD YOU LIKE TO DO ------?
    1. ADD
    2. SUBTRACT
    3. MULTIPLY
    4. DIVIDE

THE RESULT OF YOUR CALCULATION IS ------
```

Clearly, there are several information-only fields and several data fields on this screen. One field that should catch your eye is the uppermost left field on the screen, CALC. In CICS, every application is initiated through a transaction id (as you'll remember from an earlier chapter). Hence, to reinitiate our application for every user's request, we must place the transaction id for this application in the upper left of the screen. We also have to do this because our application will be written in a nonconversational programming style.

If you recall the pseudocode for the landlord system, you'll remember that after each completion of a function, the program returned to the system, placed a value in memory, and set the next tranid value to whatever was appropriate for that component of the application. That memory area is simply an area on the screen display that actually contains the transaction id for this transaction, or the map code indicator, or a function indicator. Since there's only one map and one function, the map code indicator and function indicators are not needed in this application. (In a later chapter, we'll address these items in more detail for more "sophisticated" applications.) Hence, each time that the user presses the *enter* key, CICS will reinitiate our transaction because we have placed the transaction id associated with this transaction in the first field on the terminal display.

If this information is not going to be meaningful to the user, we can hide it on the screen by specifying the attribute DRK for this field. Further, if we do not want the user to be able to change this field, we can assign the attribute ASKIP to this field. Finally, since it is *mandatory* that this field reinitiate our transaction, we *must* code the FSET attribute on this field to make it appear to CICS as though the user had entered the field himself. This coding assures us that our transaction will be restarted the next time we press the *enter* key.

To describe the initiation in another way, we can say this screen is sent out to ask the user to identify his or her values and the operation to be performed. After this screen is sent out, the only fields recognized by the CICS system or made available to the application program the next time that this screen is to be processed are those that have been modified by the terminal operator, or that appear to have been modified by the terminal operator. Since it is the transaction id that initiates our application, then our application can only be initiated if the user types in our transaction id or if it appears that the first field on the screen (first four bytes of screen data) has been typed in by the terminal operator. Since the terminal operator should *not* have to continually type in the transaction id to reinitiate the program(s) associated with this application, we'll accomplish the same thing by making the attribute for that field appear to have been modified by the terminal operator. We do so by specifying FSET as an attribute for that field. In a later chapter we'll see a different way of accomplishing the same thing without having the transaction id physically present on the terminal display. At this point, however, let's leave the transaction id on the screen as a *necessary* field in order to reemphasize the fact that it is the transaction id that causes application execution.

This is about the only tricky aspect of CICS nonconversational programming. Every screen must be equipped with a transaction id to reinitiate the application program(s) once the screen is sent out. Again, you may want to hide the tranid by specifying the attributes (FSET,ASKIP,DRK) on the DFHMDF statement for this field. If you really want to have this field visible to the user so that the user can remember what he's doing or what the procedure means, you should specify (FSET,ASKIP,NORM) as the attributes for this field. The remaining fields on the screen are straightforward. Here, then, is a display of the screen showing the location of the attributes for each field:

```
+CALC+        EXPENSIVE ON-LINE CALCULATOR

  +ENTER YOUR FIRST OPERAND HERE ------+              +

  +ENTER YOUR SECOND OPERAND HERE ------+             +

  +WHAT OPERATION WOULD YOU LIKE TO DO ------+?       +
   +1. ADD
   +2. SUBTRACT
   +3. MULTIPLY
   +4. DIVIDE

  +THE RESULT OF YOUR CALCULATION IS ------+          +

   +
```

Note that each data field is bordered either by a header field or a null field to restrict the length of the data field on the screen. Therefore, if we call the first operand VAL1, the second VAL2, the type of operation to be done CHOICE, the result of the calculation RSLT, and the message area at the bottom of the screen MSG, then our complete mapset for this application could be coded as shown below. Remember that there is only one map for this mapset. If there was more than one map, the other maps would simply follow (or precede) the map shown, but be contained *within* the DFHMSD statements.

```
0          01       11                                      7
1          90       67                                      2


CALCMAP    DFHMSD   TYPE=DSECT,MODE=INOUT,                  X
                    TIOAPFX=YES,STORAGE=AUTO,               X
                    CTRL=FREEKB,LANG=COBOL
MAINMAP    DFHMDI   SIZE=(24,80),LINE=1,COLUMN=1
```

```
          DFHMDF  POS=(1,1),LENGTH=4,              X
                  ATTRB=(ASKIP,DRK,FSET),          X
                  INITIAL='CALC'
          DFHMDF  POS=(1,25),LENGTH=27,            X
                  ATTRB=(BRT,ASKIP),               X
                  INITIAL='EXPENSIVE ON-LINE CAX
                  LCULATOR'
          DFHMDF  POS=(5,3),LENGTH=36,             X
                  ATTRB=(ASKIP,NORM),              X
                  INITIAL='ENTER YOUR FIRST OPEX
                  RAND HERE ----- '
VAL1      DFHMDF  POS=(5,40),LENGTH=7,             X
                  ATTRB=(BRT,NUM,UNPROT,IC)
          DFHMDF  POS=(5,48),LENGTH=1,             X
                  ATTRB=(ASKIP)
          DFHMDF  POS=(7,3),LENGTH=36,             X
                  ATTRB=(ASKIP,NORM),              X
                  INITIAL='ENTER YOUR SECOND OPX
                  ERAND HERE ----- '
VAL2      DFHMDF  POS=(7,40),LENGTH=7,             X
                  ATTRB=(BRT,NUM,UNPROT)
          DFHMDF  POS=(7,48),LENGTH=1,             X
                  ATTRB=(ASKIP)
          DFHMDF  POS=(10,3),LENGTH=40,            X
                  ATTRB=(ASKIP,NORM),              X
                  INITIAL='WHAT OPERATION WOULDX
                   YOU LIKE TO DO -----'
CHOICE    DFHMDF  POS=(10,44),LENGTH=1,            X
                  ATTRB=(BRT,NUM,UNPROT),          X
                  INITIAL='?'
          DFHMDF  POS=(10,46),LENGTH=1,            X
                  ATTRB=ASKIP
          DFHMDF  POS=(11,8),LENGTH=12,            X
                  ATTRB=ASKIP,INITIAL='1.   ADD'
          DFHMDF  POS=(12,8),LENGTH=12,            X
                  ATTRB=ASKIP,INITIAL='2.   SUBTX
                  RACT'
          DFHMDF  POS=(13,8),LENGTH=12,            X
                  ATTRB=ASKIP,INITIAL='3.   MULTX
                  IPLY'
          DFHMDF  POS=(14,8),LENGTH=12,            X
                  ATTRB=ASKIP,INITIAL='4.   DIVIX
                  DE'
          DFHMDF  POS=(18,3),LENGTH=37,            X
                  ATTRB=ASKIP,                     X
```

```
                               INITIAL='THE RESULT OF YOUR CX
                               ALCULATION IS -----'
RSLT          DFHMDF           POS=(18,41),LENGTH=11,          X
                               ATTRB=(ASKIP,BRT),             X
                               PICOUT='99999999.99'
MSG           DFHMDF           POS=(24,10),LENGTH=60,          X
                               ATTRB=(BRT,ASKIP)
              DFHMSD           TYPE=FINAL
              END
```

Carefully review this code to note the following: how the mapset definition and termination is identified within this mapset; how each line within the map is coded "in order" with all necessary operands for the fields specified; and finally, note the various field names, attributes, initialization, and picture input and output clauses used in the map. Next, this code must be assembled to produce the physical and symbolic mapsets to be used in supporting our applications processing.

The physical mapset is used by BMS to aid in positioning fields on the screen, assigning default values to fields including default attributes, and in associating the data on the screen with the application program's symbolic mapset. Below is a rough idea of how the physical mapset would appear to BMS and what information it would contain for our calculator mapset.

field location	attributes	initial data	
0000	FSET, ASKIP, DRK	CALC	
	ASKIP, BRT	title	
0322	ASKIP, NORM	ENTER . . . FIRST OPERAND	
0359	UNPROT, IC BRT, NUM		000000
0367	ASKIP		
0482	ASKIP, NORM	ENTER . . . SECOND OPERAND	
0519	UNPROT. BRT, NUM		000010
0527	ASKIP		

field location	attributes	initial data	
0722	ASKIP, NORM	WHAT . . . PERFORM	
0763	UNPROT, NUM, BRT	?	000020
0765	ASKIP		

(the rest of the physical map has been purposely omitted)

If you take a few minutes to compare the p~~hysical~~ mapset with the BMS code for our map, you'll see that they're **practically** identical except for appearance, field location (which is specified as a relative offset to zero), and the symbolic mapset relative offset. This last field (relative offset) is the tie between the physical and symbolic mapsets that allows BMS to prepare screen data to be used by the application program for processing, and to "pull" data *from* the storage area defined by the symbolic mapset to build a TIOA data stream to be sent to the terminal. In other words, when your application program sends data out to a terminal, BMS *merges* the data in the symbolic mapset with the data in the physical mapset to build a terminal data stream in an output TIOA according to the symbolic map relative position defined in the physical map. This resulting data stream will be in the format in which you want your information to be displayed to that terminal device.

Actually, we're cheating a little here. There really isn't a relative-position field in the physical map at all; rather, when the compiler uses the symbolic mapset in the compilation of the application program, the named fields (referenced by the application code) are translated into offsets from the beginning of the map (as I've shown in the table). This resulting machine code for the program uses "displacement addressing" to reference each field within that map.

When BMS in processing your map, BMS associates each named field (as indicated in the physical map) with an offset into the symbolic mapset, on the basis of the length of each preceding field. This is mimicked in the above example through the use of the relative field column. If you look at the data in this column carefully, you'll see that the first named field on this map is called VAL1. Since this field will be the first field in the symbolic map (since it is the first field with a name in our map definition), the number of bytes of field data preceding VAL1 in the symbolic map is zero. VAL2, on the other hand, is the next named field within this map. Hence, VAL2 is located after VAL1 in the symbolic mapset and is actually 10 positions (bytes) after the VAL1 field data.

The length is ten bytes because the length of the VAL1 data field is 7, the length of the attribute byte field is 1, and the "length" field (more about that in a moment) is 2 bytes. Hence, $1 + 2 + 7 = 10$, which matches the relative offset of VAL2 in the symbolic map.

If your application is getting data from a terminal, then BMS moves the data *from* the input TIOA data stream to the storage area defined through your symbolic mapset so that your program can access each field through a data name. In this way, your application program need not be concerned with terminal hardware characteristics, since the handling of these components is done by BMS.

Additionally, when BMS merges your symbolic map data with your physical map data to build an output display to the terminal, your symbolic map data override *any* information in the physical mapset. For example, if you specify ATTRB=(NUM,NORM) and INITIAL='000' in the physical map but you move an attribute value of (BRT,NUM) and a value of 123 in the symbolic map for that field, then when BMS merges the two maps together, the resulting output to the terminal will specify (BRT,NUM) for that field and display a value of 123 instead of 000.

Hence, whenever the application needs to change a field's attributes or displayable values, the application simply has to move the desired values to the symbolic map area and issue a send request; the results will then be displayed on the screen as desired. However, this change is effective *only* for this *one* request. That is, the physical mapset is never changed from mapping operation to mapping operation. If it is necessary to change the attributes or displayed information for a field in *every* send request to the terminal, then the application program must be coded so that it applies the new values *before every* send request for this screen. If your default attributes or initial values for a field are to be a permanent change to that map, then probably the best solution would be to change the code within that map, reassemble the maps, and then recompile the application program(s) using that mapset.

Let's look at the COBOL code for the symbolic map to support our application:

```
01  MAINMAPI.
    02  FILLER           PIC X(12).
    02  VAL1L            COMP PIC S9(4).
    02  VAL1F            PIC X.
    02  FILLER           REDEFINES VAL1F.
        03  VAL1A        PIC X.
    02  VAL1I            PIC X(7).
    02  VAL2L            COMP PIC S9(4).
    02  VAL2F            PIC X.
    02  FILLER           REDEFINES VAL2F.
        03  VAL2A        PIC X.
```

```
        02 VAL2I        PIC X(7).
        02 CHOICEL      COMP PIC S9(4).
        02 CHOICEF      PIC X.
        02 FILLER       REDEFINES CHOICEF.
           03 CHOICEA   PIC X.
        02 CHOICEI      PIC X.
        02 RSLTL        COMP PIC S9(4).
        02 RSLTF        PIC X.
        02 FILLER       REDEFINES RSLTF.
           03 RSLTA     PIC X.
        02 RSLTI        PIC X(11).
        02 MSGL         COMP PIC S9(4).
        02 MSGF         PIC X.
        02 FILLER       REDEFINES MSGF.
           03 MSGA      PIC X.
        02 MSGI         PIC X(60).
     01 MAINMAPO        REDEFINES MAINMAPI.
        02 FILLER       PIC X(12).
        02 FILLER       PIC X(3).
        02 VAL1O        PIC X(7).
        02 FILLER       PIC X(3).
        02 VAL2O        PIC X(7).
        02 FILLER       PIC X(3).
        02 CHOICEO      PIC X.
        02 FILLER       PIC X(3).
        02 RSLTO        PIC 99999999.99.
        02 FILLER       PIC X(3).
        02 MSGO         PIC X(60).
```

The first obvious feature is probably the field names. They look quite different from the ones that we assigned to these fields. But are they really different? Once you learn about each of these field names, you'll see that there's really nothing unusual about them.

You should also notice that there are really two map definitions here. The first one defines the *input* data coming from the screen to the application program. You can see why the data field names here end in "I." The second map simply redefines the same storage area, but assigns an O suffix to field names to indicate *output* areas. VAL1I and VAL1O actually address the same physical storage area within memory, so interchanging the I- and O-suffixed fields is really no problem, although the programmer may find it more meaningful to distinguish between input and output field areas.

In this symbolic map, note the A-, L-, and F-suffixed fields. The A field is used to assign a new set of attributes to a field *before* it is sent to the terminal.

Attributes for a field can be easily changed through a simple MOVE instruction (more about this a little later).

When a field is coming in from a terminal, the L and F fields may be important to your application. The L-suffixed field tells your program the number of bytes entered by the terminal operator, or the number of characters in the field if the FSET attribute was specified. Hence, if the value in the length field is zero, then no data were entered by the terminal operator, or no data were defaulted in these fields. If this is the case, your application could send the user a message something like "please enter data in field. . . ."

If the input data field is empty, that is, if it contains binary zeros (null values or low-values) and the FSET attribute was not specified, then the F-suffixed field will have a value of X'00'. If your data field was defined with the FSET attribute and has no data in it, then the F-suffixed field will contain a value of X'80'. Hence, the L- and F-suffixed fields allow your application program to determine whether any data were entered in a field and how much was entered. Thus, the user would be provided with more meaningful messages to enter in the data fields on the screen.

If you carefully compare the symbolic and the physical maps, you'll notice that the I- and O-suffixed fields for VAL2 are 10 bytes after the VAL1 fields. CHOICEL is 20 bytes after the VAL1L fields and 10 bytes after the VAL2L fields. If you understand this relationship, you should be able to see how the "relative symbolic mapset" column in the physical map presented earlier matches up with the input and output field areas associated with each one of the named data fields on this map.

Remember, a map is a component of a mapset and a field is a component of a map. Mapping operations involve two elements, a physical map and a symbolic map, of which the symbolic map is really two entities. The physical map contains default information for a field that can be overridden by the application program *if, and only if,* that field is addressable by the application program. Addressability is achieved by giving a field a name, and thus creating a set of field elements in the symbolic mapset. Finally, fields are accessed by data names through the symbolic-physical map connection supported by BMS. Each field data name really consists of several components that give the application program information about the data coming in to the application and enable the application program to change information before that map is sent out to the terminal.

Earlier in the chapter, we discussed the use of the operands STORAGE= AUTO and BASE=dataname on the DFHMSD control statement. If you refer back to the symbolic map for our calculator screen, you'll see that the main map for this application *does not* redefine any other storage area. Let's assume that this map is being processed in the WORKING-STORAGE section of our program and that move mode processing is most likely being used within the program.

If we remove the STORAGE=AUTO operand on our DFHMSD statement, replacing it with BASE=MAPAREA, then the following symbolic mapset will be generated by the assembler. Note that the only difference between this symbolic map code and the code presented earlier is the REDEFINES on MAINMAPI (first line of the code).

```
01  MAINMAPI         REDEFINES MAPAREA.
    02 FILLER        PIC X(12).
    02 VAL1L         COMP PIC S9(4).
    02 VAL1F         PIC X.
    02 FILLER        REDEFINES VAL1F.
       03 VAL1A      PIC X.
    02 VAL1I         PIC X(7).
    02 VAL2L         COMP PIC S9(4).
    02 VAL2F         PIC X.
    02 FILLER        REDEFINES VAL2F.
       03 VAL2A      PIC X.
    02 VAL2I         PIC X(7).
    02 CHOICEL       COMP PIC S9(4).
    02 CHOICEF       PIC X.
    02 FILLER        REDEFINES CHOICEF.
       03 CHOICEA    PIC X.
    02 CHOICEI       PIC X.
    02 RSLTL         COMP PIC S9(4).
    02 RSLTF         PIC X.
    02 FILLER        REDEFINES RSLTF.
       03 RSLTA      PIC X.
    02 RSLTI         PIC X(11).
    02 MSGL          COMP PIC S9(4).
    02 MSGF          PIC X.
    02 FILLER        REDEFINES MSGF.
       03 MSGA       PIC X.
    02 MSGI          PIC X(60).
01  MAINMAPO         REDEFINES MAINMAPI.
    02 FILLER        PIC X(12).
    02 FILLER        PIC X(3).
    02 VAL1O         PIC X(7).
    02 FILLER        PIC X(3).
    02 VAL2O         PIC X(7).
    02 FILLER        PIC X(3).
    02 CHOICEO       PIC X.
    02 FILLER        PIC X(3).
    02 RSLTO         PIC 99999999.99.
    02 FILLER        PIC X(3).
    02 MSGO          PIC X(60).
```

In this case, we can process the maps in the linkage section of our program by using locate-mode processing, thus improving the performance of our transaction slightly and reducing the storage requirements of our program. Although we've been discussing the differences in map processing by using move or locate mode and although the variations of implementation are many, one could function just as well by choosing one technique and becoming fluent in its use. The few hundredths of a second saved in locate-mode coding versus move-mode coding may not be a strong enough case for the problems that can arise during processing, especially for an inexperienced CICS programmer.

SCREEN GENERATOR PACKAGES

By now you either understand BMS usage and appreciate how it works, or you're so confused that you don't know how anyone could function with such a package. There is hope, however; your work can be made much easier if you use a screen generator system. Some time ago, I developed a package to produce BMS code automatically from a screen layout. In other words, you simply code a 24 by 80 screen and identify numeric fields by a dollar sign ($) and character fields by an at-sign (@), as shown below.

```
@@@@         EXPENSIVE ON-LINE CALCULATOR

ENTER YOUR FIRST OPERAND HERE ------ $$$$$$$

ENTER YOUR SECOND OPERAND HERE ------ $$$$$$$

WHAT OPERATION WOULD YOU LIKE TO DO ------ $
   1. ADD
   2. SUBTRACT
   3. MULTIPLY
   4. DIVIDE

THE RESULT OF YOUR CALCULATION IS ------ $$$$$$$$




@@@@@@@@@@@@@@@@@@@@@@@@@@@@@@@@@@@@@@@
```

The system will then produce an easier language by which you can update field attributes, or assign mapset, map, and field names; it also has many other features not found in standard BMS coding facilities. This superlanguage is then preprocessed, and out of the preprocessing comes high-quality, error-free BMS code that is fed directly into the assembler for screen generation. Earlier, we stated that BMS coding usually takes hours for even a simple screen. With a system such as the one I've just described, this time has been reduced to *minutes*. In fact, we've been using this package for some time now and have saved thousands of CPU seconds, tens of thousands of processing dollars, and hundreds of man-hours. Such packages are commercially available through various vendors. If you want to use CICS in your application development and at the same time minimize your implementation schedule, you might want to investigate such screen-generator packages. They can turn your BMS-coding phase into a minor task.

Before we leave this chapter, let me reemphasize a particularly important point. Defining screens to CICS is a rather mechanical task. The major emphasis of screen development should be on designing a set of screens that are acceptable to the user, that are easy to use, *and* that coordinate with the work activities of the user. Don't lose sight of the user, even at the outset of screen definition. Proper attributes must be set on the various fields and the information must be presented to the user in an acceptable fashion. You must get the user involved during this definition procedure. Continually have your screens reviewed by the user and match the screens to the user's work activities.

In conclusion, IBM's CICS is a powerful tool but one that is easy to use. With components such as BMS to provide the level of support needed for on-line application development, on-line implementation can be a short phase in the life cycle of your system. In this chapter we carefully studied the components of terminal-to-program communications through BMS by moving from a general overview to a specific field-level implementation. Although some of the concepts may not be entirely clear yet, the next few chapters will help resolve any questions you may have about the mapping process and map usage. We are about to find out *how* to send and receive data from a terminal through an application program. We'll do this by implementing the calculator problem presented in this chapter. Although the main application that we want to implement is the Landlord Management System, we don't have all of the tools to do that yet. Hence, we'll implement this small application first and discuss its operation; then we can apply the knowledge we gain from this application to the larger application. Let me call your attention to the questions at the end of this chapter since they are important to your understanding of BMS processing. You should carefully study and answer these questions before we go on to implement this application in the next chapter.

THOUGHT QUESTIONS

1. Why is the transaction id needed in the upper left corner of the terminal screen? What if the tranid was in the upper right corner of the screen but represented the first input field to CICS?

2. What would the symbolic map look like if there were two or more maps within this mapset?

3. Suppose that a field is originally defined without the FSET operand. When would an application program want to change the attributes for a field (to FSET) before that screen is displayed to the terminal?

4. Review the coding rules and operands for the PRINT, comment, DFHMSD, DFHMDI, DFHMDF and END statements.

5. Try to guess what would happen if you processed a screen's data using the wrong mapset definition.

6. Compare and contrast locate-mode and move-mode processing for terminal display screens in terms of usage, performance, under-standing, and ease of use.

9

PROGRAM-TO-TERMINAL COMMUNICATIONS

We are now going to finish developing the simple on-line calculator system begun in Chapter 8 by describing the mapset to be used to support that application. At the same time, we will introduce command-level statements to communicate with the terminal. Since terminal communications and nonconversational programming are probably the two most difficult aspects of CICS application development, we will carefully study how these services are used and give numerous examples of their application.

We have already developed a mapset for our calculator system that has several fields. We have categorized most of these fields as information-only or header fields, data fields, or fields specifically manipulated by the program and not by the user. One field was not manipulated by the program or the terminal operator, yet it was processed by the CICS system. This last field is, of course, the transaction id field, CALC, located in the upper left corner of the screen on next page.

Before we continue, we should explain one critical aspect of CICS programming—the way that a screen is presented to the application program by BMS.

FORMATTED AND UNFORMATTED SCREENS

In CICS on-line programming, a terminal input-output area (TIOA) can present one of two formats to the application when data are coming from the

```
CALC          EXPENSIVE ON-LINE CALCULATOR

   ENTER YOUR FIRST OPERAND HERE ------

   ENTER YOUR SECOND OPERAND HERE ------

   WHAT OPERATION WOULD YOU WANT TO DO ------?
      1. ADD
      2. SUBTRACT
      3. MULTIPLY
      4. DIVIDE

   THE RESULT OF YOUR CALCULATION IS ------
```

terminal *into* the application program to be processed. Hence, it is the responsibility of the application program to determine which format has been presented *before* it processes any data on that display screen. If the application chooses the incorrect format of the data, an abend is almost guaranteed.

The two formats are called *unformatted* and *formatted* screen displays. Determining which one has been presented to your nonconversational program is a *very* simple task. It amounts to nothing more than coding a TIOA description (FD) and conducting a simple IF-THEN test, as you'll soon see.

Generally, most of the formats presented to your application under BMS are *formatted* screen displays. A screen display is formatted when fields are defined with attributes. If you are using a special component of BMS in which attributes for fields are *not* specified, then you must be using an unformatted screen format. Hence, it is easy to determine whether a screen is formatted or unformatted *from a user's point of view*—that is, if fields are highlighted, dark, askipped, protected, or numeric, the screen is formatted; otherwise it's unformatted.

From a program's point of view, you can't look at a screen. However, you can analyze the data on that screen and look for field values. If an expected field value is found, the screen is formatted; if not, it is an unformatted screen. Let me show you an unformatted screen.

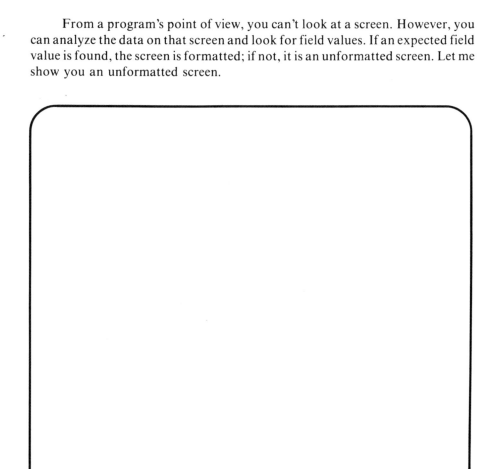

You're probably thinking that the printer forgot to type something inside the boundaries above. No, there's no error in the screen above. This is a typical unformatted screen like the one your program will probably encounter every time that it is initiated. But when will it process such a screen? The answer is simple: the first time that the user initiates your application!

PROGRAM INITIATION AND TERMINATION

When a user wants to use an on-line application, he must enter the transaction id associated with that application to get that application started. To do this, the user presses the *clear* key and gets a blank screen! Ah-ha! An unformatted screen!

The user then types in the transaction id necessary to initiate that transaction. Even though no data appear on this screen, they are still in an unformatted structure since the user didn't type in any attribute along with the transaction id. As a matter of fact, the user *cannot* make a screen formatted by typing in data. Thus, the screen *remains* unformatted, and might look like this:

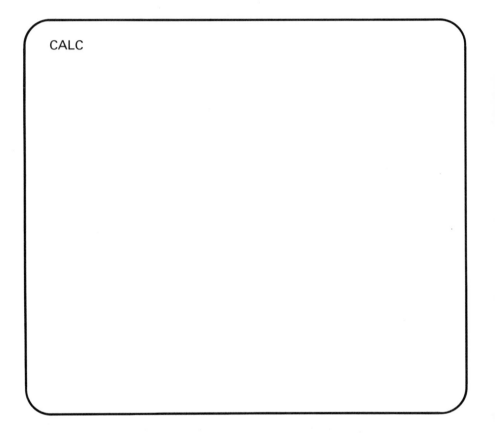

After entering the transaction id, the user presses the *enter* key. This step, of course, initiates the application program; in the example above, the program associated with the transaction id CALC (as defined in the PCT) is initiated by CICS. Therefore, the first screen processed by any on-line application program that receives control the first time it is initiated *must* be able to recognize an unformatted screen.

Although there are no meaningful applications data on the screen in the example above, it is possible to use unformatted screens to send data to the application program from the terminal operator. (We discuss this procedure in a later chapter.) When this unformatted screen comes in to the application program, the program usually sends out a formatted screen immediately to begin user processing. Many times, this first screen is a menu, but a menu may not always be applicable, as is the case in our calculator application. A menu is not needed there because only one screen is used to support the application. Hence, when the calculator program recognizes an unformatted screen, it knows that it is being initiated for the first time by this terminal operator, and that the main map should be sent out. Hence, after the user enters the letters C-A-L-C on the blank screen and presses the *enter* key, the following screen will be displayed:

```
CALC            EXPENSIVE ON-LINE CALCULATOR

ENTER YOUR FIRST OPERAND HERE ------

ENTER YOUR SECOND OPERAND HERE ------

WHAT OPERATION WOULD YOU WANT TO DO ------?
   1. ADD
   2. SUBTRACT
   3. MULTIPLY
   4. DIVIDE

THE RESULT OF YOUR CALCULATION IS ------
```

From this point on, all communication between user and program will take place through *formatted* screen displays. Only when the user presses the *clear* key to end all processing for this application will the screen revert to an unformatted mode.

Earlier we said that determining whether or not a screen is formatted or unformatted is an easy task. It amounts to analyzing the position of data fields within the input TIOA. Let's think of the data on a screen as a large record that may even be stored on some other direct access device. Let's also assume that the record is 1920 bytes long. Each time that our program is initiated, we read the record from the terminal to determine what the user wants us to do. This record contains the data fields to be processed (if there were data fields on the screen) and, of course, the transaction id, the first field on the screen. Since the transaction id will always be in this record, which we read (since we specified an attribute of FSET), we can simply analyze this one field to determine if the entire record is formatted or unformatted.

DEFINING AND PROCESSING A TIOA

To access the data in this record we need a record description. Since the record is read into a TIOA, let's call our record description TIOA-AREA. Since TIOA-AREA has fields within it, we could define some other fields within this FD; however, the only field that we really need to define is the transaction id field. On the other hand, a formatted screen may have many fields. Wouldn't it seem logical, then, to define each of these? It would, but we've already done this! When we defined our maps to the system, we generated a symbolic mapset, *which is* the definition of fields on a formatted screen. Hence, if we determine that the screen to be processed is formatted, then we'll simply have BMS move or map the data from our input TIOA to our symbolic map area so that we can process our fields with the L-, I-, F-, O-, and A-suffixed variable names. Hence, the FD called TIOA-AREA needs to reference only one field.

```
01   TIOA-AREA.
     03   UNFORMATTED-TRANID      PIC X(4).
     02   REST-OF-THE-TIOA        PIC X(1916).
```

This is clearly a simple definition of the data in the TIOA, but it isn't useful for most purposes. This definition would not work, for example, in a situation that requires the program to process several maps! Well, since we can't accept this structure, we need to define a more complete structure that will enable us to reference the data on *both* a formatted and unformatted screen and, when necessary, allow us to use the definition to determine which formatted screen within a mapset is ready to be processed by our program. The structure below would meet such a need.

```
01   TIOA-AREA.
     02   FIRST-PART-OF-TIOA      PIC X(20).
     02   UNFORMATTED-PART        REDEFINES
                                  FIRST-PART-OF-TIOA.
          03   UNFORMATTED-TRANID PIC X(4).
```

```
        03  FILLER                  PIC  X(16).
  02  FORMATTED-PART                REDEFINES
                                    FIRST-PART-OF-TIOA.
        03  FILLER                  PIC  X(3).
        03  FORMATTED-TRANID        PIC  X(4).
        03  FILLER                  PIC  X(13).
  02  REST-OF-THE-TIOA             PIC  X(1900).
```

If you carefully examine the FD above, you'll see that when the screen is unformatted, the transaction id is in the first four positions of the 1920-byte record. When the screen is formatted, the transaction id is *not* in the first four bytes of the record; when the screen is formatted, the three filler bytes precede the transaction id. These three filler bytes are made up of system control data (2-bytes) and the flag-attribute byte for the transaction id field (1-byte) coming into the application from a formatted screen. The fact that three filler bytes are *not* present for fields on an unformatted screen is the basis for determining whether a screen is formatted or unformatted. Fields on an unformatted screen do not have attributes or system control information and so the location of the field in a TIOA is different from that on a map (formatted screen). Although both the formatted screen (maps) and unformatted screen will have a tranid in the upper left corner, the tranid field will have a different offset in the TIOA when the screen is unformatted.

DISTINGUISHING BETWEEN SCREEN FORMATS

To determine whether the screen is formatted or unformatted, the program must make a simple decision:

```
if UNFORMATTED-TRANID = 'CALC' then
    — send out the "MAINMAP"
    — return

else
    — map the data from TIOA-AREA to the
      symbolic map area associated with "MAINMAP"
    — process the data in "MAINMAP"
```

This may not be a difficult decision to make for the calculator application, but consider the landlord management application in which there are many formatted screens. If we instruct BMS to map the wrong screen from our TIOA-AREA to our symbolic map area, then we could have a severe problem. Hence, even though the decision above tells us whether the screen is formatted or unformatted, it does not tell us *which* formatted screen is to be processed. Hence, we'll need to alter our TIOA-AREA FD to help us make *this* decision.

```
01  TIOA-AREA.
    02  FIRST-PART-OF-TIOA              PIC X(20).
    02  UNFORMATTED-PART               REDEFINES
                                       FIRST-PART-OF-TIOA.
        03  UNFORMATTED-TRANID         PIC X(4).
        03  FILLER                     PIC X(16).
    02  FORMATTED-PART                 REDEFINES
                                       FIRST-PART-OF-TIOA.
        03  FILLER                     PIC X(3).
        03  FORMATTED-TRANID           PIC X(4).
        03  FORMATTED-MAP-CODE         PIC X.
        03  FILLER                     PIC X(12).
    02  REST-OF-THE-TIOA               PIC X(1900).
```

In the FD above you should notice a field called FORMATTED-MAP-CODE. This field is to be used in determining *which* formatted map is to be processed. However, defining this field does not ensure that we'll process the correct map; we must also make sure that there is a special field on our maps to use along with an FD of this type. This means that within the field definition statements for every map in your mapset, you'll need to append a *unique* character to the transaction id to help you distinguish between the various formatted maps. Let's suppose that the mapset LAMSM has three maps: MENU, ADD, and DELETE. The DFHMDF statements to define the transaction id field on each of these screens might be as follows:

```
LAMSM   DFHMSD   ....

MENU    DFHMDI   SIZE=(24,80),LINE=1,COLUMN=1
        DFHMDF   POS=(1,1),LENGTH=5,                            X
                 ATTRB=(DRK,FSET,ASKIP),INITIAL='LAMSM'

         .        .
         .        .
         .        .

ADD     DFHMDI   SIZE=(24,80),LINE=1,COLUMN=1
        DFHMDF   POS=(1,1),LENGTH=5,                            X
                 ATTRB=(DRK,FSET,ASKIP),INITIAL='LAMSA'

         .        .
         .        .
         .        .

DELETE  DFHMDI   SIZE=(24,80),LINE=1,COLUMN=1
        DFHMDF   POS=(1,1),LENGTH=5,                            X
                 ATTRB=(DRK,FSET,ASKIP),INITIAL='LAMSD'
```

```
            .            .

            .            .

            .            .
        DFHMSD   TYPE=FINAL
        END
```

In the above code you see that the same transaction id is used throughout each of the maps and that it has another letter appended to it that makes it appear to be five characters long. This letter will be used by the program to distinguish between the ADD, DELETE, and MENU screens for the LAMS mapset. The transaction id for this system is LAMS; hence, the *same* program will be given control each time that the user presses the *enter* key.

Within this program, the FORMATTED-MAP-CODE field can be used to determine whether the MENU map (map code of M), the ADD map (map code of A), or the DELETE map is to be processed (map code of D). Therefore, if the extra field is appended to the transaction id, the application can easily determine which formatted map is to be processed. The logic for making such a decision is as follows:

```
if UNFORMATTED-TRANID = 'LAMS' then
    — send out the "MAINMAP"
    — return

else
    if FORMATTED-MAP-CODE = 'A' then
        — map the data from the input TIOA to the
          symbolic map area for ADD map
        — process the ADD map data

    else
        if FORMATTED-MAP-CODE = 'M' then
            — map the data from the input TIOA
              to the symbolic map area for MENU map
            — process the MENU map data

        else
            if FORMATTED-MAP-CODE = 'D' then
                — map the data from the input TIOA
                  to the symbolic map area for the
                  DELETE map
                — process the DELETE map data

            else

                . . . .

                . . . .
```

You could successfully argue that this is a cumbersome way of programming. Many installations implement their applications in conversational rather than nonconversational mode just to avoid these idiosyncrasies. Although it may seem pointless to implement such a technique, you may nonetheless want to consider it instead of sacrificing system performance by implementing your application in a conversational programming style. In a later chapter we will discuss an alternate method that is much easier and is usable in the nonconversational programming style.

If you examine the screens in the ADD and DELETE components of a system, you soon realize that it may be possible to use one map to perform both functions. One map could display all the data to a user in the case of a DELETE and the same map could accept data from the user in the case of an ADD; thus, the same map having exactly the same fields could be used for both functions. If you want to share a map among several functions within your application, however, the FORMATTED-MAP-CODE field may be misleading in that a shared map would probably have the same code. In such a situation, an additional control character may be needed to help you distinguish not only between maps, but also between the functions being performed, such as ADD or DELETE. Since this field would be constructed in the same fashion as the map code field, the previous example can be modified slightly to allow us to retain such information. Again, this situation is unique to nonconversational transactions or to systems that share a map among several functions.

Another drawback to this technique is that if you want the transaction id to be visible to the user, then the user will also see this control character and may become confused as to the reason for its presence. Another problem is that if the user changes this character, your program will map the data to the symbolic map area incorrectly and an abend will probably occur. You can, however, easily define this control letter in a different way and interrogate its value using a different TIOA-AREA FD, as shown below. In this way, the transaction id *can* be visible to the user *and* the control character can still be available to the program to aid it in determining which screen is to be processed.

```
01  TIOA-AREA.
    02  FIRST-PART-OF-TIOA          PIC X(20).
    02  UNFORMATTED-PART            REDEFINES
                                    FIRST-PART-OF-TIOA.
        03  UNFORMATTED-TRANID      PIC X(4).
        03  FILLER                  PIC X(16).
    02  FORMATTED-PART              REDEFINES
                                    FIRST-PART-OF-TIOA.
        03  FILLER                  PIC X(3).
        03  FORMATTED-TRANID        PIC X(4).
        03  FILLER                  PIC X(3).
        03  FORMATTED-MAP-CODE      PIC X.
        03  FILLER                  PIC X(9).
    02  REST-OF-THE-TIOA            PIC X(1900).
```

```
LAMSM   DFHMSD  ....
MENU    DFHMDI  SIZE=(24,80),LINE=1,COLUMN=1
        DFHMDF  POS=(1,1),LENGTH=4,ATTRB=(FSET,UNPROT), X
                INITIAL='LAMS'
        DFHMDF  POS=(1,6),LENGTH=1,                      X
                ATTRB=(DRK,FSET,ASKIP),INITIAL='M'
          .       .
          .       .
          .       .
ADD     DFHMDI  SIZE=(24,80),LINE=1,COLUMN=1
        DFHMDF  POS=(1,1),LENGTH=4,ATTRB=(FSET,UNPROT), X
                INITIAL='LAMS'
        DFHMDF  POS=(1,6),LENGTH=1,                      X
                ATTRB=(DRK,FSET,ASKIP),INITIAL='A'
          .       .
          .       .
          .       .
DELETE  DFHMDI  SIZE=(24,80),LINE=1,COLUMN=1
        DFHMDF  POS=(1,1),LENGTH=4,ATTRB=(FSET,UNPROT), X
                INITIAL='LAMS'
        DFHMDF  POS=(1,6),LENGTH=1,                      X
                ATTRB=(DRK,FSET,ASKIP),INITIAL='D'
          .       .
          .       .
          .       .
        DFHMSD  TYPE=FINAL
        END
```

Any of the above techniques or formats will work in our calculator problem since we have only one screen. It's not even necessary to place a control character within MAINMAP since only one map is needed to support the calculator application; nor is it necessary to keep information on the function to be performed since this application has just one function. Hence, we'll use the first TIOA-AREA presented because it will help us determine whether the screen to be processed is formatted or unformatted.

OUTPUT TERMINAL COMMANDS

If an application is to communicate with a terminal using formatted maps, the programmer needs to know only three commands. One command is used to send data to a terminal and the other two are used to obtain data from a terminal. There is no need for complicated commands because command-level programming and BMS processing are used in our terminal handling requests.

To send a map out to a terminal, the programmer must code a SEND MAP command. When this command is issued, BMS will *merge* any data in the symbolic map area associated with this map together with the physical map data to build a terminal data stream. This data stream will then be passed on to the system's telecommunications access methods to be transmitted to the terminal.

When this command is issued, the programmer must identify the mapset and the map within it that is to be sent out. Further, the programmer must tell BMS which symbolic map is to be used in the merge process, unless, of course, there are *no* data in the symbolic map area, in which case the programmer can tell BMS to skip the merging and send out only the physical map data. This procedure can reduce the processing performed by BMS and slightly improve your transaction response time. For example, let's suppose that in our calculator problem the program is being initiated for the first time. Since an unformatted map will reside in the TIOA, there won't be any data in the TIOA to process or computation to perform. Hence, no results need to be sent to the terminal operator. Since there are no data to send, no data exist in the symbolic map area for MAINMAP; therefore, we can send out MAINMAP by issuing the following command:

```
EXEC CICS SEND MAP('MAINMAP') MAPSET('CALCMAP')
ERASE MAPONLY END-EXEC
```

This instruction tells BMS to send out the *physical* map (MAPONLY) called 'MAINMAP' that is a member of the mapset called 'CALCMAP.' Also, BMS does not need to merge the symbolic and physical maps because there are no data in the symbolic map area to be merged. When the screen is sent to the terminal, the data on the screen shoud be erased *before* this map is displayed so that a fresh display will appear to the terminal operator.

In the command, the literals 'MAINMAP' and 'CALCMAP' identify for BMS the map and mapset to be processed. If you do not like literals in your code, then you can store these literal values in your WORKING-STORAGE section and issue the command shown below by referencing the appropriate data names. Note that if this technique is used the data name variables must be defined in WORKING-STORAGE as X(8).

```
01   CALC-MAPSET-NAME      PIC X(8) VALUE 'CALCMAP'.
01   MAIN-MAP-NAME         PIC X(8) VALUE 'MAINMAP'.
     .  .
     .  .
     .  .
```

```
EXEC CICS SEND MAP(MAIN-MAP-NAME)
     MAPSET(CALC-MAPSET-NAME) ERASE
     MAPONLY END-EXEC
```

In either version of the above commands, the cursor will be positioned at the VAL1 field on the map because when we defined the VAL1 field, we specified that the cursor should be inserted in this field when the MAINMAP is sent out. This specification was made via the IC operand within the attribute list for the VAL1 field. If we wanted to override the IC attribute from our program and position the cursor in some other field, we could code a CURSOR operand on the SEND MAP statement as follows (let's assume that we want to position the cursor at the VAL2 field instead of the VAL1 field):

```
EXEC CICS SEND MAP('MAINMAP') MAPSET('CALCMAP')
     ERASE MAPONLY CURSOR (520) END-EXEC
```

Since VAL2 has been defined with a position of (7,40), then the number of screen positions that precede the VAL2 field can be computed by the following formula:

$$\text{cursor-loc} = (\ (\text{field row number} - 1) * 80) + \text{field column number}$$

Hence, VAL2's screen location will be ($(7-1)*80)+40$, which computes to 520. In the SEND MAP command above, the number 520 for the cursor position tells BMS to place the cursor at the first byte of the VAL2 field.

Again, the value 520 is a literal. If you wish, the cursor location of VAL2 can be referenced through a variable in the WORKING-STORAGE section of the program, as shown below. Note that if this technique is used, then the WORKING-STORAGE data area *must* be defined as S9(4) COMP.

```
01   VAL2-SCREEN-LOC      PIC S9(4) COMP VALUE +520.
     .   .
     .   .
     .   .

     EXEC CICS SEND MAP(MAIN-MAP-NAME)
          MAPSET('CALCMAP') ERASE MAPONLY
          CURSOR(VAL2-SCREEN-LOC) END-EXEC
```

Incidentally, I mixed literals and nonliterals in the above command just to demonstrate that it can be done. Whatever combination appeals to you in specifying any of the above operand values is what you should use in your application development, as long as the data names are defined in the proper format in the WORKING-STORAGE section of your program.

Now let's suppose that when we send out this map we want to send with it a message such as:

ENTER YOUR VALUES, MAKE YOUR SELECTION, PRESS ENTER

If a message is to be sent out, then this is regarded as program-supplied data to BMS and, as a result, the MAPONLY operand cannot be used. To send out a message like this, the program must do the following:

- Move the message to the message field associated with the map to be sent out (this places the data into the symbolic map area associated with this map).
- Send out the map by merging the symbolic and physical maps together.

If you recall, the message area is called MSG on the MAINMAP and so the area in the symbolic map for sending out message values is called MSGO. To send out the message to the terminal, the program must move the message to the MSGO data area before issuing a SEND MAP command.

After moving the message into the symbolic map area, the program must issue a SEND MAP command, but this time the MAPONLY operand cannot be specified since a message resides in the symbolic map area. It will be merged with the physical data to produce a terminal display by BMS. Thus, a different form of the SEND MAP command will be needed so that BMS can be told which symbolic map is to be used in the merge process and where. Since MAINMAP is the map being sent out, the symbolic map area associated with MAINMAP should be used. The code used to place the message in the symbolic map area and to send out MAINMAP is shown below:

```
MOVE 'ENTER YOUR VALUES,..., PRESS ENTER' TO MSGO.
EXEC CICS SEND MAP('MAINMAP') MAPSET('CALCMAP')
    FROM(MAINMAPO) ERASE END-EXEC.
```

Again, the cursor will be positioned at the VAL1 field when this map reaches the terminal because we haven't overridden the IC operand as specified for the VAL1 field on the map.

Did you notice that there are no specific references to any fields in the SEND MAP command? As a result, this command can be used to send the results of the calculations back to the terminal. If you choose not to use the MAPONLY operand, you can get by with learning only one SEND MAP command for your on-line application processing.

Now let's suppose that MAINMAP has been sent out and that the user has entered either the VAL1 or VAL2 field incorrectly. Yet another form of the SEND MAP command can be used to avoid the merge process. Instead of sending just the physical map data (as in the MAPONLY operand), *only* the symbolic map data can be sent. Since no merging of symbolic and physical maps will occur, a physical map must already be displayed or the resulting display will look rather strange to the terminal operator. For example, let's suppose that the following data were entered on the user's screen.

```
CALC         EXPENSIVE ON-LINE CALCULATOR

    ENTER YOUR FIRST OPERAND HERE ------ 475%00

    ENTER YOUR SECOND OPERAND HERE ------ 124

    WHAT OPERATION WOULD YOU WANT TO DO ------?
        1. ADD
        2. SUBTRACT
        3. MULTIPLY
        4. DIVIDE

    THE RESULT OF YOUR CALCULATION IS ------
```

Clearly the data in the VAL1 field is invalid and the user should be told that incorrect data has been entered. Since the current display at the user's terminal has all the necessary header and information fields, there's really no need to resend a complete display screen. Hence, if the program determines that the VAL1 field is in error and that an error message should be sent back to the user's terminal to inform the user of the error, this task can be accomplished by making a simple change in the SEND MAP command.

```
MOVE 'PLEASE CORRECT YOUR FIRST FIELD' TO MSGO.
EXEC CICS SEND MAP('MAINMAP') MAPSET('CALCMAP')
    FROM(MAINMAPO) DATAONLY END-EXEC.
```

The DATAONLY operand informs BMS *not* to merge the physical and symbolic maps; it informs BMS to build a terminal data stream only from the data in the symbolic map area. Hence, the overhead associated with the merging process is saved. You should also have noticed that the ERASE operand *was not* specified on this SEND MAP command. Make sure that you do not specify ERASE; otherwise the user's screen will look like the following one when you send out your messages with the DATAONLY operand:

```
CALC


                                            475%00

                                            124

                                                ?

















      PLEASE CORRECT YOUR FIRST FIELD
```

Since the physical and symbolic map merging was skipped, no header and information-only fields appear in the terminal data stream. Since you also coded the operand ERASE, these fields were erased when this map was displayed, and only the data contained in the symbolic map area were redisplayed. You could have a rather embarrassing situation on your hands in your applications processing if you specified ERASE in a situation like this. If ERASE had not been specified, the screen would appear as originally entered by the user, except for the additional message at the bottom of the screen.

One final note about the use of the DATAONLY operand. In a later chapter we discuss the setting of field attributes from within the application program. If you use the DATAONLY operand, you should "refresh" *all* the attributes for *all* your data fields before the screen is sent out. Although this step merely consists of a series of COBOL move statements, it should be taken to avoid processing problems when the DATAONLY operand is used. In other words, there's a little more to the DATAONLY operand than meets the eye, and if you do not properly refresh or reset your field attributes, you'll have a group of frustrated users on your hands. Every time a screen is sent out using DATAONLY, the user will have to retype *every* field on the screen, even if he doesn't want the contents changed (more about this in a later chapter).

Another point to mention about sending maps to the terminal concerns cursor positioning. In previous examples, we relied either on the IC operand to position the cursor or on the actual field's screen location (we computed its offset and used this offset in the SEND MAP command). If a user doesn't like the location of a field on a screen and its location changes, that field's cursor location would undoubtedly change and hence, all SEND commands would have to be recomputed or recoded to reflect the new field locations. This may not be a feasible implementation. The solution is to use another form of cursor positioning; however, this alternate form can be used *only* if the mapset is defined with the MODE=INOUT operand.

You also have to remember that this form cannot be used with the MAPONLY operand because it requires that information be placed into the symbolic map area. Then, whenever you want to position the cursor at a particular field on your map, you move the value -1 (negative one) to the L-suffixed field associated with the data field at which the cursor is to be positioned. When you issue the SEND MAP command (a different form is required to do this), the cursor is positioned at the field with the value -1 in the L-suffixed element. If for some reason several L-suffixed fields have a value of -1, then the last field in the map with a -1 L value will be the one where the cursor will be positioned.

For example, assume that the user selected choice 5 on the menu portion of our calculator screen. Since 5 is not valid, we'll want to send out an error message and position the cursor at the choice field so that the user can now make a valid selection. The following code will accomplish this task:

```
MOVE 'ONLY 1,2,3 AND 4 ARE VALID SELECTIONS' TO MSGO.
MOVE -1  TO CHOICEL.
EXEC CICS SEND MAP('MAINMAP') MAPSET('CALCMAP')
   FROM(MAINMAPO) ERASE CURSOR END-EXEC.
```

In the code above, -1 is moved to the L-suffixed field associated with the choice that the user made. This action tells BMS to position the cursor at this field. The SEND command specifies CURSOR, but not the location. By coding

CURSOR in this fashion, BMS is instructed to position the cursor at the field whose L-suffixed field has −1 stored within it.

Since the L-suffixed field resides in the symbolic map area, the MAPONLY operand cannot be specified if this type of cursor positioning is to work. Further, since the symbolic map area must be processed to handle this type of request, the MODE=IN and MODE=OUT operands cannot be used either, since communication to and from the terminal through the symbolic map area is not allowed when these operands are specified.

One other operand can be specified on the SEND MAP command. This operand will improve the performance of your terminal output operations substantially when you are using command-level programming because it allows faster disconnection between interfacing CICS systems. Since this operand may not be available on all versions of CICS, you should verify that it is supported before using it. This operand may be used on CICS versions 1.5 and more recent ones, and is suggested particularly for nonconversational applications.

When a SEND MAP command is issued and the operand LAST is specified, the interfacing CICS systems can terminate intersystem communication much faster since the operand LAST essentially chains two commands together—your send request, and a session disconnect command. Hence, only one communication takes place between CICS systems rather than two. However, this operand can only be used on the *LAST* output operation from your application program prior to termination. If your screens are composed of three maps, for example, and you send out the first map with the operand LAST and then you send out the second map, you'll probably abend your transaction or simply lose the second and third maps from transmission. It is critical that this operand be used only on the LAST output operation from your application to the terminal and that it be coded as follows:

EXEC CICS SEND MAP('MAINMAP') MAPSET('CALCMAP')
FROM(MAINMAPO) ERASE CURSOR LAST END-EXEC.

INPUT TERMINAL OPERATIONS

Obtaining data from a terminal to be processed by an application program involves two steps in a nonconversational application. First, the data must be read from the terminal and placed into a TIOA. Secondly, the data must be analyzed in the TIOA to see whether they are formatted or unformatted. If the data are *un*formatted, the second step is *not* performed, since an unformatted screen does not require moving the field data to a symbolic map area.

If the screen data are formatted, then another command must be issued to map the formatted field data from the input TIOA to the symbolic map area. It is during this step that the control characters can be used to identify *which* map is to undergo a "mapping" operation and which function is being performed or continued. If your program becomes confused and maps the data incorrectly, you're almost certain to abend your application. Hence, you must establish *unique* map codes and process these codes properly if your input mapping operations are to be successful.

The first step in the mapping process is quite simple and unless you change the name of your TIOA-AREA description, this command never changes. To acquire the terminal data through BMS and to place the data into your defined TIOA so that you can reference the fields, you simply need to code:

```
WORKING-STORAGE SECTION.
01   TIOA-DATA-LENGTH              PIC S9(4) COMP
                                   VALUE +1920.

01   TIOA-AREA.
     02   FIRST-PART               PIC X(20).
     02   UNFORMATTED-PART         REDEFINES
                                   FIRST-PART.
          03   UNFORMATTED-TRANID  PIC X(4).
          03   FILLER             PIC X(16).
     .    .    .
     .    .    .
     .    .    .


PROCEDURE DIVISION.
  EXEC CICS RECEIVE INTO(TIOA-AREA)
    LENGTH (TIOA-DATA-LENGTH) END-EXEC.
```

The RECEIVE command informs BMS of the length of storage that you've set aside for your TIOA. Since it is possible to have 1920 bytes of data, we've set aside a 1920-byte TIOA. Through the INTO operand, the command also informs BMS where our TIOA resides. Not much more can be said about the command, other than it reads the data from the terminal and places the terminal record into the data area called TIOA-AREA.

After this command is issued, we choose the format of the screen, as we noted earlier. If the screen is formatted, we can issue a second RECEIVE command that will enable us to reference the fields on the map through our symbolic map area. In other words, we're going to map the data *from* our input TIOA area *into* our symbolic map area associated with the screen being processed. Since we have only one screen in our calculator application, our second mapping operation is issued as follows:

```
EXEC CICS RECEIVE MAP('MAINMAP') MAPSET('CALCMAP')
  FROM(TIOA-AREA) LENGTH(TIOA-DATA-LENGTH)
  INTO(MAINMAPI) END-EXEC.
```

We can now reference the fields VAL1I, VAL2I, CHOICEI, and so on, as defined in our MAINMAPI symbolic map area. This completes the mapping process for the calculator application.

If we apply these ideas to the landlord application for the MENU, ADD, and DELETE screens discussed earlier, we will have three separate mapping commands, *only one of which* is actually issued.

```
IF    FORMATTED-MAP-CODE = 'A' THEN
      EXEC CICS RECEIVE MAP('ADD') MAPSET('CALCMAP')
        FROM(TIOA-AREA) LENGTH(TIOA-DATA-LENGTH)
        INTO(ADDI) END-EXEC
      PERFORM PROCESS-ADD-MAP-DATA

  ELSE
      IF FORMATTED-MAP-CODE = 'M' THEN
        EXEC CICS RECEIVE MAP('MENU') MAPSET('CALCMAP')
          FROM(TIOA-AREA) LENGTH(TIOA-DATA-LENGTH)
          INTO(MENUI) END-EXEC
        PERFORM PROCESS-MENU-MAP-DATA

      ELSE
        IF FORMATTED-MAP-CODE = 'D' THEN
          EXEC CICS RECEIVE MAP('DELETE')
            MAPSET('CALCMAP') FROM(TIOA-AREA)
            LENGTH(TIOA-DATA-LENGTH)
            INTO(DELETEI) END-EXEC
          PERFORM PROCESS-DELETE-MAP-DATA.
```

Or, if a common screen was shared by the ADD and DELETE components, as discussed earlier, the following code might be used:

```
IF    FORMATTED-MAP-CODE = 'B'
      AND FUNCTION-CODE    = 'A' THEN
      EXEC CICS RECEIVE MAP('BIGMAP') MAPSET('CALMAP')
        FROM(TIOA-AREA) LENGTH(TIOA-DATA-LENGTH)
        INTO(BIGMAPI) END-EXEC
      PERFORM PROCESS-ADD-DATA

  ELSE
      IF  FORMATTED-MAP-CODE = 'B'
        AND FUNCTION-CODE    = 'D' THEN
        EXEC CICS RECEIVE MAP('BIGMAP') INTO('BIGMAPI')
          MAPSET('CALCMAP') FROM (TIOA-AREA)
          LENGTH(TIOA-DATA-LENGTH) END-EXEC
        PERFORM PROCESS-DELETE-DATA
```

```
        ELSE
          IF  FORMATTED-MAP-CODE = 'M' THEN
              EXEC CICS RECEIVE MAP('MENU') MAPSET('CALCMAP')
              FROM(TIOA-AREA) LENGTH(TIOA-DATA-LENGTH)
              INTO(MENUI) END-EXEC
              PERFORM PROCESS-MENU-MAP-DATA.
```

You can see that the control characters help in determining which map is finally to be received into the appropriate symbolic map area and also which function is to be performed for a map that is shared by two or more application functions.

We have now covered the basic forms of terminal communications needed for application development. In a later chapter we discuss locate-mode terminal communications that may improve your transaction performance to some degree. Before we leave this chapter, however, let's finish the calculator application by coding the complete on-line program. Also, let's identify the types of errors that can occur in terminal communications and see how they can be handled.

RESOLVING PROBLEMS WHEN MAPPING

Mapping operation problems to and from the terminal can be difficult to solve and may require the assistance of an experienced CICS programmer. Many problems can be easily handled, however, once you understand the nature of the problem and can evaluate the code. Let's start with the simple problems and then progress to more difficult ones. Some errors are hard to identify but if you understand the symptoms, you can probably fix the disease. Just imagine that you're a doctor and that your on-line application is a sick patient. Once that you thoroughly understand the sickness, you can usually treat most CICS on-line mapping problems (by attending to the code, of course).

The easiest problem to diagnose is one that causes an APCT or ABM0 CICS abend code. If this abend should result, one of a few things is usually the problem. Incidentally, if you haven't encountered the APCT or ABM0 abend codes before, don't worry, CICS abend codes are quite different from batch abend codes and we'll discuss them in a later chapter. Here is a list of the things to look for in your on-line program if it abends with one of the above codes:

- Your map or mapset name is spelled incorrectly in your SEND or RECEIVE commands.

- You've overlayed the area of your WORKING-STORAGE section that contains the name of your map or mapset if you are using variables to specify map or mapset names.

- The systems programming staff or on-line administration group did not define your mapset to the CICS system properly or they forgot to place your mapset name in the PPT.

- A map or mapset developed by someone else has a name that you did not expect.

- The mapset that you are trying to reference did not assemble properly and has not been loaded into a CICS program library. Hence, this mapset has been marked "nonusable" by CICS. You must verify that your assembly was successful and if not, fix the problem. If it was successful, you'll need to "enable" your mapset for use by using the CSMT or CEMT command, depending on the version of CICS that you are operating under. The CEMT and CSMT commands are special master commands built into the CICS system that are not programmed in your application program. Generally, one terminal in the CICS network is defined as the master terminal. From this terminal, special commands can be issued to control CICS execution, task priority, and the definition of programs to CICS. After your program has been successfully loaded into the CICS library, the CICS system must be informed that a new copy of your program has been created and that CICS can now start using that copy for applications processing. This is done through either the CSMT or CEMT commands, depending on the version of CICS that you have. Since these commands are very powerful, an explanation of these commands has been omitted from this text. Contact your systems programmer or your console operator (they may have authorization) to complete the definition of your program to the CICS system, or refer to the *CICS/VS Operator's Guide* for details about how to issue these commands.

Apart from the last situation described, these problems have obvious solutions. Most of them require a careful review of your code for misspelled map or mapset names. You may have to contact your systems or on-line staff to see that they defined your mapset to the system properly.

The next category of errors consists of somewhat more difficult problems that may require careful analysis of a dump or the use of an on-line debugging package to help you identify the problems. Since many of these problems have different solutions, the individual problems and possible solutions are listed together here:

- The data fields displayed to the terminal are offset on the screen by 12 bytes. (Your mapset TIOAPFX and symbolic map TIOAPFX specifications do not agree.)

- The program abends with an ASRA or AEI9 abend code. (You did not decide whether the screen was formatted or unformatted properly; you forgot to issue your second receive map before trying to process symbolic map data; you mapped your data into the wrong symbolic map area; the symbolic and physical maps do not agree and must be reassembled; the control character codes defined on the maps are not what you expected; some other CICS program has destroyed either your symbolic or your physical mapset.)

- Program abends with an ABMI or ABMO abend code.
  (Your map was defined as MODE=IN or MODE=OUT and you were trying to process it in the opposite way.)

- The program abends with an ABMx abend code.
  (See earlier discussion; the TIOA-DATA-LENGTH variable defined in your WORKING-STORAGE section has not been properly defined or has not been given a large enough value; the value that you specified for the cursor position was larger than the size of the terminal screen; you did not code the cursor variable correctly as PIC S9(4) COMP.)

These are some of the more common types of mapping abends, but there are others. For further information on a problem that you may have, contact your systems programming or on-line staff or IBM, or consult the *CICS/VS Messages and Codes* manual listed in the bibliography.

SAMPLE APPLICATION

By combining all the previous techniques and ideas, we should easily be able to implement a solution to our calculator problem. Before we look at the code, let's sketch out the logic for the on-line program. By the way, there is a rather obvious bug in the code below. If the user tries to divide by zero, the program can abend. To keep the flow of things simple at this point, let's forget about error handling and deal with this problem in a later chapter.

1. Receive terminal data.
2. If screen is unformatted, then
   a. send out the mainmap
   b. return
3. Receive the mainmap into the symbolic map area.
4. If any of the data do not pass editing, then
   a. move a message to the message field with respect to the field in error
   b. position the cursor at the field in error
   c. send the "mainmap" back out for data correction
   d. return
5. Perform the calculation.
6. Move the result to the screen display.
7. Send out the mainmap with the results.
8. Return control to CICS.

Implementing our application will be simple with this pseudocode, except for one command. Each time that a screen is sent to the terminal, the program returns to CICS. Hence, each time that the user presses the *enter* key, the program *starts at the beginning* and not where it last returned control. Since program execution always begins with the first statement in the PROCEDURE DIVISION and since this program returns to CICS between user processing requests, we say that this program operates in a nonconversational style. Thus, while the user is looking at the results of a computation or an error message, the program is *not* active and may not even reside in the system if there is a demand for the storage occupied by the instructions for that program. Hence, no resources are needed by this program between user requests. As we discussed in earlier chapters, this is the key to nonconversational programming style.

A program returns to CICS by issuing a RETURN command, as shown below. Because this command has only one operand, there's no need to discuss how it works. Simply stated, the program stops running.

Incidentally, notice that the code below has a STOP RUN statement, but it is *never* executed. Under CICS you do not stop a program's execution with a STOP RUN statement as is the case in a batch COBOL program; you *always* issue a CICS RETURN command.

```
IDENTIFICATION DIVISION.
  PROGRAM-ID.  CALCPRG.
  AUTHOR.        ME.
ENVIRONMENT DIVISION.
DATA DIVISION.
WORKING-STORAGE SECTION.
  01  TIOALEN                    PIC S9(4) COMP VALUE +1920.
  01  VAL1X                      PIC 9(7).
  01  VAL2X                      PIC 9(7).
  01  TIOA-AREA.
      02  FIRST-HALF             PIC X(20).
      02  UNFORMATTED-X          REDEFINES FIRST-HALF.
          03  UNFORM-TRANID      PIC X(4).
          03  FILLER             PIC X(16).
      02  REST-OF-TIOA           PIC X(1900).

  01  COPY CALCM.

PROCEDURE DIVISION.
  EXEC CICS RECEIVE INTO(TIOA-AREA) LENGTH(TIOALEN)
  END-EXEC.

  IF UNFORM-TRANID = 'CALC' THEN
      EXEC CICS SEND MAP('MAINMAP') MAPSET('CALCM')
          MAPONLY ERASE END-EXEC
      EXEC CICS RETURN END-EXEC.
```

```
EXEC CICS RECEIVE MAP('MAINMAP') MAPSET('CALCM')
  INTO(MAINMAPI) FROM(TIOA-AREA) LENGTH(TIOALEN)
  END-EXEC.

IF VAL1I NOT NUMERIC THEN
  MOVE 'INVALID FIRST VALUE' TO MSGO
  EXEC CICS SEND MAP('MAINMAP') MAPSET('CALCM')
    FROM(MAINMAPO) ERASE CURSOR(360) END-EXEC
  EXEC CICS RETURN END-EXEC.

IF VAL2I NOT NUMERIC THEN
  MOVE 'INVALID SECOND VALUE' TO MSGO
  EXEC CICS SEND MAP('MAINMAP') MAPSET('CALCM')
    FROM(MAINMAPO) ERASE CURSOR(520) END-EXEC
  EXIC CICS RETURN END-EXEC.

MOVE VAL1I TO VAL1X.
MOVE VAL2I TO VAL2X.

IF CHOICEI = '1' THEN
  COMPUTE RSLTO = VAL1X + VAL2X
ELSE
  IF CHOICEI = '2' THEN
    COMPUTE RSLTO = VAL1X - VAL2X
  ELSE
    IF CHOICEI = '3' THEN
      COMPUTE RSLTO = VAL1X * VAL2X
    ELSE
      IF CHOICEI = '4' THEN
        COMPUTE RSLTO = VAL1X / VAL2X
      ELSE
        MOVE 'INVALID MENU CHOICE' TO MSGO
        EXEC CICS SEND MAP('MAINMAP')
          MAPSET('CALCM') FROM(MAINMAPO)
          ERASE CURSOR(764) END-EXEC
        EXEC CICS RETURN END-EXEC.

EXEC CICS SEND MAP('MAINMAP') MAPSET('CALCM')
  FROM(MAINMAPO) ERASE CURSOR(360) END-EXEC.
EXEC CICS RETURN END-EXEC.
STOP RUN.
```

You should be able to understand each line of the code presented above, especially each command-level statement. Remember that the variables VAL1I, VAL2I, CHOICEI and the O-suffixed variables come from the copy member called CALCM. Although the copied-in code is not shown above, it will appear within this code after translation and compilation. You'll also see the execute interface block (EIB), transaction of command-level commands into their COBOL equivalents, and other "interesting" statements following this translation and compilation.

With the knowledge that you now have, you can expand on this application in the next chapter by considering some alternative processing methods. Also, several new processing techniques are discussed there, along with the following topics: screen attribute processing, which is used to alter a field's characteristics from *within* an application program; the coding of commands to prevent program abends and to trap mapping operation failures so as to avoid a translation abend; and the editing services available through CICS command level programming. We will also implement the calculator application in a conversational programming style!

Not to lose site of the Landlord Management System, we are leading up to an implementation of this application. However, since we don't have all of the tools to implement this application yet, we are using the on-line calculator problem as a stepping stone between our introduction to CICS programming and the Landlord Management System. By the end of the next few chapters, we'll be able to concentrate on the CICS commands needed to implement the landlord system.

In summary, we have formed the basis for implementing on-line applications in command-level CICS by allowing our application to communicate with the terminal. With the various techniques and screen formats to be handled, terminal communication is probably the most difficult aspect of developing CICS application. Therefore, if you are proficient in applying the information presented up to this point, you'll probably have no difficulty in implementing the other aspects of your on-line application.

THOUGHT QUESTIONS

1. *Suppose that a user has to enter a special password or code word on the first unformatted screen to initiate the calculator application. If the code word is eight characters long, write the TIOA description and the revised code to check this password submitted by the terminal operator.*

2. *If you do not code CTRL=FREEKB on the DFHMSD statement for your mapset, then every time that a map is sent to the terminal, the keyboard remains locked. However, the operand FREEKB can be specified on the SEND MAP command in the same way that ERASE and LAST were specified. Compare the placement of this operand in the two areas.*

3. *Suppose that a user of another application has been allowed to type over the transaction id for his or her system. If a screen for that application is currently displayed at that user's terminal and if the user accidentally types in your transaction id instead of the one that he should have, what would you expect to happen? What would that user see?*

10

SUPPORTING
APPLICATION EXECUTION

As we reexamine our calculator application in this chapter, we are going to introduce some additional processing steps that will allow us to control field attributes from the program as well as handle processing errors, attention identifier keys, field editing, and, finally, conversational implementation. These new steps should be easy to incorporate into our application. You're already familiar with some of them.

SPECIFYING FIELD ATTRIBUTES

Field attributes, as mentioned earlier, can be changed by the application program. We're ready now to put this idea to work: we want to manipulate attributes in order to control field usage, highlight errors, and control the return of data to our program.

Let's suppose that all fields on a screen are defined as normal (NORM) intensity. Further, assume that after the user enters the data on a screen and presses the *enter* key, the data must go through an edit before they are processed. Although some of this editing was done in Chapter 9, we did not discuss it.

Through the use of the attribute (A-suffixed) fields in the symbolic map, we can alter the attributes of a field simply by moving a new attribute byte to this A field *before* the map is sent to the terminal. Hence, if we detect an error in the user's data during editing, it might be advantageous to highlight this field (or many fields) before we send the screen out with an error message. This highlighting will help the user quickly identify the fields in error, correct them, and get them back into the program for processing.

Attribute byte manipulation could be used in the following situation as well. Suppose that a screen has two input fields (call the fields A and B), both of which are defined as (NUM,UNPROT). If the user enters data in both fields and the data in either field do not pass program editing, then the screen is sent back to the user for correction. *However,* if the user corrects *only* the field in error (suppose it is field A) and does not retype at least one character in field B, the program will not be returned any data from the terminal for field B. Hence, the program will edit field B and now find an error in this field. The resulting error message—no data entered in this field—will confuse the user. The screens below illustrate this situation.

If the user enters valid data in the first field and invalid data in the second field, the program will catch the error during editing and will send the screen out to the terminal with an error message, as shown in display 2.

Display 1:

```
          EXPENSIVE ON-LINE CALCULATOR

ENTER YOUR FIRST OPERAND HERE ------ 457

ENTER YOUR SECOND OPERAND HERE ------ 2%4

WHAT OPERATION DO YOU WANT TO DO ------ 2
     1. ADD
     2. SUBTRACT
     3. MULTIPLY
     4. DIVIDE

THE RESULT OF YOUR CALCULATION WAS ------
```

Display 2:

```
              EXPENSIVE ON-LINE CALCULATOR

    ENTER YOUR FIRST OPERAND HERE ------ 457

    ENTER YOUR SECOND OPERAND HERE ------ 2%4

    WHAT OPERATION DO YOU WANT TO DO ------ 2
        1. ADD
        2. SUBTRACT
        3. MULTIPLY
        4. DIVIDE

    THE RESULT OF YOUR CALCULATION WAS ------




              FIELD TWO CONTAINS INVALID CHARACTERS
```

However, since FSET attribute has not been specified in either field, the only data that will be read from the terminal screen the next time that the user presses *enter* will be the data that are in the fields in which the *user* has typed. Hence, if the user corrects field two but doesn't retype operand one or the selection, *only* data for operand two will be available for processing. In a command-level CICS environment, the only fields obtained from the terminal display are those that appear to have been modified by the terminal operator.

Each attribute byte for a field contains a special bit called a MODIFIED DATA TAG (MDT). If that bit is "on," the system assumes that the data in that field has been typed in by the terminal operator. This bit can be activated in two ways: the operator can turn the MDT on by typing data into a field, or the program can turn the MDT on via the FSET attribute, either by defining the attribute in the mapset or specifying it through move commands in the program. Therefore, as a program edits a field, it is wise to set a field's MDT to "on" if that field passes editing. Thus, if the map is sent out to correct another field in error, the user does not have to retype the data already entered. Setting a field's MDT to "on" is equivalent to marking the field FSET.

Within the COBOL program, a programmer can define attribute byte values. IBM supplies an attribute byte COPY member with CICS that assigns bit values to attribute bytes and thus allows the program to set attribute bytes to values that differ from the original mapset definition. The COPY member supplied by IBM is called DFHBMSCA. To incorporate this attribute list into your program, you merely have to code a COPY command to have these attribute definitions copied into the WORKING-STORAGE section of your program during compilation, just as you did your symbolic mapset. You can get an idea of this member from the following abbreviated version:

```
01   DFHBMSCA.
     02  DFHBMASK      PIC X VALUE '0'.
     02  DFHBMUNP      PIC X VALUE 'Q'.
     02  DFHBMFSE      PIC X VALUE '9'.
     .  .  .
     .  .  .
     .  .  .
```

In other words, the various attribute settings are defined in a list available to your program. Translated, the attribute list would read:

```
DFHBMASK  —  ASKIP
DFHBMUNP  —  UNPROT
DFHBMUNN  —  UNPROT, NUM
DFHBMPRO  —  PROT
DFHBMBRY  —  BRT
DFHBMDAR  —  DRK
DFHBMFSE  —  FSET
DFHBMPRF  —  PROT, FSET
DFHBMASF  —  ASKIP, FSET
DFHBMASB  —  ASKIP, BRT
```

Notice that the above list does not contain combinations such as (BRT,NUM,FSET) or (UNPROT,FSET) or many other possible attribute settings. Users are forced to define their own attributes if they want complete field definition capabilities, but to do so they must understand the various bit settings within an attribute byte. Most companies define a complete list of attribute byte combinations and simply replace the IBM-supplied member list for program usage. Following is a partial list of a user-defined attribute byte list:

```
01   SCREEN-ATTRIBUTES.
     02  UNPROT-BRT-FSET     PIC X VALUE 'I'.
```

```
02  UNPROT-FSET-BRT      PIC X VALUE 'I'.
02  BRT-NUM              PIC X VALUE 'Q'.
02  ASKIP-DRK-FSET       PIC X VALUE ' I '.
```

Clearly, this attribute list is more meaningful than the other one and—take my word for it—it's much more extensive. Throughout the remainder of this text, we'll use this attribute list rather than the one supplied by IBM.

If you don't have your own attribute list and don't care for the one that IBM has provided, you can define the attributes in your program yourself. Each bit within an attribute byte has a specific meaning and combinations of bit settings also result in different meanings. You'll need to define an area in the WORKING-STORAGE section of your program to hold your attribute value. Although this is a cumbersome way to do it, if you only have to develop a few unique pairs, this method will suffice. In other cases, you could define this attribute list and place this definition into a COPY library for use by other programmers.

Each attribute byte contains eight bits that can be set. However, only five bits are actually used to specify attribute settings. From left to right, we'll call the bit positions 0, 1, 2, 3, 4, 5, 6, and 7.

bit 0 — determined by bits 2–7

bit 1 — always set to 1

bit 2 — 0 value — unprotect
        1 value — protected

bit 3 — 0 value — alphnumeric data field
        1 value — numeric data field

bit 4

bit 5 — these two bits are used in combination
        00 — normal intensity, not light pen detectable
        01 — normal intensity, pen detectable
        10 — bright, pen detectable
        11 — dark, not detectable

bit 6 — reserved, must always be a 0 value

bit 7 — modified data tag bit
        0 value — field has not been modified
        1 value — field has been modified

By learning to use the bit settings above, we can build attribute bytes that have more attribute settings than do those in the DFHBMSCA list supplied by IBM. For example, let's suppose that we want a field that has the following attributes: (ASKIP,DRK,FSET). This field would require a bit setting of 0111 1101, or a hexadecimal value of X'7D'. In base ten notation, this value would be $((7*16)+13)$, or 125. Knowing this value, we can define our own attribute setting for the ASKIP, DRK, and FSET values as follows:

```
01   ASKIP-DRK-FSET-XXX        PIC S9(4) COMP
                               VALUE +125.

01   ASKIP-DRK-FSET-CHAR       REDEFINES
                               ASKIP-DRK-FSET-XXX
     02   FILLER               PIC X.
     02   ASKIP-DRK-FSET       PIC X.
```

The attribute setting that we want can now be referenced through the meaningful variable called ASKIP-DRK-FSET from our program. If this structure was an element of a copy library, all programmers could use this attribute combination. Other attribute settings can be built in the same way by simply computing the decimal value on the basis of the bit settings that you need and then defining structures as described above. You may be wondering where the ASKIP attribute came from, since no specific bit within the attribute byte means ASKIP. This attribute is really a combination of two fields, the protected (PROT) bit setting and the numeric (NUM) setting. If the field is marked both PROT and NUM, then the field is really defined as ASKIP to the 3270 terminal device.

Another implementation of the above structure that may cause fewer syntax problems in your program coding defines a series of attribute combinations as shown below. Here, no matter what order is used to specify the attributes, the proper setting will be applied to the field being processed.

```
01   ADF-NUM                PIC S9(4) COMP VALUE +125.
01   ADF0                   REDEFINES ADF-NUM.
     02   FILLER            PIC X.
     02   ASKIP-DRK-FSET    PIC X.
01   ADF1                   REDEFINES ADF-NUM.
     02   FILLER            PIC X.
     02   ASKIP-FSET-DRK    PIC X.
01   ADF2                   REDEFINES ADF-NUM.
     02   FILLER            PIC X.
     02   DRK-FSET-ASKIP    PIC X.
01   ADF3                   REDEFINES ADF-NUM.
     02   FILLER            PIC X.
     02   DRK-ASKIP-FSET    PIC X.
01   ADF4                   REDEFINES ADF-NUM.
     02   FILLER            PIC X.
     02   FSET-ASKIP-DRK    PIC X.
```

```
01   ADF5                    REDEFINES ADF-NUM.
     02  FILLER              PIC X.
     02  FSET-DRK-ASKIP      PIC X.
```

The following table should help you define attributes in the format described above. Note that the left column contains the ATTRB operand values that would be specified on the DFHMDF statement. In the first case, only the operand BRT is specified. However, in the ATTRB operand, default values of UNPROT, non-FSET, and non-NUM are supplied with this operand; they result in the bit settings that you see below.

ATTRB= VALUES	BIT SETTINGS	DECIMAL VALUE
BRT	1100 1000	200
ASKIP	1111 0000	240
FSET	1100 0001	193
NUM	0101 0000	80
PROT	0110 0000	96
ASKIP,BRT	1111 1000	248
ASKIP,FSET	1111 0001	241
ASKIP,BRT,FSET	1111 1001	249
ASKIP,DRK,FSET,NUM	0111 1101	125
UNPROT,BRT,FSET	1100 1001	201
UNPROT,DRK	0100 1100	76
UNPROT,DRK,FSET	0100 1101	77
UNPROT,DRK,FSET,NUM	0101 1101	93
UNPROT,BRT,FSET,NUM	1101 1001	217
UNPROT,NUM,NORM,FSET	1101 0001	209
PROT,NUM	1111 0000	240
PROT,NUM,BRT,FSET	1111 1001	249
PROT,FSET,DRK	0110 1101	109

Once you've established your attribute list, or even if you're going to use the list supplied by IBM, it's easy to change the attributes of a field from the program before the screen is sent out.

In our calculator example—in which one field failed editing and the first operand field didn't—we can unprotect, fset, and mark the valid field numeric by the following COBOL move statement (using the attribute list that I have defined):

```
MOVE UNPROT-NUM-FSET  TO VAL1A.
```

This statement places the specified attribute byte value into the symbolic map area housing VAL1's A-suffixed field. When the screen is then sent to the terminal, this attribute is applied to the VAL1 attribute data field, and the field becomes unprotected, fset, and numeric, regardless of how it was defined in the physical map.

Remember that when the user corrects field two and presses the *enter* key, the attribute specifications of unprotected, fset, and numeric are no longer in effect for field one. Hence, if field two again fails editing and it is necessary to send the screen out another time, the program *must again* apply the attributes of unprotected, fset, and numeric to the VAL1 A-suffixed field.

Attributes are easy enough to manipulate, as you can see, but when a field's attributes must be continually updated from the program, it may be easier to respecify the attributes within the mapset and regenerate the mapset to the system. Also, remember that only fields with field names can have their attributes changed from within the program. If it is necessary to change attributes on a heading or title field, even though the data in those fields may not change, you must assign names to those fields.

HANDLING PROGRAM ERRORS

Now and then a user causes a system to abend. Although we generally try to plan for exceptional situations, users seem to have an uncanny knack for finding those unusual bugs. Let's suppose, for example, that a user enters two very large numbers in our calculator problem, and specifies that they should be multiplied together. An overflow condition could occur and cause a program abend. If the user specifies the number 10 as the first operand and 0 as the second, and then requests the operation *divide,* our program could abend with a zero-divide condition.

Each of these are expected errors, and as our program currently stands, an abend can easily occur. We can, however, interface with CICS in order to trap these exceptional conditions; this is done through the HANDLE ABEND command.

The HANDLE ABEND command has just one operand, which specifies the name of a paragraph to be given control if the program fails. For example, if we issue the HANDLE ABEND command immediately after the PROCEDURE DIVISION statement, then if our program abends during the computation, control will be given to the paragraph called ABEND-ROUTINE, which is shown after the HANDLE ABEND statement below:

```
PROCEDURE DIVISION.

    EXEC CICS HANDLE ABEND LABEL(ABEND-ROUTINE) END-EXEC.
```

```
ABEND-ROUTINE.

    MOVE 'INVALID OPERATION, CORRECT DATA AND RETRY'
        TO MSGO.

    MOVE -1 TO VAL1L.
    EXEC CICS SEND MAP('MAINMAP') MAPSET('CALCMAP')
        FROM(MAINMAPO) ERASE CURSOR END-EXEC.
    EXEC CICS RETURN END-EXEC.
```

Incidentally, the program is not able to determine why an abend occurs or what type of abend has occurred; the program only knows that it has abended.

After the abend routine has sent out the main map, control is returned to CICS! Control does *not* return to the statement causing or following the point of abend, as is the case in other languages or with other on-line system monitors.

We can extend the handling of exceptional conditions through another command-level statement called HANDLE CONDITION. With this command, control can be transferred to a paragraph when another type of exceptional situation arises.

HANDLING "EXPECTED" ERRORS
(NOT ABENDS)

The processing for a HANDLE CONDITION statement is much the same as the HANDLE ABEND command in that control is transferred to the paragraph identified in the command operand. The HANDLE ABEND command is used to trap *abends* that occur during program processing; the HANDLE CONDITION command is used to trap failures that occur as a result of issuing a *command-level* request. For example, when a COBOL COMPUTE statement fails, an *abend* occurs, but when an EXEC CICS (command-level) statement fails, an exceptional condition occurs. As a result, two HANDLE commands may be required in some application programs.

Since we've only discussed terminal communication command-level statements, we'll restrict ourselves to the applicable HANDLE conditions for our SEND and RECEIVE commands. (Other command-level statements and their associated HANDLE conditions are discussed in later chapters.)

In general, a RECEIVE command will fail if a map other than the one you expect is being processed by your program. (See "Thought Questions," Chapter 9.) RECEIVE commands can also fail if TIOA lengths do not agree with the area to be received. Such situations are responsible for the MAPFAIL condition. Hence, if you want a special paragraph to be given control in such a situation, then you should code the following command in your program:

EXEC CICS HANDLE CONDITION MAPFAIL(MAPPING-FAILED)
    END-EXEC.

A SEND command can fail as a result of several situations. Each situation can be handled by a separate paragraph, but some programmers do not like coding many exceptional paragraphs because they clutter the code. Hence, rather than specifying individual paragraphs to handle each type of failure (actually a much better solution), we can specify a general error routine that will be given control if any condition arises that we have not specifically handled. To specify a general error paragraph you simply code:

EXEC CICS HANDLE CONDITION ERROR(GENERAL-ROUTINE)
    END-EXEC.

We can combine the two HANDLE CONDITION statements into one that will activate a transfer to a specific paragraph if a MAPFAIL occurs, and that will give control to a general routine if any other condition occurs. This is done as follows:

EXEC CICS HANDLE CONDITION MAPFAIL(MAPPING-FAILED)
    ERROR(GENERAL-ROUTINE) END-EXEC.

This procedure will not only save a little typing time, but it will also allow us to specify that the routine called GENERAL-ROUTINE will be given control for any condition *other than* the MAPFAIL.

Now let's suppose that for some reason we want to override the previous MAPFAIL command so that a different paragraph is to be given control if the condition arises. This might be done when a special map is being sent out that you want to handle in a special way. To override the previous specification, we only have to code another HANDLE statement with our new paragraph name, placing the statement in the line of executable code where appropriate, but this must be done before our "special" map is to be sent to the terminal.

EXEC CICS HANDLE CONDITION MAPFAIL(OTHER-ROUTINE) END-EXEC.

Hence, when a MAPFAIL condition now arises, OTHER-ROUTINE will be given control rather than the routine called MAPPING-FAILED, as defined in the previous HANDLE statement.

To nullify a handle condition so that if it does occur and you don't want to handle it, the program is to be abended—you simply specify the HANDLE statement without a paragraph name on your handle operand. Hence, in the statement below, after this command is issued, and once the MAPFAIL condition has arisen, the system will abend the application program; or, if the general error condition is still in effect, control will be transferred to that general routine.

EXEC CICS HANDLE CONDITION MAPFAIL END-EXEC.

Another way of undoing a handle condition is to ask CICS to ignore the condition, that is, to treat it as if it didn't occur. This can be done whenever you expect a condition to occur. For example, when you are reading records from an alternate index in which duplicates are allowed, for every read operation you issue, the DUPKEY condition arises whenever an alternate index record is read that has a duplicate key value. This condition can be rather annoying. You can handle it by informing CICS that you just don't care that this condition occurred, and simply want to ignore it. This can be done as follows:

EXEC CICS IGNORE CONDITION DUPKEY END-EXEC.

Until *you* issue a HANDLE CONDITION DUPKEY to override the action taken by this IGNORE, the DUPKEY condition will not be raised by CICS. Of course, if your task ends, all conditions will be reset by CICS on the next initiation of your application.

In Chapter 7 we discussed the contents of the execute interface block (EIB) and pointed out a series of fields that can be used to determine the source and cause of the error in your application program. The errors here are handle conditions and not program abends.

If a general error routine is specified for all handle conditions that arise, this routine might want to be able to determine why the error occurred, where it occurred, and what action should be taken. The general error routine is capable of doing this, provided that the programmer and designer take the time to identify the various conditions that are to be specifically tested, and the action to be taken if a condition arises that has not been anticipated. In any case, this routine can interrogate some fields in the execute interface block (EIB) to determine why the error occurred and (we hope) determine where the error occurred. Note that specific handle condition paragraphs for each possible handle condition would accomplish the same thing, but in this case, you're centralizing your error handling and analysis. Either method of implementation is available, and it's really up to you to choose the method of implementation. If you do not implement either option, you can expect a program to abend if a condition arises during your program processing.

The fields in the EIB to be tested are EIBDS, EIBRSRCE, EIBFN, and EIBRCODE. The last two fields are probably the most important ones. EIBFN (function code) identifies the type of operation that was being performed when the condition arose. Hence, if you were issuing a SEND MAP command and it failed, then EIBFN would have a code that specifies that a SEND MAP command was being issued when the failure occurred. Although you now know that the SEND MAP command caused the error, you don't really know why the error occurred. The EIBRCODE (response code) provides a detailed description (via coded values) of the cause of the error. Since both fields are code driven, a table of codes must be available to help you identify the type of error and its cause. Hence, rather than describe the many (more than 50) function or response codes, let me again refer you to the *CICS/VS Application Programmer's Reference Manual* for further details.

The EIBDS and EIBRSRCE fields can provide the name of the file or resource that your program was trying to process when the error occurred. These fields could contain the name of the file responsible for the condition, the mapset name that caused a MAPFAIL condition, and so on. It is important that you understand that the general routine identified must interrogate those codes *before* any other command-level statements are issued. As soon as the next command-level command is issued, most of these fields will contain new values.

ATTENTION IDENTIFIER KEYS

The last type of HANDLE command in the CICS vocabulary is the HANDLE AID command. AID stands for *attention identifier.* An AID key on the keyboard is one that can initiate program execution. These keys are the *enter* key, PF keys, PA keys, *clear* key, and LIGHT PEN. Your terminal may not be equipped with all these keys.

When a user presses the *clear* key while a screen is displayed, a problem can arise if the program is expecting the *enter* key to be pressed. This situation can be handled in much the same way that you handled mapping failures.

Usually, HANDLE AID commands are issued before any other commands in the application program, so that if the user presses the *clear* key at any time during processing, proper action can be taken. Since the HANDLE AID command has the same format as the HANDLE CONDITION command, implementation is straightforward. Also, when a HANDLE AID is raised, the same type of action occurs—namely, control is transferred to the paragraph identified within the HANDLE AID statement.

For example, to give control to the paragraph called CLEAR-KEY when a user presses the *clear* key during processing, you would code the following.

```
EXEC CICS HANDLE AID CLEAR(CLEAR-KEY) END-EXEC.
```

In many applications, the PF1 and PF2 keys are used to scroll the user's screen or to advance within a file when the user is performing browsing operations. Further, many menus are implemented with PF-key selection as fewer key strokes are required of the user when he is making a choice. To give control to the proper paragraph when either of these keys is pressed, you could code:

```
EXEC CICS HANDLE AID
    PF1(PF1-KEY-PARAGRAPH)
    PF2(PF2-KEY-PARAGRAPH) END-EXEC.
```

Now let's look at a reverse logic situation. Let's suppose that if the user presses any key other than the *enter* key, we want to give control to a special routine that sends out a message indicating that the user pressed an invalid key. We could code the HANDLE AID statement in two ways here. First, we could identify the paragraph to be given control for each of the various handle conditions, or we could simply introduce a new AID operand called ANYKEY that would perform the same task.

```
EXEC CICS HANDLE AID
    PF1(NOT-THE-ENTER-KEY)
    PF2(NOT-THE-ENTER-KEY)
    .  .  .

    .  .  .
    PF24(NOT-THE-ENTER-KEY)
    CLEAR(NOT-THE-ENTER-KEY)
    .  .  .

    .  .  .
    PA3(NOT-THE-ENTER-KEY) END-EXEC.
```

-------- OR --------

```
EXEC CICS HANDLE AID ANYKEY(NOT-THE-ENTER-KEY) END-EXEC.
```

In either situation, the proper action will be taken, but obviously the second method is much easier to code. The paragraph identified in the handle operands will be given control if any key other than the *enter* key is pressed by the user.

HANDLE AID commands are used quite often in conversational programs, and they can also be used in nonconversational applications. Your application could be designed so that as long as the user presses the *enter* key, processing continues normally. However, if the user wants to abort or discontinue a processing sequence, he can press any key (except the *enter* key) and he will be returned to the system menu or to some other starting point within the application.

Command-level CICS provides yet another way of handling AID keys that does not require the issuing of HANDLE AID commands at all. You simply code a few IF-THEN-ELSE tests to determine which key has been pressed. Depending on your style, you may prefer this method over the AID command, (which transfers control to a paragraph when it is determined that a particular key has been pressed).

To use this alternate style, you must remember that your application is interfacing with the execute interface program. Further, your communications with EIP take place through the special control block called the execute interface block. This control block contains a field that can be tested to determine whether the user pressed the *clear* key, *enter* key, PF1 through PF24 keys, PA1 through PA3 keys, or whether the user used a light pen to initiate your application. This field is called EIBAID. Along with this field, IBM supplies a set of variables that can be used to test the value of the EIBAID. These values are copied into your program in exactly the same way that the attribute list, DFHBMSCA, was copied into your program earlier in the chapter.

When you issue your COPY command, the DFHAID list is copied into your program and appears similar to the following:

```
01  COPY DFHAID.
01  DFHAID.
    02  DFHCLEAR
    02  DFHENTER
    02  DFHPA1
    02  DFHPA2
    02  DFHPA3
    02  DFHPF1
    02  DFHPF2
       .    .  .
       .    .  .
    02  DFHPF24
    02  DFHPEN
```

Hence, by using a simple IF-THEN-ELSE test as shown below, you can determine which key was pressed by the user at the terminal. If you make this decision before any of your RECEIVE commands are issued, you can avoid program failures.

```
IF EIBAID = DFHCLEAR THEN
       .   .   .
       .   .   .
```

The distinctive feature of this method of determining which AID was pressed is that control is not forcibly transferred to any other location in your program. Hence, the logic of your code can remain stable and will be easy to follow if someone else has to modify that code. Be careful, however; this method may not work in a conversational programming environment, where you'd probably be better off using the HANDLE AID commands rather than testing key depression in this fashion.

The HANDLE ABEND, AID, and CONDITION commands can be useful for controlling a variety of situations. We've covered the ABEND and AID commands but have left conditions related to other command-level commands for later chapters. When we revisit the calculator application later in this chapter, we'll use these commands in appropriate situations to provide you with more examples of their use.

CICS ABEND CODES

If your program ever fails, you'll probably be confused the first time it happens since the abend codes used by CICS are not consistent with the abend codes used in a batch environment. You really have to learn a completely new set of abend codes. The abend codes briefly described here are the ones most likely to occur when you are developing your application or running it from a user's point of view. Each code is accompanied by a brief description of the code and some guidelines for debugging your application.

ABMx — We studied these abend codes in an earlier section dealing with mapping operations. In general, they mean that a mapping request that you have issued has failed.

AEDx — If you were using the EDF on-line debugging system, you might get one of these errors. See your CICS systems programmer for help if you get one of these abends; it may not be your fault.

AEIx — These abend codes are replicas of the HANDLE CONDITION operands that may be tested for each handle condition that can arise. The last letter of the AIEx command is associated with a specific handle condition, as listed below. If you get one of these abends, it usually means that you overlooked a handle condition that should have been issued by your applications program.

L – The file that you tried to reference was not defined in the FCT (DSIDERR).

M – The record that you tried to read was not in the file (NOTFND).

N – You tried to write a new record to a file, but a record already in the file has the same key (DUPREC).

P – This is a general category for any error that occurs that does not fit into any other category. Consult the messages and codes manual for assistance (INVREQ).

Q – The I/O that you tried to issue failed because of a device I/O error (IOERR).

R – There's no space in the file to add the record you have just tried to write (NOSPACE).

S – The file that you tried to access is not open to CICS. This usually indicates that: the file is not defined properly in the FCT, it doesn't have any records in it (VSAM), or the file has something wrong with it (NOTOPEN).

U – The sequence of command-level commands that you have issued is illogical. Maybe you tried to rewrite a record that you didn't read for update or you tried to read backwards in a file that was defined as a forward browsing operation (ILLOGIC).

V – The record that you tried to write to your file is longer or shorter than the record length defined for the file. It could also mean that the calculation that you used to determine the length of your record is incorrect (LENGERR).

9 – You've seen this one before (MAPFAIL).

AICA — Your program is probably looping and the system has abended your program because CICS assumes that you are not doing productive work.

AKCP — CICS was in trouble for storage or some other resource, to the point of not being able to run any tasks. Your task was cancelled by the CICS task control program to try to restore stability in the entire environment and enable the program to run tasks again.

AMTJ — The Master Terminal Operator cancelled your task. See the MTO for information or contact your CICS systems programming group or master console operator to find out why your task was cancelled.

APCT — We discussed this one before. The program or mapset that you tried to access was not defined in the PPT, was not spelled properly in your request, or was not link-edited into the CICS program library properly under the CICS system.

ASCx — You issued either a GETMAIN or FREEMAIN to obtain or release some storage area, but the request failed.

ATAI — A terminal error was detected. If you were expecting a map to be sent out by your program, then you probably sent the map out from the wrong symbolic map area and undecodable data have gone to the terminal; or someone unplugged your terminal; or your program or someone else's program has overlayed part of your symbolic or physical map so that unrecognizable characters have been placed in the terminal data stream.

DEBUGGING CICS PROGRAMS

Since there are several CICS application debugging packages on the market, it's difficult to do justice to any one, or to say that any one is superior. You can usually learn to use one of these debugging packages in a short time, or you can get your CICS systems programmer to help you read your CICS dump if you do not have an on-line debugging package. Hence, rather than cover a particular debugging package or technique, which you may or may not have available at your installation, I'll simply omit debugging packages from this text.

In general, the on-line debugging packages allow the programmer to step through the code in an interactive execution environment. The programmer may look at storage areas at any point desired, and, in some cases, can alter values in those storage areas or alter commands in passing. This is a powerful feature and is a tremendous aid in correcting minor bugs.

Debugging on-line programs through hardcopy dumps is also an effective way of solving a problem. In this mode of debugging, however, the programmer sees only what has happened *after* the program has failed and has to rebuild the sequence of events leading up to the point of abend. Although the dump-debugging facility provided with CICS does trace these events for a transaction, it does not provide "snapshots" of storage areas used by the program. Even so, the programmer is able to trace the changing of variables during processing. Hence, the on-line debugging packages offer more reliable, more accurate, and faster problem resolution than the hardcopy dump-reading, debugging methods.

Most manuals that vendors supply on their debugging packages are both useful and readable. You should therefore consult these manuals for more information on dump reading, or the CICS on-line debugging packages.

FIELD-EDITING SERVICES

As you've seen, command-level implementation comes with a variety of service commands that can improve the reliability of the application. One editing feature is of particular interest because it can be used on fields to remove nonnumeric characters. This service is regarded as a built-in-function. What it does is simply *correct* data in a numeric field.

As we discuss this command, you should carefully think about its drawbacks. In some instances, you may *not* want to use this command in your processing because it distorts the data. Moreover, if you want the user to be able to see what has been typed in, especially if the field *is in error,* then you would not want to use this service because it also alters the contents of the data.

The command is called BIF DEEDIT (built-in-function for editing) and it works like this. Suppose that a field defined at the terminal is seven positions long and that the field is to contain *only* numeric data. If the user types in a period or a dollar sign, or if he strikes the ALPHA-shift key that is available on some keyboards, then clearly the numeric field is no longer totally numeric.

In the COBOL program, we can use the decision IF-field-IS-NUMERIC-THEN to determine whether there are invalid characters in the field, and if there are, a message can be sent to the terminal along with the data that the user entered to announce the error.

Further, assume that no matter what the user types in, we will remove all the nondigit characters from the field, right-justify it, fill remaining leading positions with zeros, and continue processing. In this case, we may actually be changing the user's data and at the same time we may be converting the data to a form that our program requires.

Suppose a field is sent to the terminal using a PICOUT clause and that its displayed value is ᵬᵬ$34.26. If the user alters the field by typing ᵬ$126.34 and presses the *enter* key, the user's intentions are clear, but if this field undergoes the IF NUMERIC test, the field will *fail* the test.

By using the built-in function to DEEDIT this field, CICS will provide us a field value of 00012634 when given the value ᵬ$126.34. In other words, the nondigit characters will be removed, the remaining digits will be right-justified, and leading positions will be filled with zeros. The resulting number will be in the proper form for processing and will not fail an edit test, and will not cause a program abend.

This function is easy to use and can be activated through one command-level request for each field to be processed. Let's suppose that the field that we want to edit is called VAL11, which is one of the input fields on the MAINMAP for our calculator application. To edit this field using the command-level edit feature, we could code:

```
EXEC CICS BIF DEEDIT FIELD(VAL11)
    LENGTH(7) END-EXEC.
```

Obviously, two operands must be specified for this command. The FIELD operand specifies the field that contains the data to be edited. Further, the result of the edit will *replace* the current contents of this field. The second operand specifies the length of the field, which in our case (VAL11) is defined as a 7-byte field.

A CONVERSATIONAL IMPLEMENTATION

You're probably wondering where conversational programming fits into this chapter. When applications are implemented in a conversational style under CICS, the application must be able to handle situations such as the one in which the user presses the *clear* key, or some key other than *enter*. You probably understand these situations now and think you know how to handle them. The danger, however, is that you might want to move ahead too quickly and brush over the details.

To encourage you to think more deeply about the topics covered in this chapter, I am going to implement these new ideas in a conversational mode. The implementation that follows applies all the ideas previously discussed in this chapter and briefly runs through the conversational programming style.

Several drastic changes occur in the structure of the application when it is implemented in a conversational style. Each of these changes needs to be carefully studied and the trade-offs in implementation styles carefully examined before you adopt either programming style.

Notice first that the decision logic used to test whether the screen is formatted or unformatted is completely removed from the program. There's no need to test this information because the program is initiated only *once* for every terminal user and does not come and go, as was the case in a nonconversational implementation. As a result, the TIOA-AREA definition is no longer needed to support this decision structure.

Since the application program never gives up control until the user informs the program that processing has ended, there's no need to place a transaction id in the upper left corner of each map display. Further, the control character used to help the program determine which screen is to be processed is no longer needed because each time a screen is sent to the terminal, *that screen* is immediately received. Obviously the screen that is to be received is the same screen that was just sent out. You'll also notice that the application program is structured like a loop in that the same functions are repeated until the user presses the *clear* key to end the transaction. Lastly, when the program ends, you'll notice that a different SEND command is used. This command may seem strange since *no data* are actually sent to the terminal (LENGTH(0)). The purpose of this command is simply to clear the screen.

What follows is the complete on-line program that can be used to implement the calculator application in a conversational mode. Many of the ideas discussed in this chapter are incorporated into the code, which includes: attribute byte manipulation, field editing, abend and condition handling, and finally, AID processing for special keys on the keyboard.

```
IDENTIFICATION DIVISION.
  PROGRAM-ID.  CALCPRG.
  AUTHOR.       ME.
ENVIRONMENT DIVISION.
DATA DIVISION.
WORKING-STORAGE SECTION.
01  VAL1X          PIC 9(7).
01  VAL2X          PIC 9(7).
01  FOREVER        PIC X(3) VALUE 'YES'.
```

```
01   COPY CALCM.
01   COPY ATTRBS.
PROCEDURE DIVISION.
    EXEC CICS SEND MAP('MAINMAP') MAPSET('CALCM')
       MAPONLY ERASE END-EXEC.

    EXEC CICS HANDLE ABEND LABEL(NASTY-PROBLEM) END-EXEC.
    EXEC CICS HANDLE AID ANYKEY(ALL-DONE) END-EXEC.

    PERFORM LOOP-THE-LOOP THRU LOOP-THE-LOOP-EXIT
       UNTIL FOREVER = 'NO'.
ALL-DONE.
    EXEC CICS SEND FROM(VAL1X) LENGTH(0) ERASE
       END-EXEC.
    EXEC CICS RETURN END-EXEC.
LOOP-THE-LOOP.
    EXEC CICS RECEIVE MAP('MAINMAP') MAPSET('CALCM')
       INTO(MAINMAPI) END-EXEC.
    IF VAL1I NOT NUMERIC THEN
       MOVE 'INVALID FIRST VALUE' TO MSGO
       MOVE -1                    TO VAL1L
       MOVE UNPROT-BRT-FSET       TO VAL2A, CHOICEA
       EXEC CICS SEND MAP('MAINMAP') MAPSET('CALCM')
          ERASE CURSOR END-EXEC
    ELSE
       IF VAL2I NOT NUMERIC THEN
          MOVE 'INVALID SECOND VALUE' TO MSGO
          MOVE -1                     TO VAL1L
          MOVE UNPROT-BRT-FSET        TO VAL1A, CHOICEA
          EXEC CICS SEND MAP('MAINMAP') MAPSET('CALCM')
             ERASE CURSOR END-EXEC
       ELSE
          MOVE VAL1I TO VAL1X
          MOVE VAL2I TO VAL2X
          MOVE -1    TO VAL2L

          IF CHOICEI = '1' THEN
             COMPUTE RSLTO = VAL1X + VAL2X
          ELSE
             IF CHOICEI = '2' THEN
                COMPUTE RSLTO = VAL1X - VAL2X
             ELSE
                IF CHOICEI = '3' THEN
                   COMPUTE RSLTO = VAL1X * VAL2X
```

```
                    ELSE
                     IF CHOICEI = '4' THEN
                        COMPUTE RSLTO = VAL1X / VAL2X
                     ELSE
                        MOVE 'INVALID MENU CHOICE' TO
                         MSGO
                        MOVE -1  TO CHOICEL.

           IF CHOICEL = -1 THEN
              MOVE +0 TO VAL1L.
           MOVE UNPROT-BRT-FSET TO VAL1A, VAL2A, CHOICEA.
           EXEC CICS SEND MAP('MAINMAP') MAPSET('CALCM')
              FROM(MAINMAPO) ERASE CURSOR END-EXEC.
           GO TO LOOP-THE-LOOP-PRE-EXIT.

       NASTY-PROBLEM.
           MOVE 'SEVERE ERROR, TRY AGAIN' TO MSGO.
           MOVE -1                        TO VAL1L.
           MOVE UNPROT-BRT-FSET   TO VAL1A, VAL2A, CHOICEA.
           EXEC CICS SEND MAP('MAINMAP') MAPSET('CALCM')
              FROM(MAINMAPO) ERASE CURSOR END-EXEC.

       LOOP-THE-LOOP-PRE-EXIT.

       LOOP-THE-LOOP-EXIT.

       STOP-RUN-DUMMY-PARAGRAPH.
           STOP RUN.
```

THOUGHT QUESTIONS

1. *In what instances would you not want to handle an abend and instead let the program abend?*

2. *What impact or impression does an abend have on a user? Does it matter to the user whether a "nice" message is displayed or a program is abended?*

3. *When an abend or exceptional condition is "handled," a transaction dump is usually not produced to aid the programmer in identifying and resolving the problem. How might this affect your decision to handle or not handle conditions?*

4. *Some installations issue the ABEND or DUMP command when an exceptional condition arises. Although we haven't addressed these commands, when do you think a forced program abend or a dump of transaction resources is appropriate? How might these commands be "abused"?*

11

PROCESSING FILES UNDER CICS

File processing is an important area of on-line application and requires a general understanding of CICS processing, which you should now have. The basic steps of file processing—such as reading, writing (adding), deleting, and updating of records—will seem easy compared with other operations that we have discussed. This chapter looks at both file requests and some exceptional conditions that may arise during the processing of file requests, as well as some elaborate types of file processing situations such as variable length record processing, generic file processing, file browsing, and alternate index file processing. By the end of the chapter you'll have enough tools to implement almost any CICS on-line application.

TESTING I/O SUCCESS

File processing under CICS is requested through the FILE MANAGE-MENT component of CICS. Using special CICS COMMAND-LEVEL file I/O statements, your file requests are communicated through EIP to FILE CONTROL. The file operation is performed by CICS, and control is returned to the next statement (if the operation is successful), or to an alternate point in the program (in the event of an error). This status can be handled either by specific handle condition establishments for each of the various conditions that could arise, or—as discussed in Chapter 7—a general error routine could be built to interrogate the return codes in the execute interface block.

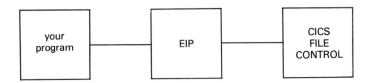

To communicate your requests to FILE CONTROL, you must issue the appropriate command-level statement. This command set consists of READ, READ for update, WRITE (add), REWRITE, and DELETE. These basic operations are easy to code with command-level programming, but you must first make sure that the files that you want to process are properly defined to the CICS system, and that your application adheres to the basic rules of file processing.

DEFINING FILES TO CICS

To define a file to CICS, you'll probably ask your systems programming staff or on-line support group to perform this definition. It is done in much the same way that a program or mapset was defined in the PPT and a transaction was defined in the PCT. File entries, however, are defined in a table called the FILE CONTROL TABLE or FCT. The *CICS/VS Systems Programmer's Reference Manual* for CICS 1.5 or the *CICS/VS Resource Definition Guide* for CICS 1.6 can assist you in this definition. Information that must be supplied to the FCT includes:

- file name (logical name)
- password
- type of file
- access method to be used to process the file
- length of the record key
- position of the key in the record
- the type of operations that you want to perform against this file
- the number of people who will be concurrently updating records in the file
- the characteristics of the records in the file
- whether this file is a component of a CICS data base that is indirectly accessed through a key in another file

These are just a few of the many options that may be specified in the FCT entry for your file, but as an application designer or programmer, you should consider each of these elements before you define your FCT entries for your files.

Since some of the elements in this list may not be clear to you, let's examine each one more closely and at the same time compare the structure of on-line file processing with that of batch processing.

In an IBM processing environment, COBOL programs access files through I/O statements such as READ and WRITE. These commands refer back to a file description and to a SELECT clause for a file. The SELECT clause contains a one-to-eight character file name that attaches the SELECT to a DD statement in your JCL. A data set name is placed (DSN) on the JCL statement. The DSN attaches the file name or DDNAME on this DD statement to the physical file. A similar situation occurs when files are processed under CICS, *but from a much different perspective.*

When an on-line file is defined in the FCT, a file name is assigned, which is coordinated between you and the person placing your file entry into the FCT. This file name must be unique with respect to all other files defined in the FCT. As well, this FCT entry is associated with a DD statement (as in a batch environment). Remember, however, that since your application operates as a subroutine to CICS, any JCL that is coded is defined to CICS and not to *your* program.

When processing files under CICS, *you should not* issue any OPEN or CLOSE or SELECT statements in your application program. *All* file requests should be handled by FILE CONTROL. If this rule is violated, you're likely to encounter terrible response times and many system failures. CICS opens, closes, and selects all files. That is, when CICS is activated, one of the first tasks it performs is to OPEN all the application files, unless your file is specified as "deferred open," in which case the application program must issue the proper command-level command to open the file. When CICS is shut down, all application files are closed. Since deferred opening and closing of files is not usually done, an application should never have to specifically request that a file be opened or closed, unless you design your system in this way. Files are generally available to any application as long as CICS is servicing transaction requests.

In general, it is not advisable to defer opening of on-line files. For example, suppose that user A initiates the system XYZ. If the files used by XYZ are defer-opened, then XYZ must first open the files before processing can begin. Assume that this was done. Now suppose that user B initiates XYZ. Since XYZ has no facility (nor does CICS) to test the openness of a file, XYZ will assume that the files are closed and try to open them. However, since they are already opened, the initiation of XYZ by user B may cause an abend if XYZ is not designed to handle this situation. IF XYZ has been designed properly, then XYZ must either wait until user A's initiation finishes, or attempt to process concurrently with the initiation by user A. In other words, it becomes difficult to coordinate the two initiations. If you now assume that XYZ can be initiated by several hundred users, the problem is compounded. In general, it is much more efficient to let CICS, rather than the application, manage file open and close processing, which then become much easier to coordinate.

Another feature of CICS is that it permits a file to be used in an on-line environment concurrently with batch. In other words, CICS does not control a file exclusively *unless* the file is being used for add, delete, or update operations. In those cases, simultaneous batch usage can only take place if the batch system is performing read-only operations. The reverse is also true. If the on-line system is performing only read-only operations (and the file is defined in the FCT as such), then a batch system can be concurrently reading, adding, deleting, or updating records in that file. Some other on-line monitors "hold" onto files and do not permit any type of concurrent batch usage.

TYPES OF FILES-SUPPORTED BY CICS

CICS supports most of the IBM file access methods that include QSAM, BDAM, ISAM, or VSAM. When choosing an access method, however, you should be careful to implement your system since one of these access structures can cause severe system performance degradation (QSAM). In general, on-line systems attempt to service random requests, and thus most application files should be either indexed, relative, or direct in nature. QSAM files are *not* usually found in a CICS environment and you should not use them for application implementation. There are ways of implementing a QSAM file structure in your CICS environment through transient data files, but because this access method leads to performance problems, these processing techniques will not be discussed in this text. The file access methods that are usually used to support application processing are:

- Sequential files
  VSAM ESDS
- Direct files
  BDAM
- Relative files
  BDAM
  VSAM RRDS
  VSAM ESDS using RBA's
- Indexed files
  ISAM
  VSAM KSDS
- Data base files
  IMS/DLI
  indirect access files

When a file is to be defined under CICS, you must identify all the types of processing that will be done on that file. For example, a file can be read, updated, or browsed; records can also be deleted or added to the file. If you do not want to give *any* on-line application the ability to update, add, or delete records from a file, then you can specify that only read and browse operations be done against that file. This specification takes place through yet another parameter in the FCT. However, *all* applications are forced to abide by this specification; that is, if you specify the type of operations that may be performed on a file, then no application (even yours) is allowed to do anything else to that file, unless you define another FCT entry for that file with a different set of processing options that only you know about. In that case, the file would be accessed in two different ways within the same CICS system. Therefore, by designing your programs to process from the other "secret" file, you can perform activities that other users cannot.

In VSAM environments, it may be necessary to know the number of users who will be concurrently updating records in the file. This number must be specified in the FCT so that some control can be placed on file access (string number). Accessing a VSAM file for update requires that a series of control blocks be managed and coordinated among all users. Too many control strings can add additional processing overhead to VSAM and waste memory resources; too few control strings may hinder application performance. This aspect of file definition should be carefully discussed with your on-line control group.

The last item on our list has to do with the characteristics of the data, such as key length, key position, logical and physical record lengths, record formats, and so on. This information is usually not required in the FCT entry for your files since it can be obtained from the volume table of contents (VTOC) for the file when the file is opened by CICS for processing.

As your FCT entry is being defined, you should create your file and place it on a direct access storage device. At the same time, you should inform your on-line control group of the name of your data set so that the proper JCL can be supplied with the running of CICS to access your file.

If your data set is a VSAM data set, then one other step might have to be taken. In some cases, depending on your VSAM structure and interfacing with CICS, your VSAM files may need to be preformatted before they are made available for CICS on-line processing. This means that *before* the file can actually be processed under CICS, you must create the file and actually store a record into that file. If you don't, it may not be possible for CICS to open the file for on-line processing.

Preloading a VSAM file simply means writing a record to the file and then deleting that record. Although the file is now physically empty, it has *had* a record in it, and thus satisfies the preformatting requirement. If you *have* data to place into the file, then, rather than start your on-line system with an empty file, simply load data into your file. As long as there are or have been records in the file, it will open normally for on-line processing.

Finally, when files are used under CICS, or any on-line system for that matter, batch and on-line processing must be carefully planned. Usually, a file that is used by CICS or other on-line systems may *not* also be available for batch processing when the on-line system is active. CICS is not quite as restrictive in this case, and in general, a file defined to CICS may be updated through CICS but not updated from a batch environment; however, the file *can* be processed for input-only operations in a batch mode. Other on-line systems totally restrict the usage of files from a batch mode during the time that the file is being used by an active on-line environment.

These are the major rules to follow when you are processing files in a CICS environment. If you adhere to these few basic restrictions, you'll have few if any problems in your file processing.

HANDLING FILE ERRORS

When an application attempts to read a record from a file but the record is not found, a file processing exceptional condition arises. Obviously, the program should be able to recover from this situation and should not abend from a normal event of this kind. In file processing, this type of situation is handled by means of the HANDLE CONDITION command.

In Chapter 10, we discussed the use of the HANDLE CONDITION command with reference to SEND and RECEIVE requests. You'll recall that the MAPFAIL condition was being tested when we used the HANDLE command to trap mapping operation failures. Since it is not appropriate to use MAPFAIL for file operations here, instead we'll identify a list of applicable conditions to test for, depending on the type of operation we intend to perform.

As mentioned earlier, the HANDLE CONDITION command transfers control to a paragraph if that condition arises during processing. As a result, that paragraph should take appropriate action in accordance with the type of error obtained. Further, if an application needs to process several files to service a user's request, it may be necessary to issue many HANDLE CONDITION statements and to have many HANDLE CONDITION paragraphs (one for each file). Thus, when a condition arises for a file, a specific action can be taken. On the other hand, we can just as easily use a general error routine with the ability to analyze the status code in the execute interface block.

For example, suppose that an application will read three files, (A, B, and C) to display information for a particular request. If it is possible that the necessary data will not be found in any one of the files, then it might be necessary to establish a NOTFND (not found) handle condition for each file. If you forget to establish such a condition and do not have a general error routine to handle the situation, an abend will occur.

This NOTFND handle condition can be specified in two general ways. One HANDLE CONDITION NOTFND can be established for all three files, and thus less coding is needed to process such an error. However, sharing a paragraph among three files may not be appropriate since you'll again have to interrogate the EIB to determine *which* file was responsible for the condition. Another solution would be to code three separate NOTFND exceptional routines, one for each file. Then, just before you issue the read request for a file, you can issue a HANDLE CONDITION NOTFND *for that file.* Thus, if the read request fails, a specific paragraph associated with that file and that read request will be given control. In the second case, three different HANDLE CONDITIONS must be coded *and* three separate routines must be defined if they are to be the target of the transfer of control. However, this offers a flexible and informative method of determining which file caused the error and what was done as a result.

If you recall, we spent a substantial amount of time discussing file conditions during the design of a system. We defined separate routines for each type of file condition and discussed the implementation of handle conditions. We said that the HANDLE CONDITION *must* be in effect before the I/O being issued. Also, to enhance understanding and readability, we established handle conditions immediately before the I/O so that later reference to the program would indicate the establishment of handle conditions for each file I/O operation.

Handle conditions are related to a type of command-level operation. We're going to discuss the handle conditions applicable to every type of file operation—read, write, or delete. In any file operation, however, there are some general handle conditions that are common to all the file I/O requests that you may not want to handle individually. Instead, you can develop a shared error paragraph to handle this group of file problems.

CONDITION	EXPLANATION
DSIDERR	The file name that you specified in your command-level statement was not found in the FCT. You probably spelled the name of the file incorrectly or your FCT entry hasn't been defined yet.
NOTOPEN	The file that you tried to process is not open to CICS for processing. There could be several reasons for this error: The FCT entry for your file is not correct. The JCL to access your file was not supplied when CICS started and so your file is not allocated to CICS. Your file has not been preloaded (only VSAM). The file name is defined in the FCT but the DDNAME on the JCL DD statement to reference your file is spelled incorrectly and so CICS can't allocate or open your file.

IOERR	A device I/O error occurred when you tried to access your file. If you are processing in direct mode, you may have computed an invalid TTR.
ILLOGIC	For VSAM files, the sequence of commands for performing the I/O that you wanted is not correct.

Of course there are other handle conditions, but these are the most common conditions to be tested. As for specific requests related to the type of operation that you are performing, these are discussed next under each file operation command.

FILE PROCESSING COMMANDS

To process a record in a file, you first need a description of that record area. You also need to build a key description in the WORKING-STORAGE section of your program that is *separate* from the record description. Once these two actions are completed, file processing is easy to do. For example, let's suppose that we have an indexed file that has the following record description. We must then define two structures that can be used against this indexed file. The first area simply forms a basis for the key of the file and must be located in the WORKING-STORAGE section of the program. The second structure is the actual file description. It can reside in one of two places: the WORKING-STORAGE section, if we are processing the file in move mode; or in the LINKAGE SECTION, if we are processing the file in locate mode. We'll discuss locate mode in a later chapter. For now, both of these structures reside in the WORKING-STORAGE section of the program.

```
01   RIDFLD-KEY                      PIC X(9).

01   MASTER-RECORD.
     02   SOCIAL-SECURITY            PIC X(9).
     02   NAME                       PIC X(30).
     02   ADDRESS-LINE-1             PIC X(30).
     02   ADDRESS-LINE-2             PIC X(30).
     02   CITY                       PIC X(20).
     02   STATE                      PIC X(2).
     02   ZIP                        PIC X(9).
     02   HOURS-WORKED               PIC S9(5)V99 COMP-3.
     02   HOURLY-SALARY              PIC S9(5)V99 COMP-3.
     02   BONUS-HOURS                PIC S9(3)V99 COMP-3.
```

In this example, the key to the record is the employee's social security number. Another field could be the key, but in this example, let's simply use the social security number. Clearly, the data names presented could be changed to something more meaningful, but they serve the purpose for the commands that we want to study. The basic commands available to an application are READ, READ for update, WRITE, REWRITE, and DELETE. Each has its own format. Again, we're going to refer to these command for move-mode processing. (In a later chapter, we address record processing using locate mode.)

When processing any file in a CICS environment, you must know the file name as defined in the FCT. In the examples that follow, let's assume that the name of our file is EMPFILE. We're now ready to process our file.

READING RECORDS

A record from a file cannot be read until a command-level READ is issued. When the read command is issued, the request is passed through EIP to CICS FILE CONTROL, the record is read, and then the record is moved to the record description in the WORKING-STORAGE section of your program. If the read is successful, the statement following the READ command will be able to process the data in the MASTER-RECORD file description area. If the read is not successful, then the paragraph identified in the HANDLE CONDITION statement will be given control. This paragraph must be identified in the HANDLE statement before the READ command is issued, and the program should establish the handle condition in the event that the record is not in the file (NOTFND). Other conditions could also be tested here, but, in general, the NOTFND condition and the conditions previously discussed (IOERR, DSIDERR, NOTOPEN, and ILLOGIC) are about the only conditions that will occur during a READ request. To issue the read command, you simply code the following:

```
EXEC CICS READ DATASET('EMPFILE')
  INTO(MASTER-RECORD) RIDFLD(RIDFLD-KEY) END-EXEC.
```

The DATASET operand specifies the name of the file that is to be processed. This must match the name of an entry in the file control table (FCT). Again, this data set name can be specified as a literal (as shown), or it can be specified as a data name defined as X(8) in the WORKING-STORAGE section of the program.

The INTO operand informs CICS where the record is to be placed if it is read correctly. After the command completes normally, the data will reside in our data structure (defined in WORKING-STORAGE) called MASTER-RECORD.

RIDFLD identifies the key of the record that is to be read. This field must *not* be contained *within* the record description in which the record is to be placed.

Further, *before* you issue this command, you must have placed the key of the record into the RIDFLD (record identification field) in order to obtain the correct record. If you forget to move the key to this area before the read is issued, the NOTFND condition will arise.

UPDATING RECORDS

Although it is a simple command, remember that records can be read only with this command. The data in this record cannot be updated. If you attempt to rewrite a record after performing a read, as shown above, an INVREQ condition will arise.

If you want to update a record in a file, then two commands are needed. You must first read the record *for update* and then issue a REWRITE command to replace the record into the same file. To read a record for update, you simply specify the operand UPDATE on the command-level READ statement, as follows:

```
EXEC CICS READ DATASET('EMPFILE') UPDATE
   INTO(MASTER-RECORD) RIDFLD(RIDFLD-KEY) END-EXEC.
```

After you issue this command, you can replace any fields within the data structure called MASTER-RECORD and then issue the following REWRITE command:

```
EXEC CICS REWRITE DATASET('EMPFILE')
   FROM(MASTER-RECORD) END-EXEC.
```

This replaces the old copy of the record in the file with the new data that you entered into the structure called MASTER-RECORD. However, this statement has several important characteristics. When you issue a READ for update and read the record INTO an area, you must REWRITE *from that same area* if the command is to work successfully. In other words, the data area identified in the FROM option on the REWRITE statement above must be the same data area identified on the INTO option on the READ-for-update command.

The REWRITE command does not contain a RIDFLD operand. Hence, you are *not* allowed to change the key of the record after performing a READ for update. You might try this if you simply want to duplicate the information in a record and then add it to the file using a different key. If this was a necessary component of your application, you'd read (not for update) and then write (add) the record to the file after changing the key and any other information within the record description area.

Finally, you should be careful in the coordination of the READ for update and the REWRITE statement, especially in a nonconversational environment, where you'll probably read and display the record to the terminal before an actual REWRITE is performed. In this interim period, someone else could READ and update that record underneath the user who is doing the same thing. Depending on how your application is written, one of the changes may not be applied to the record. Clearly, this could cause a severe synchronization problem. Further, after the record data are displayed to the terminal for the user changes, the program ends, thus releasing control of that record to the system. If the changes are to be actually applied to the record, the program must read the record a second time, update the record by moving in the modified fields, and then issue the REWRITE command to replace the record in the file. In other words, two reads are required to update a record when a nonconversational programming style is used. Since the first read does not result in any change to the data in a record, a simple READ (without update) can suffice. When the second READ is issued, however, a READ for update *must* be done so that the REWRITE will be successful. This brings up yet another drawback to nonconversational implementation.

We have already asked how you can lock out other users from a record in a nonconversational environment. Some possibilities are to read and update the record twice by building into it a special field that is zero if the record is not being used by another terminal operator and one if the record is in use. Another idea is to build another control file that keeps track of all the records currently undergoing updating. When a request to update a record is made, an entry is placed into this file. As the update is completed or if the user cancels his or her request, the entry is deleted from the file. In any case, some method of protecting a record from dual updating must be designed into your system if you are implementing applications by means of nonconversational programming style.

In a *conversational* programming style, this problem is avoided because that task does not have to give up control of the record. A typical update request in a conversational approach might be as follows:

1. Receive requested record key to be updated.
2. Read the record from the file *for update.*
3. Display the record's data to the terminal.
4. Receive the screen of modified data.
5. If the user wants to abort this operation, then
   unlock the file from this update request
   go to ??????????
6. If any of the fields fail editing, then
   move an error message to the message area on this screen
   position the cursor at the bad field
   set all field attributes appropriately
   go to step 3

7. Move the data from the screen area to the record description area, replacing all fields to be modified.

8. Rewrite the record to the file.

In this code you'll notice only one read command. This approach is much simpler than the nonconversational approach, and it is more secure because *no other users* can update this record while the user is changing the fields on the screen. However, if this record was in a control interval (VSAM) with many other records, *none* of the records in that control interval could be updated by any other user as long as this user stayed in update mode. This situation can cause severe bottlenecks within your system whenever a file is heavily used for update purposes.

You'll also notice the test for the user aborting this update request. Within this processing, the file must be unlocked (UNLOCK) so that other pending updates can be processed. If you forget to unlock the file and do not issue a REWRITE command for the record that you have READ for update, an INVREQ condition will occur on your next file request. This situation could *not* occur in a nonconversational environment because as soon as a nonconversational task returns to CICS, all resources held by that task are also returned to CICS, including file resources. Thus, in a nonconversational approach, *no* unlock command has to be issued unless you want to add unnecessary overhead to your on-line transaction processing.

To unlock a file in a conversational environment, you can issue the following command:

```
EXEC CICS UNLOCK DATASET('EMPFILE') END-EXEC.
```

ADDING RECORDS

When it is necessary to add a record to a file, the programmer must code a WRITE command. Before issuing this command, you must build a complete record in your record description area, in this case, MASTER-RECORD. You must also place the key of the record in both areas, the RIDFLD-KEY and in the MASTER-RECORD field called SOCIAL-SECURITY. Many programmers forget to do both and cause an INVREQ or ILLOGIC handle condition to arise as a result. If we assume that the record has been successfully constructed in our WORKING-STORAGE section under the name MASTER-RECORD and that the key has been placed in both key areas, the following command can be issued:

```
EXEC CICS WRITE DATASET('EMPFILE')
    FROM(MASTER-RECORD) RIDFLD(RIDFLD-KEY)
    END-EXEC.
```

The operands in this command are exactly the same as the previous ones. However, in the command above and in the REWRITE command previously described, the records that we are processing must be FIXED LENGTH records. If we attempt to write out variable length records with these commands, a LENGERR condition will result. We'll talk about variable length records later in this chapter, but for now, it's important to remember that all the commands being described deal only with fixed length records. Further, you can assume that the FCT entry for EMPFILE specifies that fixed length record processing is to be used, and hence, the LENGTH operand need not be coded on the REWRITE or WRITE commands as shown above.

When writing records to a file, you should test for the following handle conditions: DUPREC means that a record already in the file has the same key as the record that you're trying to add, and the NOSPACE condition informs your program when your file has filled up. I hope that this last condition never arises because in order to reorganize your file or expand it, you may have to take down your entire CICS system, or, if your system is equipped to do so, you may have to dynamically deallocate a file from your CICS system. Since the software to do this is relatively complex, most installations simply take down and restart the CICS system. As a precaution, you should check the space utilization for your files daily to ensure that there is adequate space for that day's processing. If you have a rigid CICS operations schedule, and if you run out of space in the middle of the day, other users may have to wait until the next day before they can add records to the file(s) supported by your application.

DELETING RECORDS

By now you should know how to delete records from a file. Many of the same operands are used to delete records, but you do not have to have *any* data in the area called MASTER-RECORD. In other words, you do not have to read the record for update before trying to delete it; in fact, you *can't* read it for update and then delete it.

To delete a record, you first move the key of the record to your special key area, which in our case is called RIDFLD-KEY. Then you issue the following command to delete the record from the file, but before you do, you should establish handle conditions in case the record with the key you specify is not in the file (NOTFND).

EXEC CICS DELETE DATASET('EMPFILE')
RIDFLD(RIDFLD-KEY) END-EXEC.

Since we've seen most of these operands before, there's no need to spend time analyzing each one. This is all there is to deleting a record from a file.

These are the basic file processing commands available through command-level CICS. The operands should be relatively familiar by this point since many of the same operands are used through the command set. The next section of this chapter addresses extended file operations. The basic command set and operands that we have just established will be used again in the next section; you should understand their use before we tackle the next step in CICS file processing.

VARIABLE LENGTH RECORD PROCESSING

Basic file processing under CICS is relatively simple and straightforward. Many people think that processing variable length records or alternate indexes is much more difficult, but as you'll soon see, these types of processing are also very simple. As long as you abide by the rules, so to speak, you won't have any problems implementing applications that use the more elaborate file processing options.

First, let's look at the handling of variable length records. If you have done variable length record processing in a batch environment, then you won't have any difficulty in performing the same task in an on-line setting. The handling of variable length records is not much different from the READ, WRITE, REWRITE, and DELETE commands that we've already seen except for one more operand, the LENGTH operand.

The LENGTH operand must be specified on the REWRITE and WRITE commands for records that are to be written back out to a file defined as variable length. This operand communicates the length of the record to CICS's FILE CONTROL component so that the proper record descriptor information can be built into the record before it is written to the file. *You* must compute the length of the record in some fashion and make sure that the value in the LENGTH operand matches exactly the amount of data in your record. LENGTH must also be specified when reading variable length records into the WORKING-STORAGE section of the program. Here, the LENGTH operand specifies the largest record that the program will accept. Further, this operand must be defined in WORKING-STORAGE as an S9(4) COMP variable. If we use the same employee description as before but with a slight change, we can derive a variable length processing situation as follows:

```
01   RIDFLD-KEY                    PIC X(9).

01   MASTER-RECORD.
     02   SOCIAL-SECURITY          PIC X(9).
     02   NAME                     PIC X(30).
     02   ADDRESS-LINE-1           PIC X(30).
     02   ADDRESS-LINE-2           PIC X(30).
     02   CITY                     PIC X(20).
```

02	STATE	PIC X(2).
02	ZIP	PIC X(9).
02	NUMBER-OF-WEEKS	PIC S9(4) COMP.
02	WEEKLY-INFO	OCCURS 1 TO 52 TIMES DEPENDING ON NUMBER-OF-WEEKS.
	03 HOURS-WORKED	PIC S9(5)V99 COMP-3.
	03 HOURLY-SALARY	PIC S9(5)V99 COMP-3.
	03 BONUS-HOURS	PIC S9(3)V99 COMP-3.

In the above structure, WEEKLY-INFO is the variable length portion of our record. This part of the record can contain up to fifty-two weeks of information for each employee. Hence, in this application it appears that we're keeping track of an employee's earnings for each week of a year. The number of segments in the record depends on the field NUMBER-OF-WEEKS, which contains a value greater than or equal to 1, less than or equal to 52. This value reflects the number of weeks throughout the year that this employee has worked and is related to the hours, salary, and bonus time accumulated. The record description above is a variable length description.

In addition to defining a RIDFLD-KEY and MASTER-RECORD area, we must define an area to hold the length of our records. Let's add the following definition to the working-storage section of our program.

```
01   LRECL    PIC S9(4) COMP.
```

In order to process variable length records, we must declare such a variable in our program and *it must* be defined as a COMP variable, as shown above.

After we establish our file and our record descriptions, we must also verify that the information for our file is properly defined in the FCT. The EMPFILE must be defined as a variable length record file; otherwise a LENGERR handle condition will arise when we try to process the file.

To read a record from the employee file, we do exactly as we did earlier. We move the key of the record to be read (the employee's social security number) to the field called RIDFLD-KEY. We then issue the following READ statement. This statement is almost the same as the READ issued for fixed-length records.

```
MOVE +704  TO LRECL.
EXEC CICS READ DATASET('EMPFILE') LENGTH(LRECL)
   INTO(MASTER-RECORD) RIDFLD(RIDFLD-KEY)
   END-EXEC.
```

If the read command is successful (the same handle conditions apply as before), the contents of the record will reside in the area called MASTER-RECORD. We can then process the record in the way that we desire.

To read a record for update, we issue the same command, but we must specify the UPDATE operand on our READ statement. Again, this statement has the same effect as in the fixed-length record processing activities.

To update a record and rewrite a record to the file, we must now change our procedure. Before a record can be written to the file, we must compute the length of the record and place this value in the variable called LRECL. Since the MASTER-RECORD description has two parts, we'll compute the record length as such in two sections:

COMPUTE LRECL = 9 + 90 + 20 + 2 + 9 + 2.
COMPUTE LRECL = LRECL + (11 * NUMBER-OF-WEEKS).

The static portion of the employee record is computed first; then, the total length of all variable segments is computed (11 * NUMBER-OF-WEEKS) and is added to the static length to derive the total length of the record to be replaced or added to the file. We're now ready to issue the REWRITE command for this record. Note, you must compute the record length before the I/O is issued or else you'll write a very long record, a very short record, or cause the LENGERR condition to arise.

EXEC CICS REWRITE DATASET('EMPFILE')
    FROM(MASTER-RECORD) LENGTH(LRECL)
    END-EXEC.

To add a new record to the file, you follow much the same procedure. Build the record in the record description area as you normally would in a batch environment. Move the key of the record into your special RIDFLD-KEY area established in the WORKING-STORAGE section of your program. Then, compute the length of the record as we did in the REWRITE example and issue the command below:

EXEC CICS WRITE DATASET('EMPFILE')
    FROM(MASTER-RECORD) RIDFLD(RIDFLD-KEY)
    LENGTH(LRECL) END-EXEC.

To delete a variable length record, you issue the same command that you did for a fixed length record since no data are transferred to or from the file.

ALTERNATE INDEX FILE PROCESSING

Obviously, variable length record processing is not much different from fixed length record processing. Processing VSAM alternate index files under

CICS is not much different from processing any other type of file. Records can be added, deleted, updated, or read from the files as necessary for application processing. Since the commands to perform these operations are like the other commands, I am going to leave their formats to you. However, there are some peculiarities of alternate index file processing that you should be aware of.

An alternate index is another way of accessing data in a primary file. Just like any other file, an alternate index file has an FCT entry, but the entry actually defines a "path" between the alternate index file and the primary data set.

In defining the FCT entry for your AIX, you should specify the proper options. The easiest way to process an AIX is to allow only read or browse access through the AIX to get to the base data set records. If you allow a record to be added to the base data set through the alternate index, your FCT entry definition must specify this type of processing requirement. Further, there must be closer coordination between the AIX and the base cluster because a user accessing the AIX to update, add, or delete records may, in fact, be locking other users out of both the AIX and the base cluster, depending on the keys of the records. This situation could weaken overall performance in your processing environment. Therefore, in an on-line environment, you should restrict the addition, deletion, and updating of base records so that they can only be done through the base FCT entry definition and not through the alternate index.

In AIX processing in which duplicate keys are allowed in the alternate index file, one must plan to handle the DUPKEY condition in program processing. Each time that a record is retrieved from the base data set in which a duplicate key exists in the alternate index, the DUPKEY condition arises. In applications having many duplicate alternate index keys, this condition could interfere with your program design and processing. You may want to ignore the DUPKEY condition, as discussed in Chapter 10.

Another great concern is the specification of buffer sharing when alternate indexes are being used. For all base and alternate index FCT entries, you'll get better performance if you do not allow buffer pooling or buffer sharing for file I/O. In some instances, sharing may *not* even be allowed, but in either case, you should try to avoid it if at all possible. Despite the cost in terms of memory requirements, system performance will be higher if buffer sharing is not allowed. Buffer sharing is not a problem, of course, *unless* the files have alternate indexes defined over them.

The last point to be made about alternate indexes is that they are expensive in terms of performance and response time. Base files having several alternate indexes require a substantial amount of I/O and could degrade the performance of your transactions to unacceptable levels. Designers who can design a flexible and high-performing system that uses alternate index file definitions are highly praised, but they can also be criticized severely if an implementation of an application requiring several alternate indexes causes severe degrading of a system.

PROCESSING FILES GENERICALLY

Under CICS, generic file processing is almost as easy to carry out as standard file operations. Generic file processing is generally used for two types of processing requests: reading records and deleting records. The commands needed here have basically the same operands, except for one additional operand, KEYLENGTH. The KEYLENGTH operand identifies a value (or it could be a data area defined as S9(4) COMP) that specifies the length of the key being supplied. For example, let's suppose that in our employee application we decide to store the records in the employee file in a different format, as shown below:

```
01   RIDFLD-KEY.
     02  RIDSSN              PIC X(9).
     02  RIDMONTH            PIC 99.

01   MASTER-RECORD.
     02  RECORD-KEY.
         03  SSNUM           PIC X(9).
         03  MONTH-OF-YEAR   PIC 99.
     02  HOURS-WORKED        PIC S9(5)V99 COMP-3.
     02  HOURLY-SALARY       PIC S9(5)V99 COMP-3.
     02  BONUS-HOURS         PIC S9(3)V99 COMP-3.
```

If we ignore the rest of the data in the record momentarily and concentrate on the key, we can see that there is one record in the file for every month that the person was employed.

Suppose now that we want to know the first month that the person worked during the year in order to determine the amount of vacation pay that individual is eligible for. In other words, some people didn't work during the first few months of the year owing to illness or some other problem and for these people, there will not be a record in the file for the first few months of the year. A person may not even be on the file because he or she was on sick-leave all year. If we do not know the first month in which the person worked, we will have to read the file for each month's record until we find the first one, or we can use generic file processing to do the same thing.

What we'll do is supply a partial key to the system, namely, the person's social security number. Then when we issue the read request, we'll inform the system that the complete key of the record has not been specified and ask that the first record in the file with a key greater than or equal to this record be returned to the program. However, the option GTEQ in the READ command below can only be replaced with the option EQUAL. Thus, finding records with keys "less than" and so on is not possible under the CICS system, but must be done in the following way:

```
MOVE EMPSSNI  TO RIDSSN.

EXEC CICS READ DATASET('EMPFILE')
   INTO(MASTER-RECORD) RIDFLD(RIDFLD-KEY)
   GENERIC KEYLENGTH(9) GTEQ END-EXEC.
```

Here we are specifying that a partial key be used in the search process; when a record is found that has a key greater than or equal to the key specified in the RIDFLD, the record will be returned to the program and placed in the area called MASTER-RECORD. Incidentally, EMPSSNI is a field on a screen that supports this application.

If this employee did not work the entire year, then there would be no records for this employee in the file. If we issue the command above, the "next" person's record in the file would be returned, instead of the record that we actually wanted. If there were no other employee records in the file with a key greater than or equal to this employee's social security number, the NOTFND condition would arise. Hence, you should issue handle conditions for processing files generically, as you did for nongeneric requests.

Generic file processing is also commonly used for deleting records from a file. Let me warn you, however, that the slightest error here can cause *total* file destruction. Let's assume that in our application above an employee leaves the company and we want to delete all of his or her records from the file. If the employee's social security number comes in from the terminal in a field called EMPSSNI, we can use this field in our deletion process, or we can use the field RIDFLD-KEY, as we have been doing. Here are two examples of what we could do:

```
MOVE EMPSSNI  TO RIDSSN.

EXEC CICS DELETE DATASET('EMPFILE')
   RIDFLD(RIDFLD-KEY) GENERIC
   KEYLENGTH(3) END-EXEC.

-------------------- OR --------------------

EXEC CICS DELETE DATASET('EMPFILE')
   RIDFLD(EMPSSNI) GENERIC
   KEYLENGTH(3) END-EXEC.
```

Did you notice the error in the above code? We probably deleted about 90 percent of our file. Since the KEYLENGTH value was incorrectly typed in by the programmer, if the *first three* digits of an employee's social security number match the three in the field EMPSSNI, that employee will be deleted from the file. Now you can see why a seemingly simple error can be so serious.

In this example we can also obtain from the system the number of records that were deleted, if we happen to want this information. To do this, we have to define a variable in WORKING-STORAGE to hold the returned number. This variable (we'll call it GONE) must be defined as S9(4) COMP. To obtain the number of records deleted, you simply have to code:

```
MOVE EMPSSNI  TO RIDSSN.

EXEC CICS DELETE DATASET('EMPFILE')
    GENERIC KEYLENGTH(9) RIDFLD(RIDFLD-KEY)
    NUMREC(GONE) END-EXEC.
```

-------------------- OR --------------------

```
EXEC CICS DELETE DATASET('EMPFILE')
    GENERIC KEYLENGTH(9) RIDFLD(EMPSSNI)
    NUMREC(GONE) END-EXEC.
```

After the records are deleted, CICS will return to you the number deleted from the file, placing this value in the field called GONE. Obviously generic deletion is a powerful feature of CICS FILE CONTROL and it could be a dangerous one as well if misused intentionally or unintentionally.

BROWSING ON-LINE FILES

Browsing is another useful service of CICS because it allows you to position yourself into a file and to read sequentially from that point on until you decide to terminate the browsing operation. For VSAM files, you can browse forward or backward, if need be.

To begin a browse operation, you must issue a STARTBR (start browse) command, which positions you into the file starting at the record whose key you've identified in the RIDFLD. You can also perform this positioning operation generically by specifying the same information as you did in the generic processing example (except for browsing the file backwards). After the command is completed successfully, the file is now ready to be browsed. Note that no records are actually read from the file until a READNEXT or READPREV command is issued against this data set. If the browse command fails with an ILLOGIC condition, then the browse command was not completed successfully because there weren't any records in the file with the key that you requested.

Careful consideration must be given to the use of browsing in a nonconversational environment since the program ends and reinitiates over and over again. It may therefore be necessary to issue several start-browse commands throughout the life of the user's requests, one or more for each reinitiation of the program.

In most cases for every start browse command that you issue, you should issue an ENDBR (end browse) command to inform the system that you have terminated your browsing. If you need to browse the file from another reference point, then you can issue another start-browse to browse another file, or even the same file, if necessary. On the other hand, if you're going to browse the same file, then you shouldn't issue an end-browse followed by another start-browse; instead, issue a reset-browse (RESETBR) and simply start processing the file again. The reset-browse is more efficient than the end-browse and start-browse combination. Do not issue the ENDBR command if the STARTBR command fails. If you do, yet another handle condition will arise.

Let's suppose that in a given application we want to browse the file to collect data about a particular type of record. Further, let's assume that only a partial key has been supplied but that we want to obtain information on all the records before displaying the results to the terminal. Incidentally, since a partial key has been supplied, we can only browse "forward" through the file. A full key must be specified in order to browse backward in the file. The following logic could be used to implement such a request:

1. Move partial key to our key area.
2. If the ILLOGIC condition arises, then don't do steps 2–7.
3. Issue the start-browse command specifying a generic key and the length of that generic key.
4. If the ENDFILE or NOTFND conditions arise during processing, then go to step 7.
5. Read the "next" record in the file.
6. Repeat as long as there are records to process:
   a. process the record.
   b. Read the "next" record in the file by using to full length of the key.
7. Issue the ENDBR command.
8. Display the information to the terminal.

You'll notice several things about this code. First, the RIDFLD actually undergoes a slight change during processing so that it continually qualifies the "next" record in the file for browsing. Although this record identification field is changed automatically by FILE CONTROL, you must be aware that it will not contain the value originally stored. You can also use this field to terminate your processing when you've advanced through the file to a particular point. Further, many handle conditions will be issued in the event that no more records are found in the file and in the event that there are no records in the file with the qualified key that we supply. Finally, the processing sequence is terminated with the end-browse command and the system is released from the control of our browsing operation. Now that we have specified the logic, let's look at the commands to implement this code.

```
          MOVE PARTIAL-KEY   TO RIDFLD-KEY.
          EXEC CICS HANDLE CONDITION ILLOGIC(STARTBR-FAILED)
            END-EXEC.

          EXEC CICS STARTBR DATASET('EMPFILE') RIDFLD(RIDFLD-KEY)
            GENERIC KEYLENGTH(N1) GTEQ END-EXEC.

          EXEC CICS HANDLE CONDITION NOTFND(STEP7)
            ENDFILE(STEP7) END-EXEC.

          EXEC CICS READNEXT DATASET('EMPFILE')
            INTO(MASTER-RECORD) RIDFLD(RIDFLD-KEY)
            KEYLENGTH(N1) END-EXEC.

AAA:  -----   PROCESS THE RECORD   -----

          —ACCUMULATE THE INFORMATION THAT WE WANT TO

          EXEC CICS READNEXT DATASET('EMPFILE')
            INTO(MASTER-RECORD) RIDFLD(RIDFLD-KEY)
            LENGTH(N2) END-EXEC.

          GO TO AAA.

          EXEC CICS ENDBR DATASET('EMPFILE') END-EXEC.

          MOVE DATA TO THE MAP AREA.

          EXEC CICS SEND MAP ------ END-EXEC.
```

You should notice that two different key length values were specified in the READNEXT commands. This procedure ensures that the records are appropriately qualified, and that we will advance through the file in the proper way and not receive the same record more than once. Finally, keep in mind that your browsing needs may not be the same as described here. In this case, the data were accumulated before a summary of the data was presented to the terminal operator. If you wanted to browse through the file and display the information to the user, you could probably get by with a version of the simple generic read command rather than browsing. Of course, this depends on the structure of the key and the records used in your files.

In our landlord application, the records are keyed by problem number. As pointed out earlier, this design may not be the most flexible one from the tenant's point of view. By using a key consisting of the tenant's name and a sequence number, or, apartment number and a sequence number, the program could be designed to browse the file by name or apartment number in order to collect all records associated with that tenant or apartment. Clearly, modifying the existing system to this alternate design is relatively simple at this point in your study of CICS services.

This chapter has introduced you to the file processing services of CICS command-level programming. There isn't much work involved in file processing from a programmer's point of view, but to a designer the structure of the file is important for maintaining a high performance system. As you have seen, file processing is relatively straightforward in basic file operations, but as we advance toward more elaborate file processing services, program reliability for the on-line user increasingly depends on program control through the use of handle conditions.

This brief overview of the file services offered through CICS command-level programming is probably adequate for most of the on-line applications that you will develop. At least, it has given you an idea of the CICS capabilities and the services that can be performed without using a data base package. In the next chapter, we try to improve the performance of our applications by using locate-mode processing in place of move-mode processing.

THOUGHT QUESTIONS

1. *Suppose that a user wants to view records from a file that meet a certain set of criteria, and thus browsing of the file is required. What would the design of such an application look like in a conversational programming style? In a nonconversational style?*

2. *Suppose that an application does not allow physical deletion of records. How would you implement a logical deletion of records using the CICS file commands described?*

3. *Since you do not have QSAM available for sequential file processing, and if we assume that VSAM-ESDS is also not allowed, how could you mimic a sequential file set-up using a relative, direct, or indexed file structure?*

4. *Prepare a handout for new employees stating how they can have files defined to a CICS system in a manner appropriate to your company organization.*

5. *Would the UNLOCK command ever be needed in a nonconversational programming environment? Describe cases in which it would be necessary and others in which it would be a waste of time.*

6. *In what situations could generic file processing work, as well as browsing an application file?*

12

MANAGING STORAGE FROM THE PROGRAM

The applications that we have developed so far in this text have been implemented with move-mode processing for terminal and file I/O requests. A much more efficient method—locate-mode processing—can be used to perform these functions, but it requires several changes to the layout of the program. In addition, several new concepts have to be understood by the programmer. The trade-offs involved may not be worth the effort required to make the change, especially for rather small applications. For larger applications, however, the outcome may be well worth the investment. As a first step in our discussion of this new method, let's briefly examine the differences between locate-mode and move-mode I/O processing.

Data records on their way from a file to a program, or from a program to a file, can be held in intermediary storage areas called buffers, which are located between the application programs and the files that they process. The movement of data from file to buffer and buffer to program can take considerable time, depending on the size of the records. When records are processed within the WORKING-STORAGE areas of the application program itself, the program is said to be using move-mode processing since the data have to be moved from the buffer into the program before being processed. When this occurs, a copy of the record exists in two places: the buffer and in the program area.

When records are processed in the buffer and are not moved from the buffer to the program areas, the program is said to be using locate-mode I/O processing. Since locate mode saves data from additional movement, the savings in time can be substantial. Hence, it is advantageous to use locate mode as much as possible for both input and output processing in order to reduce this unnecessary movement of data.

We must now learn a few new commands. One of these—GETMAIN—allows us to acquire storage from the CICS dynamic storage area to be used in building screen displays, new records to be added to a file, or tables to aid in program processing. A second command—FREEMAIN—gives that storage back to CICS so that other tasks running in CICS can obtain the storage that they require for their processing. Before we discuss the format of the commands, we should understand how and when they may be used.

When a COBOL program is initiated by CICS, the WORKING-STORAGE section of the program is allocated as a separate entity in the program. As a result, the instructions within the program can be shared by several terminal users, but each terminal user has his or her own WORKING-STORAGE section, as illustrated in the following diagram:

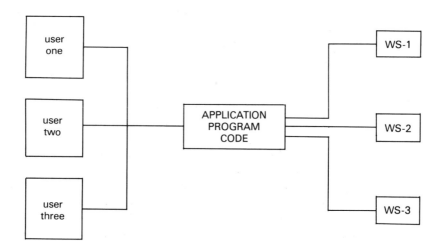

When the instructions of a program are shared by terminal users, fewer copies of the same instruction set need to be in memory at any one time, and thus memory resources are saved.

Terminal users are unaware that they are sharing instructions because each terminal user (task) has its own set of control blocks and WORKING-STORAGE areas; thus, the instructions appear unique to that particular user. Each set of control areas and WORKING-STORAGE sections is attached to the program code by a series of address pointers. The maintenance and resetting of these pointers is handled by TASK CONTROL, EXECUTE INTERFACE, and the COBOL modules needed to support your program's execution. In some instances when a optimizing compiler is used to compile your COBOL program, the programmer must also assist in this process by placing a SERVICE RELOAD command after almost every command-level statement.

ALLOCATING PROGRAM WORK AREAS

When a WORKING-STORAGE area is allocated to a program, it is initialized to LOW-VALUES or binary zeros. Every data item to which you've assigned a VALUE clause then becomes initialized. Following this procedure, your WORKING-STORAGE area is ready to support the execution of the user's request through the instruction set selected by that user via the transaction id that has been entered.

Since our mapset(s) are stored into our WORKING-STORAGE section, they, too, are initialized to binary zeros. It is important to recognize that our maps have been initialized to binary zeros whether we are using move-mode or locate-mode processing.

When a map is received, that information is placed into the symbolic map area overlying the binary zeros initially contained in that symbolic map area. As we manipulate the data in the symbolic map area, we may add more data to that storage area by moving in messages, cursor positions, or attribute bytes. Or, we can remove data from that map by blanking out a field. When we send that map out, the data in the symbolic map area are used to build a terminal data stream that is then sent to the user's terminal. We know that the data stream is built by BMS, but *how* is this done? We know this, too: BMS uses the physical mapset as a set of rules to address the various fields in the symbolic map area.

As BMS finds a field that *should* be in the resulting data stream (a named field), BMS refers to that field in the symbolic map area. If the *first character* of that data field in the symbolic map area is binary zeros (X'00'), then that field is *not* moved to the terminal data stream for eventual transmission to the terminal. Since the WORKING-STORAGE section was initialized to binary zeros, very few fields from our symbolic map area may be merged into the data stream. If the value in a field is spaces, BMS *will* place this information into the terminal data stream to be transmitted to the user's terminal because the character space or blank has a hexadecimal value of '40' and not '00'. This screen is then displayed to the terminal user with the field blanked out.

Now, let's suppose that instead of initializing the WORKING-STORAGE section with binary zeros, CICS initializes it to spaces. If we send out a map now, *all* symbolic map fields will be merged into the terminal data stream, and a large message will be sent to the terminal. This occurs because the first byte of every field is X'40', and not X'00'. As the amount of data sent to a terminal increases, the performance on that communications line decreases because of the increased traffic. Clearly, initializing a mapset area to spaces would not be an efficient method of transmitting data.

If our WORKING-STORAGE section wasn't initialized at all, then we'd inherit whatever garbage was in that location in memory when our program was initiated. This, too, could affect our display screen. Remember, then, that whenever you want to build a map and send it to the terminal, you must initialize that area to binary zeros before you use it, if you are to get the best performance from your on-line application.

File processing involves a different set of considerations. If the following record structure is used in record processing, what should each field be initialized to?

```
01   MASTER-RECORD.
     02   SSN                PIC X(9).
     02   NAME               PIC X(30).
     02   STREET-1           PIC X(30).
     02   STREET-2           PIC X(30).
     02   CITY               PIC X(20).
     02   STATE              PIC X(2).
     02   ZIP                PIC X(9).
     02   HOURS-WORKED       PIC S9(5)V99   COMP-3.
     02   HOURLY-SALARY      PIC S9(5)V99   COMP-3.
     02   BONUS-HOURS        PIC S9(3)V99   COMP-3.
     02   TAX-CODE           PIC S9(4)      COMP.
```

If the record is defined in the WORKING-STORAGE section of the program, then it will be initialized to binary zeros (as were our mapsets) as part of the normal WORKING-STORAGE initialization procedure. If the program does not move data to *every* field in this record description before the record is written to the file, then some fields will contain binary zeros. Clearly, if the HOURS-WORKED, HOURLY-SALARY, or BONUS-HOURS fields are not initialized by the program, then the next time that this record is read from the file, an abend will probably occur (data exception-ASRA) if any of these fields are referenced. This is a common error made by many programmers and it is easily corrected by initializing all fields within a new record.

Even if the WORKING-STORAGE section was initialized to spaces, Xs, or whatever, the same problem would arise. The point to be made is that now that you are able to acquire your own storage through the GETMAIN command, you must initialize your areas properly if your program is to be executed efficiently and reliably.

LOCATE-MODE PROCESSING

By using locate-mode processing, your program will run slightly faster since less movement of data will occur. With your mapsets and files in the WORKING-STORAGE section—as is the case in move-mode processing—data must be moved from buffers to WORKING-STORAGE for input operations, and from WORKING-STORAGE to buffers for output requests. To avoid moving data twice, we'll simply process the data within the buffer work areas.

We can also save a substantial amount of memory by using locate-mode processing. Consider a large mapset with ten maps, all contained within the WORKING-STORAGE section of your program. If only two of the maps are used on a regular basis, then the other eight are simply taking up space. If you want to hold any of your maps, however, CICS must allocate a WORKING-STORAGE section to your program for the duration of your task to hold your complete *mapset;* and the section must be large enough to contain all ten maps and all the other variables defined in your WORKING-STORAGE section. By using locate-mode processing, you can remove *all* maps from the WORKING-STORAGE section of the program, as well as record descriptions. *As the need* for storage arises, we can acquire it, use it, and then discard when we're done with it. Hence, our program becomes highly efficient since it uses *only* the storage resources that it needs to perform a particular function for *each* user.

This almost sounds too good to be true. There has to be some drawback to this processing. There is—it's very dangerous if it's not done correctly.

CICS STORAGE AREAS AND ALLOCATIONS

Many different types of storage areas are managed by the STORAGE CONTROL component of CICS and many different pools of storage can supply storage to applications for various purposes. When an application needs storage, STORAGE CONTROL dips into a pool (if there's any storage left in the pool) and gives that storage to your task.

Most of the storage that you request will come from a pool called the DYNAMIC STORAGE AREA or DSA. All tasks acquire storage from this area, and when a task is finished with the storage, it is returned to the DSA for use by other tasks.

DSA storage can be thought of as a long string of bytes managed by STORAGE CONTROL. When a task requests storage, that string is cut up and the amount requested assigned to that task. To reference that storage area, the system points the program to the storage area by informing the program where that storage is located in memory. In more technical terms, the program addresses or accesses data by its location in the computer. Before this can occur, special variables called "pointers" or "BLL cells" (to be discussed later in this chapter) must be set to the address or memory location of the data. When these variables are assigned values, the program has access to the data. When these variables do not have values, the program does not have access to data areas usable by the program. This is a critical factor in locate-mode processing— a pointer or cell must have an address value that correlates with the storage areas owned by the program. If it has a value that is not within the storage areas assigned to that task, then the variable is said to be in violation of storage usage. Violation of storage area boundaries is a primary cause of system failures during locate-mode processing.

To assist in program development and to help maintain system integrity, CICS and EIP generally keep track of storage areas for your task. To do this, CICS places an 8-byte area on the front and back of the area assigned to your task (see diagram below) and chains this area to your task by "placing" an entry into your TCA (Task Control Area) control block. This 8-byte area, called the STORAGE ACCOUNTING AREA (SAA), is very important in CICS execution.

SAA	THE STORAGE THAT YOU REQUESTED	SAA

Let's suppose that you requested 100 bytes of storage. The example above shows how this area would appear in the DSA; but you *do not* have to be concerned about the presence of the SAAs as far as your program is concerned. Since your storage is part of a larger storage pool, we could illustrate the complete DSA and the storage allocations for each task as follows:

TASK A OWNED	TASK B OWNED	
remaining TASK B	TASK R	
YOUR STORAGE	TASK T	
TASK T		
UNUSED		

Hence, your storage may be sandwiched between storage owned by several other tasks, in this case task R and T. This arrangement does not concern you as long as you've assigned proper values to your pointer or BLL cell variables. (We'll discuss how to do this later.) On the other hand, suppose that task R behaves abnormally and starts referencing areas not owned by task R. Further, assume that the storage area assigned to task R is being used as a table that is being built by task R. If we assume that R is in a loop, task R could fill up the storage area allocated for its table. But R doesn't stop there! Task R can continue to place data into "its" table, and in doing so it gradually destroys the *entire* dynamic storage area, including the storage being used by your task! In other words, CICS does *not* protect one task's storage area from reference or abuse by another task. If your task requests storage from the DSA, then you're on your honor to use that storage properly and not to use (abuse) anyone else's for the execution of your task.

Obviously this is a potentially disastrous situation. If any pair of SAAs were to be destroyed, the *entire* CICS system could abend! The consequences could be serious for an application that is not properly designed or coded. In our approach to locate-mode processing, we are going to make sure that we *allocate and reference* our storage areas properly so that we do not affect the execution of any task, other than our own.

Consider what happened to one company, for example, when it experienced a situation similar to task R above. At random periods throughout the week, CICS storage would be clobbered by a task that would cause a few applications to abend; on a few occassions, all of CICS was brought down. When we looked through the dumps for the problem, we could not find the task that had destroyed the DSA since it had come and gone before the "fun" began. In other words, this phantom transaction would initiate; and, during its course of running, destroy parts of the DSA, and then terminate. CICS would then terminate the task (in a normal manner) and remove any trace of that task from the CICS environment. When CICS started executing other tasks in the system or tried to assign storage through STORAGE CONTROL, tasks or CICS would abend. We hunted for that mystery transaction for months and never found it. For all I know, it may still be "running" today.

PROGRAM STRUCTURE AND BLL CELLS

To use locate-mode processing, you must change the structure of your program by adding a LINKAGE SECTION to it. You usually have to change the mapsets associated with this program as well. You do so by omitting the STORAGE=AUTO operand and replacing it with the BASE=dataname operand. You don't have to do this, but you should be familiar with this mode of processing before you try to retain the STORAGE=AUTO operand.

To support our locate-mode requests we *must* define a series of variables that will be used to point to or address the areas that we are processing. These pointer variables are called cells—specifically, base locator for linkage (BLL) cells.

Each cell will be referenced by a variable name. Each variable name will allow your program to reference *up to* 4096 bytes of storage. For example, a record layout for a file will have its own BLL cell to allow it to refer to the data in that record. Each mapset that we use can have its own BLL cell; thus, all maps within that mapset can be referenced by only one BLL cell variable. Or, if we use the STORAGE=AUTO operand for locate-mode processing, *each map* will have its own BLL cell and we will be able to process two or more maps at the same time. If we're not going to use more than one map at a time, then all maps should share the same BLL cell.

To define BLL cells, you merely need to code an "01" level structure in the LINKAGE SECTION. Let's call our structure DFHBLLDS. Here's what a typical LINKAGE SECTION would look like for an application that has one file description. All maps within this mapset share a common storage area, but redefine that area in different ways. This technique is called *overlay defining* and is a great aid in reducing the amount of storage needed to support program execution.

```
LINKAGE SECTION.

01   DFHBLLDS.
     02   RESERVED-BLL      PIC S9(8) COMP.
     02   MAPBLL            PIC S9(8) COMP.
     02   FILEBLL           PIC S9(8) COMP.

01   MAPOVERLAY            PIC X(1920).
01   COPY LAMSM.

01   MASTER-RECORD.
     02   SSN               PIC X(9).
     02   NAME              PIC X(30).
     02   STREET-1          PIC X(30).
     02   STREET-2          PIC X(30).
     02   CITY              PIC X(20).
     02   STATE             PIC X(2).
     02   ZIP               PIC X(9).
     02   HOURS-WORKED      PIC S9(5)V99   COMP-3.
     02   HOURLY-SALARY     PIC S9(5)V99   COMP-3.
     02   BONUS-HOURS       PIC S9(3)V99   COMP-3.
     02   TAX-CODE          PIC S9(4)      COMP.
```

In this example you see three BLL cells. The first BLL cell *cannot* be used by the application program and so it's simply reserved for CICS usage. The remaining BLL cells correspond to the succeeding "01"-levels that follow the DFHBLLDS definition in the LINKAGE SECTION. Hence, MAPBLL corresponds to the shared storage area for all maps called MAPOVERLAY, and FILEBLL corresponds to the next 01 level in the LINKAGE SECTION, MASTER-RECORD. In other words, there are *three* 01 level definitions in this LINKAGE SECTION: DFHBLLDS, MAPOVERLAY, and MASTER-RECORD. The copy statement for the mapset is not considered a separate 01-level (in this case) since all maps in the mapset refer to the area

MAPOVERLAY. For each 01 entity, you *must* have a BLL cell variable defined within the DFHBLLDS structure. Our three cell variables are RESERVED-BLL, MAPBLL, and FILEBLL. Finally, the order in which the 01 levels are defined *must* match the order of the BLL variables within the BLL structure. If the order does not match, you'll probably destroy some other application running under CICS, or, possibly even the entire CICS system.

Below is an example of an *incorrect* cell-to-01-level relationship. Here the MAPBLL and FILEBLL cells are out of order with respect to the succeeding 01 levels.

```
*******   THIS EXAMPLE CONTAINS ERRORS   *******

LINKAGE SECTION.

01   DFHBLLDS.
     02   RESERVED-BLL      PIC S9(8) COMP.
     02   FILEBLL           PIC S9(8) COMP.
     02   MAPBLL            PIC S9(8) COMP.

01   MAPOVERLAY            PIC X(1920).
01   COPY LAMSM.

01   MASTER-RECORD.
     02   SSN               PIC X(9).
     02   NAME              PIC X(30).
     02   STREET-1          PIC X(30).
     02   STREET-2          PIC X(30).
     02   CITY              PIC X(20).
     02   STATE             PIC X(2).
     02   ZIP               PIC X(9).
     02   HOURS-WORKED      PIC S9(5)V99   COMP-3.
     02   HOURLY-SALARY     PIC S9(5)V99   COMP-3.
     02   BONUS-HOURS       PIC S9(3)V99   COMP-3.
     02   TAX-CODE          PIC S9(4)      COMP.
```

In each of these examples, the DFHMSD statement for our mapset called LAMSM was:

```
LAMSM   DFHMSD   TYPE=DSECT,MODE=INOUT,          X
                 LANG=COBOL,CTRL=FREEKB,         X
                 TIOAPFX=YES,BASE=MAPOVERLAY
```

If you recall, the Landlord Management System mapset had several maps. Assume that there are three maps in this mapset called ADD, DELETE, and MENU. In the example above, only the data for one map can be processed at any one time since all maps share the same area. If you were processing the data on the MENU map and accidentally moved data to a field on the ADD or DELETE map, you'd probably destroy a field or two on the MENU map screen and when you tried to send out that MENU map a MAPFAIL condition or ATAI abend (terminal error) could occur, or the user might see an unidentified data element somewhere on the screen.

If it *is* necessary to process two screens of data at the same time, you could define your screens in WORKING-STORAGE, or you could change your DFHMSD statement and at the same time alter your LINKAGE SECTION to reflect *three separate* map 01 areas instead of the one, shared 01 area, as follows:

```
LAMSM   DFHMSD  TYPE=DSECT,MODE=INOUT,      X
                LANG=COBOL,CTRL=FREEKB,     X
                TIOAPFX=YES,STORAGE=AUTO
```

```
LINKAGE SECTION.
01  DFHBLLDS.
    02   RESERVED-BLL        PIC S9(8) COMP.
    02   ADDMAP-BLL          PIC S9(8) COMP.
    02   DELETEMAP-BLL       PIC S9(8) COMP.
    02   MENUMAP-BLL         PIC S9(8) COMP.
    02   FILEBLL             PIC S9(8) COMP.

01  COPY LAMSM.

01  MASTER-RECORD.
    02   SSN                 PIC X(9).
    02   NAME                PIC X(30).
    02   STREET-1            PIC X(30).
    02   STREET-2            PIC X(30).
    02   CITY                PIC X(20).
    02   STATE               PIC X(2).
    02   ZIP                 PIC X(9).
    02   HOURS-WORKED        PIC S9(5)V99   COMP-3.
    02   HOURLY-SALARY       PIC S9(5)V99   COMP-3.
    02   BONUS-HOURS         PIC S9(3)V99   COMP-3.
    02   TAX-CODE            PIC S9(4)      COMP.
```

Problems arise in file processing just as easily as they do in map processing. One common errror in file processing occurs when the record length exceeds 4096 bytes. Since one BLL cell can only reference *up to* 4096 bytes, only part of our record will be addressable unless we modify our LINKAGE SECTION to accommodate the extra-long records.

Let's assume that our records are 10,000 bytes long! Since each BLL will address up to 4096 bytes, we'll need *three* BLL cells to reference the entire record area. The LINKAGE SECTION for this situation would appear as follows:

```
LINKAGE SECTION.
01  DFHBLLDS.
    02  RESERVED-BLL          PIC S9(8) COMP.
    02  MAPBLL                PIC S9(8) COMP.
    02  FILEBLL1              PIC S9(8) COMP.
    02  FILEBLL2              PIC S9(8) COMP.
    02  FILEBLL3              PIC S9(8) COMP.

01  MAPOVERLAY               PIC X(1920).
01  COPY LAMSM.

01  MASTER-RECORD.
    02  SSN                   PIC X(9).
    02  NAME                  PIC X(30).
    02  STREET-1              PIC X(30).
    02  STREET-2              PIC X(30).
    02  CITY                  PIC X(20).
    02  STATE                 PIC X(2).
    02  ZIP                   PIC X(9).
    02  BIG-FILLER-XXXXXXX    PIC X(9857).
    02  HOURS-WORKED          PIC S9(5)V99  COMP-3.
    02  HOURLY-SALARY         PIC S9(5)V99  COMP-3.
    02  BONUS-HOURS           PIC S9(3)V99  COMP-3.
    02  TAX-CODE              PIC S9(4)     COMP.
```

In the situation above, *it is the responsibility of the programmer* to coordinate the three BLL cells for file operations since only the first BLL for each 01 area is maintained through CICS command-level instructions. This means that if the program issues a read request to retrieve a record from the file, *the program must also* establish addressability for the other BLL cells *before* trying to process the record. This would be done with the following logic:

Read the record from the file and set the first BLL cell

COMPUTE FILEBLL2 = FILEBLL1 + 4096.

COMPUTE FILEBLL3 = FILEBLL2 + 4096.

Here, the record is read and the first 4096 bytes are automatically addressable through the operand in the READ statement. Since the next two lines establish addressability to the rest of the record area, the entire range of the three BLL cells is at least 10,000 bytes. The record can now be processed by the application program.

Now that you understand *how* to use locate-mode processing and BLL cells in your environment, you may still be wondering *when* you need to obtain or release storage areas.

In a nonconversational transaction, you never have to issue a FREEMAIN command to release storage that you are using. CICS will release your resources when your task ends. You can let CICS "clean up" after your transaction rather than issue this command and risk having your task hurt its response time.

In a conversational environment, you should release storage whenever it is no longer needed. However, if your application is designed to iteratively acquire storage, process, and then release that storage, you should probably redesign your application. This design structure has a substantial overhead as you have to issue several requests to CICS for services. Each storage acquisition and release amounts to several thousand machine instructions. This operation could amount to many *seconds* of CPU time, depending on how iterative your system is. Indeed, most of your transaction's response time could be expended in CICS overhead and not in the execution of worthwhile applications.

Storage should be obtained through a GETMAIN command in the following situations: in building a record to be *added* to a file; in sending out a map—*not* one just received—with data in the symbolic map area; or in the construction of a table to be used throughout the application. GETMAIN storage is *not* necessary for passing data between one module and another within an application. (In the next chapter we'll discuss a less expensive way to pass parameters and return codes between application programs.)

You do not need to obtain storage if you are reading a record from a file, reading a record to be updated, deleting a record, browsing a file, expanding or shrinking a variable length record, or sending out a map that was just received. The last may be a case in which the screen has to be sent out with an error message because it was edited when it came into the program and the data were found to be invalid. You do not have to obtain storage before you send out this map since you already have a map storage area that contains your symbolic map data. This area was automatically provided to your task by BMS when you issued your RECEIVE MAP command. If you *do* issue a GETMAIN before you send out this map for user data correction, you'll erase all the fields typed in by the user, who will then have to reenter the entire screen. This method would undoubtedly teach the user to be more careful in entering the data!

Finally, you do not need to obtain storage for a map being sent out with the MAPONLY operand. Since no symbolic area processing has to be done, there's no reason to acquire a storage area for the map when you're not going to use it anyway.

Since we are using a nonconversational programming style, we must include one other important storage area in the LINKAGE SECTION of our programs. If you recall, a definition of a TIOA was required to help us determine whether the input screen was formatted or unformatted and to identify the format being used. It is now time to fit this data structure into the LINKAGE SECTION and describe how it should be used:

```
WORKING-STORAGE SECTION.
01  HEX-00                      PIC X VALUE LOW-VALUES.
01  RIDFLD-KEY                  PIC X(9).
01  TIOALEN                     PIC S9(4) COMP VALUE +1920.

LINKAGE SECTION.
01  DFHBLLDS.
    02  RESERVED-BLL            PIC S9(8) COMP.
    02  TIOABLL                 PIC S9(8) COMP.
    02  MAPBLL                  PIC S9(8) COMP.
    02  FILEBLL                 PIC S9(8) COMP.

01  TIOA-AREA.
    02  FIRST-PART-OF-TIOA      PIC X(20).
    02  UNFORMATTED-PART        REDEFINES
                                FIRST-PART-OF-TIOA.
        03  UNFORMATTED-TRANID  PIC X(4).
        03  FILLER              PIC X(16).
    02  FORMATTED-PART          REDEFINES
                                FIRST-PART-OF-TIOA.
        03  FILLER              PIC X(3).
        03  FORMATTED-TRANID    PIC X(4).
        03  FILLER              PIC X(3).
        03  FORMATTED-MAP-CODE  PIC X.
        03  FILLER              PIC X(9).
    02  REST-OF-THE-TIOA        PIC X(1900).

01  MAPOVERLAY                  PIC X(1920).
01  COPY LAMSM.

01  MASTER-RECORD.
    02  SSN                     PIC X(9).
    02  NAME                    PIC X(30).
    02  STREET-1                PIC X(30).
    02  STREET-2                PIC X(30).
    02  CITY                    PIC X(20).
    02  STATE                   PIC X(2).
    02  ZIP                     PIC X(9).
    02  HOURS-WORKED            PIC S9(5)V99  COMP-3.
    02  HOURLY-SALARY           PIC S9(5)V99  COMP-3.
    02  BONUS-HOURS             PIC S9(3)V99  COMP-3.
    02  TAX-CODE                PIC S9(4)     COMP.
```

```
PROCEDURE DIVISION.
    EXEC CICS RECEIVE SET(TIOABLL) LENGTH(TIOALEN)
    END-EXEC.

IF UNFORMATTED-TRANID = 'LAMS' THEN
    EXEC CICS SEND MAP('MENU') MAPSET('LAMSM')
       ERASE END-EXEC
    EXEC CICS RETURN END-EXEC.

IF FORMATTED-MAP-CODE = 'M' THEN
    EXEC CICS RECEIVE MAP('MENU') MAPSET('LAMSM')
       SET(MAPBLL) FROM(TIOA-AREA)
       LENGTH(TIOALEN) END-EXEC

ELSE
    IF FORMATTED-MAP-CODE = 'A' THEN
       EXEC CICS RECEIVE MAP('ADD') MAPSET('LAMSM')
          SET(MAPBLL) FROM(TIOA-AREA)
          LENGTH(TIOALEN) END-EXEC

    .   .   .
    .   .   .
    .   .   .
```

In the above code, we see that the terminal data are first placed into the area called TIOA-AREA but that this operation is performed in locate mode; in this way we can avoid the transfer of data to the WORKING-STORAGE section of our program. We then reference the fields UNFORMATTED-TRANID and FORMATTED-MAP-CODE as appropriate to the action to be taken, depending on the screen to be processed. This logic and coding are similar to that presented in an earlier chapter, except that we are setting (SET) BLL cell variables rather than moving data into a data area for processing. Also, the variable called TIOALEN defined in the WORKING-STORAGE section of the program can now play a valuable role in applications processing. When the RECEIVE command is issued, TIOALEN will contain the number of bytes of data coming in from the terminal screen. Hence, if the user enters transaction id (4 characters), the value of TIOALEN will be four. The program can check for excess data and void the user's transaction if this type of processing is appropriate.

The last item to note is the definition of the BLL cells and their reference to the 01 levels that follow. Note that each 01-level has its own BLL cell and that the order of the BLL cell variables corresponds to the order of the 01 data structures following DFHBLLDS.

STORAGE MANAGEMENT COMMANDS

Two simple commands are used to obtain or release storage resources for your program: GETMAIN and FREEMAIN. The GETMAIN command requests storage from CICS and must identify the amount of storage desired and the BLL cell to be set to the address of the storage area returned. Additionally, one can specify whether this area should be initialized and what it should be initialized to. For example, suppose that we want to obtain storage to build a record that is to be added to a file. If the record is 143 bytes long and we want the storage area initialized to spaces, we must define a variable in WORKING-STORAGE to hold our initial value, and then issue the GETMAIN command as shown below.

```
01   BLANKS      PIC X VALUE ' '
          .  .  .

          .  .  .

     EXEC CICS GETMAIN SET(FILEBLL)
        LENGTH(143) INITIMG(BLANKS) END-EXEC.

        --- BUILD THE RECORD HERE ---

     EXEC CICS WRITE DATASET('EMPFILE')
        FROM(MASTER-RECORD) RIDFLD(RIDSSN)
        LENGTH(143) END-EXEC.
```

With the command above, the BLL cell variable called FILEBLL will be set to point to our 143-byte storage area that has been initialized to blanks. If there was not enough storage in the DSA to satisfy your request, the NOSTG condition would be raised *if* you issued a HANDLE CONDITION for NOSTG. If you don't issue the NOSTG handle condition command, CICS will delay the continued processing of your task until your storage request has been satisfied. If the delay is long, it could upset the user or cause him to become excited and press the *clear* key, turn off the terminal, or even call you. (We discuss an alternative method in a later section on how to handle such a storage failure.) In almost all cases, however, the NOSTG condition need not be handled; CICS will take care of queuing your storage request and providing storage to your task when it becomes available from another transaction.

After you write the record to the file, you should not free that storage area by using a FREEMAIN command as it will be automatically freed for you by CICS.

If FILEBLL is the BLL cell variable for the 01-level called MASTER-RECORD, then at some point when we've acquired storage and built a record, the user might decide to cancel his or her request and do some other processing.

To release a storage area *that you have obtained* simply free that storage area with a FREEMAIN command. *Do not free the BLL cell variable,* as many programmers try to do. You'd issue the following command to free the area called MASTER-RECORD pointed to by the BLL cell variable, FILEBLL:

EXEC CICS FREEMAIN DATA(MASTER-RECORD) END-EXEC.

When you are processing screens, you can use a GETMAIN command to create a symbolic map area for a screen. Again, a FREEMAIN command is not required because the storage area containing your symbolic map is automatically freed by CICS when you issue your SEND command.

If, for example, we want to send out the menu screen with a message at the bottom of the screen, then we can't use the MAPONLY operand. As a result, we must acquire storage for a symbolic map area, initialize it to binary zeros, move the message into the symbolic map area, and then send out that map. The commands to do this are shown below.

```
01  HEX-00     PIC X VALUE LOW-VALUES.
     .   .
     .   .
     .   .
IF UNFORMATTED-TRANID = 'LAMS' THEN
     EXEC CICS GETMAIN SET(MAPBLL) LENGTH(2000)
        INITIMG(HEX-00) END-EXEC
     MOVE 'SELECT YOUR OPTION AND PRESS ENTER' TO
        MENUMSGO
     MOVE -1 TO CHOICEL
     EXEC CICS SEND MAP('MENUMAP') MAPSET('LAMSM')
        FROM(MENUMAPO) ERASE CURSOR END-EXEC
     EXEC CICS RETURN END-EXEC.
```

Suppose that a request screen has come from a user's terminal and that the request contains the key of a record to be displayed. If we assume that the screen with the key is different from the screen that would display that record's information, the following commands will be required to perform this function:

```
WORKING-STORAGE SECTION.
01  HEX-00            PIC X VALUE LOW-VALUES.
01  RIDFLD-KEY        PIC X(9).
01  TIOALEN           PIC S9(4) COMP VALUE +1920.

LINKAGE SECTION.
01  DFHBLLDS.
     02  RESERVED-BLL    PIC S9(8) COMP.
```

```
      02   TIOABLL                          PIC S9(8) COMP.
      02   MAPBLL                           PIC S9(8) COMP.
      02   FILEBLL                          PIC S9(8) COMP.

  01  TIOA-AREA.
      02   FIRST-PART-OF-TIOA               PIC X(20).
      02   UNFORMATTED-PART                 REDEFINES
                                            FIRST-PART-OF-TIOA.

           03   UNFORMATTED-TRANID          PIC X(4).
           03   FILLER                      PIC X(16).
      02   FORMATTED-PART                   REDEFINES
                                            FIRST-PART-OF-TIOA.

           03   FILLER                      PIC X(3).
           03   FORMATTED-TRANID            PIC X(4).
           03   FILLER                      PIC X(3).
           03   FORMATTED-MAP-CODE          PIC X.
           03   FILLER                      PIC X(9).
      02   REST-OF-THE-TIOA                 PIC X(1900).

  01  MAPOVERLAY                            PIC X(1920).
  01  COPY LAMSM.

  01  MASTER-RECORD.
      02   SSN                              PIC X(9).
      02   NAME                             PIC X(30).
      02   STREET-1                         PIC X(30).
      02   STREET-2                         PIC X(30).
      02   CITY                             PIC X(20).
      02   STATE                            PIC X(2).
      02   ZIP                              PIC X(9).
      02   HOURS-WORKED                     PIC S9(5)V99  COMP-3.
      02   HOURLY-SALARY                    PIC S9(5)V99  COMP-3.
      02   BONUS-HOURS                      PIC S9(3)V99  COMP-3.
      02   TAX-CODE                         PIC S9(4)     COMP.

  PROCEDURE DIVISION.
      .  .
      .  .
      .  .

  EXEC CICS RECEIVE MAP('KEYMAP') MAPSET('LAMSM')
      SET(MAPBLL) FROM(TIOA-AREA) LENGTH(TIOALEN)
      END-EXEC.

  MOVE KEYSSNI   TO RIDFLD-KEY.

  MOVE CICS HANDLE CONDITION NOTFND(A) END-EXEC.
```

```
    EXEC CICS READ DATASET('EMPFILE') SET(FILEBLL)
        RIDFLD(RIDFLD-KEY) END-EXEC.

    EXEC CICS GETMAIN SET(MAPBLL) LENGTH(2000)
        INITIMG(HEX-00) END-EXEC.

    ---- MOVE DATA FROM RECORD TO THE DISPLAY SCREEN

    EXEC CICS SEND MAP('DISPLAY') MAPSET('LAMSM')
        FROM(DISPLAYO) ERASE CURSOR END-EXEC.

    EXEC CICS RETURN END-EXEC.

A.

    MOVE 'RECORD NOT FOUND IN THE FILE' TO KEYMSGO.
    MOVE -1 TO KEYSSNL.
    EXEC CICS SEND MAP('KEYMAP') MAPSET('LAMSM')
        FROM(KEYMAPO) ERASE CURSOR END-EXEC.
    EXEC CICS RETURN END-EXEC.
```

In the example above, notice that if a NOTFND condition arises, the GETMAIN to acquire new map storage is not performed, and the paragraph called A is allowed to send out the key screen with a message telling the user that the record was not found in the file. Also notice how the BLL cells are set when storage is obtained and when a record is read, but no FREEMAIN commands are coded in this nonconversational program.

PURPOSELY STALLING YOUR TASK EXECUTION

In some instances, a resource that your program needs may not be available because it is being used by another task. When this occurs, CICS may simply stop the execution of your task until that resource becomes available, and place your task into a queue. If the queue is long, it may be a while before the terminal operator receives a response from your transaction. In some cases, especially if the user is accustomed to a more or less immediate response, the user may become impatient and press the *clear* key or PF key, turn the terminal off, or even call you to find out if he did something wrong or if the system went down.

To avoid these problems, *you* can be "friendly" to the user and inform him that there has been a delay and that you'll satisfy his request as soon as you can. Such a delay could occur if you are trying to obtain a piece of storage for building a record.

What we're going to do now is describe a process by which you can actually wait for a resource to become available as well as tell the user that you know he's there and that you're still working on his request.

Execution of a task within CICS can be temporarily halted for any length of time that you desire. You can halt the transaction for twenty-four hours if you want to, but this would not be a good idea from a user's point of view; also, the terminal would be tied up for that amount of time. On the other hand, we might want to take a two-second break from processing and then retry a request that failed just a short time ago. We hope that when we try our request again it will be completed because the task that was holding that resource has now released it to other users.

Let's suppose that we need some storage to build a record but that when we issue the GETMAIN request, there is not enough storage to satisfy our request. Normally CICS would suspend the execution of our task, place our task in a storage queue, and when the needed storage became available, start our task executing again. If other tasks running in the system don't release enough storage for quite some time, our task waits and waits and waits—and so does the user. Instead of blindly waiting, we'll keep the user informed of the fact that we're still working on the problem and ask him to be patient. However, if after an extended period of waiting the request is still not satisfied, we will have to tell the user that we can't finish his or her request because the system is bogged down. The logic might go something like this:

1. Set counter to 0.
2. If the GETMAIN fails with NOSTG then go to step 7.
3. Issue GETMAIN request.
4. Process record normally.
5. Send back positive response.
6. End the task.
7. Counter = counter + 1.
8. If counter = 10, then
   a. Tell user that the system is bogged down and to try again tomorrow.
   b. End the task.
9. Tell user that the system is busy and that there will be a two-second delay.
10. Delay processing two seconds.
11. Go to step 2.

There are two important points about the code. First, if you don't code a counter, as we did above, make sure that everything else is all right; otherwise you may be looping forever. Secondly, to the user, you will have to use a screen display. Screens can be sent from the program to the terminal at any time, as many times as you'd like, but you can't receive the data unless the user presses an AID key. Hence, the data that the user typed in—which we are going to use to build the record—simply stays in memory as we loop through our GETMAIN request code. Make sure that you don't free this storage or end your task in the delay routine if you code such a routine into your program.

To delay the processing of your program, you simply code the DELAY command, as shown below. The INTERVAL operand is in the form HHMMSS, where HH is hours, MM is minutes and SS is the seconds to be delayed. To delay your task by two seconds, you would specify 000002 in this parameter, as follows:

EXEC CICS DELAY INTERVAL(000002) END-EXEC.

This command is obviously simple but if coded incorrectly could cause you or the user to wait a long time for a transaction response. This command may also entice some of you to play games with your transactions rather than perform simple, straightforward coding. Such endeavors are no problem as long as they do not affect the performance of other, more important transactions running in the system at the same time.

In this chapter we have covered a substantial amount of processing and many new concepts in the operation of CICS. The application program can manage storage effectively and efficiently by using CICS resources, but, as you've seen, it can also cause problems if not used properly. With the background that you now have about CICS processing and addressing storage areas, you can turn your attention to some rather special processing techniques such as addressing CICS control areas and passing parameters between application programs. These techniques are not much different from those used in obtaining and freeing storage for your task, but, again, if they are used incorrectly, the results can be disastrous. The next chapter is especially important for users who want to improve the performance of their transactions as much as possible by using the various techniques of this chapter.

THOUGHT QUESTIONS

1. *The SERVICE RELOAD command must be used whenever your COBOL code is optimized. What do you think that this command does for the execution of your program? What do you think happens if you omit or forget to issue this command if you optimize your code?*

2. *Apart from the file and mapping operations used to obtain or release storage, what other applications for storage management commands can you see in your environment?*

3. *What criteria should you use in analyzing a program's resource needs to determine whether the program* must *use locate-mode processing to complete its functions?*

4. *Suppose that your environment has a phantom transaction, as I've described. What do you think you'd have to do to determine which application caused a storage problem?*

5. *What role should locate-mode processing play in conversational implementation versus the nonconversational style that we've explored here? Would there be more or less reason to use locate mode in a conversational environment over a nonconversational environment?*

13

PROGRAM-TO-PROGRAM COMMUNICATIONS

Most of the system structures in this text contain elements called modules that communicate with each other. Data are transferred between these modules to request a service and to return either data or an indicator describing how well that activity was completed. Many entities—for example, a paragraph in a COBOL program, or a *truly* external program or subroutine—can be considered modules. Even EIP and CICS are considered to be modules by our programs, and our programs are modules to them. This text, however, has dealt exclusively with paragraph modules and not with external programs.

Calling, linking, or transferring control to a module with or without parameters is a straightforward procedure in command-level CICS. However, each module that you want to invoke must be defined as an entry in the PPT and *should not* be link-edited with any other module. In a batch environment, we compile and link each module in a system separately and then composite-link all of the modules to form our execution package. This *is not* the approach taken here. Each module should be defined as its own entity in on-line processing and all communications with that module should be transmitted through a command-level statement.

Invoking other programs in CICS is a costly endeavor as well. Each invocation may take two to three thousand machine instructions! In this era of fast computers, that may not seem excessive, but as our system development strives for more modular systems, you may want to consider what you're doing to the overall performance of your computer. If your system is designed in a highly modular fashion, you could be wasting considerable computer resources through

269

your program-to-program communications. Calling modules should be kept to a minimum, possibly no more than ten to twenty calls per initiation. Consider the experience of one company, in which a rather large system performed upwards of 600 program calls per transaction enter, in some cases more than 2000! After careful analysis, it was determined that more than 70 percent of the computer time used by that transaction was attributable to program-to-program communications. Average response time was upwards of 25 seconds on a very fast computer. Obviously, this is not the level of module calling that you want to strive for.

COMMUNICATING WITH "YOURSELF"

A program talks not only to other programs, but many times must also talk to itself. For example, in our previous programming examples, the transaction id was placed in the upper left corner of the screen on our maps so that our program would be initiated the next time that the user pressed the *enter* key. This field helped us determine whether the screen was formatted or unformatted. Although we pointed out that this is a cumbersome method and less efficient than an alternative method that is available, it works, and no system intervention is required to carry this out.

This is a case in which a program communicated with itself in order to let the program (since it was nonconversational) remember what it was doing the last time it was executed. You'll recall that we also placed control characters somewhere on the screen to help us determine which map was displayed at the terminal at any given point and which function we were performing.

These fields are called hidden fields and are an effective way for a program to supply itself with data, whether they be transaction ids, control characters, or record keys. The user is not aware that the program needs this information and, in some cases, the data may not even be visible to the user. If this method does not appeal to you or if your communication lines can't handle this unnecessary data transfer, then there are many other ways to accomplish the same thing.

USING COMMAREAS IN PROGRAM EXECUTION

Under CICS command-level programming, a program can establish a communication area in which data can be stored for later reference by the program. Since there are no restrictions on what can be placed into this area, many command-level users are turning to COMMAREAS for data storage rather than storing information in hidden fields on the screens. There are several advantages in doing so. First, the transaction id does *not* have to be placed on each screen in your mapset; instead, the program will communicate to CICS information about the transaction id that is to be used when the next initiation occurs from that user's terminal. Your screens can then be used in other applications, if necessary. Secondly, you don't have to place control characters on the maps either; in fact, no hidden fields are necessary at all to help you determine which screen is being used or what function you are performing. Finally, this technique can help you document the program since you *will know* whether a program is to be reinitiated after a SEND command is issued, or whether it has actually finished its tasks.

To use a COMMAREA, the programmer must define two 01-level structures that look exactly the same, one in the WORKING-STORAGE section of the program, and the other in the LINKAGE-SECTION of the program. These structures should represent the information that is to be carried from session to session, or, if you want to think of it in a nonconversational programming style, from initiation to initiation. In our earlier examples, the only information that we needed to carry from session to session was a single character that aided our program in determining which map was on the screen, and a character to help us determine the function being performed. Hence, the structure that we might use for this purpose may look like this:

```
01   REMEMBER-LIST.
     02   SCREEN-CODE     PIC X.
     02   FUNCTION-CODE   PIC X.
```

Although simple, this structure serves the purpose of communicating the necessary information to the program. In other words, immediately before the program sends out a screen, it will place a character code into these two fields. When the program ends, it will request that *CICS* remember these codes for the program. When the user initiates the program again, CICS will make these codes available, and the program can test them and determine what is to be done.

When the program is initiated for the *first* time, the program cannot check the codes in these fields because there aren't any codes for CICS to remember. Hence, the program must make a precode-check to see if a set of codes was remembered by CICS. This is easily done by testing a value in the execute interface block, as follows:

```
IF EIBCALEN = 0 THEN
   ---  SEND OUT THE "FIRST SCREEN"
   ---  SET SCREEN-CODE TO "FIRST TIME"
   ---  SET FUNCTION-CODE TO "?"
   ---  END THE TASK
```

The EIBCALEN field (communication area length) contains a value of zero if no set of fields is remembered by CICS; and the value is greater than zero if CICS remembers something for the program.

Finally, another structure similar to our REMEMBER-LIST *must* be defined in the LINKAGE-SECTION of our program. If locate-mode processing is being used, *this structure must be defined before* the BLL cell structure. The structure in the LINKAGE-SECTION *must* be called DFHCOMMAREA. Hence, to completely define a structure that the program can use to communicate with itself, we have to design the program as follows:

```
WORKING-STORAGE SECTION.
01  REMEMBER-LIST.
        02  SCREEN-CODE          PIC X.
        02  FUNCTION-CODE        PIC X.

LINKAGE SECTION.
01  DFHCOMMAREA.
        02  COMM-SCREEN-CODE     PIC X.
        02  COMM-FUNCTION-CODE   PIC X.

01  DFHBLLDS.
        .    .    .
```

The critical factor here is that the structure REMEMBER-LIST and DFHCOMMAREA must be identical; otherwise you'll not be able to reference the data in the format that you desire. Clearly, other information can be placed into these structures to aid the program in its communications. A record key could be stored in this area to be carried from screen to screen. If a user must enter a password or code word to perform a certain function, this, too, can be carried from function to function so that the user doesn't have to enter the code word repeatedly. If a large record is to be built from several input screens of information, this record can be built in this COMMAREA. As each screen of data comes into the program, the program constructs the record in the COMMAREA. After the last screen is processed, the program builds a copy of the record in WORKING-STORAGE, or, if locate-mode I/O is to be used, in the LINKAGE-SECTION, and then writes the record out to disk. Since the COMMAREA storage is in memory, optimal performance is obtained during processing; thus an external file is not needed to retain information from screen to screen or invocation to invocation.

To use this communications area in your program, you must change the form of your RETURN statement. In the RETURN statement you will request—through EIP—that your data be remembered from session to session. You must also inform CICS which transaction is to be invoked the next time the user presses an initiator key on the terminal. This is done by informing CICS which transaction id to be used on the next enter. In other words, when you RETURN from your program, you tell CICS the data that you want remembered and you give CICS a transaction id to remember. When the user presses an AID key, *that* transaction id will be used in transaction initiation, even if a transaction id is stored in the upper left of the screen! CICS remembers both the data that you wanted to remember and the transaction id to be associated with the next execution. In this way, your program or another application program could be given control, depending on the transaction id value that you return with.

In the design component of this text, we devoted a substantial amount of time to this discussion, especially when multiple transaction ids were used to support an application. Let me refer you back to that discussion and to the pseudocode presented so that you can fully understand how other applications are initiated through this method.

If all the above information is combined, a typical program that uses the COMMAREA for communicating with itself will look like the one shown below. Let's assume that it was first initiated with the transaction id of LAMS.

```
WORKING-STORAGE SECTION.
01   REMEMBER-LIST.
     02   SCREEN-CODE          PIC X.
     02   FUNCTION-CODE        PIC X.

LINKAGE SECTION.
01   DFHCOMMAREA.
     02   COMM-SCREEN-CODE     PIC X.
     02   COMM-FUNCTION-CODE   PIC X.

01   DFHBLLDS.
       .   .   .
       .   .   .
       .   .   .

PROCEDURE DIVISION.
   IF EIBCALEN = 0 THEN
      EXEC CICS SEND MAP('MENU') MAPSET('LAMSM')
         ERASE MAPONLY END-EXEC
      MOVE 'M'    TO SCREEN-CODE
      MOVE 'M'    TO FUNCTION-CODE
      EXEC CICS RETURN COMMAREA(REMEMBER-LIST)
         LENGTH(2) TRANSID('LAMS') END-EXEC.

   MOVE COMM-SCREEN-CODE   TO SCREEN-CODE.
   MOVE COMM-FUNCTION-CODE   TO FUNCTION-CODE.

   IF SCREEN-CODE = 'M' THEN
      EXEC CICS RECEIVE MAP('MENU')
         MAPSET('LAMSM') SET(MAPBLL) END-EXEC
      PERFORM PROCESS-MENU-MAP-DATA
   ELSE
      IF SCREEN-CODE = 'D' THEN
```

EXEC CICS RECEIVE MAP('MAINMAP')
MAPSET('LAMSM') SET(MAPBLL) END-EXEC
PERFORM PROCESS-MAIN-MAP-DATA
　　.　.　.
　　.　.　.
　　.　.　.

In the code above, EIBCALEN is tested first to make sure that a COMMAREA has been passed from session to session. If it has not, then the user is invoking this application program for the first time and there is no map on the user's screen. As a result, the system menu (or first screen for your application) should be sent out. At this time, the program places values into the REMEMBER-LIST so that the next time that the program is initiated, the program will know that the MENU screen is the screen that is to be processed (screen code value of M) and that the function being performed is menu processing.

In the RETURN statement, the REMEMBER-LIST area is identified to CICS as the data area containing the information to be remembered; the length of this data area is set at two-bytes long. These parameters must be coded in order to use COMMAREA in your processing. Finally, the TRANSID option is coded (and must be) so that CICS knows which transaction id is to be associated with initiation on the *next* user's enter. In this case, since the same transaction id as the one that caused initiation in the first place is being specified in this option, this same program will be given control. Hence, this processing has the same effect as placing the transaction id on each screen in the mapset with the characteristic of FSET.

You should also have noticed that the processing of TIOA-AREA has been removed from this program. Since the COMMAREA helps us determine which screen is to be processed, we *do not* need to receive the data into TIOA-AREA in order to test for formatting and the code values. Instead, we *know* what screen is to be processed and we can immediately RECEIVE that MAP rather than issue two RECEIVE commands, as was formerly required. This, of course, saves processing time as less interaction with BMS will be required in this processing situation.

Despite its apparent simplicity, this program does have a bug in it. The program will abend if the user presses any key on the keyboard other than the *enter* key. As shown, CICS will initiate this program no matter what key has been pressed as a result of using TRANSID. Since you have no choice here in whether or not to specify the TRANSID option, something must be done. You'll recall from our previous examples for nonconversational programs that when the user pressed the *clear* key, the program was *not* initiated by CICS; instead, the screen was simply cleared by the terminal. In this case, whenever the user presses the *enter* key, *clear* keys, PF keys, or PA keys, or uses the light pen, our program *will* be initiated. This is about the only drawback of COMMAREA in program processing. With this in mind, we'll have to issue the appropriate HANDLE conditions or perform the appropriate processing to take care of the situation in which the user presses a key other than *enter.* Here are two ways of handling this situation:

Version 1

```
WORKING-STORAGE SECTION.
01  REMEMBER-LIST.
    02  SCREEN-CODE           PIC X.
    02  FUNCTION-CODE         PIC X.

01  NO-SCREEN-DATA            PIC X VALUE ' '.

01  COPY DFHAID.

LINKAGE SECTION.
01  DFHCOMMAREA.
    02  COMM-SCREEN-CODE      PIC X.
    02  COMM-FUNCTION-CODE    PIC X.

01  DFHBLLDS.
    .  .  .
    .  .  .

PROCEDURE DIVISION.
  IF EIBAID NOT = DFHENTER THEN
     EXEC CICS SEND FROM(NO-SCREEN-DATA)
        LENGTH(0) ERASE END-EXEC
     EXEC CICS RETURN END-EXEC.

  IF EIBCALEN = 0 THEN
     EXEC CICS SEND MAP('MENU') MAPSET('LAMSM')
        ERASE MAPONLY END-EXEC
     MOVE 'M'    TO SCREEN-CODE
     MOVE 'M'    TO FUNCTION-CODE
     EXEC CICS RETURN COMMAREA(REMEMBER-LIST)
        LENGTH(2) TRANSID('LAMS') END-EXEC.

  MOVE COMM-SCREEN-CODE     TO SCREEN-CODE.
  MOVE COMM-FUNCTION-CODE   TO FUNCTION-CODE.

  IF SCREEN-CODE = 'M' THEN
     EXEC CICS RECEIVE MAP('MENU')
        MAPSET('LAMSM') SET(MAPBLL) END-EXEC
     PERFORM PROCESS-MENU-MAP-DATA
  ELSE
```

```
            IF SCREEN-CODE = 'D' THEN
               EXEC CICS RECEIVE MAP('MAINMAP')
                 MAPSET('LAMSM') SET(MAPBLL) END-EXEC
               PERFORM PROCESS-MAIN-MAP-DATA
            .   .   .
            .   .   .
```

Version 2

```
WORKING-STORAGE SECTION.
01   REMEMBER-LIST.
     02   SCREEN-CODE          PIC X.
     02   FUNCTION-CODE        PIC X.

01   NO-SCREEN-DATA            PIC X VALUE ' '

LINKAGE SECTION.
01   DFHCOMMAREA.
     02   COMM-SCREEN-CODE     PIC X.
     02   COMM-FUNCTION-CODE   PIC X.

01   DFHBLLDS.
     .   .   .
     .   .   .

PROCEDURE DIVISION.
   EXEC CICS HANDLE CONDITION
      ANYKEY(NOT-THE-ENTER-KEY) END-EXEC.

   IF EIBCALEN = 0 THEN
      EXEC CICS SEND MAP('MENU') MAPSET('LAMSM')
         ERASE MAPONLY END-EXEC
      MOVE 'M'    TO SCREEN-CODE
      MOVE 'M'    TO FUNCTION-CODE
      EXEC CICS RETURN COMMAREA(REMEMBER-LIST)
         LENGTH(2) TRANSID('LAMS') END-EXEC.

   MOVE COMM-SCREEN-CODE      TO SCREEN-CODE.
   MOVE COMM-FUNCTION-CODE    TO FUNCTION-CODE.

   IF SCREEN-CODE = 'M' THEN
      EXEC CICS RECEIVE MAP('MENU')
         MAPSET('LAMSM') SET(MAPBLL) END-EXEC
      PERFORM PROCESS-MENU-MAP-DATA
   ELSE
      IF SCREEN-CODE = 'D' THEN
         EXEC CICS RECEIVE MAP('MAINMAP')
```

```
    MAPSET('LAMSM') SET(MAPBLL) END-EXEC
    PERFORM PROCESS-MAIN-MAP-DATA
.   .   .

.   .   .

NOT-THE-ENTER-KEY.
    EXEC CICS SEND FROM(NO-SCREEN-DATA)
        LENGTH(0) ERASE END-EXEC.
    EXEC CICS RETURN END-EXEC.
```

When it was determined that the *enter* key was not pressed, the screen was simply blanked out in both examples by writing out a data area that has a length of zero. No map was sent at this time and the RETURN statement did not have the TRANID or COMMAREA options specified on it because we *really wanted* to *end* this transaction's processing. Hence, when this data stream is sent to the terminal (actually no data are sent other than terminal control characters), the screen is erased and ready for the user's next request. No automatic return to the program will occur in the above situations.

Clearly, version one does not use the HANDLE command to test the pressing of the keys, but instead uses a single IF-THEN-ELSE test. Depending on your preference, either version will work.

Hidden fields and COMMAREAS are not the only channels that a program uses to pass information to itself. Two others are commonly used as well. Records can be stored into a data set that can later be retrieved, analyzed, updated, or deleted, or information can be placed into a special area (similar to COMMAREA) so that the next time that the program is initiated, this area can be interrogated for instructions.

TEMPORARY STORAGE PROCESSING

This first alternative uses a facility of CICS called temporary storage processing, which involves the creation, writing, reading, updating, and deletion of records into a file. This file can be defined in two ways by the staff that installs CICS, and the file can reside totally in memory or on disk. If the file resides in memory, data can be accessed faster and more efficiently than by the disk storage technique. If CICS storage is limited, however, the disk option may be more desirable.

In general, you do not want to use temporary storage if COMMAREAs could serve you just as well. Temporary storage records not only require more overhead, but they involve learning many more commands and coordinating those commands through handle conditions. On the other hand, temporary storage records can be used to retain data throughout a complete session or from transaction to transaction at a particular user's terminal. COMMAREAs could not allow this since the COMMAREA is eventually destroyed when a user presses any key other than *enter* (in our example). In general, COMMAREAs are related to a specific application and are not carried between applications. Hence, if your needs require this, temporary storage may be your answer.

An application generally needs to retain only one record in a temporary storage file, although as many records as desired can be retained if necessary. Further, each record in this file has an associated key that must be coordinated between the various applications wanting to use that file. System designers and programmers may want to coordinate the keys to be used for temporary storage records; some have suggested using a combination of predefined prefix and the current date for a key, unless, of course, your transaction could run from one day into the next. Another possibility is to use the terminal id (from the EIBTRMID field in the execute interface block) for the key of the record. Any combination of fields can be used for a temporary storage key as long as the length of the key is less than or equal to 8 bytes.

To use the temporary storage facility, let's suppose that the key for our application's temporary storage record will be "LAMSXXXX" so that we fill the 8 bytes. If we want to store the screen code in a temporary storage record, we can issue the following sequence of commands:

```
WORKING-STORAGE SECTION.
01   REMEMBER-LIST.
     02   SCREEN-CODE          PIC X.
     02   FUNCTION-CODE        PIC X.

01   TEMP-STORAGE-KEY          PIC X(8) VALUE 'LAMSXXXX'.

PROCEDURE DIVISION.
     .  .  .
     .  .  .
     .  .  .

     MOVE 'M' TO SCREEN CODE, FUNCTION-CODE.

     EXEC CICS WRITEQ TS FROM(REMEMBER-LIST)
          QUEUE(TEMP-STORAGE-KEY) LENGTH(2) END-EXEC.
```

This sequence places a record into the temporary storage file (also called a queue) for later referencing by the program. Again, much more data can be placed into this record than the amount shown here. As stated earlier, we could store data from several screens in this record, and thus could gradually build a record to be added to a file, or we could carry a code word or record key along with program processing so that the user wouldn't have to enter the same information repeatedly.

Additionally, we could revise the program code above for locate-mode processing by first performing a GETMAIN command for REMEMBER-LIST storage, moving in the various codes, and then issuing the WRITEQ command. Either implementation will work for entering data in a temporary storage file. We should also issue a handle condition before this command is issued in case the file is full (NOSPACE) or in case the queue key that we have specified has a matching record in the temporary storage file (DUPREC).

To read a record from the queue, you must issue a READQ command that is similar to the READ command discussed in earlier chapters. However, since the key of the record is not identified through a RIDFLD option, as it was for standard application file accesses, we must code the QUEUE operand in place of the RIDFLD operand. For example:

```
EXEC CICS READQ TS QUEUE(TEMP-STORAGE-KEY)
   INTO(REMEMBER-LIST) END-EXEC.
```

Again, this command could be modified to work for locate-mode processing by simply changing the INTO operand to a SET operand and adding the proper descriptions to the LINKAGE-SECTION of your program.

You can update a temporary storage record by issuing a READQ on that record, modifying it, and then issuing a rewrite command, as we did in the previous cases. However, the rewrite command has a different form here than in the application processing examples used earlier in the text. In our example, the following code would read, update, and rewrite the temporary storage record for the LAMS application:

```
EXEC CICS HANDLE CONDITION
   QIDERR(TEMP-STORAGE-RECORD-NOT-FOUND) END-EXEC.

EXEC CICS READQ TS QUEUE(TEMP-STORAGE-KEY)
   INTO(REMEMBER-LIST) END-EXEC.

MOVE 'D' TO SCREEN-CODE.
MOVE 'A' TO FUNCTION-CODE.

EXEC CICS WRITEQ TS QUEUE(TEMP-STORAGE-KEY)
   FROM(REMEMBER-LIST) LENGTH(2) REWRITE END-EXEC.
```

Several points should be made about the above code. First, a handle condition has been issued in the event that the queue record that we want to process is not in the file. If this condition should arise, it would mean that there was no queue record in the file and that it was the first time that this program was executed. This situation is comparable to the unformatted-formatted screen decision or the EIBCALEN decision made in other program reinitiation situations. You should also notice that the result of the WRITEQ command is much like adding a record to the file. The only difference is in the operand REWRITE, which tells CICS to replace the contents of the existing record with the current contents of the REMEMBER-LIST. Again, the QUEUE identifier and the LENGTH of the data area must be specified for this WRITEQ operation.

The last command for temporary storage processing allows the program to DELETE records from the file. The command to do this is simple and similar to the standard file delete command discussed earlier. Again, the QIDERR condition should be tested in the event that the record to be deleted is not found in the temporary storage file.

```
EXEC CICS DELETEQ TS
    QUEUE(TEMP-STORAGE-KEY) END-EXEC.
```

TERMINAL CONTROL TABLE PROCESSING

Still another channel for program-to-itself communications is a special area within the terminal control table (TCT). For every terminal defined in the TCT, there is a work area associated with that definition. This area can be used by programs to communicate information from a program to itself, or from a program to another program within the same or different transaction, as long as they're invoked from the same terminal. Since this area is in memory, it offers fast processing, versus the file I/O drawbacks that may be present for temporary storage processing. However, you should check with your systems programmer or CICS systems programmer before using this area because it may already be in use, retaining information about the work that you are doing at your terminal. Also, you'll need to contact these staff members to determine the length of this area. If you blindly use this area to store 100 bytes of data and the area is only capable of handling 50 bytes of data, again you could be destroying parts of another application, or even components of CICS. (The ASSIGN command can also aid you in determining the amount of area available.)

The TCT user area (TCTUA) *cannot* be used outside of locate-mode processing since this area is accessible only through a SET command. Let's suppose that in our application, we want to retain the SCREEN-CODE field, as we have been doing (dropping the FUNCTION-CODE from our examples just for variety). To define the structure to be used within the LINKAGE-SECTION of our program, we'd code the following:

```
LINKAGE SECTION.
    .  .  .

    .  .  .

    .  .  .

01  DFHBLLDS.
    02  RESERVED-BLL    PIC S9(8) COMP.
    02  TCTBLL          PIC S9(8) COMP.
```

```
           .  .  .
         .  .  .
   01   REMEMBER-LIST.
        02   SCREEN-CODE   PIC X.
```

Here, REMEMBER-LIST is again used to hold the information necessary to keep our task informed about what to do next. Associated with REMEMBER-LIST is a BLL cell variable, as required for locate-mode processing. In this case, our BLL cell variable is called TCTBLL.

To access the TCT user area (in order to determine if anything exists in that area, and, if so, what the value is), we must learn a new command-level command. This command will return the address of the TCT user area and set the variable TCTBLL. After setting, we can refer to the REMEMBER-LIST area to determine the value of SCREEN-CODE. This is done as follows:

```
   LINKAGE SECTION.
        .   .   .
        .   .   .
        .   .   .

   01   DFHBLLDS.
        02   RESERVED-BLL   PIC S9(8) COMP.
        02   TCTBLL         PIC S9(8) COMP.
              .   .   .
              .   .   .
   01   REMEMBER-LIST.
        02   SCREEN-CODE   PIC X.

   PROCEDURE DIVISION.

        EXEC CICS ADDRESS TCTUA(TCTBLL) END-EXEC.

        IF SCREEN-CODE = LOW-VALUES THEN
           MOVE 'M' TO SCREEN-CODE
           EXEC CICS SEND MAP('MENU') MAPSET('LAMS')
              MAPONLY ERASE END-EXEC
           EXEC CICS RETURN TRANSID('LAMS') END-EXEC.
```

Again, the same decision structure is used to determine if any value is in the user area or if this marks the first time through the program. Since the command required to perform this function is quick and easy, you may be inclined to use it immediately. However, let me emphasize again that you *must* first check with your system staffs to determine if that area is already in use or if there are any restrictions on your use of that area, and to establish its size.

More commonly, the ADDRESS command is used in sequence with the ASSIGN command to verify that sufficient work area exists, and if so, address the desired area. The following code illustrates the use of the ASSIGN and ADDRESS command sequence.

```
WORKING-STORAGE SECTION.
01  TCTUA-LENGTH            PIC S9(4) COMP.
01  TCTUA-AMOUNT-NEEDED     PIC S9(4) COMP VALUE +???

LINKAGE SECTION.
    .  .  .
    .  .  .
    .  .  .

01  DFHBLLDS.
    02  RESERVED-BLL        PIC S9(8) COMP.
    02  TCTBLL             PIC S9(8) COMP.
        .  .  .
        .  .  .
01  REMEMBER-LIST.
    02  SCREEN-CODE         PIC X.
PROCEDURE DIVISION.
    EXEC CICS ASSIGN TCTUA(TCTUA-LENGTH) END-EXEC.
    IF TCTUA-LENGTH NOT < TCTUA-AMOUNT-NEEDED THEN
        EXEC CICS ADDRESS TCTUA(TCTBLL) END-EXEC
    ELSE
        ???????? -- WHAT DO WE DO HERE -- ????????

    IF SCREEN-CODE = LOW-VALUES THEN
        MOVE 'M' TO SCREEN-CODE
        EXEC CICS SEND MAP('MENU') MAPSET('LAMS')
            MAPONLY ERASE END-EXEC
        EXEC CICS RETURN TRANSID('LAMS') END-EXEC.
```

The variable TCTUA-LENGTH will contain the length of the TCT user area after initiation of the ASSIGN command. The variable is tested for sufficient storage and appropriate action (should be) taken.

Other common uses of the ASSIGN command are to: determine the length of available CWA or TWA storage (as well as TCT user area); to obtain operator security ids to be used in securing access to transactions; and to determine whether a terminal is able to support extended attribute processing (which will be discussed in Chapter 14).

INVOKING OTHER CICS PROGRAMS

Now that we can communicate with ourselves, let's concentrate on communicating with other programs in our system. We will have to use the CALL and XCTL commands, and perhaps some parameter lists, to pass data to and from the various programs. In our previous examples, where data were transmitted from a module to itself or one component of a system to another (within the same system), we found that only temporary storage and the TCT user area could be used for this purpose. In other words, program A could place data into a temporary storage record and program B could interrogate that data, and even update that information. Similarly, program A could place data into the TCT user area and B could reference or update this information.

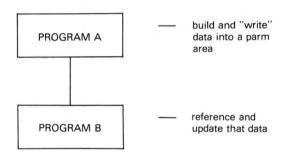

| PROGRAM A | —— build and "write" data into a parm area |
| PROGRAM B | —— reference and update that data |

Although these techniques can be used, they are not the standard means of passing data from one program to another under the command-level approach. Another method is to use a parameter list defined in the WORKING-STORAGE section of program A (the *calling* program), and defined in the LINKAGE-SECTION of program B (the *called* program). As a result, program B would not be able to call program A unless the same WORKING-STORAGE to LINKAGE-SECTION relationship existed between the programs using that type of calling structure.

Another program can be given control from your program in two ways: you can CALL the other program, or you can XCTL (transfer control) to that other program. Although in both cases the other program gets control, each technique has a different end result. In the example below we see three programs, A, B, and C. Program A *calls* program B; program B *transfers control* to program C. If program A calls program B and B issues a return, control goes back to program A. If program A calls program B and B transfers control to program C, then when C issues a return, control goes back to program *A*.

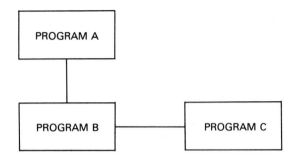

The structure of your application may be such that both commands may be appropriate. In any case, make sure that the proper command has been issued. Transferring control to a program is rather handy when an error condition occurs, specifically an abend. If you recall from our earlier discussion, the HANDLE ABEND statement identified the name of a paragraph to be given control in the event of an abend. We can modify this so that a completely new program gets control instead if an abend should occur during processing. However, if this method is used, you must be aware that the transfer to another program through the HANDLE ABEND command is a *total* transfer of control—that is, no return to your program will occur, unless that module transfers control back to you, at which point your program starts from the *beginning* again. To code the HANDLE ABEND command so that control can be transferred to another program in the event of failure, you simply code:

EXEC CICS HANDLE ABEND PROGRAM('CLEANUP') END-EXEC.

If you want to transfer control to a program in situations other than an abend, you would code (as in the case of program B above):

EXEC CICS XCTL PROGRAM('C') END-EXEC.

If you want to *call* a program, as in the case of program A to B, program A would contain the following code:

EXEC CICS CALL PROGRAM('B') END-EXEC.

Obviously, no parameters are being passed between any of the modules in the statements above. We'll discuss the various methods shortly.

When a program CALL or XCTL is issued, the program name that you want to transfer to *must* be defined in the PPT, and it must be possible to execute the program (the program must reside in the library in the proper form). This program must adhere to command-level conventions. As long as it does, your COBOL program can call an assembler or PLI program to perform some function and return the result (or not return) to the calling module. This communication ability between languages is taken care of by the execute interface system for supporting your applications.

If you issue a CALL or XCTL command and the program that you are trying to invoke is not in the PPT or it cannot be executed, then a PGMIDERR condition will arise. Unless you want your calling program to abend, you should issue a HANDLE CONDITION to trap such a problem.

The program-to-program communications structure available through command-level CICS is rather simple, as you have seen, although no parameters are passed in either case. In most systems, some data are passed between most modules, and in a CICS on-line environment, there are many ways to transfer these data along with your control.

Earlier in the chapter we saw two methods of communicating between programs: by passing data in a file (temporary storage) from program to program or system to system, or by passing data in a TCT user area from program to program. Program-to-program communication can take place in three more ways.

STANDARD METHOD OF PASSING PARAMETERS

First, the WORKING-STORAGE section of the calling program can be used to pass data into the LINKAGE-SECTION of the program to be called. In this case, the structure of the parameters must be coordinated between programs so that proper communication takes place. This is the most commonly used method of passing data among command-level applications and it's about the easiest to understand.

Suppose that program A wants to pass data to program B. In this case, A wants to send a 15-byte key of a record to be read. Program B will read the record from a file and place the address of that record into a variable, which will be returned to program A. Also, B will inform A as to the success of the operation through a return code variable. The value, if the operation is successful, will be zero, if not successful, 8. The code to implement such a situation is shown below along with the commands to call B from A:

Program A

```
IDENTIFICATION DIVISION.
  PROGRAM-ID.  A.
ENVIRONMENT DIVISION.
DATA DIVISION.
```

```
WORKING-STORAGE SECTION.
01   A-PARM-LIST.
      02   RETURN-CODE        PIC S9(4) COMP.
      02   RECORD-ADDR        PIC S9(8) COMP.
      02   RECORD-KEY         PIC X(15).

LINKAGE SECTION.
01   DFHBLLDS.
      02   RESERVED-BLL       PIC S9(8) COMP.
      02   FILEBLL            PIC S9(8) COMP.
      02   MAPBLL             PIC S9(8) COMP.

01   MASTER-RECORD.
      02   .......
      02   .......

01   MAPAREA               PIC X(1920).
01   COPY LAMSM.

PROCEDURE DIVISION.

    .   .   .
    .   .   .
    .   .   .

    MOVE SCRNKEYI  TO RECORD-KEY.
    EXEC CICS HANDLE CONDITION PGMIDERR(B-IS-BAD)
      END-EXEC.
    EXEC CICS CALL PROGRAM('B') COMMAREA(A-PARM-LIST)
      LENGTH(21) END-EXEC.
    MOVE RECORD-ADDR   TO FILEBLL.
```

Program B

```
IDENTIFICATION DIVISION.
  PROGRAM-ID.   B.
ENVIRONMENT DIVISION.
DATA DIVISION.

WORKING-STORAGE SECTION.
01   KEY-OF-THE-RECORD.  PIC X(15).

LINKAGE SECTION.
01   DFHCOMMAREA.
      02   RETURN-CODE        PIC S9(4) COMP.
      02   RECORD-ADDR        PIC S9(8) COMP.
      02   RECORD-KEY         PIC X(15).
```

```
01   DFHBLLDS.
     02   RESERVED-BLL    PIC S9(8) COMP.
     02   FILEBLL         PIC S9(8) COMP.

01   MASTER-RECORD.
     02   .......
     02   .......

PROCEDURE DIVISION.

   MOVE RECORD-KEY   TO KEY-OF-THE-RECORD.

   EXEC CICS HANDLE CONDITION NOTFND(NOT-ON-FILE)
     END-EXEC.

   EXEC CICS READ DATASET('MSTRFILE')
     SET(FILEBLL) RIDFLD(KEY-OF-THE-RECORD)
     END-EXEC.

   MOVE +0      TO RETURN-CODE.
   MOVE FILEBLL  TO RECORD-ADDR.
   EXEC CICS RETURN END-EXEC.

NOT-ON-FILE.
   MOVE +8      TO RETURN-CODE.
   MOVE +0      TO RECORD-ADDR.
   EXEC CICS RETURN END-EXEC.
   STOP RUN.
```

Notice in the example above that the structure of the parameter list is exactly the same in both programs. Also, the parameter list resides in the WORKING-STORAGE section of the calling program, program A, and in the LINKAGE-SECTION under the heading DFHCOMMAREA in the called program, program B.

In program A, the CALL to program B is done through the CALL command-level statement passing the parameter list, which becomes the COMMAREA in program B. Hence, in program A, the COMMAREA option used in the CALL statement informs CICS that data are to be passed from A to B, and that the length of this data is 21 bytes. If the call to program B is not successful, A has established a handle condition routine to take care of the problem.

In program B, the record key must be moved to WORKING-STORAGE in order to issue the READ command for the file. Remember—this was a requirement for the I/O command. B establishes a handle condition in the event that the record desired by A is not in the file.

Depending on the outcome of the file operation, B appropriately sets the return code, establishes an address for the record (or, no address, if applicable), and returns to A as a normal return command would be issued. This completes the calling sequence for A and B.

Clearly, the parameter list between the two programs can be manipulated for your application as desired. Although you may not want to perform the processing described, typically, I/O is done in subroutines.

To demonstrate A transferring control to B (not calling), we simply have to change the operand CALL to the operand XCTL. But wait a minute. If A transfers control to B, then when B returns, B returns to CICS or to the program that called program A. Since A expects B to return to it, this application would not work with the XCTL command. An application that may be appropriate is the one described in Chapter 5 for the Landlord Management System, in which several modules were used to implement the application—a driver program that processed the menu and then transferred control to the other functional modules, depending on the user's choice. Once the driver module relinquished control to the functional modules, the return from those functional modules was to CICS and not back to the driver module.

Rather than engage in a lengthy discussion of program structure and design and the use of XCTL versus CALL, let me simply refer you to earlier chapters in this text. You should have a sufficient understanding of program-to-program communications by this point.

USING THE CWA TO PASS PARAMETERS

Another way of passing data from module to module—and one that is quite dangerous—requires the use of the primary control area for all of CICS. If, for example, too much information is moved into *your* assigned area, or if you violate storage here, it's almost guaranteed that CICS will abend. Nonetheless this is an efficient way of passing data not only from program to program within the same system, but also from system to system; however, it's not as easy as it sounds!

The primary control block for CICS is called the COMMON SYSTEM AREA (CSA). This is sacred ground as far as you're concerned; this area should be used with great care, *and* this use must be coordinated with your system programmers or CICS system programmers. If you can and must use this area, processing is simple enough, but you be careful.

We have already discussed a command that will allow us to refer to the TCT user area. This command is called the ADDRESS command. It returns the address of the user area available to us. We can use the same command to address the CWA or COMMON WORK AREA (a component of the CSA) as follows:

EXEC CICS ADDRESS CWA(CWABLL) END-EXEC.

If we have established the proper LINKAGE-SECTION for our processing, we'll be able to pass data between A and B in our earlier example as follows:

Program A

```
IDENTIFICATION DIVISION.
   PROGRAM-ID.   A.
ENVIRONMENT DIVISION.
DATA DIVISION.

WORKING-STORAGE SECTION.

LINKAGE SECTION.
01   DFHBLLDS.
     02   RESERVED-BLL     PIC S9(8) COMP.
     02   FILEBLL          PIC S9(8) COMP.
     02   CWABLL           PIC S9(8) COMP.
     02   MAPBLL           PIC S9(8) COMP.

01   MASTER-RECORD.
     02   .......
     02   .......

01   A-PARM-LIST.
     02   RETURN-CODE      PIC S9(4) COMP.
     02   RECORD-ADDR      PIC S9(8) COMP.
     02   RECORD-KEY       PIC X(15).

01   MAPAREA              PIC X(1920).
01   COPY LAMSM.

PROCEDURE DIVISION.
     .   .   .
     .   .   .
     .   .   .

     EXEC CICS ADDRESS CWA(CWABLL) END-EXEC.
     MOVE SCRNKEYI   TO RECORD-KEY.
     EXEC CICS HANDLE CONDITION PGMIDERR(B-IS-BAD)
        END-EXEC.
     EXEC CICS CALL PROGRAM('B') COMMAREA(A-PARM-LIST)
        LENGTH(21) END-EXEC.
     MOVE RECORD-ADDR   TO FILEBLL.
```

Program B

```
IDENTIFICATION DIVISION.
  PROGRAM-ID.  B.
ENVIRONMENT DIVISION.
DATA DIVISION.

WORKING-STORAGE SECTION.

01  KEY-OF-THE-RECORD   PIC X(15).

LINKAGE SECTION.
01  DFHBLLDS.
      02  RESERVED-BLL     PIC S9(8) COMP.
      02  CWABLL           PIC S9(8) COMP.
      02  FILEBLL          PIC S9(8) COMP.

01  CWA-PARM-LIST.
      02  RETURN-CODE      PIC S9(4) COMP.
      02  RECORD-ADDR      PIC S9(8) COMP.
      02  RECORD-KEY       PIC X(15).

01  MASTER-RECORD.
      02  .......
      02  .......

PROCEDURE DIVISION.
    EXEC CICS ADDRESS CWA(CWABLL) END-EXEC.
    MOVE RECORD-KEY   TO KEY-OF-THE-RECORD.

    EXEC CICS HANDLE CONDITION NOTFND(NOT-ON-FILE)
        END-EXEC.

    EXEC CICS READ DATASET('MSTRFILE')
        SET(FILEBLL) RIDFLD(KEY-OF-THE-RECORD)
        END-EXEC.

    MOVE +0          TO RETURN-CODE.
    MOVE FILEBLL     TO RECORD-ADDR.
    EXEC CICS RETURN END-EXEC.

NOT-ON-FILE.
    MOVE +8          TO RETURN-CODE.
    MOVE +0          TO RECORD-ADDR.
    EXEC CICS RETURN END-EXEC.
    STOP RUN.
```

But there's a serious problem here! Only one CWA is being shared by *all* transactions in the system. As soon as A moves in the key of the record to be read from the file, that key will probably be replaced by another user who is running the same transaction at *his or her* terminal. Although the CWA does serve as a means of passing data from program to program, some critical restrictions are imposed on applications processing and design:

- Only one copy of your transaction is being used in the system at any given time.
- No other transactions use the CWA for supporting their program-to-program communications.
- Before attempting to use, the user should test the availability of CWA storage by using the ASSIGN command as discussed in an earlier section.

As a result, you are advised *not to use* the CWA to pass information between programs within a CICS environment. Rather, the CWA should be restricted to system-to-system communications, and coordination between systems must be handled carefully.

PASSING PARAMETERS USING THE TWA

The last method of passing data between programs (*not* systems) via the ADDRESS command can be used to obtain addressability to yet another storage area. One drawback to this procedure is that it *cannot* be used for passing data to "yourself" in a nonconversational application. In other words, the storage disappears between initiations. Each time that your transaction is initiated by a user, the area is set to binary zeros. Hence, you can only use this area to pass data from program to program while your task is active.

The last method is faster than using the DFHCOMMAREA and passing parameters with the CALL or XCTL command. Since all passing is done via BLL cells, no data movement occurs, and processing is fast. Moreover, you do not have to worry about interference from other tasks or systems running under CICS control because you have your own copy of this area.

The area that we'll be using in this example is attached to your TCA (task control area). It is a working area or "scratch pad" for applications and is created by CICS when your task is initiated. This area can be as long as you want it to be, although most parameter lists are kept under 4096 bytes to make addressing storage areas easier. Again, the ASSIGN command can be used to determine the length of TWA storage available for your transaction.

Before you use this area, however, you should contact your systems programmer or CICS systems programmer. The transaction work area (TWA) is not usually allocated as part of normal task initiation unless a specific request for a TWA area is made through the PCT entry for your transaction. In the PCT entry, the systems programmer simply identifies the amount or size of the TWA that you need to support your application. After this entry is specified, your application is ready to use one of the easiest and cheapest forms of program-to-program communications under CICS.

Using the TWA is exactly like using the CWA, except that the drawbacks of the CWA are eliminated. You don't have to worry about any other user's terminal destroying your TWA because a TWA is task dependent; that is, each task in CICS has its own TWA area. Hence, another user using the same transaction at another terminal will have a different task association and therefore his or her own TWA. Since the CWA processing and TWA processing are almost identical, here's the same application using the TWA to pass parameters:

Program A

```
IDENTIFICATION DIVISION.
   PROGRAM-ID.   A.
ENVIRONMENT DIVISION.
DATA DIVISION.

WORKING-STORAGE SECTION.

LINKAGE SECTION.
01   DFHBLLDS.
        02   RESERVED-BLL   PIC S9(8) COMP.
        02   FILEBLL        PIC S9(8) COMP.
        02   TWABLL         PIC S9(8) COMP.
        02   MAPBLL         PIC S9(8) COMP.

01   MASTER-RECORD.
        02   .......
        02   .......

01   A-PARM-LIST.
        02   RETURN-CODE    PIC S9(4) COMP.
        02   RECORD-ADDR    PIC S9(8) COMP.
        02   RECORD-KEY     PIC X(15).

01   MAPAREA              PIC X(1920).
01   COPY LAMSM.

PROCEDURE DIVISION.
      .   .   .

      .   .   .

      .   .   .


      EXEC CICS ADDRESS TWA(TWABLL) END-EXEC.
      MOVE SCRNKEYI   TO RECORD-KEY.
      EXEC CICS HANDLE CONDITION PGMIDERR(B-IS-BAD)
         END-EXEC.
```

```
    EXEC CICS CALL PROGRAM('B') COMMAREA(A-PARM-LIST)
       LENGTH(21) END-EXEC.
    MOVE RECORD-ADDR   TO FILEBLL.
```

Program B

```
IDENTIFICATION DIVISION.
  PROGRAM-ID.   B.
ENVIRONMENT DIVISION.
DATA DIVISION.

WORKING-STORAGE SECTION.
01   KEY-OF-THE-RECORD   PIC X(15).

LINKAGE SECTION.
01   DFHBLLDS.
     02   RESERVED-BLL    PIC S9(8) COMP.
     02   TWABLL          PIC S9(8) COMP.
     02   FILEBLL         PIC S9(8) COMP.

01   TWA-PARM-LIST.
     02   RETURN-CODE     PIC S9(4) COMP.
     02   RECORD-ADDR     PIC S9(8) COMP.
     02   RECORD-KEY      PIC X(15).

01   MASTER-RECORD.
     02   .......
     02   .......

PROCEDURE DIVISION.
    EXEC CICS ADDRESS TWA(TWABLL) END-EXEC.
    MOVE RECORD-KEY   TO KEY-OF-THE-RECORD.

    EXEC CICS HANDLE CONDITION NOTFND(NOT-ON-FILE)
       END-EXEC.

    EXEC CICS READ DATASET('MSTRFILE')
       SET(FILEBLL) RIDFLD(KEY-OF-THE-RECORD)
       END-EXEC.

    MOVE +0           TO RETURN-CODE.
    MOVE FILEBLL      TO RECORD-ADDR.
    EXEC CICS RETURN END-EXEC.

NOT-ON-FILE.
    MOVE +8           TO RETURN-CODE.
    MOVE +0           TO RECORD-ADDR.
    EXEC CICS RETURN END-EXEC.
    STOP RUN.
```

This concludes our discussion of program-to-program communications and the many different ways to pass data between modules. Some of these techniques are very easy to use and do not affect the execution of other tasks within the CICS system. As for the others, you are urged to examine these techniques carefully and discuss them thoroughly with your systems programmer before using them.

By now, you should have a sufficient background to implement almost any on-line application under CICS using command-level programming. Some techniques should be discussed with your system staffs before you use them, but in most cases simply defining the proper entries in the table should prepare you for on-line processing. CICS has developed tremendously in the last few years and continues to support more and more application needs. Basic on-line processing has been our main theme up to this point, but some of you may want to consider "fancier" items. The next chapter is devoted to those special touches.

THOUGHT QUESTIONS

1. *Describe several situations in which the XCTL command would be valuable in your environment.*

2. *Compare each method of passing parameters in the following way: number of file I/Os; number of instructions required to use; overall difficulty of understanding; number of CICS instructions necessary to carry out the request. The* CICS/VS System Programmer's Reference Manual *contains statistics about how long it takes to process a typical CICS request. To help you determine which method may be most efficient and to help you develop a sense of how much time your transactions spend in "overhead" through program calls or whatever, refer to the statistics in this manual.*

3. *On the basis of your results in Question 2, what changes in design structure or implementation are you going to propose to your standards and performance groups? How about to your manager?*

14

SPECIAL CICS
PROCESSING FEATURES

We now turn to the fine points of CICS command-level services, some of which you may not even have available on your CICS system. These features will include color for screen fields, reverse video field display, underlining fields, controlling access to resources, loading and accessing programs and paging terminal operations. Operations added to the latest release of CICS (1.6) include sending control characters to erase a screen (SEND CONTROL), and stacking handle conditions when subroutine processing requires a different set of handle conditions than a calling module. In the last section of this chapter we learn how to communicate with a terminal *without* using maps. Many programmers spend a substantial amount of time coding maps and mapsets for a simple application, when maps may not be needed. This section will show you how to process unformatted screen displays and how to communicate with a terminal as if a map was being used.

USING COLOR ON SCREEN DISPLAYS

CICS programmers can greatly enhance the friendliness of a system by incorporating color into the screen displays where color terminals are available. Blue or green for information-only fields, white or pink for data fields, and red for error messages or fields in error may greatly help point out user errors and enhance the readability of the screen. Further, allowing users to pick their colors will get them more involved in the development of the application and make them take more interest in it. However, be prepared to do a lot of color changing after the system is implemented because the colors often clash and you'll probably end up redoing the entire thing anyway.

To specify extended field processing for your screen displays when using BMS, you simply have to code EXTATT=YES on the DFHMSD statement for your mapsets. Our mapset definition statement from earlier chapters would now look like this:

```
LAMSM   DFHMSD   TYPE=DSECT,MODE=INOUT,LANG=COBOL,   X
                 CTRL=FREEKB,TIOAPFX=YES,             X
                 STORAGE=AUTO,EXTATT=YES
```

Now you're ready to begin processing your extended fields. These are fields that have been defined with extended attributes. That is, in some systems, not only can a screen field be marked fset, numeric, bright, and so on, but the field can also support color, reverse video, field underlining, and validation. If your terminals do not support these features, these options will be ignored by CICS when you issue your request. You'll also be wasting computer time by generating your screens with this support.

When using these features, you can specify that all fields within the mapset be the same color by coding COLOR on the DFHMSD statement; you can specify that each map within a mapset have a different color by coding the COLOR operand on the DFHMDI statement, or you can specify colors for individual fields within a map by coding COLOR on the DFHMDF statement. In general, most users like different colors and will want color specified at the field level rather than the map or mapset level. Further, the other extended processing options may be treated in much the same way—at the mapset, map, or field level. You can decide how global your specifications should be.

One possibility is to color-coordinate all maps for a type of function to be performed. For example, if a user can perform four functions (add, change, delete, and inquire), these might be color-coordinated as follows: all add screens have BLUE fields; all change screens have PINK fields; all delete screens have RED fields; all inquire screens have WHITE fields. Hence, if users pick a function from the menu and think they are choosing inquire and a RED screen is displayed, they'll know that they chose the wrong menu option.

Along with the EXTATT operand on the DFHMSD statement, the programmer must be aware of a new set of symbolic map fields that are generated as a result of specifying this operand. If you recall, the general symbolic map fields ended in I, O, A, F, and L. Four additional fields may be manipulated by the program to set individual field characteristics, much like attributes could be specified from within the application program. These fields and their suffixes are:

'C — color of the field

'H — highlighting

'V — validation specification

'P — not discussed for 327x communication

Since a new set of fields is defined for a mapset, all programs using this mapset must be recompiled to incorporate these additional fields into their symbolic mapset definition before processing can begin.

In addition to these new fields, the programmer can refer to another set of variables within the DFHBMSCA structure discussed earlier. If you recall, DFHBMSCA supplied attribute byte settings that the programmer could move to the attribute byte field (A-suffixed) within the symbolic map to apply a new set of attributes to that field. Another set of fields can be supplied within this same structure to support extended terminal processing:

DFHBLUE   — assigns the color blue

DFHRED   — assigns the color red

DFHPINK   — assigns the color pink

DFHGREEN — assigns the color green

DFHTURQ   — assigns the color turquoise

DFHYELLO — assigns the color yellow

DFHNEUTR — assigns the color white

DFHBLINK — causes the field to blink

DFHREVRS — reverse video specification

DFHUNDLN — field underline specification

DFHMFIL   — user must completely fill the field before going to the next field

DFHMENT — user must enter some data into the field

DFHMFE   — user must completely fill and must enter data into the field

MUSTFILL AND MUSTENTER FIELD SPECIFICATIONS

You may be wondering what the highlighting and validation fields do. Assume that you've just sent out the system menu or a screen in which it is mandatory to make a selection or enter something into a field before processing on this function can continue. In our current situation, if the user doesn't enter any data and presses the *enter* key, the program must edit that field; when it does and finds that the user hasn't entered any data into the field, the screen will be sent back out and a message displayed stating that the user *must* enter data into that field. Instead of letting the program control this editing, the extended attributes can do some of this editing for you. In our example, we can specify that the field is a mandatory enter field (DFHMENT) so that the program will not be given control unless the user enters something into the field. Clearly it may not be the "correct" item that the programs want, but the fact that it is an item will eliminate the need for more program processing in the CPU.

Now assume that the user is looking at a screen in which he must enter a key of a record. The keys for all the records are 5 positions long, and generic processing is not used to obtain a record. If the user enters only four positions, the record will not be found. In fact, no record will be found unless the user enters all five positions. For such a field, you can specify that the user *must* enter *all* five positions of the field by moving the attribute DFHMFIL to the V-suffixed field within the symbolic map before you send the map out.

If the user must enter data into a field *and* must enter data in every position of the field, then your program should move the element DFHMFE to the V-suffixed field in your symbolic map.

If it is necessary to permanently apply these attributes to your screen fields, you can code color, validation, and highlighting on the DFHMDF statements for the fields in your maps. The color values are obvious. The validation values are MUSTFILL and MUSTENTER.

Obviously, the fields are not completely edited but instead of invoking the program only to find no data or only partial data in a field, you can, with the proper specifications and proper terminal equipment, perform this editing at the terminal.

HIGHLIGHTING A FIELD

The highlighting of a field can also enhance the meaning or importance of a field. Take this text, for example. Black ink is used on a white background. If we reversed the colors in this text—that is, print white letters on a black page—we would have reverse video display. This option is especially useful for indicating the length of a field on the screen. In most of the screens that you've seen throughout this text, the boundaries of a field were never fully visible to the user. In other words, the user really doesn't know how many characters can be typed in the screen on next page, for the person's name, address, city, and so on.

```
                      HIGHLIGHTING EXAMPLE
   ENTER THE PERSON'S NAME - - - - - - - - - - - - - - - - - - - -
   WHAT IS HIS ADDRESS - - - - - - - - - - - - - - - - - - - - - - -
   IN WHAT CITY DOES HE LIVE - - - - - - - - - - - - - - - - - - -
   ENTER THE STATE HERE - - - - - - - - - - - - - - - - - - - - - -
   THE ZIP CODE IS - - - - - - - - - - - - - - - - - - - - - - - - - - -
```

REVERSE VIDEO AND UNDERLINED FIELDS

With reverse video, the data field forms a box that the user types into, clearly showing him the length of the field and the amount of data that has been typed in.

With the underline feature, the screen would appear like this:

```
┌──────────────────────────────────────────────────────────────┐
│                     HIGHLIGHTING EXAMPLE                       │
│   ENTER THE PERSON'S NAME_____    SMITH, JOHN _____     │
│   WHAT IS HIS ADDRESS _____     102 N. MAPLE _____     │
│   IN WHAT CITY DOES HE LIVE_____    NEW YORK _____       │
│   ENTER THE STATE HERE _____     NY                      │
│   THE ZIP CODE IS  _____      10022                   │
│                                                                │
│                                                                │
│                                                                │
│                                                                │
└──────────────────────────────────────────────────────────────┘
```

In each of the fields above, the user knows how much data can be entered. Without this feature, a position on the screen can hold only one character. Hence, it would not be possible for a field to contain both an underline and a character in the same position, as shown above.

The last feature, BLINK, causes the field to blink off and on in order to draw attention to a field. This device is useful for fields that the user must enter and completely fill, for a field that the user has entered incorrectly, for fields that compose the key of a record, or for error messages. You have to decide how you're going to use each of these extended processing attributes in your applications. These options can be specified on the DFHMDF statement as BLINK, REVERSE, or UNDERLINE, as necessary.

SPECIAL TERMINAL I/O COMMANDS

In several examples, we found it necessary to clear a terminal display screen when the user pressed any key other than *enter*. We did this by using a different form of the SEND command, and we did not send a map out during this operation. This SEND request appeared as follows:

EXEC CICS SEND FROM (TIOALEN) LENGTH (0)
ERASE END-EXEC.

You'll notice that no data are actually sent to the terminal here. The only thing this command does is to erase the screen, leaving it unformatted. This function can be accomplished more easily and less expensively with a new command available only with release 1.6 or later of CICS. The command is called SEND CONTROL.

This command allows the programmer to perform the following operations without using maps in the processing:

ERASE — Erase the entire screen leaving the screen unformatted. It's like pressing the *clear* key.

ALARM — Sound the alarm at a terminal, if that terminal is equipped with the alarm feature. Won't this be an opportunity to get back at a nagging user!

FREEKB — Free the keyboard at the user's terminal. Usually specified with the ERASE operand described above.

ERASEAUP — Erase all unprotected (and only unprotected) fields on the screen.

CURSOR (n) — Position the cursor at a field.

In our previous example, we'd want to erase the screen and free the keyboard. This could be accomplished as follows:

EXEC CICS SEND CONTROL ERASE FREEKB END-EXEC.

Although the command is simple, one operand—CURSOR—needs to be given special attention. Since no map is needed for the SEND CONTROL operand, you cannot move negative one (-1) to the symbolic map area and issue a SEND CONTROL command. You *must* know the exact offset at which the cursor is to be positioned on the terminal display. Some tend to forget this and want to kick themselves when, after several hours of trying to fix the "mapping" operation, they find this error.

SPECIAL HANDLE-CONDITION OPTIONS

Suppose that while you're processing you send out a map, but that the mapping operation fails with a MAPFAIL condition. Since you've established a handle condition for MAPFAIL, your mapfail routine takes control. This routine tries to send out another map, but because your mapset has been destroyed by another CICS application, this mapping request also fails, and the MAPFAIL condition arises again. Your mapfail routine takes control, tries to send out the map, and so on. The problem behind this situation has led many applications into an infinite loop. The 1.6 release of CICS has introduced a new set of commands to help the application program solve this problem. These commands are PUSH HANDLE and POP HANDLE.

The handle-condition, abend-condition, and AID-condition commands established in your program can be thought of as a *set* of exceptional condition actions that are to be taken whenever the condition arises. However, in some situations you may want to temporarily "turn off" these conditions in order to try something else. If you succeed, then you may want to restore the former conditions and continue processing.

This could also apply to subroutine linkage. Suppose that when program A calls program B, both programs perform I/O to different files or to the same file. In order for A to process the file, A must establish handle-condition commands for that file request in the event that the record isn't found, for example, or there isn't any space. When A calls B, B has a different routine to handle the situation when the file I/O issued by B fails. However, when B issues the HANDLE-CONDITION command, B destroys the method of handling conditions established by A. As a result, A must reissue any HANDLE-CONDITION commands when B returns to A in the event that they were reset by B's processing.

With the PUSH and POP commands, this sequence can be avoided. A can establish A's handle-conditions. When A calls B, B can PUSH the current handle conditions, specify its own set of handle-conditions and then perform its processing. Before B returns to A, B POPs the handle conditions so that when A gets control back from B, the handle conditions are as they were when B was called.

In the case of our MAPFAIL situation, the mapfail routine can PUSH the current handle-conditions, turn off or ignore the MAPFAIL handle-conditions or specify a new routine to be given control if that SEND MAP request fails. After it is determined that the task should be abended or that control should be returned to the control program, the conditions can be popped, and they will be as they were when the first condition arose.

The commands to perform the stacking of conditions and unstacking are as follows:

EXEC CICS PUSH HANDLE END-EXEC.

EXEC CICS POP   HANDLE END-EXEC.

When you PUSH or POP HANDLE-CONDITIONS you are also PUSHing and POPping the ABEND-condition, AID key actions, and the general CONDITION actions. Further, the stack has many levels, so that if A calls B and B calls C and C calls D and D calls E, all of these modules can PUSH and POP these HANDLE elements so that the depth of the stack increases as we increase our level of calling, and the depth of the stack decreases as control goes back to A from E.

ENQUEUING RESOURCES

In some situations, an application may require controlled access to a resource. For example, if an application is updating a set of records in a file, then the application may want exclusive control of that file for the duration of the update process. This would prevent any other user from accessing the same file and undoing the changes made by this application. In Chapter 11, we noted that in a nonconversational update request, a record could be deleted from underneath a user between transaction initiations. I do not mean to imply that we are going to resolve that problem here—on the contrary—a nonconversational application will *always* have this problem. What I do mean is—an application *can* control access to a resource while it is being executed by CICS.

Let's assume that a financial status file can be updated by several transactions simultaneously. If the file consists of several sets of records, each set composing a financial table, then an application that is updating one of the records in that set may not have control over all other records in that set unless each record has been read for update. If it *is* necessary that the application control *all* records associated with this table, then until the update is completed, this transaction must *enqueue* or lock out all other users from this set of records, which we will now refer to as a *resource*. To obtain control over a resource, the program can issue the ENQ command to lock out all others until updating is finished. This can be done as follows:

```
WORKING-STORAGE SECTION.
01   TABLE-RECORD-KEY.
     05   TABLE-PREFIX        PIC X(5).
     05   TABLE-SEQUENCE      PIC 99.

01   TABLE-PREFIX-LENGTH      PIC S9(4) COMP
                              VALUE +5.

     .  .  .

     .  .  .

PROCEDURE DIVISION.
     EXEC CICS ENQ RESOURCE(TABLE-RECORD-KEY)
     LENGTH(TABLE-PREFIX-LENGTH) END-EXEC.
```

In this example, the key of each financial table record is 7 positions: consisting of a 5-character prefix (to identify a specific table within the file) and a 2-digit sequence number (within that table). The ENQ command informs CICS that our application wants exclusive control over the resource whose first *five* characters are the table prefix. Hence, as long as our task is active, no other application may access any resource having this name. Note that we are not locking other applications from the entire file, rather, we are only preventing others from using the same set of table records that we are using at this time. As a result, all other transactions trying to access the financial status table being used by this program will be suspended until our task releases the resource, terminates, or abends. The resource can be released as follows:

EXEC CICS DEQ RESOURCE(TABLE-RECORD-KEY)
LENGTH(TABLE-PREFIX-LENGTH) END-EXEC.

When a program attempts to enqueue a resource, the program can first issue a handle condition command to determine if the resource is being used by testing the condition ENQBUSY. If a handle condition is not issued, CICS will simply suspend the task until the resource is available. Since task suspension may result in long user response times, the program may be designed to pause for a few seconds and then retry the request until it is successful; notifying the user periodically of the delay and assuring the user that processing continues. (An example of such a design was presented in Chapter 12 when storage was requested through the GETMAIN command.)

If applications share resources, as illustrated above, then the applications should be designed to enqueue and dequeue resources when control of those resources is required. Testing the availability of a resource is a question of program design which I'll leave to you.

LOADING PROGRAMS OR TABLES

Recall the financial status example discussed in the last section. Each financial status record could be considered to be a row of a two-dimensional table. Each data element would be associated with a column of the table. If the application was now designed in this fashion, access to all financial status records within a specific set could be done at one time and would be much easier.

Assume that the two-dimensional table is called FTABL and is defined as a program to the CICS system; thus, it requires a PPT entry. If this module has been compiled and link-edited into a CICS program library, then it can be loaded into CICS memory and made available to any application by using the LOAD command-level statement. As a result, the application can gain access to the entire set of records associated with a financial status set in one command, rather than having access to only one record at a time. The LOAD command must be used with BLL cells as illustrated below:

```
WORKING-STORAGE SECTION.
01   TABLE-NAME                      PIC X(8).
                                     VALUE 'FTABL'.

         .   .   .

         .   .   .

LINKAGE SECTION.
01   DFHBLLDS.
        05   FILLER                  PIC S9(8) COMP.
        05   TABLEBLL                PIC S9(8) COMP.

01   TABLE-DEFINITION.
        05   TABLE-ROWS              OCCURS 10 TIMES.
            10   TABLE-COLUMNS       OCCURS 20 TIMES.
                20   ELEMENT-A       PIC XXX.
                20   ELEMENT-B       PIC XXX.
                20   ELEMENT-C       PIC XXX.

PROCEDURE DIVISION.
    EXEC CICS LOAD PROGRAM(TABLE-NAME)
    SET(TABLEBLL) END-EXEC.
```

Data is now referenced as any 10-row by 20-column table might be. For example, ELEMENT-C in row 4 and column 10 would be referenced as: ELEMENT-C(4,10). Obviously, referencing a table is easy, but if we now assume that many applications will be using the table, possibly for update purposes; other factors must be considered. First; the table *cannot* be replaced in the CICS library and thus, no *permanent* updates to this table can be made (as could be done with records in a file). Second; if several people are updating the table at the same time, update synchronization would have to be performed by using the ENQ and DEQ commands. Finally, this table could be released from CICS memory if at some point there were no applications using the table and there is a demand on CICS memory, thus, all updates could be lost. Hence, in the design of an application using a table such as this, the following considerations must be made:

- The table should be defined in the PPT as a permanently resident module or should be held in CICS memory by the application.
- All applications must enqueue and dequeue the table resource to ensure that data are not unknowingly changed during usage.
- If permanent updates *are* to be reflected in such a table, do not design your application in this manner.

The first item is easily accomplished by the CICS systems programming or on-line administration group by defining the module as a permanent-resident module in the PPT. Details on this specification are available in the *CICS/VS Resource Definition Guide* for CICS versions 1.6 and later; and the *CICS/VS System Programmer's Reference Manual* for earlier versions of CICS. However, the application program has the ability to load and hold such a module if desired, thus having the same affect as defining the module resident! As a result, the table can be held in CICS memory throughout the day and can remain in control by the application. To load, hold, and address a module in memory, the application program must issue the LOAD command as follows:

EXEC CICS LOAD PROGRAM('FTABL')
SET(TABLEBLL) HOLD END-EXEC.

On the other hand, if it is desired that this module not be retained in memory, then the application need not load the program with the HOLD option.

The HOLD option can have a negative effect on processing in that it will not allow a module to be new-copied (as discussed in a previous chapter). Without the HOLD option, the module can be deleted by CICS (if storage is needed) once the task has ended or abended. However, a module that has been loaded with the HOLD option can only be deleted from memory (or new-copied) when it has been released from its hold status. This can be done as follows:

EXEC CICS RELEASE PROGRAM('FTABL') END-EXEC.

Therefore, the ability to load and release programs or tables can greatly increase the capabilities of CICS applications, especially when such tables are used as a communication feature between applications. Incidentally, have you realized that this facility allows: a program to communicate with itself; a program to communicate with another program; one transaction to communicate with another; or a heavily used mapset to be retained in memory to improve performance? This advanced topic may have been more appropriately placed in Chapter 13 when we discussed program-to-program communications or earlier in the text when we discussed performance considerations. However, it is placed here due to the fact that you now have the background to understand its uses; and, since it requires careful coordination between applications, may require the use of ENQ and DEQ to provide integrity to your system.

TERMINAL PAGING OPERATIONS

In many applications it may be necessary to display several screens of data to the user, as in the case shown on next page:

```
                    PRODUCT INVENTORY              PAGE 001
    ITEM                             QUANTITY   COST
    NUMBER         DESCRIPTION       IN STOCK   (RETAIL)
    XXXXX    XXXXXXXXXXXXXXXXXXX     XXXXXX    XXXXX.XX
    XXXXX    XXXXXXXXXXXXXXXXXXX     XXXXXX    XXXXX.XX
    XXXXX    XXXXXXXXXXXXXXXXXXX     XXXXXX    XXXXX.XX
    XXXXX    XXXXXXXXXXXXXXXXXXX     XXXXXX    XXXXX.XX
    XXXXX    XXXXXXXXXXXXXXXXXXX     XXXXXX    XXXXX.XX
    XXXXX    XXXXXXXXXXXXXXXXXXX     XXXXXX    XXXXX.XX
    XXXXX    XXXXXXXXXXXXXXXXXXX     XXXXXX    XXXXX.XX
    XXXXX    XXXXXXXXXXXXXXXXXXX     XXXXXX    XXXXX.XX
    XXXXX    XXXXXXXXXXXXXXXXXXX     XXXXXX    XXXXX.XX
    XXXXX    XXXXXXXXXXXXXXXXXXX     XXXXXX    XXXXX.XX
    XXXXX    XXXXXXXXXXXXXXXXXXX     XXXXXX    XXXXX.XX
    XXXXX    XXXXXXXXXXXXXXXXXXX     XXXXXX    XXXXX.XX

    PRESS ENTER TO SEE NEXT PAGE OF ITEMS
```

To implement such an application, the program generally keeps track of the last item displayed on the terminal (maybe in the COMMAREA); when the user presses the *enter* key, the program reads the next set of records from the file and displays those records to the terminal, again saving information about the last record displayed on PAGE 2. For each screen display, the program must be restarted, must remember where it left off, reposition itself in the file, and accumulate the records moving the data to the screen. Finally, when the screen is full or when the records are exhausted in the file, the program must display the screen.

This type of processing operation can be simplified through BMS by a procedure called *paging*. When paging is used, the program simply operates as if it were in a loop, as indicated by the logic that follows:

1. Position into the file.
2. Read the first record.
3. Set screen line count to 0.

4. Repeat until the last record is found:
   a. Move record data to screen
   b. Add 1 to screen line count
   c. If screen line count > 15, then
      i. send out this screen
      ii. set screen line count to 0
   d. read the next record from the file

5. End of processing.

When the program sends out a screen, the screen does not go to the user's terminal immediately. With the paging option, the screen goes into a temporary storage file managed by BMS. When your program finishes this processing, the program informs BMS that the paging operation has ceased and that the first screen can now be displayed at the terminal. The application program then ends by returning to CICS.

BMS retrieves the first page and displays it at the user's terminal. To go from screen one to screen two, the user presses the *enter* key and *BMS* is called upon to retrieve the next screen display from temporary storage and display that screen to the user's terminal, *without any initiation or intervention by the application program.* As a result, the program logic does not have to remember the last piece of information displayed; furthermore, understanding of the program is enhanced. Also, the overhead associated with reinitiating the program and repositioning into the file is eliminated from the program's activities.

The commands needed to perform this type of processing are as easy as issuing the SEND MAP command—as a matter of fact, the command *is* the SEND MAP command.

To send out a map to the user's terminal in a paging mode (one or more pages to be displayed), the programmer alters the SEND MAP command by adding the operand PAGING, as follows:

EXEC CICS SEND MAP('INVENT') MAPSET('BUSINES')
FROM(INVENTO) ERASE PAGING END-EXEC.

After the program has determined that there are no more pages to be sent *and has sent its last page* (screen display), the program must issue the following command:

EXEC CICS SEND PAGE RELEASE NOAUTOPAGE END-EXEC.

This command informs BMS that the paging has been completed and that BMS can now display the first page to the terminal. The user can then page through the various screen displays. To stop, the user simply presses the *clear* key and enters the next transaction id. When the next transaction is entered, BMS will delete all the pages stored in temporary storage for that user's terminal before beginning to process the next transaction request from that user. If the user wants to see this "paged" data again, he will have to reinitiate the transaction.

This feature of BMS can substantially reduce the amount of processing and overhead involved in accomplishing the same thing under application program control. However, there is one item that can't be overlooked in using this command.

When each screen is sent to the terminal, the program *must* place the character string P/+1 in the upper left corner of the screen (the transaction id area) for each screen other than the last one. On the last screen, the program should place the characters P/1ø. With this information, BMS knows that the operator is performing a paging operation and not trying to initiate a transaction. Further, the P/+1 informs BMS to display the *next* screen in the paging set. The P/1ø characters tell BMS to display page *one* of the paging set. Hence, if there are three pages in your paging set, the operator would see page one, press the *enter* key to see page two, press the *enter* key to see page three, and press the *enter* key to return to page one.

This field must also be defined as FSET by the program on that map to ensure that BMS recognizes that paging is being done at this user's terminal.

Paging has another interesting feature. Suppose that your program has processed a tremendous number of records and now there are 100 pages of screen displays. (A page is equivalent to one screen display.) Suppose that the operator wants to start looking at page 75 rather than starting at page one and proceeding through the data to page 75. With the paging support provided by BMS, the operator does *not* have to page through the first 74 pages before getting to page 75, because he is in control of the page that he would like to see. Hence, the operator can press the *clear* key to clear the screen, enter the command P/75, and press the *enter* key. This action tells BMS to display page 75 in the page set to this user's terminal. The user can then page forward from that point on the basis of the P/+1 data stored in the upper part of the terminal screen.

If the user is currently looking at page 20 in the page set and wants to go back five pages, the user presses the *clear* key (unless you've allowed the user to type over the P/xx data area), enters the command P/−5, and presses the *enter* key. The next page displayed at the terminal will be page 15. Thus, *the user* gains control of the data he or she wants to look at by means of a few very simple commands.

TERMINAL COMMUNICATIONS WITHOUT MAPS

If a user is familiar with screen usage and if an application requires only a few data fields, it may not be necessary, in some applications, to code a complete map or mapset and define a PPT entry for that mapset. There is an easier way to provide users with an on-line processing environment, but it does not have the features provided by BMS. We'll call it unformatted screen processing. In this mode, you cannot define attributes or fields on the screen and request mapping services from BMS. Data will come from the terminal into a TIOA definition and *you* will manipulate the data, process them, and then send an unformatted response to the user's terminal. In many cases, it may be all that the user wants.

Let's suppose that we have an application in which information about an apartment problem is to be reported to the terminal user. The user enters a problem number and the system returns some basic information about that problem. This can be done with map displays, as you know from earlier chapters, in which this situation is a subset of the Landlord Management System. Further, the application is an inquiry application, which is one of the most common types of applications that can be supported through this terminal communications technique.

When data come in from a screen the first time that the program is initiated, they are in an unformatted mode. If the user understands how to enter the information, there's no reason why the program couldn't process the input data from this unformatted screen. In other words, if the user can enter a problem number made up of four positions, the program can define an area called TIOA-AREA in the following way:

```
01   TIOA-AREA.
     02   UNFORMATTED-TRANID       PIC X(4).
     02   USERS-PROBLEM-NUMBER     PIC X(4).
     02   REST-OF-TIOA             PIC X(1912).
```

This structure is all that is needed to carry out a simple inquiry. After the user types in the transaction id and the problem number on the screen, he presses the *clear* key and then types in the transaction id, followed immediately by the four position problem number. If the problem number is 25, then the user enters 0025 so that four positions are accounted for. The screen would appear like this:

When the user presses the *enter* key, the application program will RECEIVE the screen data into the TIOA-AREA and then process the data as if they were a regular field on any other screen.

```
IDENTIFICATION DIVISION.
  PROGRAM-ID.  XXXX.
ENVIRONMENT DIVISION.
DATA DIVISION.

WORKING-STORAGE SECTION.
01   KEY-OF-THE-RECORD              PIC X(5).
01   TIOALEN                        PIC S9(4) COMP
                                    VALUE +1920.

LINKAGE SECTION.
01   DFHBLLDS.
     02   RESERVED                  PIC S9(8) COMP.
```

```
        02  TIOABLL                      PIC S9(8) COMP.
        02  FILEBLL                      PIC S9(8) COMP.

    01  TIOA-AREA.
        02  UNFORMATTED-TRANID           PIC X(4).
        02  USERS-PROBLEM-NUMBER         PIC X(4).
        02  REST-OF-TIOA                 PIC X(1912).

    01  FILE-AREA.
        02  NUMBER                       PIC X(4).
        02  ......
        02  ......

    PROCEDURE DIVISION.

        EXEC CICS RECEIVE SET(TIOABLL) LENGTH(TIOALEN)
          END-EXEC.
        IF USERS-PROBLEM-NUMBER NOT NUMERIC THEN
        ?????????
          EXEC CICS RETURN END-EXEC.

        MOVE USERS-PROBLEM-NUMBER TO KEY-OF-THE-RECORD.
        EXEC CICS HANDLE CONDITION NOTFND(REC-NOT-FND)
          ERROR(OTHER-PROBLEM) END-EXEC.
        EXEC CICS READ DATASET('LAMSFILE')
          RIDFLD(KEY-OF-THE-RECORD) SET(FILEBLL) END-EXEC.

        ------- PROCESS THE RECORD AS USUAL -------
```

In the example above, many pieces of the puzzle are clearly missing, but the program does accept the user's data and can process those data as a regular data field on a display screen. This process has its limitations, however, since the data must be carefully typed by the user so that they can be processed by the program.

Perhaps we can allow the user to enter several fields of data, separated by blanks, and use some of the STRING commands of COBOL to unstring and examine these fields. *No, we can't!!!!* Many of the COBOL string processing commands are *not* allowed under CICS and, if issued, will likely cause a CICS system failure. Well, since that won't work, we'll write our own subroutine, pass it these data and have this routine (written in assembler) return the data to the program in the format that the program requires. This could be done, but why go through all that effort? BMS was designed to do this for you. Use a map if you need this type of processing! The point to be made is that unformatted screen processing is limited in scope and should only be used for a limited number of data fields on a screen. If you can adapt to this type of processing, then fine; if not, use BMS to provide better assistance in your screen processing.

Now that we have data in the program, how can we send a message out from the program to the terminal? Believe it or not, you already know the command. Let's see if you can remember where it was used before:

EXEC CICS SEND FROM(XXXXXXX)
LENGTH(XXXX) ERASE END-EXEC.

The command above was used to clear the screen when the user wanted to terminate a transaction. By adopting this command to send information out to the terminal, we can provide a cheap way of implementing an on-line application:

```
IDENTIFICATION DIVISION.
  PROGRAM-ID.  SIMPLE.
  AUTHOR.        ME.
ENVIRONMENT DIVISION.
DATA DIVISION.
WORKING-STORAGE SECTION.
01  KEY-OF-THE-RECORD      PIC X(4).
01  TIOALEN                PIC S9(4) COMP
                           VALUE +1920.

01  OUTPUT-SCREEN.
      02  LINE1       PIC X(80) VALUE SPACES.
      02  LINE2       PIC X(30) VALUE
                      'PROBLEM NUMBER - - - - - - - - - - - - - - - - - - - - -'.
      02  PNUM        PIC X(4).
      02  FILLER      PIC X(46) VALUE SPACES.
      02  LINE3       PIC X(30) VALUE
                      'REPORTED BY - - - - - - - - - - - - - - - - - - - - - - - -'.
      02  PNAME       PIC X(25).
      02  FILLER      PIC X(25) VALUE SPACES.
      02  LINE4       PIC X(30) VALUE
                      'APARTMENT NUMBER - - - - - - - - - - - - - - - - - - -'.
      02  PAPT        PIC X(3).
      02  FILLER      PIC X(47) VALUE SPACES.
      02  LINE5       PIC X(30) VALUE
                      'WILL BE FIXED BY - - - - - - - - - - - - - - - - - - - - - -'.
      02  PFIXEDBY    PIC X(30).
      02  FILLER      PIC X(20) VALUE SPACES.
      02  LINE6       PIC X(30) VALUE
                      'PROBLEM WILL BE FIXED ON - - - - - - - - - - - - -'.
      02  PFIXEDON    PIC X(8).
      02  FILLER      PIC X(42) VALUE SPACES.
```

```
    02   FILLER        PIC X(1200) VALUE SPACES.
    02   FILLER        PIC X(80) VALUE
         'YOU MUST PRESS CLEAR AND ENTER THE'.
    02   FILLER        PIC X(80) VALUE
         'TRANID AND THE NEXT NUMBER FOR YOUR'.
    02   FILLER        PIC X(80) VALUE
         'NEXT PROBLEM REPORT REQUEST.'.

01  ERROR-MSG.
    02   ETRANID       PIC X(4).
    02   EPNUM         PIC X(4).
    02   FILLER        PIC X(71) VALUE SPACES.
    02   FILLER        PIC X(80) VALUE SPACES.
    02   MSGAREA       PIC X(80) VALUE SPACES.
    02   FILLER        PIC X(80) VALUE SPACES.
    02   FILLER        PIC X(80) VALUE
         'PRESS CLEAR AND TRY ALL OVER AGAIN PLEASE.'.

LINKAGE SECTION.
01  DFHBLLDS.
    02   RESERVED                 PIC S9(8) COMP.
    02   TIOABLL                  PIC S9(8) COMP.
    02   FILEBLL                  PIC S9(8) COMP.

01  TIOA-AREA.
    02   UNFORMATTED-TRANID       PIC X(4).
    02   USERS-PROBLEM-NUMBER     PIC X(4).
    02   REST-OF-TIOA             PIC X(1912).

01  FILE-AREA.
    02   FNUM                     PIC X(4).
    02   FNAME                    PIC X(20).
    02   FAPT                     PIC X(3).
    02   FFIXEDBY                 PIC X(30).
    02   FFIXEDWHEN               PIC X(8).

PROCEDURE DIVISION.

    EXEC CICS RECEIVE SET(TIOABLL) LENGTH(TIOALEN)
      END-EXEC.
    MOVE UNFORMATTED-TRANID      TO ETRANID.
    MOVE USERS-PROBLEM-NUMBER  TO EPNUM.

    IF USERS-PROBLEM-NUMBER NOT NUMERIC THEN
      MOVE 'ERROR IN PROBLEM NUMBER, BAD DATA' TO
        MSGAREA
      EXEC CICS SEND FROM(ERROR-MSG) LENGTH(400)
        ERASE END-EXEC
```

```
        EXEC CICS RETURN END-EXEC.

    MOVE USERS-PROBLEM-NUMBER TO KEY-OF-THE-RECORD.

    EXEC CICS HANDLE CONDITION NOTFND(BAD-READ) END-EXEC.

    EXEC CICS READ DATASET('LAMSFILE')
        RIDFLD(KEY-OF-THE-RECORD) SET(FILEBLL) END-EXEC.

    MOVE FNUM       TO PNUM.
    MOVE FNAME      TO PNAME.
    MOVE FAPT       TO PAPT.
    MOVE FFIXEDBY   TO PFIXEDBY.
    MOVE FFIXEDON   TO PFIXEDON.

    EXEC CICS SEND FROM(OUTPUT-SCREEN) LENGTH(1920)
        ERASE END-EXEC.
    EXEC CICS RETURN END-EXEC.

BAD-READ.
    MOVE 'RECORD NOT FOUND IN THE FILE' TO MSGAREA.
    EXEC CICS SEND FROM(ERROR-MSG) LENGTH(400)
        ERASE END-EXEC.
    EXEC CICS RETURN END-EXEC.
    STOP RUN.
```

The program's output to the terminal is much like a report to a printer in a batch environment. Since terminal screens are usually 24 lines long by 80 columns wide, the output is structured in 80-column record layouts. In the event that an error occurs, the user must clear the screen and retype the transaction id and the problem number in order to reinitiate the transaction because there are no attributes on the screen displays, and thus there are no FSET fields to cause the transaction to be reinitiated. All initiation *must* be done by the user.

The SEND command simply identifies the area to be written out and the length of that area. The data are transferred to the terminal, through BMS, but no mapping operations or reformatting of the data from physical or symbolic maps will occur because these areas don't exist! Hence, processing is simple and results in a high-performing transaction.

Lastly, the processing within the program is much like that in any other program in that handle-condition actions are established and the program obtains and gives up control in the same way; the only thing that has changed is the way that data come in and go out of the program.

Instead of focusing on unformatted screen processing, this text has displayed many different ways—one of which could be unformatted processing—of implementing applications in a CICS processing environment. We have investigated several methods of communicating information to the user, some simple, others difficult. You should now have the ability and knowledge to implement almost any application under CICS, under any type of IBM 327x compatible device. As you reflect on the ideas, techniques, and commands, you may find that you favor one over another, but be careful. On-line processing should be approached thoughtfully, with due consideration for the many possible approaches to a situation. One approach may have advantages over another, but yet its disadvantages may make it unsuitable for your given application.

The final chapter of this text presents the Landlord Management System from several implementation viewpoints. Although you are probably aware of my biases from the text, I want you to decide on the implementation technique most suited to your interests and applications. The implementations in Chapter 15 do not contain any of the elaborate capabilities of CICS that were presented in this chapter. I leave you the task of incorporating the techniques discussed here into the implementations that follow. Good Luck.

THOUGHT QUESTIONS

1. *The discussion of attribute byte manipulation in an earlier chapter and the use of extended attributes in this chapter have a lot in common. Compare the setting of field color, highlighting, attributes at the mapset, map and field level from outside and inside the application program.*

2. *Derive a list of standards to be used in setting the attributes, color, and extended highlighting for a header or data field on a screen display.*

3. *If the unformatted screen processing discussion at the end of this chapter was combined with conversational programming, what additional types of processing could be done in an application program?*

15

THE LANDLORD MANAGEMENT APPLICATION

The final chapter is devoted to implementing the Landlord Management On-line System as described throughout the text. Many different implementation styles follow, some in nonconversational mode, others in conversational mode; and some in locate mode, others in move mode. Since we've already discussed the trade-offs throughout the chapters on each of the implementation approaches that follow, I'll let you decide which implementation method you will use in your environment.

The mapset that follows will be used for all examples of implementation of the Landlord Management System.

MAPSET CODE FOR THE SYSTEM

```
LAMSM     DFHMSD TYPE=DSECT,LANG=COBOL,CTRL=FREEKB,
                 BASE=MAPAREA,MODE=INOUT,TIOAPFX=YES
MENU      DFHMDI SIZE=(24,80),LINE=01,COLUMN=01
          DFHMDF POS=(01,001),                               C
                 ATTRB=(ASKIP,DRK,FSET),                      C
                 INITIAL='LAMS',                              C
                 LENGTH=04
MENUX     DFHMDF POS=(01,006),                               C
                 ATTRB=(ASKIP,DRK,FSET),                      C
                 INITIAL='M ',                                C
                 LENGTH=02
```

```
            DFHMDF POS=(01,009),                                    C
                   ATTRB=(ASKIP),                                   C
                   INITIAL='       LANDLORD MANAGEMENT ONLINE SYC
                   STEM',                                           C
                   LENGTH=39
            DFHMDF POS=(02,025),                                    C
                   ATTRB=(ASKIP),                                   C
                   INITIAL='SYSTEM MENU',                           C
                   LENGTH=11
            DFHMDF POS=(07,001),                                    C
                   ATTRB=(ASKIP),                                   C
                   INITIAL='CHOOSE ONE OF THE NUMBERED OPTIONS C
                   BELOW AND ENTER YOUR',                           C
                   LENGTH=55
            DFHMDF POS=(08,001),                                    C
                   ATTRB=(ASKIP),                                   C
                   INITIAL='SELECTION HERE ------------->'          C
                   ,LENGTH=29
CHOICE      DFHMDF POS=(08,031),                                    C
                   ATTRB=(BRT,NUM,UNPROT,IC),                       C
                   LENGTH=01
            DFHMDF POS=(08,033),                                    C
                   ATTRB=(ASKIP),                                   C
                   LENGTH=01
            DFHMDF POS=(11,007),                                    C
                   ATTRB=(ASKIP),                                   C
                   INITIAL='1.   INQUIRE ABOUT A PROBLEM',          C
                   LENGTH=27
            DFHMDF POS=(12,007),                                    C
                   ATTRB=(ASKIP),                                   C
                   INITIAL='2.   REPORT A NEW PROBLEM',             C
                   LENGTH=24
            DFHMDF POS=(13,007),                                    C
                   ATTRB=(ASKIP),                                   C
                   INITIAL='3.   UPDATE A PROBLEMS INFORMATION',C
                   LENGTH=33
            DFHMDF POS=(14,007),                                    C
                   ATTRB=(ASKIP),                                   C
                   INITIAL='4.   DELETE AN OLD PROBLEM THAT HAS C
                   BEEN FIXED',                                     C
                   LENGTH=45
MENUMSG     DFHMDF POS=(24,003),                                    C
                   ATTRB=(ASKIP,BRT),                               C
                   LENGTH=67
            DFHMDF POS=(24,071),                                    C
                   ATTRB=(ASKIP),                                   C
                   LENGTH=01
DISPLAY     DFHMDI SIZE=(24,80),LINE=01,COLUMN=01
            DFHMDF POS=(01,001),                                    C
```

```
                  ATTRB= (ASKIP,DRK,FSET),                          C
                  INITIAL='LAMS',                                   C
                  LENGTH=04
DISX       DFHMDF POS=(01,006),                                     C
                  ATTRB=(ASKIP,DRK,FSET),                           C
                  INITIAL='D ',                                     C
                  LENGTH=02
           DFHMDF POS=(01,009),                                     C
                  ATTRB=(ASKIP),                                    C
                  INITIAL='          LANDLORD MANAGEMENT ONLINE SC
                  YSTEM',                                           C
                  LENGTH=40
DISSUB     DFHMDF POS=(02,021),                                     C
                  ATTRB=(ASKIP,BRT,FSET),                           C
                  LENGTH=23
           DFHMDF POS=(02,045),                                     C
                  ATTRB=(ASKIP),                                    C
                  LENGTH=01
           DFHMDF POS=(05,001),                                     C
                  ATTRB=(ASKIP),                                    C
                  INITIAL='REPORT NUMBER --------------------C
                  ----------->',                                   C
                  LENGTH=47
PROBNUM    DFHMDF POS=(05,049),                                     C
                  ATTRB=(BRT,NUM,UNPROT,IC),                        C
                  LENGTH=05
           DFHMDF POS=(05,055),                                     C
                  ATTRB=(ASKIP),                                    C
                  LENGTH=01
           DFHMDF POS=(06,001),                                     C
                  ATTRB=(ASKIP),                                    C
                  INITIAL='REPORTED ON (DATE PROBLEM OCCURRED)C
                  ---------->'                                     C
                  LENGTH=47
MM         DFHMDF POS=(06,049),                                     C
                  ATTRB=(BRT,NUM,UNPROT),                           C
                  LENGTH=02
           DFHMDF POS=(06,052),                                     C
                  ATTRB=(ASKIP),                                    C
                  INITIAL='-',                                      C
                  LENGTH=01
DD         DFHMDF POS=(06,054),                                     C
                  ATTRB=(BRT,NUM,UNPROT),                           C
                  LENGTH=02
           DFHMDF POS=(06,057),                                     C
                  ATTRB=(ASKIP),                                    C
                  INITIAL='-',                                      C
                  LENGTH=01
YY         DFHMDF POS=(06,059),                                     C
```

```
                     ATTRB=(BRT,NUM,UNPROT),                         C
                     LENGTH=02
              DFHMDF POS=(06,062),                                   C
                     ATTRB=(ASKIP),                                  C
                     LENGTH=01
              DFHMDF POS=(08,001),                                   C
                     ATTRB=(ASKIP),                                  C
                     INITIAL='REPORTED BY (TENNANTS NAME) -------C
                     ----------->',                                  C
                     LENGTH=47
TENNANT       DFHMDF POS=(08,049),                                   C
                     ATTRB=(BRT,UNPROT),                             C
                     LENGTH=20
              DFHMDF POS=(08,070),                                   C
                     ATTRB=(ASKIP),                                  C
                     LENGTH=01
              DFHMDF POS=(09,001),                                   C
                     ATTRB=(ASKIP),                                  C
                     INITIAL='APARTMENT NUMBER HAVING THE PROBLEMC
                     ----------->',                                  C
                     LENGTH=47
APTNO         DFHMDF POS=(09,049),                                   C
                     ATTRB=(BRT,NUM,UNPROT),                         C
                     LENGTH=03
              DFHMDF POS=(09,053),                                   C
                     ATTRB=(ASKIP),                                  C
                     LENGTH=01
              DFHMDF POS=(11,001),                                   C
                     ATTRB=(ASKIP),                                  C
                     INITIAL='DESCRIPTION OF THE PROBLEM:',          C
                     LENGTH=27
              DFHMDF POS=(12,001),                                   C
                     ATTRB=(ASKIP),                                  C
                     INITIAL='---->',                                C
                     LENGTH=05
DESC1         DFHMDF POS=(12,007),                                   C
                     ATTRB=(BRT,UNPROT),                             C
                     LENGTH=50
              DFHMDF POS=(12,058),                                   C
                     ATTRB=(ASKIP),                                  C
                     INITIAL='<----',                                C
                     LENGTH=05
              DFHMDF POS=(13,001),                                   C
                     ATTRB=(ASKIP),                                  C
                     INITIAL='---->',                                C
                     LENGTH=05
DESC2         DFHMDF POS=(13,007),                                   C
                     ATTRB=(BRT,UNPROT),                             C
                     LENGTH=50
```

```
            DFHMDF POS=(13,058),                                   C
                   ATTRB=(ASKIP),                                  C
                   INITIAL='<----',                                C
                   LENGTH=05
            DFHMDF POS=(16,001),                                   C
                   ATTRB=(ASKIP),                                  C
                   INITIAL='REPAIR INFORMATION:   FIXED ON -----C
                   ------------>',                                 C
                   LENGTH=47
FIXMM       DFHMDF POS=(16,049),                                   C
                   ATTRB=(BRT,NUM,UNPROT),                         C
                   LENGTH=02
            DFHMDF POS=(16,052),                                   C
                   ATTRB=(ASKIP),                                  C
                   INITIAL='-',                                    C
                   LENGTH=01
FIXDD       DFHMDF POS=(16,054),                                   C
                   ATTRB=(BRT,NUM,UNPROT),                         C
                   LENGTH=02
            DFHMDF POS=(16,057),                                   C
                   ATTRB=(ASKIP),                                  C
                   INITIAL='-',                                    C
                   LENGTH=01
FIXYY       DFHMDF POS=(16,059),                                   C
                   ATTRB=(BRT,NUM,UNPROT),                         C
                   LENGTH=02
            DFHMDF POS=(16,062),                                   C
                   ATTRB=(ASKIP),                                  C
                   LENGTH=01
            DFHMDF POS=(17,022),                                   C
                   ATTRB=(ASKIP),                                  C
                   INITIAL='FIXED BY ---------------->',           C
                   LENGTH=26
STAFF       DFHMDF POS=(17,049),                                   C
                   ATTRB=(BRT,UNPROT),                             C
                   LENGTH=20
            DFHMDF POS=(17,070),                                   C
                   ATTRB=(ASKIP),                                  C
                   LENGTH=01
            DFHMDF POS=(18,022),                                   C
                   ATTRB=(ASKIP),                                  C
                   INITIAL='TIME REQUIRED TO FIX ---->',           C
                   LENGTH=26
FIXTIME     DFHMDF POS=(18,049),                                   C
                   ATTRB=(BRT,NUM,UNPROT),                         C
                   LENGTH=02
            DFHMDF POS=(18,052),                                   C
                   ATTRB=(ASKIP),                                  C
                   INITIAL='  (IN HOURS)',                         C
```

```
                   LENGTH=12
             DFHMDF POS=(19,022),                                    C
                   ATTRB=(ASKIP),                                    C
                   INITIAL='QUALITY OF WORK --------->',             C
                   LENGTH=26
QUALITY     DFHMDF POS=(19,049),                                    C
                   ATTRB=(BRT,UNPROT),                              C
                   LENGTH=01
             DFHMDF POS=(19,051),                                    C
                   ATTRB=(ASKIP),                                    C
                   INITIAL='   (E,G,A,P,T)',                         C
                   LENGTH=14
DELHDR1     DFHMDF POS=(22,005),                                    C
                   ATTRB=(ASKIP,DRK),                               C
                   INITIAL='ARE YOU SURE THIS IS THE RECORD TO      C
                   BE DELETED ? --->',                              C
                   LENGTH=52
YESNO       DFHMDF POS=(22,058),                                    C
                   ATTRB=(ASKIP,DRK,FSET),                          C
                   INITIAL='NO ',                                    C
                   LENGTH=03
DELHDR2     DFHMDF POS=(22,062),                                    C
                   ATTRB=(ASKIP,DRK),                               C
                   INITIAL='<---',                                   C
                   LENGTH=04
DISMSG      DFHMDF POS=(24,003),                                    C
                   ATTRB=(ASKIP,BRT),                               C
                   LENGTH=67
             DFHMDF POS=(24,071),                                    C
                   ATTRB=(ASKIP),                                    C
                   LENGTH=01
KEY         DFHMDI SIZE=(24,80),LINE=01,COLUMN=01
             DFHMDF POS=(01,001),                                    C
                   ATTRB=(ASKIP,DRK,FSET),                          C
                   INITIAL='LAMS',                                   C
                   LENGTH=04
KEYX        DFHMDF POS=(01,006),                                    C
                   ATTRB=(ASKIP,DRK,FSET),                          C
                   INITIAL='K ',                                     C
                   LENGTH=02
             DFHMDF POS=(01,009),                                    C
                   ATTRB=(ASKIP),                                    C
                   INITIAL='          LANDLORD MANAGEMENT ONLINE    C
                   SYSTEM',                                          C
                   LENGTH=41
KEYSUB      DFHMDF POS=(02,021),                                    C
                   ATTRB=(ASKIP,BRT,FSET),                          C
                   LENGTH=26
             DFHMDF POS=(02,048),                                    C
```

```
                     ATTRB=(ASKIP),                              C
                     LENGTH=01
           DFHMDF POS=(06,003),                                 C
                     ATTRB=(ASKIP),                             C
                     INITIAL='IN THE AREA SHOWN BELOW, ENTER THE C
                     NUMBER OF THE PROBLEM THAT',               C
                     LENGTH=61
           DFHMDF POS=(07,003),                                 C
                     ATTRB=(ASKIP),                             C
                     INITIAL='YOU WOULD LIKE TO LOOK AT.   AFTER YC
                     OU HAVE ENTERED THE PROBLEM',              C
                     LENGTH=62
           DFHMDF POS=(08,003),                                 C
                     ATTRB=(ASKIP),                             C
                     INITIAL='NUMBER, PRESS THE ENTER KEY TO CONTC
                     INUE WITH YOR REQUEST.',                   C
                     LENGTH=58
           DFHMDF POS=(11,019),                                 C
                     ATTRB=(ASKIP),                             C
                     INITIAL='---------->',                     C
                     LENGTH=11
KEYVAL     DFHMDF POS=(11,031),                                 C
                     ATTRB=(BRT,NUM,UNPROT,IC),                 C
                     LENGTH=05
           DFHMDF POS=(11,037),                                 C
                     ATTRB=(ASKIP),                             C
                     INITIAL='<----------',                     C
                     LENGTH=11
KEYMSG     DFHMDF POS=(24,004),                                 C
                     ATTRB=(ASKIP,BRT),                         C
                     LENGTH=66
           DFHMDF POS=(24,071),                                 C
                     ATTRB=(ASKIP),                             C
                     LENGTH=01
           DFHMSD TYPE=FINAL
           END
```

SYMBOLIC MAPSET DEFINITION
AFTER ASSEMBLY

```
      01  MENUI.
          02  FILLER PIC X(12).
          02  MENUXL             COMP  PIC  S9(4).
          02  MENUXF             PICTURE X.
          02  FILLER REDEFINES MENUXF.
            03 MENUXA             PICTURE X.
          02  MENUXI             PIC X(2).
```

```
02  CHOICEL              COMP  PIC  S9(4).
02  CHOICEF              PICTURE X.
02  FILLER REDEFINES CHOICEF.
    03 CHOICEA           PICTURE X.
02  CHOICEI              PIC X(1).
02  MENUMSGL             COMP  PIC  S9(4).
02  MENUMSGF             PICTURE X.
02  FILLER REDEFINES MENUMSGF.
    03 MENUMSGA          PICTURE X.
02  MENUMSGI             PIC X(67).
01  MENUO REDEFINES MENUI.
02  FILLER               PIC X(12).
02  FILLER               PICTURE X(3).
02  MENUXO               PIC X(2).
02  FILLER               PICTURE X(3).
02  CHOICEO              PIC X(1).
02  FILLER               PICTURE X(3).
02  MENUMSGO             PIC X(67).
01  DISPLAYI.
02  FILLER               PIC X(12).
02  DISXL                COMP  PIC  S9(4).
02  DISXF                PICTURE X.
02  FILLER REDEFINES DISXF.
    03 DISXA             PICTURE X.
02  DISXI                PIC X(2).
02  DISSUBL              COMP  PIC  S9(4).
02  DISSUBF              PICTURE X.
02  FILLER REDEFINES DISSUBF.
    03 DISSUBA           PICTURE X.
02  DISSUBI              PIC X(23).
02  PROBNUML             COMP  PIC  S9(4).
02  PROBNUMF             PICTURE X.
02  FILLER REDEFINES PROBNUMF.
    03 PROBNUMA          PICTURE X.
02  PROBNUMI             PIC X(5).
02  MML                  COMP  PIC  S9(4).
02  MMF                  PICTURE X.
02  FILLER REDEFINES MMF.
    03 MMA               PICTURE X.
02  MMI                  PIC X(2).
02  DDL                  COMP  PIC  S9(4).
02  DDF                  PICTURE X.
02  FILLER REDEFINES DDF.
    03 DDA               PICTURE X.
02  DDI                  PIC X(2).
02  YYL                  COMP  PIC  S9(4).
02  YYF                  PICTURE X.
02  FILLER REDEFINES YYF.
    03 YYA               PICTURE X.
```

```
02  YYI                    PIC X(2).
02  TENNANTL               COMP  PIC   S9(4).
02  TENNANTF               PICTURE X.
02  FILLER REDEFINES TENNANTF.
    03 TENNANTA            PICTURE X.
02  TENNANTI               PIC X(20).
02  APTNOL                 COMP  PIC   S9(4).
02  APTNOF                 PICTURE X.
02  FILLER REDEFINES APTNOF.
    03 APTNOA              PICTURE X.
02  APTNOI                 PIC X(3).
02  DESC1L                 COMP  PIC   S9(4).
02  DESC1F                 PICTURE X.
02  FILLER REDEFINES DESC1F.
    03 DESC1A              PICTURE X.
02  DESC1I                 PIC X(50).
02  DESC2L                 COMP  PIC   S9(4).
02  DESC2F                 PICTURE X.
02  FILLER REDEFINES DESC2F.
    03 DESC2A              PICTURE X.
02  DESC2I                 PIC X(50).
02  FIXMML                 COMP  PIC   S9(4).
02  FIXMMF                 PICTURE X.
02  FILLER REDEFINES FIXMMF.
    03 FIXMMA              PICTURE X.
02  FIXMMI                 PIC X(2).
02  FIXDDL                 COMP  PIC   S9(4).
02  FIXDDF                 PICTURE X.
02  FILLER REDEFINES FIXDDF.
    03 FIXDDA              PICTURE X.
02  FIXDDI  PIC X(2).
02  FIXYYL                 COMP  PIC   S9(4).
02  FIXYYF                 PICTURE X.
02  FILLER REDEFINES FIXYYF.
    03 FIXYYA              PICTURE X.
02  FIXYYI  PIC X(2).
02  STAFFL                 COMP  PIC   S9(4).
02  STAFFF                 PICTURE X.
02  FILLER REDEFINES STAFFF.
    03 STAFFA              PICTURE X.
02  STAFFI                 PIC X(20).
02  FIXTIMEL               COMP  PIC   S9(4).
02  FIXTIMEF               PICTURE X.
02  FILLER REDEFINES FIXTIMEF.
    03 FIXTIMEA            PICTURE X.
02  FIXTIMEI               PIC X(2).
02  QUALITYL               COMP  PIC   S9(4).
02  QUALITYF               PICTURE X.
02  FILLER REDEFINES QUALITYF.
```

```
          03  QUALITYA              PICTURE X.
      02  QUALITYI                  PIC X(1).
      02  DELHDR1L                  COMP  PIC   S9(4).
      02  DELHDR1F                  PICTURE X.
      02  FILLER REDEFINES DELHDR1F.
          03  DELHDR1A              PICTURE X.
      02  DELHDR1I                  PIC X(52).
      02  YESNOL                    COMP  PIC   S9(4).
      02  YESNOF                    PICTURE X.
      02  FILLER REDEFINES YESNOF.
          03  YESNOA                PICTURE X.
      02  YESNOI                    PIC X(3).
      02  DELHDR2L                  COMP  PIC   S9(4).
      02  DELHDR2F                  PICTURE X.
      02  FILLER REDEFINES DELHDR2F.
          03  DELHDR2A              PICTURE X.
      02  DELHDR2I                  PIC X(4).
      02  DISMSGL                   COMP  PIC   S9(4).
      02  DISMSGF                   PICTURE X.
      02  FILLER REDEFINES DISMSGF.
          03  DISMSGA               PICTURE X.
      02  DISMSGI                   PIC X(67).
  01  DISPLAYO REDEFINES DISPLAYI.
      02  FILLER                    PIC X(12).
      02  FILLER                    PICTURE X(3).
      02  DISXO                     PIC X(2).
      02  FILLER                    PICTURE X(3).
      02  DISSUBO                   PIC X(23).
      02  FILLER                    PICTURE X(3).
      02  PROBNUMO                  PIC X(5).
      02  FILLER                    PICTURE X(3).
      02  MMO                       PIC X(2).
      02  FILLER                    PICTURE X(3).
      02  DDO                       PIC X(2).
      02  FILLER                    PICTURE X(3).
      02  YYO                       PIC X(2).
      02  FILLER                    PICTURE X(3).
      02  TENNANTO                  PIC X(20).
      02  FILLER                    PICTURE X(3).
      02  APTNOO                    PIC X(3).
      02  FILLER                    PICTURE X(3).
      02  DESC1O                    PIC X(50).
      02  FILLER                    PICTURE X(3).
      02  DESC2O                    PIC X(50).
      02  FILLER                    PICTURE X(3).
      02  FIXMMO                    PIC X(2).
      02  FILLER                    PICTURE X(3).
      02  FIXDDO                    PIC X(2).
      02  FILLER                    PICTURE X(3).
```

```
      02   FIXYYO              PIC X(2).
      02   FILLER             PICTURE X(3).
      02   STAFFO             PIC X(20).
      02   FILLER             PICTURE X(3).
      02   FIXTIMEO           PIC X(2).
      02   FILLER             PICTURE X(3).
      02   QUALITYO           PIC X(1).
      02   FILLER             PICTURE X(3).
      02   DELHDR1O           PIC X(52).
      02   FILLER             PICTURE X(3).
      02   YESNOO             PIC X(3).
      02   FILLER             PICTURE X(3).
      02   DELHDR2O           PIC X(4).
      02   FILLER             PICTURE X(3).
      02   DISMSGO            PIC X(67).
01  KEYI.
      02   FILLER PIC X(12).
      02   KEYXL              COMP  PIC  S9(4).
      02   KEYXF              PICTURE X.
      02   FILLER REDEFINES KEYXF.
        03 KEYXA              PICTURE X.
      02   KEYXI  PIC X(2).
      02   KEYSUBL            COMP  PIC  S9(4).
      02   KEYSUBF            PICTURE X.
      02   FILLER REDEFINES KEYSUBF.
        03 KEYSUBA            PICTURE X.
      02   KEYSUBI            PIC X(26).
      02   KEYVALL            COMP  PIC  S9(4).
      02   KEYVALF            PICTURE X.
      02   FILLER REDEFINES KEYVALF.
        03 KEYVALA            PICTURE X.
      02   KEYVALI            PIC X(5).
      02   KEYMSGL            COMP  PIC  S9(4).
      02   KEYMSGF            PICTURE X.
      02   FILLER REDEFINES KEYMSGF.
        03 KEYMSGA            PICTURE X.
      02   KEYMSGI            PIC X(66).
01  KEYO REDEFINES KEYI.
      02   FILLER             PIC X(12).
      02   FILLER             PICTURE X(3).
      02   KEYXO              PIC X(2).
      02   FILLER             PICTURE X(3).
      02   KEYSUBO            PIC X(26).
      02   FILLER             PICTURE X(3).
      02   KEYVALO            PIC X(5).
      02   FILLER             PICTURE X(3).
      02   KEYMSGO            PIC X(66).
```

NONCONVERSATIONAL, SINGLE PROGRAM, MOVE MODE

The program that follows is an implementation of the landlord system in a nonconversational programming style. Further, there is just one program for the entire system and it is driven by a single transaction id. Finally, the program uses move-mode processing to communicate with the terminal or to perform any file operations needed for this system.

```
IDENTIFICATION DIVISION.
    PROGRAM-ID.  LAMS.
    AUTHOR.      ME.
ENVIRONMENT DIVISION.
DATA DIVISION.
WORKING-STORAGE SECTION.
01   TIOALEN                        PIC S9(4) COMP VALUE +1920.
01   LAMS                           PIC X(4)   VALUE 'LAMS'.
01   MENUMAP                        PIC X(8)   VALUE 'MENU'.
01   DISPLAYMAP                     PIC X(8)   VALUE 'DISPLAY'.
01   KEYMAP                         PIC X(8)   VALUE 'KEY'.
01   MAPSETNAME                     PIC X(8)   VALUE 'LAMSM'.
01   FILENAME                       PIC X(8)   VALUE 'MASTERF'.
01   DATA-FLAG                      PIC X(4).
01   LRECL                          PIC S9(4) COMP VALUE +300.

01   DATE-FROM-SYSTEM.
     02   SYSMM                     PIC X(2).
     02   FILLER                    PIC X.
     02   SYSDD                     PIC X(2).
     02   FILLER                    PIC X.
     02   SYSYY                     PIC X(2).

01   TIOA-AREA.
     02   FIRST-HALF-OF-TIOA        PIC X(20).
     02   UNFORMATTED-TIOA          REDEFINES FIRST-HALF-OF-TIOA.
          03   UNFORMATTED-TRANID   PIC X(4).
          03   FILLER               PIC X(16).
     02   FORMATTED-TIOA            REDEFINES FIRST-HALF-OF-TIOA.
          03   FILLER               PIC X(3).
          03   FORMATTED-TRANID     PIC X(4).
          03   FILLER               PIC X(3).
          03   FORMATTED-MAP-CODE   PIC X.
          03   FUNCTION-INDICATOR   PIC X.
          03   FILLER               PIC X(8).
     02   REST-OF-TIOA              PIC X(1900).

01   MF-KEY                         PIC 9(5).
```

```
01   MASTER-FILE.
     02   MF-PROBLEM             PIC 9(5).
     02   MF-REPORTED-ON.
          03   MF-REPORT-MM      PIC X(2).
          03   MF-REPORT-DD      PIC X(2).
          03   MF-REPORT-YY      PIC X(2).
     02   MF-TENNANT             PIC X(20).
     02   MF-APARTMENT           PIC X(3).
     02   MF-DESCRIPTION.
          03   MF-DESCRIPTION-1  PIC X(50).
          03   MF-DESCRIPTION-2  PIC X(50).
     02   MF-DATE-FIXED.
          03   MF-FIX-MM         PIC X(2).
          03   MF-FIX-DD         PIC X(2).
          03   MF-FIX-YY         PIC X(2).
     02   MF-STAFF               PIC X(20).
     02   MF-TIME-TO-FIX         PIC X(2).
     02   MF-QUALITY             PIC X.
     02   MF-FILLER              PIC X(138).

01   COPY ATTRBS.
01   COPY LAMSM.

PROCEDURE DIVISION.
     EXEC CICS RECEIVE INTO(TIOA-AREA)
         LENGTH(TIOALEN) END-EXEC.

     IF UNFORMATTED-TRANID = LAMS THEN
         EXEC CICS SEND MAP(MENUMAP) MAPSET(MAPSETNAME)
             MAPONLY ERASE END-EXEC
     ELSE
     IF FORMATTED-MAP-CODE = 'M' THEN
         EXEC CICS RECEIVE MAP(MENUMAP) MAPSET(MAPSETNAME)
             FROM(TIOA-AREA) LENGTH(TIOALEN)
             INTO(MENUI) END-EXEC
         PERFORM PROCESS-MENU-MAP THRU MENU-MAP-EXIT
     ELSE
         IF FORMATTED-MAP-CODE = 'K' THEN
             EXEC CICS RECEIVE MAP(KEYMAP) MAPSET(MAPSETNAME)
                 FROM(TIOA-AREA) LENGTH(TIOALEN) INTO(KEYI)
                 END-EXEC
             PERFORM PROCESS-KEY-MAP THRU KEY-MAP-EXIT
         ELSE
             EXEC CICS RECEIVE MAP(DISPLAYMAP)
                 FROM(TIOA-AREA) LENGTH(TIOALEN)
                 MAPSET(MAPSETNAME) INTO(DISPLAYI) END-EXEC
             PERFORM PROCESS-DISPLAY-MAP THRU DISPLAY-MAP-EXIT.

     EXEC CICS RETURN END-EXEC.
     STOP RUN.
```

```
PROCESS-MENU-MAP.
    IF CHOICEI < '1' OR CHOICEI > '4' THEN
        MOVE 'INVALID CHOICE ENTERED, CORRECT AND REENTER'
            TO MENUMSGO
        MOVE -1   TO CHOICEL
        EXEC CICS SEND MAP(MENUMAP) MAPSET(MAPSETNAME)
          FROM(MENUO) ERASE CURSOR END-EXEC
    ELSE
    IF CHOICEI = '1' THEN
        MOVE '   INQUIRE ON A PROBLEM   ' TO KEYSUBO
        MOVE 'KI' TO KEYXO
        MOVE -1   TO KEYVALL
        EXEC CICS SEND MAP(KEYMAP) MAPSET(MAPSETNAME)
          FROM(KEYO) ERASE CURSOR END-EXEC
    ELSE
        IF CHOICEI = '2' THEN
            MOVE '   REPORT A PROBLEM   ' TO DISSUBO
            MOVE 'DA'  TO DISXO
            MOVE -1    TO PROBNUML
            MOVE CURRENT-DATE TO DATE-FROM-SYSTEM
            MOVE SYSMM   TO MMO
            MOVE SYSDD   TO DDO
            MOVE SYSYY   TO YYO
            MOVE UNPROT-BRT-FSET TO MMA
            MOVE UNPROT-BRT-FSET TO DDA
            MOVE UNPROT-BRT-FSET TO YYA
            EXEC CICS SEND MAP(DISPLAYMAP) MAPSET(MAPSETNAME)
              FROM(DISPLAYO) ERASE CURSOR END-EXEC
        ELSE
            IF CHOICEI = '3' THEN
                MOVE '   UPDATE A PROBLEM   ' TO KEYSUBO
                MOVE 'KU'  TO KEYXO
                MOVE -1    TO KEYVALL
                EXEC CICS SEND MAP(KEYMAP) MAPSET(MAPSETNAME)
                  FROM(KEYO) ERASE CURSOR END-EXEC
            ELSE
                MOVE '   DELETE A PROBLEM   ' TO KEYSUBO
                MOVE 'KD'  TO KEYXO
                MOVE -1    TO KEYVALL
                EXEC CICS SEND MAP(KEYMAP) MAPSET(MAPSETNAME)
                    FROM(KEYO) ERASE CURSOR END-EXEC.
MENU-MAP-EXIT.


PROCESS-KEY-MAP.
    IF KEYVALI NOT NUMERIC THEN
        MOVE 'PROBLEM NUMBER NOT VALID, REENTER' TO KEYMSGO
        MOVE -1            TO KEYVALL
        MOVE ASKIP-BRT-FSET  TO KEYVALA
```

```
                 EXEC CICS SEND MAP(KEYMAP) MAPSET(MAPSETNAME)
                     FROM(KEYO) ERASE CURSOR END-EXEC
             ELSE
                 IF KEYXI = 'KI' THEN
                 PERFORM  DISPLAY-RECORD-TO-SCREEN THRU DISPLAY-EXIT
             ELSE
                 IF KEYXI = 'KD' THEN
                     PERFORM DELETE-RECORD-FROM-FILE THRU DELETE-EXIT
                 ELSE
                     PERFORM UPDATE-RECORD-IN-FILE THRU UPDATE-EXIT.
     KEY-MAP-EXIT.


     DISPLAY-RECORD-TO-SCREEN.
         MOVE KEYVALI   TO   MF-KEY.
         EXEC CICS HANDLE CONDITION NOTFND(INQR-NOTFND) END-EXEC.
         EXEC CICS READ DATASET(FILENAME) INTO(MASTER-FILE)
             RIDFLD(MF-KEY) END-EXEC.
         PERFORM MOVE-MASTER-DATA-TO-SCREEN.
         PERFORM SET-ATTRIBUTES-FOR-INQUIRY.
         MOVE 'DI' TO DISXO.
         MOVE 'PRESS ENTER TO RETURN TO SYSTEM MENU' TO DISMSGO.
         EXEC CICS SEND MAP(DISPLAYMAP) MAPSET(MAPSETNAME)
             FROM(DISPLAYO) ERASE CURSOR(0) END-EXEC.
         GO TO DISPLAY-EXIT.

     INQR-NOTFND.
         MOVE 'SORRY, RECORD NOT IN THE FILE' TO KEYMSGO.
         MOVE -1    TO KEYVALL.
         EXEC CICS SEND MAP(KEYMAP) MAPSET(MAPSETNAME)
             FROM(KEYO) ERASE CURSOR END-EXEC.

     DISPLAY-EXIT. EXIT.

     DELETE-RECORD-FROM-FILE.
         MOVE KEYVALI   TO   MF-KEY.
         EXEC CICS HANDLE CONDITION NOTFND(DELT-NOTFND) END-EXEC.
         EXEC CICS READ DATASET(FILENAME) INTO(MASTER-FILE)
             RIDFLD(MF-KEY) END-EXEC.
         PERFORM MOVE-MASTER-DATA-TO-SCREEN.
         PERFORM SET-ATTRIBUTES-FOR-DELETE.
         MOVE ASKIP-NORM         TO DELHDR1A.
         MOVE ASKIP-NORM         TO DELHDR2A.
         MOVE UNPROT-BRT-FSET    TO YESNOA.
         MOVE 'DD'               TO DISXO.
         MOVE -1                 TO YESNOL.
         MOVE 'ENTER YES TO DELETE THIS RECORD      ' TO DISMSGO.
         EXEC CICS SEND MAP(DISPLAYMAP) MAPSET(MAPSETNAME)
```

```
            FROM(DISPLAYO) ERASE CURSOR END-EXEC.
        GO TO DELETE-EXIT.

    DELT-NOTFND.
        MOVE 'RECORD NOT IN FILE, CANT BE DELETED' TO KEYMSGO.
        MOVE -1    TO KEYVALL.
        EXEC CICS SEND MAP(KEYMAP) MAPSET(MAPSETNAME)
            FROM(KEYO) ERASE CURSOR END-EXEC.

    DELETE-EXIT.
        EXIT.

    UPDATE-RECORD-IN-FILE.
        MOVE KEYVALI    TO    MF-KEY.
        EXEC CICS HANDLE CONDITION NOTFND(UPDT-NOTFND) END-EXEC.
        EXEC CICS READ DATASET(FILENAME) INTO(MASTER-FILE)
            RIDFLD(MF-KEY) END-EXEC.
        PERFORM MOVE-MASTER-DATA-TO-SCREEN.
        PERFORM SET-ATTRIBUTES-FOR-UPDATE.
        MOVE 'DU'              TO DISXO.
        MOVE -1                TO FIXMML.
        MOVE 'MAKE CHANGES DESIRED, THEN ENTER.   ' TO DISMSGO.
        EXEC CICS SEND MAP(DISPLAYMAP) MAPSET(MAPSETNAME)
            FROM(DISPLAYO) ERASE CURSOR END-EXEC.
        GO TO UPDATE-EXIT.

    UPDT-NOTFND.
        MOVE 'RECORD NOT IN FILE, CANT BE UPDATED' TO KEYMSGO.
        MOVE -1    TO KEYVALL.
        EXEC CICS SEND MAP(KEYMAP) MAPSET(MAPSETNAME)
            FROM(KEYO) ERASE CURSOR END-EXEC.
    UPDATE-EXIT.
        EXIT.

    PROCESS-DISPLAY-MAP.
        IF DISXI = 'DI' THEN
            EXEC CICS SEND MAP(MENUMAP) MAPSET(MAPSETNAME)
                MAPONLY ERASE END-EXEC
        ELSE
            IF DISXI = 'DA' THEN
                PERFORM ADD-2 THRU ADD-EXIT
            ELSE
                IF DISXI = 'DD' THEN
                    PERFORM DELETE-2   THRU DELETE-2-EXIT
                ELSE
                    PERFORM UPDATE-2   THRU UPDATE-2-EXIT.
    DISPLAY-MAP-EXIT.
```

```
ADD-2.
    MOVE 'GOOD'          TO DATA-FLAG.
    PERFORM  EDIT-MASTER-SCREEN-DATA.
    IF DATA-FLAG = 'BAD' THEN
        PERFORM SET-ATTRIBUTES-FOR-ADD
        EXEC CICS SEND MAP (DISPLAYMAP) MAPSET (MAPSETNAME)
          FROM (DISPLAYO) ERASE CURSOR END-EXEC
        GO TO ADD-EXIT.

    PERFORM MOVE-SCREEN-DATA-TO-MASTER.
    MOVE MF-PROBLEM    TO MF-KEY.
    EXEC CICS HANDLE CONDITION NOSPACE(ADD-NOSPACE)
        DUPREC (ADD-DUPREC) END-EXEC.
    EXEC CICS WRITE DATASET(FILENAME) FROM(MASTER-FILE)
        RIDFLD (MF-KEY) LENGTH(LRECL) END-EXEC.
    MOVE 'RECORD ADDED, ENTER NEXT REQUEST' TO MENUMSGO.
    EXEC CICS SEND MAP(MENUMAP) MAPSET(MAPSETNAME)
      FROM (MENUO) ERASE END-EXEC.
    GO TO ADD-EXIT.

ADD-NOSPACE.
    MOVE 'NO SPACE IN FILE, CONTACT PROGRAMMER' TO MENUMSGO.
    EXEC CICS SEND MAP(MENUMAP) MAPSET(MAPSETNAME)
        FROM (MENUO) ERASE END-EXEC.
    GO TO ADD-EXIT.

ADD-DUPREC.
    MOVE 'RECORD ALREADY EXISTS, CHANGE KEY AND RETRY' TO
        DISMSGO.
    MOVE -1  TO PROBNUML.
    PERFORM SET-ATTRIBUTES-FOR-ADD.
    MOVE UNPROT-BRT-FSET   TO PROBNUMA.
    EXEC CICS SEND MAP(DISPLAYMAP) MAPSET(MAPSETNAME)
        FROM (DISPLAYO) ERASE CURSOR END-EXEC.

ADD-EXIT.
    EXIT.

DELETE-2.

    IF YESNOI NOT = 'YES' AND YESNOI NOT = 'NO' THEN
        MOVE 'YES OR NO NOT ENTERED, PLEASE ENTER AGAIN' TO
            DISMSGO
        MOVE -1    TO YESNOL
        MOVE ASKIP-NORM       TO DELHDR1A
        MOVE ASKIP-NORM       TO DELHDR2A
        MOVE UNPROT-BRT-FSET  TO YESNOA
```

```
      EXEC CICS SEND MAP(DISPLAYMAP) MAPSET(MAPSETNAME)
        FROM(DISPLAYO) ERASE END-EXEC
      GO TO DELETE-2-EXIT.

   IF YESNOI = 'NO' THEN

      MOVE 'DELETE NOT DONE AS REQUESTED' TO MENUMSGO
      EXEC CICS SEND MAP(MENUMAP) MAPSET(MAPSETNAME)
         FROM(MENUO) ERASE END-EXEC
      GO TO DELETE-2-EXIT.

   MOVE PROBNUMI  TO MF-KEY.
   EXEC CICS HANDLE CONDITION NOTFND(DEL2-NOTFND) END-EXEC.
   EXEC CICS DELETE DATASET(FILENAME) RIDFLD(MF-KEY)
      END-EXEC.
   MOVE 'RECORD DELETED AS REQUESTED' TO MENUMSGO.
   EXEC CICS SEND MAP(MENUMAP) MAPSET(MAPSETNAME)
     FROM(MENUO) ERASE END-EXEC.
   GO TO DELETE-2-EXIT.

DEL2-NOTFND.
   MOVE 'RECORD WAS DELETED BY ANOTHER USER' TO MENUMSGO.
   EXEC CICS SEND MAP(MENUMAP) MAPSET(MAPSETNAME)
      FROM(MENUO) ERASE END-EXEC.
DELETE-2-EXIT.
   EXIT.

UPDATE-2.
   MOVE 'GOOD'        TO DATA-FLAG.
   PERFORM  EDIT-MASTER-SCREEN-DATA.
   IF DATA-FLAG = 'BAD' THEN
      PERFORM SET-ATTRIBUTES-FOR-UPDATE
      EXEC CICS SEND MAP(DISPLAYMAP) MAPSET(MAPSETNAME)
        FROM(DISPLAYO) ERASE CURSOR END-EXEC
      GO TO UPDATE-2-EXIT.

   MOVE PROBNUMI     TO MF-KEY.
   EXEC CICS HANDLE CONDITION NOTFND(UPDT-2-NOTFND) END-EXEC.
   EXEC CICS READ DATASET(FILENAME) INTO(MASTER-FILE)
      RIDFLD(MF-KEY) UPDATE END-EXEC.

   PERFORM MOVE-SCREEN-DATA-TO-MASTER.
   EXEC CICS HANDLE CONDITION NOSPACE(UPDT-2-NOSPACE) END-EXEC.
   EXEC CICS REWRITE DATASET(FILENAME) FROM(MASTER-FILE)
      LENGTH(LRECL) END-EXEC.
   MOVE 'RECORD UPDATED, ENTER NEXT REQUEST' TO MENUMSGO.
   EXEC CICS SEND MAP(MENUMAP) MAPSET(MAPSETNAME)
     FROM(MENUO) ERASE END-EXEC.
   GO TO UPDATE-2-EXIT.
```

```
UPDT-2-NOSPACE.
    MOVE 'NO SPACE IN FILE, CONTACT PROGRAMMER' TO MENUMSGO.
    EXEC CICS SEND MAP(MENUMAP) MAPSET(MAPSETNAME)
        FROM(MENUO) ERASE END-EXEC.
    GO TO UPDATE-2-EXIT.

UPDT-2-NOTFND.
    MOVE 'RECORD DELETED FROM UNDERNEATH YOU, SORRY'   TO
        MENUMSGO.
    EXEC CICS SEND MAP(MENUMAP) MAPSET(MAPSETNAME)
        FROM(MENUO) ERASE CURSOR END-EXEC.
UPDATE-2-EXIT.
    EXIT.


MOVE-MASTER-DATA-TO-SCREEN.
    MOVE MF-PROBLEM       TO PROBNUMO.
    MOVE MF-REPORT-MM     TO MMO.
    MOVE MF-REPORT-DD     TO DDO.
    MOVE MF-REPORT-YY     TO YYO.
    MOVE MF-TENNANT       TO TENNANTO.
    MOVE MF-APARTMENT     TO APTNOO.
    MOVE MF-DESCRIPTION-1 TO DESC1O.
    MOVE MF-DESCRIPTION-2 TO DESC2O.
    MOVE MF-FIX-MM        TO FIXMMO.
    MOVE MF-FIX-DD        TO FIXDDO.
    MOVE MF-FIX-YY        TO FIXYYO.
    MOVE MF-STAFF         TO STAFFO.
    MOVE MF-TIME-TO-FIX   TO FIXTIMEO.
    MOVE MF-QUALITY       TO QUALITYO.


MOVE-SCREEN-DATA-TO-MASTER.
    MOVE PROBNUMI        TO MF-PROBLEM.
    MOVE MMI             TO MF-REPORT-MM.
    MOVE DDI             TO MF-REPORT-DD.
    MOVE YYI             TO MF-REPORT-YY.
    MOVE TENNANTI        TO MF-TENNANT.
    MOVE APTNOI          TO MF-APARTMENT.
    MOVE DESC1I          TO MF-DESCRIPTION-1.
    MOVE DESC2I          TO MF-DESCRIPTION-2.
    MOVE FIXMMI          TO MF-FIX-MM.
    MOVE FIXDDI          TO MF-FIX-DD.
    MOVE FIXYYI          TO MF-FIX-YY.
    MOVE STAFFI          TO MF-STAFF.
    MOVE FIXTIMEI        TO MF-TIME-TO-FIX.
    MOVE QUALITYI        TO MF-QUALITY.
    MOVE SPACES          TO MF-FILLER.


SET-ATTRIBUTES-FOR-INQUIRY.
    MOVE ASKIP-BRT       TO PROBNUMA.
```

```
      MOVE ASKIP-BRT          TO MMA.
      MOVE ASKIP-BRT          TO DDA.
      MOVE ASKIP-BRT          TO YYA.
      MOVE ASKIP-BRT          TO TENNANTA.
      MOVE ASKIP-BRT          TO APTNOA.
      MOVE ASKIP-BRT          TO DESC1A.
      MOVE ASKIP-BRT          TO DESC2A.
      MOVE ASKIP-BRT          TO FIXMMA.
      MOVE ASKIP-BRT          TO FIXDDA.
      MOVE ASKIP-BRT          TO FIXYYA.
      MOVE ASKIP-BRT          TO STAFFA.
      MOVE ASKIP-BRT          TO FIXTIMEA.
      MOVE ASKIP-BRT          TO QUALITYA.

  SET-ATTRIBUTES-FOR-DELETE.
      MOVE ASKIP-BRT-FSET     TO PROBNUMA.
      MOVE ASKIP-BRT-FSET     TO MMA.
      MOVE ASKIP-BRT-FSET     TO DDA.
      MOVE ASKIP-BRT-FSET     TO YYA.
      MOVE ASKIP-BRT-FSET     TO TENNANTA.
      MOVE ASKIP-BRT-FSET     TO APTNOA.
      MOVE ASKIP-BRT-FSET     TO DESC1A.
      MOVE ASKIP-BRT-FSET     TO DESC2A.
      MOVE ASKIP-BRT-FSET     TO FIXMMA.
      MOVE ASKIP-BRT-FSET     TO FIXDDA.
      MOVE ASKIP-BRT-FSET     TO FIXYYA.
      MOVE ASKIP-BRT-FSET     TO STAFFA.
      MOVE ASKIP-BRT-FSET     TO FIXTIMEA.
      MOVE ASKIP-BRT-FSET     TO QUALITYA.

  SET-ATTRIBUTES-FOR-UPDATE.
      MOVE ASKIP-BRT-FSET     TO PROBNUMA.
      MOVE UNPROT-BRT-FSET    TO MMA.
      MOVE UNPROT-BRT-FSET    TO DDA.
      MOVE UNPROT-BRT-FSET    TO YYA.
      MOVE UNPROT-BRT-FSET    TO TENNANTA.
      MOVE UNPROT-BRT-FSET    TO APTNOA.
      MOVE UNPROT-BRT-FSET    TO DESC1A.
      MOVE UNPROT-BRT-FSET    TO DESC2A.
      MOVE UNPROT-BRT-FSET    TO FIXMMA.
      MOVE UNPROT-BRT-FSET    TO FIXDDA.
      MOVE UNPROT-BRT-FSET    TO FIXYYA.
      MOVE UNPROT-BRT-FSET    TO STAFFA.
      MOVE UNPROT-BRT-FSET    TO FIXTIMEA.
      MOVE UNPROT-BRT-FSET    TO QUALITYA.

  SET-ATTRIBUTES-FOR-ADD.
      MOVE UNPROT-BRT-FSET    TO PROBNUMA.
      MOVE UNPROT-BRT-FSET    TO MMA.
      MOVE UNPROT-BRT-FSET    TO DDA.
```

```
     MOVE  UNPROT-BRT-FSET     TO YYA.
     MOVE  UNPROT-BRT-FSET     TO TENNANTA.
     MOVE  UNPROT-BRT-FSET     TO APTNOA.
     MOVE  UNPROT-BRT-FSET     TO DESC1A.
     MOVE  UNPROT-BRT-FSET     TO DESC2A.
     MOVE  UNPROT-BRT-FSET     TO FIXMMA.
     MOVE  UNPROT-BRT-FSET     TO FIXDDA.
     MOVE  UNPROT-BRT-FSET     TO FIXYYA.
     MOVE  UNPROT-BRT-FSET     TO STAFFA.
     MOVE  UNPROT-BRT-FSET     TO FIXTIMEA.
     MOVE  UNPROT-BRT-FSET     TO QUALITYA.

EDIT-MASTER-SCREEN-DATA.
     IF PROBNUMI NOT NUMERIC THEN
        MOVE 'PROBLEM NUMBER IS NOT ALL DIGITS' TO DISMSGO
        MOVE -1  TO PROBNUMA
        MOVE 'BAD'   TO DATA-FLAG
     ELSE
      IF MMI NOT NUMERIC OR MMI < '01' OR MMI > '12' THEN
        MOVE 'MONTH ENTERED IS NOT VALID' TO DISMSGO
        MOVE -1  TO MML
        MOVE 'BAD'  TO DATA-FLAG
       ELSE
        IF DDI NOT NUMERIC OR DDI < '01' OR DDI > '31' THEN
          MOVE 'DAY ENTERED IS NOT VALID' TO DISMSGO
          MOVE -1   TO DDL
          MOVE 'BAD' TO DATA-FLAG
         ELSE
          IF YYI NOT NUMERIC OR YYI < '01' THEN
            MOVE 'YEAR IS NOT VALID' TO DISMSGO
            MOVE -1  TO DDL
            MOVE 'BAD' TO DATA-FLAG
           ELSE
            IF TENNANTL = +0 OR TENNANTI = LOW-VALUES OR
               TENNANTI = SPACES THEN
              MOVE 'A TENNANTS NAME MUST BE ENTERED' TO DISMSGO
              MOVE -1  TO TENNANTL
              MOVE 'BAD' TO DATA-FLAG
             ELSE
              IF APTNOI NOT NUMERIC OR APTNOL = +0 THEN
                MOVE 'PLEASE ENTER AN APARTMENT NUMBER' TO
                        DISMSGO
                MOVE -1  TO APTNOL
                MOVE 'BAD' TO DATA-FLAG
               ELSE
                IF DESC1L = +0 AND DESC2L = +0 THEN
                  MOVE 'A DESCIPTION MUST BE ENTERED' TO
                          DISMSGO
                  MOVE -1  TO DESC1L
                  MOVE 'BAD' TO DATA-FLAG.
```

NONCONVERSATIONAL, SINGLE PROGRAM, LOCATE MODE

The implementation that follows is that of a single program and, again, a single transaction for the entire system. In this version, however, locate-mode processing is the implementation method, and thus much less storage is required for this system during execution.

```
IDENTIFICATION DIVISION.
      PROGRAM-ID.  LAMS.
      AUTHOR.      ME.
ENVIRONMENT DIVISION.
DATA DIVISION.
WORKING-STORAGE SECTION.
01  TIOALEN                          PIC S9(4)  COMP VALUE +1920.
01  LAMS                             PIC X(4)   VALUE 'LAMS'.
01  MENUMAP                          PIC X(8)   VALUE 'MENU'.
01  DISPLAYMAP                       PIC X(8)   VALUE 'DISPLAY'.
01  KEYMAP                           PIC X(8)   VALUE 'KEY'.
01  MAPSETNAME                       PIC X(8)   VALUE 'LAMSM'.
01  FILENAME                         PIC X(8)   VALUE 'MASTERF'.
01  DATA-FLAG                        PIC X(4).
01  LRECL                            PIC S9(4)  COMP VALUE +300.
01  HEX00                            PIC X      VALUE LOW-VALUES.

01  DATE-FROM-SYSTEM.
      02  SYSMM                      PIC X(2).
      02  FILLER                     PIC X.
      02  SYSDD                      PIC X(2).
      02  FILLER                     PIC X.
      02  SYSYY                      PIC X(2).

01  MF-KEY                           PIC 9(5).
01  COPY ATTRBS.

LINKAGE SECTION.
01  DFHBLLDS.
      02  RESERVED-BLL               PIC S9(8)  COMP.
      02  TIOABLL                    PIC S9(8)  COMP.
      02  MAPBLL                     PIC S9(8)  COMP.
      02  FILEBLL                    PIC S9(8)  COMP.

01  TIOA-AREA.
      02  FIRST-HALF-OF-TIOA         PIC X(20).
      02  UNFORMATTED-TIOA           REDEFINES FIRST-HALF-OF-TIOA.
          03  UNFORMATTED-TRANID     PIC X(4).
          03  FILLER                 PIC X(16).
```

```
      02   FORMATTED-TIOA            REDEFINES FIRST-HALF-OF-TIOA.
           03   FILLER               PIC X(3).
           03   FORMATTED-TRANID     PIC X(4).
           03   FILLER               PIC X(3).
           03   FORMATTED-MAP-CODE   PIC X.
           03   FUNCTION-INDICATOR   PIC X.
           03   FILLER               PIC X(8).
      02   REST-OF-TIOA             PIC X(1900).
01   MAPAREA                        PIC X(1920).
01   COPY LAMSM.

01   MASTER-FILE.
      02   MF-PROBLEM               PIC 9(5).
      02   MF-REPORTED-ON.
           03   MF-REPORT-MM         PIC X(2).
           03   MF-REPORT-DD         PIC X(2).
           03   MF-REPORT-YY         PIC X(2).
      02   MF-TENNANT               PIC X(20).
      02   MF-APARTMENT             PIC X(3).
      02   MF-DESCRIPTION.
           03   MF-DESCRIPTION-1     PIC X(50).
           03   MF-DESCRIPTION-2     PIC X(50).
      02   MF-DATE-FIXED.
           03   MF-FIX-MM            PIC X(2).
           03   MF-FIX-DD            PIC X(2).
           03   MF-FIX-YY            PIC X(2).
      02   MF-STAFF                 PIC X(20).
      02   MF-TIME-TO-FIX           PIC X(2).
      02   MF-QUALITY               PIC X.
      02   MF-FILLER                PIC X(138).


PROCEDURE DIVISION.
    EXEC CICS RECEIVE SET (TIOABLL)
       LENGTH (TIOALEN) END-EXEC.

    IF UNFORMATTED-TRANID = LAMS THEN
       EXEC CICS SEND MAP (MENUMAP) MAPSET (MAPSETNAME)
           MAPONLY ERASE END-EXEC
    ELSE
    IF FORMATTED-MAP-CODE = 'M' THEN
       EXEC CICS RECEIVE MAP (MENUMAP) MAPSET (MAPSETNAME)
           FROM (TIOA-AREA) LENGTH (TIOALEN)
           SET (MAPBLL) END-EXEC
       PERFORM PROCESS-MENU-MAP THRU MENU-MAP-EXIT
    ELSE
       IF FORMATTED-MAP-CODE = 'K' THEN
           EXEC CICS RECEIVE MAP (KEYMAP) MAPSET (MAPSETNAME)
               FROM (TIOA-AREA) LENGTH (TIOALEN) SET (MAPBLL)
```

```
                END-EXEC
            PERFORM PROCESS-KEY-MAP THRU KEY-MAP-EXIT
        ELSE
            EXEC CICS RECEIVE MAP(DISPLAYMAP)
                FROM(TIOA-AREA) LENGTH(TIOALEN)
                MAPSET(MAPSETNAME) SET(MAPBLL) END-EXEC
            PERFORM PROCESS-DISPLAY-MAP THRU DISPLAY-MAP-EXIT.

    EXEC CICS RETURN END-EXEC.
    STOP RUN.


PROCESS-MENU-MAP.
    IF CHOICEI < '1' OR CHOICEI > '4' THEN
        MOVE 'INVALID CHOICE ENTERED, CORRECT AND REENTER'
            TO MENUMSGO
        MOVE -1    TO CHOICEL
        EXEC CICS SEND MAP(MENUMAP) MAPSET(MAPSETNAME)
            FROM(MENUO) ERASE CURSOR END-EXEC
    ELSE
    IF CHOICEI = '1' THEN
        EXEC CICS GETMAIN SET(MAPBLL) LENGTH(2000)
            INITIMG(HEX00) END-EXEC
        MOVE '    INQUIRE ON A PROBLEM    ' TO KEYSUBO
        MOVE 'KI' TO KEYXO
        MOVE -1    TO KEYVALL
        EXEC CICS SEND MAP(KEYMAP) MAPSET(MAPSETNAME)
            FROM(KEYO) ERASE CURSOR END-EXEC
    ELSE
        IF CHOICEI = '2' THEN
            EXEC CICS GETMAIN SET(MAPBLL) LENGTH(2000)
                INITIMG(HEX00) END-EXEC
            MOVE '    REPORT A PROBLEM    ' TO DISSUBO
            MOVE 'DA'    TO DISXO
            MOVE -1      TO PROBNUML
            MOVE CURRENT-DATE TO DATE-FROM-SYSTEM
            MOVE SYSMM    TO MMO
            MOVE SYSDD    TO DDO
            MOVE SYSYY    TO YYO
            MOVE UNPROT-BRT-FSET TO MMA
            MOVE UNPROT-BRT-FSET TO DDA
            MOVE UNPROT-BRT-FSET TO YYA
            EXEC CICS SEND MAP(DISPLAYMAP) MAPSET(MAPSETNAME)
                FROM(DISPLAYO) ERASE CURSOR END-EXEC
        ELSE
            IF CHOICEI = '3' THEN
                EXEC CICS GETMAIN SET(MAPBLL) LENGTH(2000)
                    INITIMG(HEX00) END-EXEC
                MOVE '    UPDATE A PROBLEM    ' TO KEYSUBO
                MOVE 'KU'    TO KEYXO
```

```
            MOVE -1        TO KEYVALL
            EXEC CICS SEND MAP(KEYMAP) MAPSET(MAPSETNAME)
                FROM(KEYO) ERASE CURSOR END-EXEC
        ELSE
            EXEC CICS GETMAIN SET(MAPBLL) LENGTH(2000)
                INITIMG(HEX00) END-EXEC
            MOVE '     DELETE A PROBLEM     ' TO KEYSUBO
            MOVE 'KD'    TO KEYXO
            MOVE -1      TO KEYVALL
            EXEC CICS SEND MAP(KEYMAP) MAPSET(MAPSETNAME)
                FROM(KEYO) ERASE CURSOR END-EXEC.
MENU-MAP-EXIT.


PROCESS-KEY-MAP.
    IF KEYVALI NOT NUMERIC THEN
        MOVE 'PROBLEM NUMBER NOT VALID, REENTER' TO KEYMSGO
        MOVE -1              TO KEYVALL
        MOVE ASKIP-BRT-FSET  TO KEYVALA
        EXEC CICS SEND MAP(KEYMAP) MAPSET(MAPSETNAME)
            FROM(KEYO) ERASE CURSOR END-EXEC
    ELSE
        IF KEYXI = 'KI' THEN
        PERFORM  DISPLAY-RECORD-TO-SCREEN THRU DISPLAY-EXIT
        ELSE
            IF KEYXI = 'KD' THEN
                PERFORM DELETE-RECORD-FROM-FILE THRU DELETE-EXIT
            ELSE
                PERFORM UPDATE-RECORD-IN-FILE THRU UPDATE-EXIT.
KEY-MAP-EXIT.


DISPLAY-RECORD-TO-SCREEN.
    MOVE KEYVALI    TO    MF-KEY.
    EXEC CICS HANDLE CONDITION NOTFND(INQR-NOTFND) END-EXEC.
    EXEC CICS READ DATASET(FILENAME) SET(FILEBLL)
        RIDFLD(MF-KEY) END-EXEC.
    EXEC CICS GETMAIN SET(MAPBLL) LENGTH(2000)
        INITIMG(HEX00) END-EXEC.
    PERFORM MOVE-MASTER-DATA-TO-SCREEN.
    PERFORM SET-ATTRIBUTES-FOR-INQUIRY.
    MOVE 'DI' TO DISXO.
    MOVE 'PRESS ENTER TO RETURN TO SYSTEM MENU' TO DISMSGO.
    EXEC CICS SEND MAP(DISPLAYMAP) MAPSET(MAPSETNAME)
        FROM(DISPLAYO) ERASE CURSOR(0) END-EXEC.
    GO TO DISPLAY-EXIT.

INQR-NOTFND.
    MOVE 'SORRY, RECORD NOT IN THE FILE' TO KEYMSGO.
```

```
      MOVE -1     TO KEYVALL.
      EXEC CICS SEND MAP(KEYMAP) MAPSET(MAPSETNAME)
         FROM(KEYO) ERASE CURSOR END-EXEC.

DISPLAY-EXIT. EXIT.

DELETE-RECORD-FROM-FILE.
      MOVE KEYVALI   TO   MF-KEY.
      EXEC CICS HANDLE CONDITION NOTFND(DELT-NOTFND) END-EXEC.
      EXEC CICS READ DATASET(FILENAME) SET(FILEBLL)
         RIDFLD(MF-KEY) END-EXEC.
      EXEC CICS GETMAIN SET(MAPBLL) LENGTH(2000)
         INITIMG(HEX00) END-EXEC.
      PERFORM MOVE-MASTER-DATA-TO-SCREEN.
      PERFORM SET-ATTRIBUTES-FOR-DELETE.
      MOVE ASKIP-NORM        TO DELHDR1A.
      MOVE ASKIP-NORM        TO DELHDR2A.
      MOVE UNPROT-BRT-FSET   TO YESNOA.
      MOVE 'DD'              TO DISXO.
      MOVE -1               TO YESNOL.
      MOVE 'ENTER YES TO DELETE THIS RECORD     ' TO DISMSGO.
      EXEC CICS SEND MAP(DISPLAYMAP) MAPSET(MAPSETNAME)
         FROM(DISPLAYO) ERASE CURSOR END-EXEC.
      GO TO DELETE-EXIT.

DELT-NOTFND.
      MOVE 'RECORD NOT IN FILE, CANT BE DELETED' TO KEYMSGO.
      MOVE -1     TO KEYVALL.
      EXEC CICS SEND MAP(KEYMAP) MAPSET(MAPSETNAME)
         FROM(KEYO) ERASE CURSOR END-EXEC.

DELETE-EXIT.
      EXIT.

UPDATE-RECORD-IN-FILE.
      MOVE KEYVALI   TO   MF-KEY.
      EXEC CICS HANDLE CONDITION NOTFND(UPDT-NOTFND) END-EXEC.
      EXEC CICS READ DATASET(FILENAME) SET(FILEBLL)
         RIDFLD(MF-KEY) END-EXEC.
      EXEC CICS GETMAIN SET(MAPBLL) LENGTH(2000)
         INITIMG(HEX00) END-EXEC.
      PERFORM MOVE-MASTER-DATA-TO-SCREEN.
      PERFORM SET-ATTRIBUTES-FOR-UPDATE.
      MOVE 'DU'             TO DISXO.
      MOVE -1               TO FIXMML.
      MOVE 'MAKE CHANGES DESIRED, THEN ENTER.   ' TO DISMSGO.
      EXEC CICS SEND MAP(DISPLAYMAP) MAPSET(MAPSETNAME)
         FROM(DISPLAYO) ERASE CURSOR END-EXEC.
      GO TO UPDATE-EXIT.
```

```
UPDT-NOTFND.
    MOVE 'RECORD NOT IN FILE, CANT BE UPDATED' TO KEYMSGO.
    MOVE -1    TO KEYVALL.
    EXEC CICS SEND MAP(KEYMAP) MAPSET(MAPSETNAME)
        FROM(KEYO) ERASE CURSOR END-EXEC.
UPDATE-EXIT.
    EXIT.


PROCESS-DISPLAY-MAP.
    IF DISXI = 'DI' THEN
        EXEC CICS SEND MAP(MENUMAP) MAPSET(MAPSETNAME)
            MAPONLY ERASE END-EXEC
    ELSE
        IF DISXI = 'DA' THEN
            PERFORM ADD-2 THRU ADD-EXIT
        ELSE
            IF DISXI = 'DD' THEN
                PERFORM DELETE-2  THRU DELETE-2-EXIT
            ELSE
                PERFORM UPDATE-2  THRU UPDATE-2-EXIT.
DISPLAY-MAP-EXIT.


ADD-2.
    MOVE 'GOOD'       TO DATA-FLAG.
    PERFORM  EDIT-MASTER-SCREEN-DATA.
    IF DATA-FLAG = 'BAD' THEN
        PERFORM SET-ATTRIBUTES-FOR-ADD
        EXEC CICS SEND MAP(DISPLAYMAP) MAPSET(MAPSETNAME)
          FROM(DISPLAYO) ERASE CURSOR END-EXEC
        GO TO ADD-EXIT.

    EXEC CICS GETMAIN SET(FILEBLL) LENGTH(300)
        INITIMG(HEX00) END-EXEC.
    PERFORM MOVE-SCREEN-DATA-TO-MASTER.
    MOVE MF-PROBLEM    TO MF-KEY.
    EXEC CICS HANDLE CONDITION NOSPACE(ADD-NOSPACE)
        DUPREC(ADD-DUPREC) END-EXEC.
    EXEC CICS WRITE DATASET(FILENAME) FROM(MASTER-FILE)
        RIDFLD(MF-KEY) LENGTH(LRECL) END-EXEC.
    EXEC CICS GETMAIN SET(MAPBLL) LENGTH(2000)
        INITIMG(HEX00) END-EXEC.
    MOVE 'RECORD ADDED, ENTER NEXT REQUEST' TO MENUMSGO.
    EXEC CICS SEND MAP(MENUMAP) MAPSET(MAPSETNAME)
      FROM(MENUO) ERASE END-EXEC.
    GO TO ADD-EXIT.


ADD-NOSPACE.
    EXEC CICS GETMAIN SET(MAPBLL) LENGTH(2000)
        INITIMG(HEX00) END-EXEC.
```

```
        MOVE 'NO SPACE IN FILE, CONTACT PROGRAMMER' TO MENUMSGO.
        EXEC CICS SEND MAP(MENUMAP) MAPSET(MAPSETNAME)
            FROM(MENUO) ERASE END-EXEC.
        GO TO ADD-EXIT.

ADD-DUPREC.
        MOVE 'RECORD ALREADY EXISTS, CHANGE KEY AND RETRY' TO
            DISMSGO.
        MOVE -1   TO PROBNUML.
        PERFORM SET-ATTRIBUTES-FOR-ADD.
        MOVE UNPROT-BRT-FSET    TO PROBNUMA.
        EXEC CICS SEND MAP(DISPLAYMAP) MAPSET(MAPSETNAME)
            FROM(DISPLAYO) ERASE CURSOR END-EXEC.

ADD-EXIT.
        EXIT.

DELETE-2.

        IF YESNOI NOT = 'YES' AND YESNOI NOT = 'NO' THEN
            MOVE 'YES OR NO NOT ENTERED, PLEASE ENTER AGAIN' TO
                DISMSGO
            MOVE -1   TO YESNOL
            MOVE ASKIP-NORM         TO DELHDR1A
            MOVE ASKIP-NORM         TO DELHDR2A
            MOVE UNPROT-BRT-FSET    TO YESNOA
            EXEC CICS SEND MAP(DISPLAYMAP) MAPSET(MAPSETNAME)
                FROM(DISPLAYO) ERASE END-EXEC
            GO TO DELETE-2-EXIT.

        IF YESNOI = 'NO' THEN
            EXEC CICS GETMAIN SET(MAPBLL) LENGTH(2000)
                INITIMG(HEX00) END-EXEC
            MOVE 'DELETE NOT DONE AS REQUESTED' TO MENUMSGO
            EXEC CICS SEND MAP(MENUMAP) MAPSET(MAPSETNAME)
                FROM(MENUO) ERASE END-EXEC
            GO TO DELETE-2-EXIT.

        MOVE PROBNUMI  TO MF-KEY.
        EXEC CICS HANDLE CONDITION NOTFND(DEL2-NOTFND) END-EXEC.
        EXEC CICS DELETE DATASET(FILENAME) RIDFLD(MF-KEY)
            END-EXEC.
        EXEC CICS GETMAIN SET(MAPBLL) LENGTH(2000)
            INITIMG(HEX00) END-EXEC.
        MOVE 'RECORD DELETED AS REQUESTED' TO MENUMSGO.
        EXEC CICS SEND MAP(MENUMAP) MAPSET(MAPSETNAME)
            FROM(MENUO) ERASE END-EXEC.
        GO TO DELETE-2-EXIT.
```

```
 DEL2-NOTFND.
     EXEC CICS GETMAIN SET (MAPBLL) LENGTH(2000)
         INITIMG(HEX00) END-EXEC.
     MOVE 'RECORD WAS DELETED BY ANOTHER USER' TO MENUMSGO.
     EXEC CICS SEND MAP(MENUMAP) MAPSET(MAPSETNAME)
         FROM(MENUO) ERASE END-EXEC.
 DELETE-2-EXIT.
     EXIT.


 UPDATE-2.
     MOVE 'GOOD'        TO DATA-FLAG.
     PERFORM  EDIT-MASTER-SCREEN-DATA.
     IF DATA-FLAG = 'BAD' THEN
         PERFORM SET-ATTRIBUTES-FOR-UPDATE
         EXEC CICS SEND MAP(DISPLAYMAP) MAPSET(MAPSETNAME)
           FROM(DISPLAYO) ERASE CURSOR END-EXEC
         GO TO UPDATE-2-EXIT.

     MOVE PROBNUMI       TO MF-KEY.
     EXEC CICS HANDLE CONDITION NOTFND(UPDT-2-NOTFND) END-EXEC.
     EXEC CICS READ DATASET(FILENAME) SET(FILEBLL)
         RIDFLD(MF-KEY) UPDATE END-EXEC.
     PERFORM MOVE-SCREEN-DATA-TO-MASTER.
     EXEC CICS HANDLE CONDITION NOSPACE(UPDT-2-NOSPACE) END-EXEC.
     EXEC CICS REWRITE DATASET(FILENAME) FROM(MASTER-FILE)
         LENGTH(LRECL) END-EXEC.
     EXEC CICS GETMAIN SET(MAPBLL) LENGTH(2000)
         INITIMG(HEX00) END-EXEC.
     MOVE 'RECORD UPDATED, ENTER NEXT REQUEST' TO MENUMSGO.
     EXEC CICS SEND MAP(MENUMAP) MAPSET(MAPSETNAME)
        FROM(MENUO) ERASE END-EXEC.
     GO TO UPDATE-2-EXIT.

 UPDT-2-NOSPACE.
     EXEC CICS GETMAIN SET(MAPBLL) LENGTH(2000)
         INITIMG(HEX00) END-EXEC.
     MOVE 'NO SPACE IN FILE, CONTACT PROGRAMMER' TO MENUMSGO.
     EXEC CICS SEND MAP(MENUMAP) MAPSET(MAPSETNAME)
         FROM(MENUO) ERASE END-EXEC.
     GO TO UPDATE-2-EXIT.

 UPDT-2-NOTFND.
     EXEC CICS GETMAIN SET(MAPBLL) LENGTH(2000)
         INITIMG(HEX00) END-EXEC.
     MOVE 'RECORD DELETED FROM UNDERNEATH YOU, SORRY'    TO
         MENUMSGO.
     EXEC CICS SEND MAP(MENUMAP) MAPSET(MAPSETNAME)
         FROM(MENUO) ERASE CURSOR END-EXEC.
```

```
UPDATE-2-EXIT.
    EXIT.

MOVE-MASTER-DATA-TO-SCREEN.
    MOVE  MF-PROBLEM         TO  PROBNUMO.
    MOVE  MF-REPORT-MM       TO  MMO.
    MOVE  MF-REPORT-DD       TO  DDO.
    MOVE  MF-REPORT-YY       TO  YYO.
    MOVE  MF-TENNANT         TO  TENNANTO.
    MOVE  MF-APARTMENT       TO  APTNOO.
    MOVE  MF-DESCRIPTION-1   TO  DESC1O.
    MOVE  MF-DESCRIPTION-2   TO  DESC2O.
    MOVE  MF-FIX-MM          TO  FIXMMO.
    MOVE  MF-FIX-DD          TO  FIXDDO.
    MOVE  MF-FIX-YY          TO  FIXYYO.
    MOVE  MF-STAFF           TO  STAFFO.
    MOVE  MF-TIME-TO-FIX     TO  FIXTIMEO.
    MOVE  MF-QUALITY         TO  QUALITYO.

MOVE-SCREEN-DATA-TO-MASTER.
    MOVE  PROBNUMI           TO  MF-PROBLEM.
    MOVE  MMI                TO  MF-REPORT-MM.
    MOVE  DDI                TO  MF-REPORT-DD.
    MOVE  YYI                TO  MF-REPORT-YY.
    MOVE  TENNANTI           TO  MF-TENNANT.
    MOVE  APTNOI             TO  MF-APARTMENT.
    MOVE  DESC1I             TO  MF-DESCRIPTION-1.
    MOVE  DESC2I             TO  MF-DESCRIPTION-2.
    MOVE  FIXMMI             TO  MF-FIX-MM.
    MOVE  FIXDDI             TO  MF-FIX-DD.
    MOVE  FIXYYI             TO  MF-FIX-YY.
    MOVE  STAFFI             TO  MF-STAFF.
    MOVE  FIXTIMEI           TO  MF-TIME-TO-FIX.
    MOVE  QUALITYI           TO  MF-QUALITY.
    MOVE  SPACES             TO  MF-FILLER.

SET-ATTRIBUTES-FOR-INQUIRY.
    MOVE  ASKIP-BRT          TO  PROBNUMA.
    MOVE  ASKIP-BRT          TO  MMA.
    MOVE  ASKIP-BRT          TO  DDA.
    MOVE  ASKIP-BRT          TO  YYA.
    MOVE  ASKIP-BRT          TO  TENNANTA.
    MOVE  ASKIP-BRT          TO  APTNOA.
    MOVE  ASKIP-BRT          TO  DESC1A.
    MOVE  ASKIP-BRT          TO  DESC2A.
    MOVE  ASKIP-BRT          TO  FIXMMA.
    MOVE  ASKIP-BRT          TO  FIXDDA.
    MOVE  ASKIP-BRT          TO  FIXYYA.
```

```
      MOVE ASKIP-BRT        TO STAFFA.
      MOVE ASKIP-BRT        TO FIXTIMEA.
      MOVE ASKIP-BRT        TO QUALITYA.

SET-ATTRIBUTES-FOR-DELETE.
      MOVE ASKIP-BRT-FSET   TO PROBNUMA.
      MOVE ASKIP-BRT-FSET   TO MMA.
      MOVE ASKIP-BRT-FSET   TO DDA.
      MOVE ASKIP-BRT-FSET   TO YYA.
      MOVE ASKIP-BRT-FSET   TO TENNANTA.
      MOVE ASKIP-BRT-FSET   TO APTNOA.
      MOVE ASKIP-BRT-FSET   TO DESC1A.
      MOVE ASKIP-BRT-FSET   TO DESC2A.
      MOVE ASKIP-BRT-FSET   TO FIXMMA.
      MOVE ASKIP-BRT-FSET   TO FIXDDA.
      MOVE ASKIP-BRT-FSET   TO FIXYYA.
      MOVE ASKIP-BRT-FSET   TO STAFFA.
      MOVE ASKIP-BRT-FSET   TO FIXTIMEA.
      MOVE ASKIP-BRT-FSET   TO QUALITYA.


SET-ATTRIBUTES-FOR-UPDATE.
      MOVE ASKIP-BRT-FSET    TO PROBNUMA.
      MOVE UNPROT-BRT-FSET   TO MMA.
      MOVE UNPROT-BRT-FSET   TO DDA.
      MOVE UNPROT-BRT-FSET   TO YYA.
      MOVE UNPROT-BRT-FSET   TO TENNANTA.
      MOVE UNPROT-BRT-FSET   TO APTNOA.
      MOVE UNPROT-BRT-FSET   TO DESC1A.
      MOVE UNPROT-BRT-FSET   TO DESC2A.
      MOVE UNPROT-BRT-FSET   TO FIXMMA.
      MOVE UNPROT-BRT-FSET   TO FIXDDA.
      MOVE UNPROT-BRT-FSET   TO FIXYYA.
      MOVE UNPROT-BRT-FSET   TO STAFFA.
      MOVE UNPROT-BRT-FSET   TO FIXTIMEA.
      MOVE UNPROT-BRT-FSET   TO QUALITYA.

SET-ATTRIBUTES-FOR-ADD.
      MOVE UNPROT-BRT-FSET   TO PROBNUMA.
      MOVE UNPROT-BRT-FSET   TO MMA.
      MOVE UNPROT-BRT-FSET   TO DDA.
      MOVE UNPROT-BRT-FSET   TO YYA.
      MOVE UNPROT-BRT-FSET   TO TENNANTA.
      MOVE UNPROT-BRT-FSET   TO APTNOA.
      MOVE UNPROT-BRT-FSET   TO DESC1A.
      MOVE UNPROT-BRT-FSET   TO DESC2A.
      MOVE UNPROT-BRT-FSET   TO FIXMMA.
      MOVE UNPROT-BRT-FSET   TO FIXDDA.
      MOVE UNPROT-BRT-FSET   TO FIXYYA.
```

```
      MOVE  UNPROT-BRT-FSET    TO STAFFA.
      MOVE  UNPROT-BRT-FSET    TO FIXTIMEA.
      MOVE  UNPROT-BRT-FSET    TO QUALITYA.


EDIT-MASTER-SCREEN-DATA.
      IF PROBNUMI NOT NUMERIC THEN
          MOVE 'PROBLEM NUMBER IS NOT ALL DIGITS' TO DISMSGO
          MOVE -1  TO PROBNUMA
          MOVE 'BAD'   TO DATA-FLAG
      ELSE
        IF MMI NOT NUMERIC OR MMI < '01' OR MMI > '12' THEN
           MOVE 'MONTH ENTERED IS NOT VALID' TO DISMSGO
           MOVE -1  TO MML
           MOVE 'BAD'  TO DATA-FLAG
        ELSE
          IF DDI NOT NUMERIC OR DDI < '01' OR DDI > '31' THEN
             MOVE 'DAY ENTERED IS NOT VALID' TO DISMSGO
             MOVE -1   TO DDL
             MOVE 'BAD' TO DATA-FLAG
          ELSE
            IF YYI NOT NUMERIC OR YYI < '01' THEN
               MOVE 'YEAR IS NOT VALID' TO DISMSGO
               MOVE -1  TO DDL
               MOVE 'BAD' TO DATA-FLAG
            ELSE
              IF TENNANTL = +0 OR TENNANTI = LOW-VALUES OR
                 TENNANTI = SPACES THEN
                 MOVE 'A TENNANTS NAME MUST BE ENTERED' TO DISMSGO
                 MOVE -1  TO TENNANTL
                 MOVE 'BAD' TO DATA-FLAG
              ELSE
                IF APTNOI NOT NUMERIC OR APTNOL = +0 THEN
                   MOVE 'PLEASE ENTER AN APARTMENT NUMBER' TO
                         DISMSGO
                   MOVE -1  TO APTNOL
                   MOVE 'BAD' TO DATA-FLAG
                ELSE
                  IF DESC1L = +0 AND DESC2L = +0 THEN
                     MOVE 'A DESCIPTION MUST BE ENTERED' TO
                          DISMSGO
                     MOVE -1  TO DESC1L
                     MOVE 'BAD'  TO DATA-FLAG.
```

NONCONVERSATIONAL, SINGLE PROGRAM, LOCATE MODE, COMMAREAS

Communication areas were a major topic in the latter chapters of this text and the single program and single transaction that follows uses COMMAREAs to help the program remember what it was doing the last time it left off. Hence, this version is also a nonconversational implementation using locate-mode processing for file and terminal I/O, but instead of hiding the fields on the screen to initiate the transaction and to remember what screen was being processed and which function was being performed, communication areas provide this support.

```
IDENTIFICATION DIVISION.
      PROGRAM-ID.   LAMS.
      AUTHOR.        ME.
ENVIRONMENT DIVISION.
DATA DIVISION.
WORKING-STORAGE SECTION.
01    TIOALEN                     PIC S9(4) COMP VALUE +1920.
01    LAMS                        PIC X(4)   VALUE 'LAMS'.
01    MENUMAP                     PIC X(8)   VALUE 'MENU'.
01    DISPLAYMAP                  PIC X(8)   VALUE 'DISPLAY'.
01    KEYMAP                      PIC X(8)   VALUE 'KEY'.
01    MAPSETNAME                  PIC X(8)   VALUE 'LAMSM'.
01    FILENAME                    PIC X(8)   VALUE 'MASTERF'.
01    DATA-FLAG                   PIC X(4).
01    LRECL                       PIC S9(4) COMP VALUE +300.
01    HEX00                       PIC X      VALUE LOW-VALUES.

01    DATE-FROM-SYSTEM.
      02   SYSMM                  PIC X(2).
      02   FILLER                 PIC X.
      02   SYSDD                  PIC X(2).
      02   FILLER                 PIC X.
      02   SYSYY                  PIC X(2).

01    MF-KEY                      PIC 9(5).
01    COPY ATTRBS.
01    COPY DFHAID.

01    MYCOMMAREA.
      02   BRAIN                  PIC X(2).
      02   XXX                    REDEFINES BRAIN.
           03   FORMATTED-MAP-CODE PIC X.
           03   FORMATTED-FUNCTION PIC X.
```

```
LINKAGE SECTION.
01  DFHCOMMAREA.
    02  BRAIN2                      PIC X(2).


01  DFHBLLDS.
    02  RESERVED-BLL                PIC S9(8) COMP.
    02  MAPBLL                      PIC S9(8) COMP.
    02  FILEBLL                     PIC S9(8) COMP.


01  MAPAREA                         PIC X(1920).
01  COPY LAMSM.
01  MASTER-FILE.
    02  MF-PROBLEM                  PIC 9(5).
    02  MF-REPORTED-ON.
        03  MF-REPORT-MM            PIC X(2).
        03  MF-REPORT-DD            PIC X(2).
        03  MF-REPORT-YY            PIC X(2).
    02  MF-TENNANT                  PIC X(20).
    02  MF-APARTMENT                PIC X(3).
    02  MF-DESCRIPTION.
        03  MF-DESCRIPTION-1        PIC X(50).
        03  MF-DESCRIPTION-2        PIC X(50).
    02  MF-DATE-FIXED.
        03  MF-FIX-MM               PIC X(2).
        03  MF-FIX-DD               PIC X(2).
        03  MF-FIX-YY               PIC X(2).
    02  MF-STAFF                    PIC X(20).
    02  MF-TIME-TO-FIX              PIC X(2).
    02  MF-QUALITY                  PIC X.
    02  MF-FILLER                   PIC X(138).



PROCEDURE DIVISION.
    IF EIBAID NOT = DFHENTER THEN
        EXEC CICS SEND FROM(HEX00) LENGTH(0)
            ERASE END-EXEC
        EXEC CICS RETURN END-EXEC.


    IF EIBCALEN = +0 THEN
        MOVE 'M ' TO BRAIN
        EXEC CICS SEND MAP(MENUMAP) MAPSET(MAPSETNAME)
            MAPONLY ERASE END-EXEC
    ELSE
    MOVE BRAIN2 TO BRAIN
    IF FORMATTED-MAP-CODE = 'M' THEN
        EXEC CICS RECEIVE MAP(MENUMAP) MAPSET(MAPSETNAME)
            SET(MAPBLL) END-EXEC
        PERFORM PROCESS-MENU-MAP THRU MENU-MAP-EXIT
```

```
    ELSE
        IF FORMATTED-MAP-CODE = 'K' THEN
            EXEC CICS RECEIVE MAP(KEYMAP) MAPSET(MAPSETNAME)
                SET(MAPBLL) END-EXEC
            PERFORM PROCESS-KEY-MAP THRU KEY-MAP-EXIT
        ELSE
            EXEC CICS RECEIVE MAP(DISPLAYMAP)
                MAPSET(MAPSETNAME) SET(MAPBLL) END-EXEC
            PERFORM PROCESS-DISPLAY-MAP THRU DISPLAY-MAP-EXIT.
    EXEC CICS RETURN COMMAREA(MYCOMMAREA) LENGTH(2)
        TRANSID(LAMS) END-EXEC.
    STOP RUN.


PROCESS-MENU-MAP.
    IF CHOICEI < '1' OR CHOICEI > '4' THEN
        MOVE 'INVALID CHOICE ENTERED, CORRECT AND REENTER'
            TO MENUMSGO
        MOVE -1   TO CHOICEL
        MOVE 'M ' TO BRAIN
        EXEC CICS SEND MAP(MENUMAP) MAPSET(MAPSETNAME)
            FROM(MENUO) ERASE CURSOR END-EXEC
    ELSE
    IF CHOICEI = '1' THEN
        EXEC CICS GETMAIN SET(MAPBLL) LENGTH(2000)
            INITIMG(HEX00) END-EXEC
        MOVE '    INQUIRE ON A PROBLEM    ' TO KEYSUBO
        MOVE 'KI' TO BRAIN
        MOVE -1   TO KEYVALL
        EXEC CICS SEND MAP(KEYMAP) MAPSET(MAPSETNAME)
            FROM(KEYO) ERASE CURSOR END-EXEC
    ELSE
        IF CHOICEI = '2' THEN
            EXEC CICS GETMAIN SET(MAPBLL) LENGTH(2000)
                INITIMG(HEX00) END-EXEC
            MOVE '      REPORT A PROBLEM      ' TO DISSUBO
            MOVE 'DA'  TO BRAIN
            MOVE -1    TO PROBNUML
            MOVE CURRENT-DATE TO DATE-FROM-SYSTEM
            MOVE SYSMM    TO MMO
            MOVE SYSDD    TO DDO
            MOVE SYSYY    TO YYO
            MOVE UNPROT-BRT-FSET TO MMA
            MOVE UNPROT-BRT-FSET TO DDA
            MOVE UNPROT-BRT-FSET TO YYA
            EXEC CICS SEND MAP(DISPLAYMAP) MAPSET(MAPSETNAME)
                FROM(DISPLAYO) ERASE CURSOR END-EXEC
        ELSE
            IF CHOICEI = '3' THEN
                EXEC CICS GETMAIN SET(MAPBLL) LENGTH(2000)
```

```
                    INITIMG(HEX00)  END-EXEC
           MOVE '       UPDATE A PROBLEM        ' TO KEYSUBO
           MOVE 'KU'    TO BRAIN
           MOVE -1      TO KEYVALL
           EXEC CICS SEND MAP(KEYMAP) MAPSET(MAPSETNAME)
               FROM(KEYO) ERASE CURSOR END-EXEC
       ELSE
           EXEC CICS GETMAIN SET(MAPBLL) LENGTH(2000)
                    INITIMG(HEX00) END-EXEC
           MOVE '       DELETE A PROBLEM        ' TO KEYSUBO
           MOVE 'KD'    TO BRAIN
           MOVE -1      TO KEYVALL
           EXEC CICS SEND MAP(KEYMAP) MAPSET(MAPSETNAME)
               FROM(KEYO) ERASE CURSOR END-EXEC.
MENU-MAP-EXIT.


PROCESS-KEY-MAP.
    IF KEYVALI NOT NUMERIC THEN
        MOVE 'PROBLEM NUMBER NOT VALID, REENTER' TO KEYMSGO
        MOVE -1                 TO KEYVALL
        MOVE ASKIP-BRT-FSET     TO KEYVALA
        EXEC CICS SEND MAP(KEYMAP) MAPSET(MAPSETNAME)
            FROM(KEYO) ERASE CURSOR END-EXEC
    ELSE
        IF BRAIN = 'KI' THEN
            PERFORM  DISPLAY-RECORD-TO-SCREEN THRU DISPLAY-EXIT
        ELSE
            IF BRAIN = 'KD' THEN
                PERFORM DELETE-RECORD-FROM-FILE THRU DELETE-EXIT
            ELSE
                PERFORM UPDATE-RECORD-IN-FILE THRU UPDATE-EXIT.
KEY-MAP-EXIT.


DISPLAY-RECORD-TO-SCREEN.
    MOVE KEYVALI    TO   MF-KEY.
    EXEC CICS HANDLE CONDITION NOTFND(INQR-NOTFND) END-EXEC.
    EXEC CICS READ DATASET(FILENAME) SET(FILEBLL)
        RIDFLD(MF-KEY) END-EXEC.
    EXEC CICS GETMAIN SET(MAPBLL) LENGTH(2000)
        INITIMG(HEX00) END-EXEC.
    PERFORM MOVE-MASTER-DATA-TO-SCREEN.
    PERFORM SET-ATTRIBUTES-FOR-INQUIRY.
    MOVE 'DI' TO BRAIN.
    MOVE 'PRESS ENTER TO RETURN TO SYSTEM MENU' TO DISMSGO.
    EXEC CICS SEND MAP(DISPLAYMAP) MAPSET(MAPSETNAME)
        FROM(DISPLAYO) ERASE CURSOR(0) END-EXEC.
    GO TO DISPLAY-EXIT.
```

```
INQR-NOTFND.
    MOVE 'SORRY, RECORD NOT IN THE FILE'  TO KEYMSGO.
    MOVE -1     TO KEYVALL.
    EXEC CICS SEND MAP(KEYMAP) MAPSET(MAPSETNAME)
        FROM(KEYO) ERASE CURSOR END-EXEC.

DISPLAY-EXIT. EXIT.

DELETE-RECORD-FROM-FILE.
    MOVE KEYVALI   TO   MF-KEY.
    EXEC CICS HANDLE CONDITION NOTFND(DELT-NOTFND) END-EXEC.
    EXEC CICS READ DATASET(FILENAME) SET(FILEBLL)
        RIDFLD(MF-KEY) END-EXEC.
    EXEC CICS GETMAIN SET(MAPBLL) LENGTH(2000)
        INITIMG(HEX00) END-EXEC.
    PERFORM MOVE-MASTER-DATA-TO-SCREEN.
    PERFORM SET-ATTRIBUTES-FOR-DELETE.
    MOVE ASKIP-NORM        TO DELHDR1A.
    MOVE ASKIP-NORM        TO DELHDR2A.
    MOVE UNPROT-BRT-FSET   TO YESNOA.
    MOVE 'DD'              TO BRAIN.
    MOVE -1                TO YESNOL.
    MOVE 'ENTER YES TO DELETE THIS RECORD    ' TO DISMSGO.
    EXEC CICS SEND MAP(DISPLAYMAP) MAPSET(MAPSETNAME)
        FROM(DISPLAYO) ERASE CURSOR END-EXEC.
    GO TO DELETE-EXIT.

DELT-NOTFND.
    MOVE 'RECORD NOT IN FILE, CAN'T BE DELETED' TO KEYMSGO.
    MOVE -1     TO KEYVALL.
    MOVE 'KD'   TO BRAIN.
    EXEC CICS SEND MAP(KEYMAP) MAPSET(MAPSETNAME)
        FROM(KEYO) ERASE CURSOR END-EXEC.

DELETE-EXIT.
    EXIT.

UPDATE-RECORD-IN-FILE.
    MOVE KEYVALI   TO   MF-KEY.
    EXEC CICS HANDLE CONDITION NOTFND(UPDT-NOTFND) END-EXEC.
    EXEC CICS READ DATASET(FILENAME) SET(FILEBLL)
        RIDFLD(MF-KEY) END-EXEC.
    EXEC CICS GETMAIN SET(MAPBLL) LENGTH(2000)
        INITIMG(HEX00) END-EXEC.
    PERFORM MOVE-MASTER-DATA-TO-SCREEN.
    PERFORM SET-ATTRIBUTES-FOR-UPDATE.
    MOVE 'DU'              TO BRAIN.
    MOVE -1                TO FIXMML.
    MOVE 'MAKE CHANGES DESIRED, THEN ENTER.    ' TO DISMSGO.
```

```
    EXEC CICS SEND MAP(DISPLAYMAP) MAPSET(MAPSETNAME)
        FROM(DISPLAYO) ERASE CURSOR END-EXEC.
    GO TO UPDATE-EXIT.

UPDT-NOTFND.
    MOVE 'RECORD NOT IN FILE, CANT BE UPDATED' TO KEYMSGO.
    MOVE -1    TO KEYVALL.
    MOVE 'KU'   TO BRAIN.
    EXEC CICS SEND MAP(KEYMAP) MAPSET(MAPSETNAME)
        FROM(KEYO) ERASE CURSOR END-EXEC.
UPDATE-EXIT.
    EXIT.

PROCESS-DISPLAY-MAP.
    IF BRAIN = 'DI' THEN
        MOVE 'M ' TO BRAIN
        EXEC CICS SEND MAP(MENUMAP) MAPSET(MAPSETNAME)
            MAPONLY ERASE END-EXEC
    ELSE
        IF BRAIN = 'DA' THEN
            PERFORM ADD-2 THRU ADD-EXIT
        ELSE
            IF BRAIN = 'DD' THEN
                PERFORM DELETE-2 THRU DELETE-2-EXIT
            ELSE
                PERFORM UPDATE-2 THRU UPDATE-2-EXIT.
DISPLAY-MAP-EXIT.

ADD-2.
    MOVE 'GOOD'        TO DATA-FLAG.
    PERFORM  EDIT-MASTER-SCREEN-DATA.
    IF DATA-FLAG = 'BAD' THEN
        PERFORM SET-ATTRIBUTES-FOR-ADD
        EXEC CICS SEND MAP(DISPLAYMAP) MAPSET(MAPSETNAME)
            FROM(DISPLAYO) ERASE CURSOR END-EXEC
        GO TO ADD-EXIT.

    EXEC CICS GETMAIN SET(FILEBLL) LENGTH(300)
        INITIMG(HEX00) END-EXEC.
    PERFORM MOVE-SCREEN-DATA-TO-MASTER.
    MOVE MF-PROBLEM    TO MF-KEY.
    EXEC CICS HANDLE CONDITION NOSPACE(ADD-NOSPACE)
        DUPREC(ADD-DUPREC) END-EXEC.
    EXEC CICS WRITE DATASET(FILENAME) FROM(MASTER-FILE)
        RIDFLD(MF-KEY) LENGTH(LRECL) END-EXEC.
    EXEC CICS GETMAIN SET(MAPBLL) LENGTH(2000)
        INITIMG(HEX00) END-EXEC.
    MOVE 'RECORD ADDED, ENTER NEXT REQUEST' TO MENUMSGO.
    MOVE 'M ' TO BRAIN.
```

```
      EXEC CICS SEND MAP(MENUMAP) MAPSET(MAPSETNAME)
        FROM(MENUO) ERASE END-EXEC.
      GO TO ADD-EXIT.

ADD-NOSPACE.
      EXEC CICS GETMAIN SET(MAPBLL) LENGTH(2000)
          INITIMG(HEX00) END-EXEC.
      MOVE 'NO SPACE IN FILE, CONTACT PROGRAMMER' TO MENUMSGO.
      MOVE 'M ' TO BRAIN.
      EXEC CICS SEND MAP(MENUMAP) MAPSET(MAPSETNAME)
          FROM(MENUO) ERASE END-EXEC.
      GO TO ADD-EXIT.

ADD-DUPREC.
      MOVE 'RECORD ALREADY EXISTS, CHANGE KEY AND RETRY' TO
          DISMSGO.
      MOVE -1  TO PROBNUML.
      PERFORM SET-ATTRIBUTES-FOR-ADD.
      MOVE UNPROT-BRT-FSET   TO PROBNUMA.
      EXEC CICS SEND MAP(DISPLAYMAP) MAPSET(MAPSETNAME)
          FROM(DISPLAYO) ERASE CURSOR END-EXEC.

ADD-EXIT.
      EXIT.

DELETE-2.

      IF YESNOI NOT = 'YES' AND YESNOI NOT = 'NO' THEN
          MOVE 'YES OR NO NOT ENTERED, PLEASE ENTER AGAIN' TO
              DISMSGO
          MOVE -1   TO YESNOL
          MOVE ASKIP-NORM         TO DELHDR1A
          MOVE ASKIP-NORM         TO DELHDR2A
          MOVE UNPROT-BRT-FSET    TO YESNOA
          EXEC CICS SEND MAP(DISPLAYMAP) MAPSET(MAPSETNAME)
            FROM(DISPLAYO) ERASE END-EXEC
          GO TO DELETE-2-EXIT.

      IF YESNOI = 'NO' THEN
          EXEC CICS GETMAIN SET(MAPBLL) LENGTH(2000)
              INITIMG(HEX00) END-EXEC
          MOVE 'DELETE NOT DONE AS REQUESTED' TO MENUMSGO
          MOVE 'M ' TO BRAIN
          EXEC CICS SEND MAP(MENUMAP) MAPSET(MAPSETNAME)
              FROM(MENUO) ERASE END-EXEC
          GO TO DELETE-2-EXIT.

      MOVE PROBNUMI  TO MF-KEY.
      EXEC CICS HANDLE CONDITION NOTFND(DEL2-NOTFND) END-EXEC.
```

```
      EXEC CICS DELETE DATASET(FILENAME) RIDFLD(MF-KEY)
         END-EXEC.
      EXEC CICS GETMAIN SET(MAPBLL) LENGTH(2000)
         INITIMG(HEX00) END-EXEC.
      MOVE 'RECORD DELETED AS REQUESTED' TO MENUMSGO.
      MOVE 'M ' TO BRAIN.
      EXEC CICS SEND MAP(MENUMAP) MAPSET(MAPSETNAME)
        FROM(MENUO) ERASE END-EXEC.
      GO TO DELETE-2-EXIT.

  DEL2-NOTFND.
      EXEC CICS GETMAIN SET(MAPBLL) LENGTH(2000)
         INITIMG(HEX00) END-EXEC.
      MOVE 'RECORD WAS DELETED BY ANOTHER USER' TO MENUMSGO.
      MOVE 'M ' TO BRAIN.
      EXEC CICS SEND MAP(MENUMAP) MAPSET(MAPSETNAME)
         FROM(MENUO) ERASE END-EXEC.
  DELETE-2-EXIT.
      EXIT.


  UPDATE-2.
      MOVE 'GOOD'          TO DATA-FLAG.
      PERFORM   EDIT-MASTER-SCREEN-DATA.
      IF DATA-FLAG = 'BAD' THEN
         PERFORM SET-ATTRIBUTES-FOR-UPDATE
         EXEC CICS SEND MAP(DISPLAYMAP) MAPSET(MAPSETNAME)
           FROM(DISPLAYO) ERASE CURSOR END-EXEC
         GO TO UPDATE-2-EXIT.

      MOVE PROBNUMI      TO MF-KEY.
      EXEC CICS HANDLE CONDITION NOTFND(UPDT-2-NOTFND) END-EXEC.
      EXEC CICS READ DATASET(FILENAME) SET(FILEBLL)
          RIDFLD(MF-KEY) UPDATE END-EXEC.
      PERFORM MOVE-SCREEN-DATA-TO-MASTER.
      EXEC CICS HANDLE CONDITION NOSPACE(UPDT-2-NOSPACE) END-EXEC.
      EXEC CICS REWRITE DATASET(FILENAME) FROM(MASTER-FILE)
         LENGTH(LRECL) END-EXEC.
      EXEC CICS GETMAIN SET(MAPBLL) LENGTH(2000)
         INITIMG(HEX00) END-EXEC.
      MOVE 'RECORD UPDATED, ENTER NEXT REQUEST' TO MENUMSGO.
      MOVE 'M '  TO BRAIN.
      EXEC CICS SEND MAP(MENUMAP) MAPSET(MAPSETNAME)
        FROM(MENUO) ERASE END-EXEC.
      GO TO UPDATE-2-EXIT.

  UPDT-2-NOSPACE.
      EXEC CICS GETMAIN SET(MAPBLL) LENGTH(2000)
         INITIMG(HEX00) END-EXEC.
      MOVE 'NO SPACE IN FILE, CONTACT PROGRAMMER' TO MENUMSGO.
      MOVE 'M ' TO BRAIN.
```

```
        EXEC CICS SEND MAP(MENUMAP) MAPSET(MAPSETNAME)
           FROM(MENUO) ERASE END-EXEC.
        GO TO UPDATE-2-EXIT.

    UPDT-2-NOTFND.
        EXEC CICS GETMAIN SET(MAPBLL) LENGTH(2000)
           INITIMG(HEX00) END-EXEC.
        MOVE 'RECORD DELETED FROM UNDERNEATH YOU, SORRY'   TO
           MENUMSGO.
        MOVE 'M ' TO BRAIN.
        EXEC CICS SEND MAP(MENUMAP) MAPSET(MAPSETNAME)
           FROM(MENUO) ERASE CURSOR END-EXEC.
    UPDATE-2-EXIT.
        EXIT.


    MOVE-MASTER-DATA-TO-SCREEN.
        MOVE MF-PROBLEM        TO PROBNUMO.
        MOVE MF-REPORT-MM      TO MMO.
        MOVE MF-REPORT-DD      TO DDO.
        MOVE MF-REPORT-YY      TO YYO.
        MOVE MF-TENNANT        TO TENNANTO.
        MOVE MF-APARTMENT      TO APTNOO.
        MOVE MF-DESCRIPTION-1  TO DESC1O.
        MOVE MF-DESCRIPTION-2  TO DESC2O.
        MOVE MF-FIX-MM         TO FIXMMO.
        MOVE MF-FIX-DD         TO FIXDDO.
        MOVE MF-FIX-YY         TO FIXYYO.
        MOVE MF-STAFF          TO STAFFO.
        MOVE MF-TIME-TO-FIX    TO FIXTIMEO.
        MOVE MF-QUALITY        TO QUALITYO.


    MOVE-SCREEN-DATA-TO-MASTER.
        MOVE PROBNUMI          TO MF-PROBLEM.
        MOVE MMI               TO MF-REPORT-MM.
        MOVE DDI               TO MF-REPORT-DD.
        MOVE YYI               TO MF-REPORT-YY.
        MOVE TENNANTI          TO MF-TENNANT.
        MOVE APTNOI            TO MF-APARTMENT.
        MOVE DESC1I            TO MF-DESCRIPTION-1.
        MOVE DESC2I            TO MF-DESCRIPTION-2.
        MOVE FIXMMI            TO MF-FIX-MM.
        MOVE FIXDDI            TO MF-FIX-DD.
        MOVE FIXYYI            TO MF-FIX-YY.
        MOVE STAFFI            TO MF-STAFF.
        MOVE FIXTIMEI          TO MF-TIME-TO-FIX.
        MOVE QUALITYI          TO MF-QUALITY.
        MOVE SPACES            TO MF-FILLER.


    SET-ATTRIBUTES-FOR-INQUIRY.
```

```
        MOVE ASKIP-BRT           TO PROBNUMA.
        MOVE ASKIP-BRT           TO MMA.
        MOVE ASKIP-BRT           TO DDA.
        MOVE ASKIP-BRT           TO YYA.
        MOVE ASKIP-BRT           TO TENNANTA.
        MOVE ASKIP-BRT           TO APTNOA.
        MOVE ASKIP-BRT           TO DESC1A.
        MOVE ASKIP-BRT           TO DESC2A.
        MOVE ASKIP-BRT           TO FIXMMA.
        MOVE ASKIP-BRT           TO FIXDDA.
        MOVE ASKIP-BRT           TO FIXYYA.
        MOVE ASKIP-BRT           TO STAFFA.
        MOVE ASKIP-BRT           TO FIXTIMEA.
        MOVE ASKIP-BRT           TO QUALITYA.

SET-ATTRIBUTES-FOR-DELETE.
        MOVE ASKIP-BRT-FSET      TO PROBNUMA.
        MOVE ASKIP-BRT-FSET      TO MMA.
        MOVE ASKIP-BRT-FSET      TO DDA.
        MOVE ASKIP-BRT-FSET      TO YYA.
        MOVE ASKIP-BRT-FSET      TO TENNANTA.
        MOVE ASKIP-BRT-FSET      TO APTNOA.
        MOVE ASKIP-BRT-FSET      TO DESC1A.
        MOVE ASKIP-BRT-FSET      TO DESC2A.
        MOVE ASKIP-BRT-FSET      TO FIXMMA.
        MOVE ASKIP-BRT-FSET      TO FIXDDA.
        MOVE ASKIP-BRT-FSET      TO FIXYYA.
        MOVE ASKIP-BRT-FSET      TO STAFFA.
        MOVE ASKIP-BRT-FSET      TO FIXTIMEA.
        MOVE ASKIP-BRT-FSET      TO QUALITYA.

SET-ATTRIBUTES-FOR-UPDATE.
        MOVE ASKIP-BRT-FSET       TO PROBNUMA.
        MOVE UNPROT-BRT-FSET      TO MMA.
        MOVE UNPROT-BRT-FSET      TO DDA.
        MOVE UNPROT-BRT-FSET      TO YYA.
        MOVE UNPROT-BRT-FSET      TO TENNANTA.
        MOVE UNPROT-BRT-FSET      TO APTNOA.
        MOVE UNPROT-BRT-FSET      TO DESC1A.
        MOVE UNPROT-BRT-FSET      TO DESC2A.
        MOVE UNPROT-BRT-FSET      TO FIXMMA.
        MOVE UNPROT-BRT-FSET      TO FIXDDA.
        MOVE UNPROT-BRT-FSET      TO FIXYYA.
        MOVE UNPROT-BRT-FSET      TO STAFFA.
        MOVE UNPROT-BRT-FSET      TO FIXTIMEA.
        MOVE UNPROT-BRT-FSET      TO QUALITYA.

SET-ATTRIBUTES-FOR-ADD.
```

```
MOVE UNPROT-BRT-FSET    TO PROBNUMA.
MOVE UNPROT-BRT-FSET    TO MMA.
MOVE UNPROT-BRT-FSET    TO DDA.
MOVE UNPROT-BRT-FSET    TO YYA.
MOVE UNPROT-BRT-FSET    TO TENNANTA.
MOVE UNPROT-BRT-FSET    TO APTNOA.
MOVE UNPROT-BRT-FSET    TO DESC1A.
MOVE UNPROT-BRT-FSET    TO DESC2A.
MOVE UNPROT-BRT-FSET    TO FIXMMA.
MOVE UNPROT-BRT-FSET    TO FIXDDA.
MOVE UNPROT-BRT-FSET    TO FIXYYA.
MOVE UNPROT-BRT-FSET    TO STAFFA.
MOVE UNPROT-BRT-FSET    TO FIXTIMEA.
MOVE UNPROT-BRT-FSET    TO QUALITYA.

EDIT-MASTER-SCREEN-DATA.
    IF PROBNUMI NOT NUMERIC THEN
        MOVE 'PROBLEM NUMBER IS NOT ALL DIGITS' TO DISMSGO
        MOVE -1  TO PROBNUMA
        MOVE 'BAD'    TO DATA-FLAG
    ELSE
      IF MMI NOT NUMERIC OR MMI < '01' OR MMI > '12' THEN
        MOVE 'MONTH ENTERED IS NOT VALID' TO DISMSGO
        MOVE -1  TO MML
        MOVE 'BAD'  TO DATA-FLAG
      ELSE
        IF DDI NOT NUMERIC OR DDI < '01' OR DDI > '31' THEN
          MOVE 'DAY ENTERED IS NOT VALID' TO DISMSGO
          MOVE -1   TO DDL
          MOVE 'BAD' TO DATA-FLAG
        ELSE
          IF YYI NOT NUMERIC OR YYI < '01' THEN
            MOVE 'YEAR IS NOT VALID' TO DISMSGO
            MOVE -1   TO DDL
            MOVE 'BAD' TO DATA-FLAG
          ELSE
            IF TENNANTL = +0 OR TENNANTI = LOW-VALUES OR
               TENNANTI = SPACES THEN
              MOVE 'A TENNANT'S NAME MUST BE ENTERED' TO DISMSGO
              MOVE -1   TO TENNANTL
              MOVE 'BAD' TO DATA-FLAG
            ELSE
              IF APTNOI NOT NUMERIC OR APTNOL = +0 THEN
                MOVE 'PLEASE ENTER AN APARTMENT NUMBER' TO
                         DISMSGO
                MOVE -1   TO APTNOL
                MOVE 'BAD' TO DATA-FLAG
              ELSE
```

```
        IF DESC1L = +0 AND DESC2L = +0 THEN
            MOVE 'A DESCIPTION MUST BE ENTERED' TO
                DISMSGO
            MOVE -1  TO DESC1L
            MOVE 'BAD' TO DATA-FLAG.
```

CONVERSATIONAL, SINGLE PROGRAM, LOCATE MODE, COMMAREAS

Conversational programming was a controversial topic throughout the text. An earlier example of implementation was the on-line calculator system. Below is an implementation of the landlord system in a conversational style with a single program using locate-mode processing and communication areas to help the program remember what it was doing. Communications areas are usually not needed in a conversational mode since conversational programs never "lose" data from initiation to initiation (they're only initiated once). Hence, they never lose track of what they were doing and what they were working on. Further, most conversational programs pause at appropriate points in the program and regain control from that point. Therefore, the code is designed to expect activities during processing, whereas a nonconversational program is reinitiated, from the beginning, after each request. One final point should be made about this program, though: although this program is categorized as a conversational program, it is designed as a nonconversational program. As you follow the logic, you'll see that the program does "restart" itself rather than continuing from where it "left off." Because of the way in which this program is structured, communication areas are needed to help the program determine what is to be done next.

```
IDENTIFICATION DIVISION.
    PROGRAM-ID.   LAMS.
    AUTHOR.       ME.
ENVIRONMENT DIVISION.
DATA DIVISION.
WORKING-STORAGE SECTION.
01    TIOALEN                 PIC S9(4)  COMP VALUE +1920.
01    LAMS                    PIC X(4)   VALUE 'LAMS'.
01    MENUMAP                 PIC X(8)   VALUE 'MENU'.
01    DISPLAYMAP              PIC X(8)   VALUE 'DISPLAY'.
01    KEYMAP                  PIC X(8)   VALUE 'KEY'.
01    MAPSETNAME              PIC X(8)   VALUE 'LAMSM'.
01    FILENAME                PIC X(8)   VALUE 'MASTERF'.
01    DATA-FLAG               PIC X(4).
01    LRECL                   PIC S9(4)  COMP VALUE +300.
01    HEX00                   PIC X      VALUE LOW-VALUES.
```

```
01   DATE-FROM-SYSTEM.
     02   SYSMM                    PIC X(2).
     02   FILLER                   PIC X.
     02   SYSDD                    PIC X(2).
     02   FILLER                   PIC X.
     02   SYSYY                    PIC X(2).

01   MF-KEY                        PIC 9(5).
01   COPY ATTRBS.

01   MYCOMMAREA.
     02   BRAIN                    PIC X(2).
     02   XXX                      REDEFINES BRAIN.
          03   FORMATTED-MAP-CODE  PIC X.
          03   FORMATTED-FUNCTION  PIC X.


LINKAGE SECTION.

01   DFHBLLDS.
     02   RESERVED-BLL             PIC S9(8) COMP.
     02   MAPBLL                   PIC S9(8) COMP.
     02   FILEBLL                  PIC S9(8) COMP.

01   MAPAREA                       PIC X(1920).
01   COPY LAMSM.

01   MASTER-FILE.
     02   MF-PROBLEM               PIC 9(5).
     02   MF-REPORTED-ON.
          03   MF-REPORT-MM        PIC X(2).
          03   MF-REPORT-DD        PIC X(2).
          03   MF-REPORT-YY        PIC X(2).
     02   MF-TENNANT               PIC X(20).
     02   MF-APARTMENT             PIC X(3).
     02   MF-DESCRIPTION.
          03   MF-DESCRIPTION-1    PIC X(50).
          03   MF-DESCRIPTION-2    PIC X(50).
     02   MF-DATE-FIXED.
          03   MF-FIX-MM           PIC X(2).
          03   MF-FIX-DD           PIC X(2).
          03   MF-FIX-YY           PIC X(2).
     02   MF-STAFF                 PIC X(20).
     02   MF-TIME-TO-FIX           PIC X(2).
     02   MF-QUALITY               PIC X.
     02   MF-FILLER                PIC X(138).


PROCEDURE DIVISION.
     EXEC CICS SEND MAP(MENUMAP) MAPSET(MAPSETNAME)
```

```
        MAPONLY ERASE END-EXEC.
    MOVE 'M' TO BRAIN.

    EXEC CICS HANDLE AID ANYKEY (ALL-DONE) END-EXEC.
    PERFORM PROCESS-USER-REQUEST THRU
            USER-REQUEST-EXIT  9999 TIMES.


ALL-DONE.
    EXEC CICS SEND FROM (HEX00) LENGTH (0)  ERASE END-EXEC.
    EXEC CICS RETURN END-EXEC.
    STOP RUN.


PROCESS-USER-REQUEST.
    IF FORMATTED-MAP-CODE = 'M' THEN
        EXEC CICS RECEIVE MAP (MENUMAP) MAPSET (MAPSETNAME)
            SET (MAPBLL) END-EXEC
        PERFORM PROCESS-MENU-MAP THRU MENU-MAP-EXIT
    ELSE
        IF FORMATTED-MAP-CODE = 'K' THEN
            EXEC CICS RECEIVE MAP (KEYMAP) MAPSET (MAPSETNAME)
                SET (MAPBLL) END-EXEC
            PERFORM PROCESS-KEY-MAP THRU KEY-MAP-EXIT
        ELSE
            EXEC CICS RECEIVE MAP (DISPLAYMAP)
                MAPSET (MAPSETNAME) SET (MAPBLL) END-EXEC
            PERFORM PROCESS-DISPLAY-MAP THRU DISPLAY-MAP-EXIT.

USER-REQUEST-EXIT.
    EXIT.

PROCESS-MENU-MAP.
    IF CHOICEI < '1' OR CHOICEI > '4' THEN
        MOVE 'INVALID CHOICE ENTERED, CORRECT AND REENTER'
            TO MENUMSGO
        MOVE -1   TO CHOICEL
        MOVE 'M ' TO BRAIN
        EXEC CICS SEND MAP (MENUMAP) MAPSET (MAPSETNAME)
            FROM (MENUO) ERASE CURSOR END-EXEC
    ELSE
    IF CHOICEI = '1' THEN
        EXEC CICS GETMAIN SET (MAPBLL) LENGTH (2000)
            INITIMG (HEX00) END-EXEC
        MOVE '   INQUIRE ON A PROBLEM   '  TO KEYSUBO
        MOVE 'KI' TO BRAIN
        MOVE -1   TO KEYVALL
        EXEC CICS SEND MAP (KEYMAP) MAPSET (MAPSETNAME)
            FROM (KEYO) ERASE CURSOR END-EXEC
```

```
        ELSE
            IF CHOICEI = '2' THEN
                EXEC CICS GETMAIN SET(MAPBLL) LENGTH(2000)
                    INITIMG(HEX00) END-EXEC
                MOVE '        REPORT A PROBLEM    ' TO DISSUBO
                MOVE 'DA'  TO BRAIN
                MOVE -1    TO PROBNUML
                MOVE CURRENT-DATE TO DATE-FROM-SYSTEM
                MOVE SYSMM   TO MMO
                MOVE SYSDD   TO DDO
                MOVE SYSYY   TO YYO
                MOVE UNPROT-BRT-FSET TO MMA
                MOVE UNPROT-BRT-FSET TO DDA
                MOVE UNPROT-BRT-FSET TO YYA
                EXEC CICS SEND MAP(DISPLAYMAP) MAPSET(MAPSETNAME)
                    FROM(DISPLAYO) ERASE CURSOR END-EXEC
            ELSE
                IF CHOICEI = '3' THEN
                    EXEC CICS GETMAIN SET(MAPBLL) LENGTH(2000)
                        INITIMG(HEX00) END-EXEC
                    MOVE '      UPDATE A PROBLEM       ' TO KEYSUBO
                    MOVE 'KU'   TO BRAIN
                    MOVE -1     TO KEYVALL
                    EXEC CICS SEND MAP(KEYMAP) MAPSET(MAPSETNAME)
                        FROM(KEYO) ERASE CURSOR END-EXEC
                ELSE
                    EXEC CICS GETMAIN SET(MAPBLL) LENGTH(2000)
                        INITIMG(HEX00) END-EXEC
                    MOVE '      DELETE A PROBLEM      ' TO KEYSUBO
                    MOVE 'KD'   TO BRAIN
                    MOVE -1     TO KEYVALL
                    EXEC CICS SEND MAP(KEYMAP) MAPSET(MAPSETNAME)
                        FROM(KEYO)  ERASE CURSOR END-EXEC.
MENU-MAP-EXIT.


PROCESS-KEY-MAP.
    IF KEYVALI NOT NUMERIC THEN
        MOVE 'PROBLEM NUMBER NOT VALID, REENTER' TO KEYMSGO
        MOVE -1              TO KEYVALL
        MOVE ASKIP-BRT-FSET  TO KEYVALA
        EXEC CICS SEND MAP(KEYMAP) MAPSET(MAPSETNAME)
            FROM(KEYO) ERASE CURSOR END-EXEC
    ELSE
        IF BRAIN = 'KI' THEN
            PERFORM  DISPLAY-RECORD-TO-SCREEN THRU DISPLAY-EXIT
        ELSE
            IF BRAIN = 'KD' THEN
                PERFORM DELETE-RECORD-FROM-FILE THRU DELETE-EXIT
```

```
          ELSE
              PERFORM UPDATE-RECORD-IN-FILE THRU UPDATE-EXIT.
KEY-MAP-EXIT.


DISPLAY-RECORD-TO-SCREEN.
     MOVE KEYVALI    TO    MF-KEY.
     EXEC CICS HANDLE CONDITION NOTFND(INQR-NOTFND)  END-EXEC.
     EXEC CICS READ DATASET(FILENAME)  SET(FILEBLL)
        RIDFLD(MF-KEY)  END-EXEC.
     EXEC CICS GETMAIN SET(MAPBLL)  LENGTH(2000)
        INITIMG(HEX00)  END-EXEC.
     PERFORM MOVE-MASTER-DATA-TO-SCREEN.
     PERFORM SET-ATTRIBUTES-FOR-INQUIRY.
     MOVE 'DI' TO BRAIN.
     MOVE 'PRESS ENTER TO RETURN TO SYSTEM MENU' TO DISMSGO.
     EXEC CICS SEND MAP(DISPLAYMAP)  MAPSET(MAPSETNAME)
        FROM(DISPLAYO)  ERASE CURSOR(0)  END-EXEC.
     GO TO DISPLAY-EXIT.

INQR-NOTFND.
     MOVE 'SORRY, RECORD NOT IN THE FILE'  TO KEYMSGO.
     MOVE -1    TO KEYVALL.
     EXEC CICS SEND MAP(KEYMAP)  MAPSET(MAPSETNAME)
        FROM(KEYO)  ERASE CURSOR  END-EXEC.

DISPLAY-EXIT.  EXIT.

DELETE-RECORD-FROM-FILE.
     MOVE KEYVALI     TO    MF-KEY.
     EXEC CICS HANDLE CONDITION NOTFND(DELT-NOTFND)  END-EXEC.
     EXEC CICS READ DATASET(FILENAME)  SET(FILEBLL)
        RIDFLD(MF-KEY)  END-EXEC.
     EXEC CICS GETMAIN SET(MAPBLL)  LENGTH(2000)
        INITIMG(HEX00)  END-EXEC.
     PERFORM MOVE-MASTER-DATA-TO-SCREEN.
     PERFORM SET-ATTRIBUTES-FOR-DELETE.
     MOVE ASKIP-NORM        TO DELHDR1A.
     MOVE ASKIP-NORM        TO DELHDR2A.
     MOVE UNPROT-BRT-FSET   TO YESNOA.
     MOVE 'DD'              TO BRAIN.
     MOVE -1                TO YESNOL.
     MOVE 'ENTER YES TO DELETE THIS RECORD    ' TO DISMSGO.
     EXEC CICS SEND MAP(DISPLAYMAP)  MAPSET(MAPSETNAME)
        FROM(DISPLAYO)  ERASE CURSOR  END-EXEC.
     GO TO DELETE-EXIT.

DELT-NOTFND.
     MOVE 'RECORD NOT IN FILE, CANT BE DELETED' TO KEYMSGO.
```

```
      MOVE  -1     TO  KEYVALL.
      MOVE  'KD'   TO  BRAIN.
      EXEC CICS SEND MAP(KEYMAP) MAPSET(MAPSETNAME)
          FROM(KEYO) ERASE CURSOR END-EXEC.

  DELETE-EXIT.
      EXIT.


  UPDATE-RECORD-IN-FILE.
      MOVE KEYVALI    TO    MF-KEY.
      EXEC CICS HANDLE CONDITION NOTFND(UPDT-NOTFND) END-EXEC.
      EXEC CICS READ DATASET(FILENAME) SET(FILEBLL)
          RIDFLD(MF-KEY) END-EXEC.
      EXEC CICS GETMAIN SET(MAPBLL) LENGTH(2000)
          INITIMG(HEX00) END-EXEC.
      PERFORM MOVE-MASTER-DATA-TO-SCREEN.
      PERFORM SET-ATTRIBUTES-FOR-UPDATE.
      MOVE 'DU'               TO BRAIN.
      MOVE -1                 TO FIXMML.
      MOVE 'MAKE CHANGES DESIRED, THEN ENTER.   ' TO DISMSGO.
      EXEC CICS SEND MAP(DISPLAYMAP) MAPSET(MAPSETNAME)
          FROM(DISPLAYO) ERASE CURSOR END-EXEC.
      GO TO UPDATE-EXIT.


  UPDT-NOTFND.
      MOVE 'RECORD NOT IN FILE, CAN'T BE UPDATED' TO KEYMSGO.
      MOVE -1    TO KEYVALL.
      MOVE 'KU'  TO BRAIN.
      EXEC CICS SEND MAP(KEYMAP) MAPSET(MAPSETNAME)
          FROM(KEYO) ERASE CURSOR END-EXEC.
  UPDATE-EXIT.
      EXIT.


  PROCESS-DISPLAY-MAP.
      IF BRAIN = 'DI' THEN
          MOVE 'M ' TO BRAIN
          EXEC CICS SEND MAP(MENUMAP) MAPSET(MAPSETNAME)
              MAPONLY ERASE END-EXEC
      ELSE
          IF BRAIN = 'DA' THEN
              PERFORM ADD-2 THRU ADD-EXIT
          ELSE
              IF BRAIN = 'DD' THEN
                  PERFORM DELETE-2  THRU DELETE-2-EXIT
              ELSE
                  PERFORM UPDATE-2  THRU UPDATE-2-EXIT.
  DISPLAY-MAP-EXIT.
```

```
ADD-2.
    MOVE 'GOOD'          TO DATA-FLAG.
    PERFORM  EDIT-MASTER-SCREEN-DATA.
    IF DATA-FLAG = 'BAD' THEN
        PERFORM SET-ATTRIBUTES-FOR-ADD
        EXEC CICS SEND MAP(DISPLAYMAP) MAPSET(MAPSETNAME)
          FROM(DISPLAYO) ERASE CURSOR END-EXEC
        GO TO ADD-EXIT.

    EXEC CICS GETMAIN SET(FILEBLL) LENGTH(300)
        INITIMG(HEX00) END-EXEC.
    PERFORM MOVE-SCREEN-DATA-TO-MASTER.
    MOVE MF-PROBLEM     TO MF-KEY.
    EXEC CICS HANDLE CONDITION NOSPACE(ADD-NOSPACE)
        DUPREC(ADD-DUPREC) END-EXEC.
    EXEC CICS WRITE DATASET(FILENAME) FROM(MASTER-FILE)
        RIDFLD(MF-KEY) LENGTH(LRECL) END-EXEC.
    EXEC CICS GETMAIN SET(MAPBLL) LENGTH(2000)
        INITIMG(HEX00) END-EXEC.
    MOVE 'RECORD ADDED, ENTER NEXT REQUEST' TO MENUMSGO.
    MOVE 'M ' TO BRAIN.
    EXEC CICS SEND MAP(MENUMAP) MAPSET(MAPSETNAME)
      FROM(MENUO) ERASE END-EXEC.
    GO TO ADD-EXIT.

ADD-NOSPACE.
    EXEC CICS GETMAIN SET(MAPBLL) LENGTH(2000)
        INITIMG(HEX00) END-EXEC.
    MOVE 'NO SPACE IN FILE, CONTACT PROGRAMMER' TO MENUMSGO.
    MOVE 'M ' TO BRAIN.
    EXEC CICS SEND MAP(MENUMAP) MAPSET(MAPSETNAME)
        FROM(MENUO) ERASE END-EXEC.
    GO TO ADD-EXIT.

ADD-DUPREC.
    MOVE 'RECORD ALREADY EXISTS, CHANGE KEY AND RETRY' TO
        DISMSGO.
    MOVE -1 TO PROBNUML.
    PERFORM SET-ATTRIBUTES-FOR-ADD.
    MOVE UNPROT-BRT-FSET    TO PROBNUMA.
    EXEC CICS SEND MAP(DISPLAYMAP) MAPSET(MAPSETNAME)
        FROM(DISPLAYO) ERASE CURSOR END-EXEC.

ADD-EXIT.
    EXIT.

DELETE-2.

    IF YESNOI NOT = 'YES' AND YESNOI NOT = 'NO' THEN
```

```
      MOVE 'YES OR NO NOT ENTERED, PLEASE ENTER AGAIN' TO
          DISMSGO
      MOVE -1    TO YESNOL
      MOVE ASKIP-NORM            TO DELHDR1A
      MOVE ASKIP-NORM            TO DELHDR2A
      MOVE UNPROT-BRT-FSET     TO YESNOA
      EXEC CICS SEND MAP(DISPLAYMAP) MAPSET(MAPSETNAME)
        FROM(DISPLAYO) ERASE END-EXEC
      GO TO DELETE-2-EXIT.

  IF YESNOI = 'NO' THEN
      EXEC CICS GETMAIN SET(MAPBLL) LENGTH(2000)
          INITIMG(HEX00) END-EXEC
      MOVE 'DELETE NOT DONE AS REQUESTED' TO MENUMSGO
      MOVE 'M ' TO BRAIN
      EXEC CICS SEND MAP(MENUMAP) MAPSET(MAPSETNAME)
        FROM(MENUO) ERASE END-EXEC
      GO TO DELETE-2-EXIT.


  MOVE PROBNUMI  TO MF-KEY.
  EXEC CICS HANDLE CONDITION NOTFND(DEL2-NOTFND) END-EXEC.
  EXEC CICS DELETE DATASET(FILENAME) RIDFLD(MF-KEY)
     END-EXEC.
  EXEC CICS GETMAIN SET(MAPBLL) LENGTH(2000)
     INITIMG(HEX00) END-EXEC.
  MOVE 'RECORD DELETED AS REQUESTED' TO MENUMSGO.
  MOVE 'M ' TO BRAIN.
  EXEC CICS SEND MAP(MENUMAP) MAPSET(MAPSETNAME)
    FROM(MENUO) ERASE END-EXEC.
  GO TO DELETE-2-EXIT.

DEL2-NOTFND.
  EXEC CICS GETMAIN SET(MAPBLL) LENGTH(2000)
     INITIMG(HEX00) END-EXEC.
  MOVE 'RECORD WAS DELETED BY ANOTHER USER' TO MENUMSGO.
  MOVE 'M ' TO BRAIN.
  EXEC CICS SEND MAP(MENUMAP) MAPSET(MAPSETNAME)
     FROM(MENUO) ERASE END-EXEC.
DELETE-2-EXIT.
  EXIT.

UPDATE-2.
  MOVE 'GOOD'        TO DATA-FLAG.
  PERFORM  EDIT-MASTER-SCREEN-DATA.
  IF DATA-FLAG = 'BAD' THEN
      PERFORM SET-ATTRIBUTES-FOR-UPDATE
      EXEC CICS SEND MAP(DISPLAYMAP) MAPSET(MAPSETNAME)
        FROM(DISPLAYO) ERASE CURSOR END-EXEC
      GO TO UPDATE-2-EXIT.
```

```
MOVE PROBNUMI     TO MF-KEY.
EXEC CICS HANDLE CONDITION NOTFND(UPDT-2-NOTFND) END-EXEC.
EXEC CICS READ DATASET(FILENAME) SET(FILEBLL)
    RIDFLD(MF-KEY) UPDATE END-EXEC.
PERFORM MOVE-SCREEN-DATA-TO-MASTER.
EXEC CICS HANDLE CONDITION NOSPACE(UPDT-2-NOSPACE) END-EXEC.
EXEC CICS REWRITE DATASET(FILENAME) FROM(MASTER-FILE)
    LENGTH(LRECL) END-EXEC.
EXEC CICS GETMAIN SET(MAPBLL) LENGTH(2000)
    INITIMG(HEX00) END-EXEC.
MOVE 'RECORD UPDATED, ENTER NEXT REQUEST' TO MENUMSGO.
MOVE 'M ' TO BRAIN.
EXEC CICS SEND MAP(MENUMAP) MAPSET(MAPSETNAME)
  FROM(MENUO) ERASE END-EXEC.
GO TO UPDATE-2-EXIT.

UPDT-2-NOSPACE.
EXEC CICS GETMAIN SET(MAPBLL) LENGTH(2000)
    INITIMG(HEX00) END-EXEC.
MOVE 'NO SPACE IN FILE, CONTACT PROGRAMMER' TO MENUMSGO.
MOVE 'M ' TO BRAIN.
EXEC CICS SEND MAP(MENUMAP) MAPSET(MAPSETNAME)
    FROM(MENUO) ERASE END-EXEC.
GO TO UPDATE-2-EXIT.

UPDT-2-NOTFND.
EXEC CICS GETMAIN SET(MAPBLL) LENGTH(2000)
    INITIMG(HEX00) END-EXEC.
MOVE 'RECORD DELETED FROM UNDERNEATH YOU, SORRY'    TO
    MENUMSGO.
MOVE 'M ' TO BRAIN.
EXEC CICS SEND MAP(MENUMAP) MAPSET(MAPSETNAME)
    FROM(MENUO) ERASE CURSOR END-EXEC.
UPDATE-2-EXIT.
EXIT.

MOVE-MASTER-DATA-TO-SCREEN.
    MOVE MF-PROBLEM        TO PROBNUMO.
    MOVE MF-REPORT-MM      TO MMO.
    MOVE MF-REPORT-DD      TO DDO.
    MOVE MF-REPORT-YY      TO YYO.
    MOVE MF-TENNANT        TO TENNANTO.
    MOVE MF-APARTMENT      TO APTNOO.
    MOVE MF-DESCRIPTION-1  TO DESC10.
    MOVE MF-DESCRIPTION-2  TO DESC20.
    MOVE MF-FIX-MM         TO FIXMMO.
    MOVE MF-FIX-DD         TO FIXDDO.
    MOVE MF-FIX-YY         TO FIXYYO.
    MOVE MF-STAFF          TO STAFFO.
```

```
        MOVE MF-TIME-TO-FIX     TO FIXTIMEO.
        MOVE MF-QUALITY         TO QUALITYO.

MOVE-SCREEN-DATA-TO-MASTER.
        MOVE PROBNUMI           TO MF-PROBLEM.
        MOVE MMI                TO MF-REPORT-MM.
        MOVE DDI                TO MF-REPORT-DD.
        MOVE YYI                TO MF-REPORT-YY.
        MOVE TENNANTI           TO MF-TENNANT.
        MOVE APTNOI             TO MF-APARTMENT.
        MOVE DESC1I             TO MF-DESCRIPTION-1.
        MOVE DESC2I             TO MF-DESCRIPTION-2.
        MOVE FIXMMI             TO MF-FIX-MM.
        MOVE FIXDDI             TO MF-FIX-DD.
        MOVE FIXYYI             TO MF-FIX-YY.
        MOVE STAFFI             TO MF-STAFF.
        MOVE FIXTIMEI           TO MF-TIME-TO-FIX.
        MOVE QUALITYI           TO MF-QUALITY.
        MOVE SPACES             TO MF-FILLER.

SET-ATTRIBUTES-FOR-INQUIRY.
        MOVE ASKIP-BRT          TO PROBNUMA.
        MOVE ASKIP-BRT          TO MMA.
        MOVE ASKIP-BRT          TO DDA.
        MOVE ASKIP-BRT          TO YYA.
        MOVE ASKIP-BRT          TO TENNANTA.
        MOVE ASKIP-BRT          TO APTNOA.
        MOVE ASKIP-BRT          TO DESC1A.
        MOVE ASKIP-BRT          TO DESC2A.
        MOVE ASKIP-BRT          TO FIXMMA.
        MOVE ASKIP-BRT          TO FIXDDA.
        MOVE ASKIP-BRT          TO FIXYYA.
        MOVE ASKIP-BRT          TO STAFFA.
        MOVE ASKIP-BRT          TO FIXTIMEA.
        MOVE ASKIP-BRT          TO QUALITYA.

SET-ATTRIBUTES-FOR-DELETE.
        MOVE ASKIP-BRT-FSET     TO PROBNUMA.
        MOVE ASKIP-BRT-FSET     TO MMA.
        MOVE ASKIP-BRT-FSET     TO DDA.
        MOVE ASKIP-BRT-FSET     TO YYA.
        MOVE ASKIP-BRT-FSET     TO TENNANTA.
        MOVE ASKIP-BRT-FSET     TO APTNOA.
        MOVE ASKIP-BRT-FSET     TO DESC1A.
        MOVE ASKIP-BRT-FSET     TO DESC2A.
        MOVE ASKIP-BRT-FSET     TO FIXMMA.
        MOVE ASKIP-BRT-FSET     TO FIXDDA.
        MOVE ASKIP-BRT-FSET     TO FIXYYA.
        MOVE ASKIP-BRT-FSET     TO STAFFA.
```

```
        MOVE ASKIP-BRT-FSET     TO FIXTIMEA.
        MOVE ASKIP-BRT-FSET     TO QUALITYA.

SET-ATTRIBUTES-FOR-UPDATE.
        MOVE ASKIP-BRT-FSET     TO PROBNUMA.
        MOVE UNPROT-BRT-FSET    TO MMA.
        MOVE UNPROT-BRT-FSET    TO DDA.
        MOVE UNPROT-BRT-FSET    TO YYA.
        MOVE UNPROT-BRT-FSET    TO TENNANTA.
        MOVE UNPROT-BRT-FSET    TO APTNOA.
        MOVE UNPROT-BRT-FSET    TO DESC1A.
        MOVE UNPROT-BRT-FSET    TO DESC2A.
        MOVE UNPROT-BRT-FSET    TO FIXMMA.
        MOVE UNPROT-BRT-FSET    TO FIXDDA.
        MOVE UNPROT-BRT-FSET    TO FIXYYA.
        MOVE UNPROT-BRT-FSET    TO STAFFA.
        MOVE UNPROT-BRT-FSET    TO FIXTIMEA.
        MOVE UNPROT-BRT-FSET    TO QUALITYA.

SET-ATTRIBUTES-FOR-ADD.
        MOVE UNPROT-BRT-FSET    TO PROBNUMA.
        MOVE UNPROT-BRT-FSET    TO MMA.
        MOVE UNPROT-BRT-FSET    TO DDA.
        MOVE UNPROT-BRT-FSET    TO YYA.
        MOVE UNPROT-BRT-FSET    TO TENNANTA.
        MOVE UNPROT-BRT-FSET    TO APTNOA.
        MOVE UNPROT-BRT-FSET    TO DESC1A.
        MOVE UNPROT-BRT-FSET    TO DESC2A.
        MOVE UNPROT-BRT-FSET    TO FIXMMA.
        MOVE UNPROT-BRT-FSET    TO FIXDDA.
        MOVE UNPROT-BRT-FSET    TO FIXYYA.
        MOVE UNPROT-BRT-FSET    TO STAFFA.
        MOVE UNPROT-BRT-FSET    TO FIXTIMEA.
        MOVE UNPROT-BRT-FSET    TO QUALITYA.

EDIT-MASTER-SCREEN-DATA.
    IF PROBNUMI NOT NUMERIC THEN
        MOVE 'PROBLEM NUMBER IS NOT ALL DIGITS' TO DISMSGO
        MOVE -1  TO PROBNUMA
        MOVE 'BAD'   TO DATA-FLAG
    ELSE
      IF MMI NOT NUMERIC OR MMI < '01' OR MMI > '12' THEN
        MOVE 'MONTH ENTERED IS NOT VALID' TO DISMSGO
        MOVE -1  TO MML
        MOVE 'BAD'   TO DATA-FLAG
      ELSE
        IF DDI NOT NUMERIC OR DDI < '01' OR DDI > '31' THEN
          MOVE 'DAY ENTERED IS NOT VALID' TO DISMSGO
          MOVE -1   TO DDL
```

```
       MOVE 'BAD' TO DATA-FLAG
   ELSE
     IF YYI NOT NUMERIC OR YYI < '01' THEN
        MOVE 'YEAR IS NOT VALID' TO DISMSGO
        MOVE -1  TO DDL
        MOVE 'BAD' TO DATA-FLAG
     ELSE
       IF TENNANTL = +0 OR TENNANTI = LOW-VALUES OR
          TENNANTI = SPACES THEN
          MOVE 'A TENNANTS NAME MUST BE ENTERED' TO DISMSGO
          MOVE -1  TO TENNANTL
          MOVE 'BAD' TO DATA-FLAG
       ELSE
         IF APTNOI NOT NUMERIC OR APTNOL = +0 THEN
            MOVE 'PLEASE ENTER AN APARTMENT NUMBER' TO
                 DISMSGO
            MOVE -1  TO APTNOL
            MOVE 'BAD' TO DATA-FLAG
         ELSE
           IF DESC1L = +0 AND DESC2L = +0 THEN
              MOVE 'A DESCIPTION MUST BE ENTERED' TO
                   DISMSGO
              MOVE -1  TO DESC1L
              MOVE 'BAD' TO DATA-FLAG.
```

NONCONVERSATIONAL, MULTIPROGRAM, LOCATE MODE, COMMAREAS, SPECIAL SCREEN HANDLING

The final implementation is a complete interacting system composed of several modules, one for each of the functions in the system. Hence, ADD, DELETE, UPDATE, INQUIRY, and driver components are implemented as individual programs for the same application. Locate-mode processing is again used for terminal and file I/O and COMMAREAs are used so that these nonconversational modules are able to determine and to remember what they were doing when they last gave up control.

Finally, this version is different from all other versions in that it also defines each screen individually rather than all screens sharing the same storage area, as is normally done in locate mode. This was accomplished by the operand STORAGE=AUTO on the DFHMSD statement rather than by omitting this operand and coding BASE=dataname, as was done in the previous locate-mode implementations.

```
IDENTIFICATION DIVISION.
    PROGRAM-ID.  LAMS.
    AUTHOR.       ME.
*----------------------------------------------------------
*     LAMS - DRIVER PROGRAM FOR THE MULTI PROGRAM SYSTEM
*----------------------------------------------------------
ENVIRONMENT DIVISION.
DATA DIVISION.
WORKING-STORAGE SECTION.
01   TIOALEN                      PIC S9(4)  COMP VALUE +1920.
01   LAMS                         PIC X(4)   VALUE 'LAMS'.
01   MENUMAP                      PIC X(8)   VALUE 'MENU'.
01   MAPSETNAME                   PIC X(8)   VALUE 'LAMSM'.
01   HEX00                        PIC X      VALUE LOW-VALUES.
01   ADDROUTINE                   PIC X(8)   VALUE 'LAMA'.
01   DELETEROUTINE                PIC X(8)   VALUE 'LAMD'.
01   UPDATEROUTINE                PIC X(8)   VALUE 'LAMU'.
01   INQUIREROUTINE               PIC X(8)   VALUE 'LAMI'.

01   COPY ATTRBS.
01   COPY DFHAID.

01   MYCOMMAREA.
     02   BRAIN                    PIC X(2).
     02   XXX                      REDEFINES BRAIN.
          03   FORMATTED-MAP-CODE PIC X.
          03   FORMATTED-FUNCTION PIC X.


LINKAGE SECTION.
01 DFHCOMMAREA.
     02   BRAIN2                   PIC X(2).

01 DFHBLLDS.
     02   RESERVED-BLL             PIC S9(8) COMP.
     02   MENUBLL                  PIC S9(8) COMP.
     02   DISPBLL                  PIC S9(8) COMP.
     02   KEYBLL                   PIC S9(8) COMP.

01   COPY LAMSM.


PROCEDURE DIVISION.

     EXEC CICS HANDLE AID ANYKEY(ALL-DONE) END-EXEC.
     IF EIBCALEN = +0 THEN
        MOVE 'M ' TO BRAIN
        EXEC CICS SEND MAP(MENUMAP) MAPSET(MAPSETNAME)
           MAPONLY ERASE END-EXEC
```

```
            EXEC CICS RETURN COMMAREA(MYCOMMAREA) LENGTH(2)
                TRANSID(LAMS) END-EXEC.

        IF EIBTRNID NOT = LAMS THEN
            EXEC CICS RETURN END-EXEC.

        MOVE BRAIN2    TO    BRAIN.
        IF FORMATTED-MAP-CODE = 'M' THEN
            EXEC CICS RECEIVE MAP(MENUMAP) MAPSET(MAPSETNAME)
                SET(MENUBLL) END-EXEC
            PERFORM PROCESS-MENU-MAP THRU MENU-MAP-EXIT.

        EXEC CICS RETURN COMMAREA(MYCOMMAREA) LENGTH(2)
            TRANSID(LAMS) END-EXEC.
        STOP RUN.

    ALL-DONE.
        EXEC CICS SEND FROM(HEX00) LENGTH(0) ERASE END-EXEC.
        EXEC CICS RETURN END-EXEC.


    PROCESS-MENU-MAP.
        IF CHOICEI < '1' OR CHOICEI > '4' THEN
            MOVE 'INVALID CHOICE ENTERED, CORRECT AND REENTER'
                TO MENUMSGO
            MOVE -1    TO CHOICEL
            MOVE 'M ' TO BRAIN
            EXEC CICS SEND MAP(MENUMAP) MAPSET(MAPSETNAME)
                FROM(MENUO) ERASE CURSOR END-EXEC
        ELSE
        IF CHOICEI = '1' THEN
            EXEC CICS XCTL PROGRAM(INQUIREROUTINE) END-EXEC
        ELSE
            IF CHOICEI = '2' THEN
                EXEC CICS XCTL PROGRAM(ADDROUTINE) END-EXEC
            ELSE
                IF CHOICEI = '3' THEN
                    EXEC CICS XCTL PROGRAM(UPDATEROUTINE) END-EXEC
                ELSE
                    EXEC CICS XCTL PROGRAM(DELETEROUTINE) END-EXEC.
    MENU-MAP-EXIT.

    IDENTIFICATION DIVISION.
        PROGRAM-ID.  LAMA.
        AUTHOR.      ME.
    *-------------------------------------------------------------------
    *|                      LAMA - ADD SUBROUTINE
    *-------------------------------------------------------------------
    ENVIRONMENT DIVISION.
    DATA DIVISION.
```

```
WORKING-STORAGE SECTION.
01    TIOALEN                      PIC S9(4)  COMP VALUE +1920.
01    LAMA                         PIC X(4)   VALUE 'LAMA'.
01    MENUMAP                      PIC X(8)   VALUE 'MENU'.
01    DISPLAYMAP                   PIC X(8)   VALUE 'DISPLAY'.
01    KEYMAP                       PIC X(8)   VALUE 'KEY'.
01    MAPSETNAME                   PIC X(8)   VALUE 'LAMSM'.
01    FILENAME                     PIC X(8)   VALUE 'MASTERF'.
01    DATA-FLAG                    PIC X(4).
01    LRECL                        PIC S9(4)  COMP VALUE +300.
01    HEX00                        PIC X      VALUE LOW-VALUES.
01    MENUROUTINE                  PIC X(8)   VALUE 'LAMS'.
01    ADDROUTINE                   PIC X(8)   VALUE 'LAMA'.
01    DELETEROUTINE                PIC X(8)   VALUE 'LAMD'.
01    UPDATEROUTINE                PIC X(8)   VALUE 'LAMU'.
01    INQUIREROUTINE               PIC X(8)   VALUE 'LAMI'.

01    DATE-FROM-SYSTEM.
      02   SYSMM                   PIC X(2).
      02   FILLER                  PIC X.
      02   SYSDD                   PIC X(2).
      02   FILLER                  PIC X.
      02   SYSYY                   PIC X(2).

01    MF-KEY                       PIC 9(5).
01    COPY ATTRBS.
01    COPY DFHAID.

01    MYCOMMAREA.
      02   BRAIN                   PIC X(2).
      02   XXX                     REDEFINES BRAIN.
           03   FORMATTED-MAP-CODE PIC X.
           03   FORMATTED-FUNCTION PIC X.


LINKAGE SECTION.
01    DFHCOMMAREA.
      02   BRAIN2                  PIC X(2).

01    DFHBLLDS.
      02   RESERVED-BLL            PIC S9(8)  COMP.
      02   MENUBLL                 PIC S9(8)  COMP.
      02   DISPBLL                 PIC S9(8)  COMP.
      02   KEYBLL                  PIC S9(8)  COMP.
      02   FILEBLL                 PIC S9(8)  COMP.

01    COPY LAMSM.
```

```
01   MASTER-FILE.
     02   MF-PROBLEM                 PIC 9 (5).
     02   MF-REPORTED-ON.
          03   MF-REPORT-MM          PIC X (2).
          03   MF-REPORT-DD          PIC X (2).
          03   MF-REPORT-YY          PIC X (2).
     02   MF-TENNANT                 PIC X (20).
     02   MF-APARTMENT               PIC X (3).
     02   MF-DESCRIPTION.
          03   MF-DESCRIPTION-1      PIC X (50).
          03   MF-DESCRIPTION-2      PIC X (50).
     02   MF-DATE-FIXED.
          03   MF-FIX-MM             PIC X (2).
          03   MF-FIX-DD             PIC X (2).
          03   MF-FIX-YY             PIC X (2).
     02   MF-STAFF                   PIC X (20).
     02   MF-TIME-TO-FIX             PIC X (2).
     02   MF-QUALITY                 PIC X.
     02   MF-FILLER                  PIC X (138).


PROCEDURE DIVISION.
     EXEC CICS HANDLE AID ANYKEY (ALL-DONE) END-EXEC.

     IF EIBTRNID NOT = LAMA THEN
        EXEC CICS GETMAIN SET (DISPBLL) LENGTH (2000)
           INITIMG (HEX00) END-EXEC
        MOVE CURRENT-DATE TO DATE-FROM-SYSTEM
        MOVE SYSMM    TO MMO
        MOVE SYSDD    TO DDO
        MOVE SYSYY    TO YYO
        MOVE UNPROT-BRT-NUM-FSET TO MMA
        MOVE UNPROT-BRT-NUM-FSET TO DDA
        MOVE UNPROT-BRT-NUM-FSET TO YYA
        MOVE -1                 TO PROBNUML
        EXEC CICS SEND MAP (DISPLAYMAP) MAPSET (MAPSETNAME)
           FROM (DISPLAYO) ERASE CURSOR END-EXEC
        MOVE 'DA' TO BRAIN
        EXEC CICS RETURN COMMAREA (MYCOMMAREA) LENGTH (2)
              TRANSID (LAMA) END-EXEC.
        EXEC CICS RECEIVE MAP (DISPLAYMAP)
           MAPSET (MAPSETNAME) SET (DISPBLL) END-EXEC
        PERFORM ADD-2 THRU ADD-EXIT.

        EXEC CICS RETURN COMMAREA (MYCOMMAREA) LENGTH (2)
              TRANSID (LAMA) END-EXEC.
        STOP RUN.
```

```
ALL-DONE.
    EXEC CICS SEND FROM(HEX00) LENGTH(0) ERASE END-EXEC.
    EXEC CICS RETURN END-EXEC.


ADD-2.
    MOVE 'GOOD'        TO DATA-FLAG.
    PERFORM  EDIT-MASTER-SCREEN-DATA.
    IF DATA-FLAG = 'BAD' THEN
        PERFORM SET-ATTRIBUTES-FOR-ADD
        EXEC CICS SEND MAP(DISPLAYMAP) MAPSET(MAPSETNAME)
          FROM(DISPLAYO) ERASE CURSOR END-EXEC
        GO TO ADD-EXIT.

    EXEC CICS GETMAIN SET(FILEBLL) LENGTH(300)
        INITIMG(HEX00) END-EXEC.
    PERFORM MOVE-SCREEN-DATA-TO-MASTER.
    MOVE MF-PROBLEM     TO MF-KEY.
    EXEC CICS HANDLE CONDITION NOSPACE(ADD-NOSPACE)
        DUPREC(ADD-DUPREC) END-EXEC.
    EXEC CICS WRITE DATASET(FILENAME) FROM(MASTER-FILE)
        RIDFLD(MF-KEY) LENGTH(LRECL) END-EXEC.
    EXEC CICS GETMAIN SET(MENUBLL) LENGTH(2000)
        INITIMG(HEX00) END-EXEC.
    MOVE 'RECORD ADDED, ENTER NEXT REQUEST' TO MENUMSGO.
    MOVE 'M ' TO BRAIN.
    EXEC CICS SEND MAP(MENUMAP) MAPSET(MAPSETNAME)
      FROM(MENUO) ERASE END-EXEC.
    MOVE MENUROUTINE    TO LAMA.
    GO TO ADD-EXIT.

ADD-NOSPACE.
    EXEC CICS GETMAIN SET(MENUBLL) LENGTH(2000)
        INITIMG(HEX00) END-EXEC.
    MOVE 'NO SPACE IN FILE, CONTACT PROGRAMMER' TO MENUMSGO.
    MOVE 'M ' TO BRAIN.
    EXEC CICS SEND MAP(MENUMAP) MAPSET(MAPSETNAME)
        FROM(MENUO) ERASE END-EXEC.
    MOVE MENUROUTINE    TO LAMA.
    GO TO ADD-EXIT.

ADD-DUPREC.
    MOVE 'RECORD ALREADY EXISTS, CHANGE KEY AND RETRY' TO
        DISMSGO.
    MOVE -1  TO PROBNUML.
    PERFORM SET-ATTRIBUTES-FOR-ADD.
    MOVE UNPROT-BRT-NUM-FSET    TO PROBNUMA.
    EXEC CICS SEND MAP(DISPLAYMAP) MAPSET(MAPSETNAME)
        FROM(DISPLAYO) ERASE CURSOR END-EXEC.
```

```
ADD-EXIT.
    EXIT.



MOVE-SCREEN-DATA-TO-MASTER.
    MOVE PROBNUMI          TO MF-PROBLEM.
    MOVE MMI               TO MF-REPORT-MM.
    MOVE DDI               TO MF-REPORT-DD.
    MOVE YYI               TO MF-REPORT-YY.
    MOVE TENNANTI          TO MF-TENNANT.
    MOVE APTNOI            TO MF-APARTMENT.
    MOVE DESC1I            TO MF-DESCRIPTION-1.
    MOVE DESC2I            TO MF-DESCRIPTION-2.
    MOVE FIXMMI            TO MF-FIX-MM.
    MOVE FIXDDI            TO MF-FIX-DD.
    MOVE FIXYYI            TO MF-FIX-YY.
    MOVE STAFFI            TO MF-STAFF.
    MOVE FIXTIMEI          TO MF-TIME-TO-FIX.
    MOVE QUALITYI          TO MF-QUALITY.
    MOVE SPACES            TO MF-FILLER.


SET-ATTRIBUTES-FOR-ADD.
    MOVE UNPROT-BRT-NUM-FSET      TO PROBNUMA.
    MOVE UNPROT-BRT-NUM-FSET      TO MMA.
    MOVE UNPROT-BRT-NUM-FSET      TO DDA.
    MOVE UNPROT-BRT-NUM-FSET      TO YYA.
    MOVE UNPROT-BRT-FSET          TO TENNANTA.
    MOVE UNPROT-BRT-NUM-FSET      TO APTNOA.
    MOVE UNPROT-BRT-FSET          TO DESC1A.
    MOVE UNPROT-BRT-FSET          TO DESC2A.
    MOVE UNPROT-BRT-NUM-FSET      TO FIXMMA.
    MOVE UNPROT-BRT-NUM-FSET      TO FIXDDA.
    MOVE UNPROT-BRT-NUM-FSET      TO FIXYYA.
    MOVE UNPROT-BRT-FSET          TO STAFFA.
    MOVE UNPROT-BRT-NUM-FSET      TO FIXTIMEA.
    MOVE UNPROT-BRT-FSET          TO QUALITYA.


EDIT-MASTER-SCREEN-DATA.
    IF PROBNUMI NOT NUMERIC THEN
        MOVE 'PROBLEM NUMBER IS NOT ALL DIGITS' TO DISMSGO
        MOVE -1 TO PROBNUMA
        MOVE 'BAD'  TO DATA-FLAG
    ELSE
      IF MMI NOT NUMERIC OR MMI < '01' OR MMI > '12' THEN
         MOVE 'MONTH ENTERED IS NOT VALID' TO DISMSGO
         MOVE -1  TO MML
         MOVE 'BAD'  TO DATA-FLAG
```

```
              ELSE
                IF DDI NOT NUMERIC OR DDI < '01' OR DDI > '31' THEN
                  MOVE 'DAY ENTERED IS NOT VALID' TO DISMSGO
                  MOVE -1   TO DDL
                  MOVE 'BAD' TO DATA-FLAG
                ELSE
                IF YYI NOT NUMERIC OR YYI < '01' THEN
                  MOVE 'YEAR IS NOT VALID' TO DISMSGO
                  MOVE -1  TO DDL
                  MOVE 'BAD' TO DATA-FLAG
                ELSE
                IF TENNANTL = +0 OR TENNANTI = LOW-VALUES OR
                   TENNANTI = SPACES THEN
                  MOVE 'A TENNANTS NAME MUST BE ENTERED' TO DISMSGO
                  MOVE -1   TO TENNANTL
                  MOVE 'BAD' TO DATA-FLAG
                ELSE
                IF APTNOI NOT NUMERIC OR APTNOL = +0 THEN
                  MOVE 'PLEASE ENTER AN APARTMENT NUMBER' TO
                        DISMSGO
                  MOVE -1   TO APTNOL
                  MOVE 'BAD' TO DATA-FLAG
                ELSE
                IF DESC1L = +0 AND DESC2L = +0 THEN
                  MOVE 'A DESCRIPTION MUST BE ENTERED' TO
                        DISMSGO
                  MOVE -1  TO DESC1L
                  MOVE 'BAD' TO DATA-FLAG.


IDENTIFICATION DIVISION.
      PROGRAM-ID.  LAMD.
      AUTHOR.      ME.
*----------------------------------------------------------------
*|               LAMD  -  DELETE ROUTINE
*----------------------------------------------------------------
ENVIRONMENT DIVISION.
DATA DIVISION.
WORKING-STORAGE SECTION.
01   TIOALEN                     PIC S9(4) COMP VALUE +1920.
01   LAMD                        PIC X(4)    VALUE 'LAMD'.
01   MENUMAP                     PIC X(8)    VALUE 'MENU'.
01   DISPLAYMAP                  PIC X(8)    VALUE 'DISPLAY'.
01   KEYMAP                      PIC X(8)    VALUE 'KEY'.
01   MAPSETNAME                  PIC X(8)    VALUE 'LAMSM'.
01   FILENAME                    PIC X(8)    VALUE 'MASTERF'.
01   DATA-FLAG                   PIC X(4).
01   LRECL                       PIC S9(4) COMP VALUE +300.
01   HEX00                       PIC X       VALUE LOW-VALUES.
```

```
01  MENUROUTINE                PIC X(8)   VALUE 'LAMS'.
01  ADDROUTINE                 PIC X(8)   VALUE 'LAMA'.
01  DELETEROUTINE              PIC X(8)   VALUE 'LAMD'.
01  UPDATEROUTINE              PIC X(8)   VALUE 'LAMU'.
01  INQUIREROUTINE             PIC X(8)   VALUE 'LAMI'.

01  DATE-FROM-SYSTEM.
    02  SYSMM                  PIC X(2).
    02  FILLER                 PIC X.
    02  SYSDD                  PIC X(2).
    02  FILLER                 PIC X.
    02  SYSYY                  PIC X(2).

01  MF-KEY                     PIC 9(5).
01  COPY ATTRBS.
01  COPY DFHAID.

01  MYCOMMAREA.
    02  BRAIN                  PIC X(2).
    02  XXX                    REDEFINES BRAIN.
        03  FORMATTED-MAP-CODE PIC X.
        03  FORMATTED-FUNCTION PIC X.


LINKAGE SECTION.
01  DFHCOMMAREA.
    02  BRAIN2                 PIC X(2).

01  DFHBLLDS.
    02  RESERVED-BLL           PIC S9(8) COMP.
    02  MENUBLL                PIC S9(8) COMP.
    02  DISPBLL                PIC S9(8) COMP.
    02  KEYBLL                 PIC S9(8) COMP.
    02  FILEBLL                PIC S9(8) COMP.

01  COPY LAMSM.

01  MASTER-FILE.
    02  MF-PROBLEM             PIC 9(5).
    02  MF-REPORTED-ON.
        03  MF-REPORT-MM       PIC X(2).
        03  MF-REPORT-DD       PIC X(2).
        03  MF-REPORT-YY       PIC X(2).
    02  MF-TENNANT             PIC X(20).
    02  MF-APARTMENT           PIC X(3).
    02  MF-DESCRIPTION.
        03  MF-DESCRIPTION-1   PIC X(50).
        03  MF-DESCRIPTION-2   PIC X(50).
```

```
02   MF-DATE-FIXED.
     03   MF-FIX-MM              PIC X(2).
     03   MF-FIX-DD              PIC X(2).
     03   MF-FIX-YY              PIC X(2).
02   MF-STAFF                    PIC X(20).
02   MF-TIME-TO-FIX             PIC X(2).
02   MF-QUALITY                 PIC X.
02   MF-FILLER                  PIC X(138).


PROCEDURE DIVISION.
     EXEC CICS HANDLE AID ANYKEY(ALL-DONE) END-EXEC.

     IF EIBTRNID NOT = LAMD THEN
         EXEC CICS GETMAIN SET(KEYBLL) LENGTH(2000)
             INITIMG(HEX00) END-EXEC
         MOVE '       DELETE A PROBLEM       ' TO KEYSUBO
         MOVE 'KD'    TO BRAIN
         MOVE -1      TO KEYVALL
         EXEC CICS SEND MAP(KEYMAP) MAPSET(MAPSETNAME)
             FROM(KEYO) ERASE END-EXEC
         EXEC CICS RETURN COMMAREA(MYCOMMAREA) LENGTH(2)
             TRANSID(LAMD) END-EXEC.

     MOVE BRAIN2   TO   BRAIN.
     IF FORMATTED-MAP-CODE = 'K' THEN
         EXEC CICS RECEIVE MAP(KEYMAP) MAPSET(MAPSETNAME)
             SET(KEYBLL) END-EXEC
         PERFORM PROCESS-KEY-MAP THRU KEY-MAP-EXIT
     ELSE
         EXEC CICS RECEIVE MAP(DISPLAYMAP)
             MAPSET(MAPSETNAME) SET(DISPBLL) END-EXEC
         PERFORM DELETE-2 THRU DELETE-2-EXIT.

     EXEC CICS RETURN COMMAREA(MYCOMMAREA) LENGTH(2)
         TRANSID(LAMD) END-EXEC.
     STOP RUN.

ALL-DONE.
     EXEC CICS SEND FROM(HEX00) LENGTH(0) ERASE END-EXEC.
     EXEC CICS RETURN END-EXEC.

PROCESS-KEY-MAP.
     IF KEYVALI NOT NUMERIC THEN
         MOVE 'PROBLEM NUMBER NOT VALID, REENTER' TO KEYMSGO
         MOVE -1              TO KEYVALL
         MOVE ASKIP-BRT-FSET  TO KEYVALA
         EXEC CICS SEND MAP(KEYMAP) MAPSET(MAPSETNAME)
             FROM(KEYO) ERASE CURSOR END-EXEC
```

```
        ELSE
            PERFORM DELETE-RECORD-FROM-FILE THRU DELETE-EXIT.
KEY-MAP-EXIT.
        EXIT.


DELETE-RECORD-FROM-FILE.
        MOVE KEYVALI    TO    MF-KEY.
        EXEC CICS HANDLE CONDITION NOTFND(DELT-NOTFND) END-EXEC.
        EXEC CICS READ DATASET(FILENAME) SET(FILEBLL)
            RIDFLD(MF-KEY) END-EXEC.
        EXEC CICS GETMAIN SET(DISPBLL) LENGTH(2000)
            INITING(HEX00) END-EXEC.
        PERFORM MOVE-MASTER-DATA-TO-SCREEN.
        PERFORM SET-ATTRIBUTES-FOR-DELETE.
        MOVE ASKIP-NORM        TO DELHDR1A.
        MOVE ASKIP-NORM        TO DELHDR2A.
        MOVE UNPROT-BRT-FSET   TO YESNOA.
        MOVE 'DD'              TO BRAIN.
        MOVE -1                TO YESNOL.
        MOVE 'ENTER YES TO DELETE THIS RECORD      ' TO DISMSGO.
        EXEC CICS SEND MAP(DISPLAYMAP) MAPSET(MAPSETNAME)
            FROM(DISPLAYO) ERASE CURSOR END-EXEC.
        GO TO DELETE-EXIT.

DELT-NOTFND.
        MOVE 'RECORD NOT IN FILE, CANT BE DELETED' TO KEYMSGO.
        MOVE -1    TO KEYVALL.
        MOVE 'KD'  TO BRAIN.
        EXEC CICS SEND MAP(KEYMAP) MAPSET(MAPSETNAME)
            FROM(KEYO) ERASE CURSOR END-EXEC.

DELETE-EXIT.
        EXIT.


DELETE-2.


        IF YESNOI NOT = 'YES' AND YESNOI NOT = 'NO' THEN
            MOVE 'YES OR NO NOT ENTERED, PLEASE ENTER AGAIN' TO
                DISMSGO
            MOVE -1    TO YESNOL
            MOVE ASKIP-NORM            TO DELHDR1A
            MOVE ASKIP-NORM            TO DELHDR2A
            MOVE UNPROT-BRT-FSET       TO YESNOA
            EXEC CICS SEND MAP(DISPLAYMAP) MAPSET(MAPSETNAME)
                FROM(DISPLAYO) ERASE END-EXEC
            GO TO DELETE-2-EXIT.
```

```
     IF YESNOI = 'NO' THEN
        EXEC CICS GETMAIN SET (MENUBLL) LENGTH (2000)
           INITIMG (HEX00) END-EXEC
        MOVE 'DELETE NOT DONE AS REQUESTED' TO MENUMSGO
        MOVE 'M ' TO BRAIN
        EXEC CICS SEND MAP (MENUMAP) MAPSET (MAPSETNAME)
           FROM (MENUO) ERASE END-EXEC
        MOVE MENUROUTINE TO LAMD
        GO TO DELETE-2-EXIT.

     MOVE PROBNUMI  TO MF-KEY.
     EXEC CICS HANDLE CONDITION NOTFND (DEL2-NOTFND) END-EXEC.
     EXEC CICS DELETE DATASET (FILENAME) RIDFLD (MF-KEY)
        END-EXEC.
     EXEC CICS GETMAIN SET (MENUBLL) LENGTH (2000)
        INITIMG (HEX00) END-EXEC.
     MOVE 'RECORD DELETED AS REQUESTED' TO MENUMSGO.
     MOVE 'M ' TO BRAIN.
     MOVE MENUROUTINE  TO LAMD.
     EXEC CICS SEND MAP (MENUMAP) MAPSET (MAPSETNAME)
       FROM (MENUO) ERASE END-EXEC.
     GO TO DELETE-2-EXIT.

 DEL2-NOTFND.
     EXEC CICS GETMAIN SET (MENUBLL) LENGTH (2000)
        INITIMG (HEX00) END-EXEC.
     MOVE 'RECORD WAS DELETED BY ANOTHER USER' TO MENUMSGO.
     MOVE 'M ' TO BRAIN.
     MOVE MENUROUTINE TO LAMD.
     EXEC CICS SEND MAP (MENUMAP) MAPSET (MAPSETNAME)
        FROM (MENUO) ERASE END-EXEC.
 DELETE-2-EXIT.
     EXIT.

 MOVE-MASTER-DATA-TO-SCREEN.
     MOVE MF-PROBLEM        TO PROBNUMO.
     MOVE MF-REPORT-MM      TO MMO.
     MOVE MF-REPORT-DD      TO DDO.
     MOVE MF-REPORT-YY      TO YYO.
     MOVE MF-TENNANT        TO TENNANTO.
     MOVE MF-APARTMENT      TO APTNOO.
     MOVE MF-DESCRIPTION-1 TO DESC1O.
     MOVE MF-DESCRIPTION-2 TO DESC2O.
     MOVE MF-FIX-MM         TO FIXMMO.
     MOVE MF-FIX-DD         TO FIXDDO.
     MOVE MF-FIX-YY         TO FIXYYO.
     MOVE MF-STAFF          TO STAFFO.
     MOVE MF-TIME-TO-FIX    TO FIXTIMEO.
     MOVE MF-QUALITY        TO QUALITYO.
```

```
MOVE-SCREEN-DATA-TO-MASTER.
      MOVE PROBNUMI          TO MF-PROBLEM.
      MOVE MMI               TO MF-REPORT-MM.
      MOVE DDI               TO MF-REPORT-DD.
      MOVE YYI               TO MF-REPORT-YY.
      MOVE TENNANTI          TO MF-TENNANT.
      MOVE APTNOI            TO MF-APARTMENT.
      MOVE DESC1I            TO MF-DESCRIPTION-1.
      MOVE DESC2I            TO MF-DESCRIPTION-2.
      MOVE FIXMMI            TO MF-FIX-MM.
      MOVE FIXDDI            TO MF-FIX-DD.
      MOVE FIXYYI            TO MF-FIX-YY.
      MOVE STAFFI            TO MF-STAFF.
      MOVE FIXTIMEI          TO MF-TIME-TO-FIX.
      MOVE QUALITYI          TO MF-QUALITY.
      MOVE SPACES            TO MF-FILLER.


SET-ATTRIBUTES-FOR-DELETE.
      MOVE ASKIP-BRT-NUM-FSET    TO PROBNUMA.
      MOVE ASKIP-BRT-NUM-FSET    TO MMA.
      MOVE ASKIP-BRT-NUM-FSET    TO DDA.
      MOVE ASKIP-BRT-NUM-FSET    TO YYA.
      MOVE ASKIP-BRT-FSET        TO TENNANTA.
      MOVE ASKIP-BRT-NUM-FSET    TO APTNOA.
      MOVE ASKIP-BRT-FSET        TO DESC1A.
      MOVE ASKIP-BRT-FSET        TO DESC2A.
      MOVE ASKIP-BRT-NUM-FSET    TO FIXMMA.
      MOVE ASKIP-BRT-NUM-FSET    TO FIXDDA.
      MOVE ASKIP-BRT-NUM-FSET    TO FIXYYA.
      MOVE ASKIP-BRT-FSET        TO STAFFA.
      MOVE ASKIP-BRT-NUM-FSET    TO FIXTIMEA.
      MOVE ASKIP-BRT-FSET        TO QUALITYA.



IDENTIFICATION DIVISION.
      PROGRAM-ID.  LAMU.
      AUTHOR.      ME.
*-----------------------------------------------------------------
*|                 LAMU - UPDATE ROUTINE
*-----------------------------------------------------------------
ENVIRONMENT DIVISION.
DATA DIVISION.
WORKING-STORAGE SECTION.
01  TIOALEN                PIC S9(4) COMP VALUE +1920.
01  LAMU                   PIC X(4)  VALUE 'LAMU'.
01  MENUMAP                PIC X(8)  VALUE 'MENU'.
01  DISPLAYMAP             PIC X(8)  VALUE 'DISPLAY'.
01  KEYMAP                 PIC X(8)  VALUE 'KEY'.
01  MAPSETNAME             PIC X(8)  VALUE 'LAMSM'.
```

```
01   FILENAME                      PIC X(8)    VALUE 'MASTERF'.
01   DATA-FLAG                     PIC X(4).
01   LRECL                         PIC S9(4) COMP VALUE +300.
01   HEX00                         PIC X       VALUE LOW-VALUES.
01   MENUROUTINE                   PIC X(8)    VALUE 'LAMS'.
01   ADDROUTINE                    PIC X(8)    VALUE 'LAMA'.
01   DELETEROUTINE                 PIC X(8)    VALUE 'LAMD'.
01   UPDATEROUTINE                 PIC X(8)    VALUE 'LAMU'.
01   INQUIREROUTINE                PIC X(8)    VALUE 'LAMI'.

01   DATE-FROM-SYSTEM.
     02   SYSMM                    PIC X(2).
     02   FILLER                   PIC X.
     02   SYSDD                    PIC X(2).
     02   FILLER                   PIC X.
     02   SYSYY                    PIC X(2).

01   MF-KEY                        PIC 9(5).
01   COPY ATTRBS.
01   COPY DFHAID.

01   MYCOMMABEA.
     02   BRAIN                    PIC X(2).
     02   XXX                      REDEFINES BRAIN.
          03   FORMATTED-MAP-CODE  PIC X.
          03   FORMATTED-FUNCTION  PIC X.


LINKAGE SECTION.
01   DFHCOMMAREA.
     02   BRAIN2                   PIC X(2).

01   DFHBLLDS.
     02   RESERVED-BLL             PIC S9(8) COMP.
     02   MENUBLL                  PIC S9(8) COMP.
     02   DISPBLL                  PIC S9(8) COMP.
     02   KEYBLL                   PIC S9(8) COMP.
     02   FILEBLL                  PIC S9(8) COMP.

01   COPY LAMSM.

01   MASTER-FILE.
     02   MF-PROBLEM               PIC 9(5).
     02   MF-REPORTED-ON.
          03   MF-REPORT-MM        PIC X(2).
          03   MF-REPORT-DD        PIC X(2).
          03   MF-REPORT-YY        PIC X(2).
     02   MF-TENNANT               PIC X(20).
     02   MF-APARTMENT             PIC X(3).
```

```
    02  MF-DESCRIPTION.
        03  MF-DESCRIPTION-1      PIC X(50).
        03  MF-DESCRIPTION-2      PIC X(50).
    02  MF-DATE-FIXED.
        03  MF-FIX-MM             PIC X(2).
        03  MF-FIX-DD             PIC X(2).
        03  MF-FIX-YY             PIC X(2).
    02  MF-STAFF                  PIC X(20).
    02  MF-TIME-TO-FIX           PIC X(2).
    02  MF-QUALITY               PIC X.
    02  MF-FILLER                PIC X(138).


PROCEDURE DIVISION.
    EXEC CICS HANDLE AID ANYKEY(ALL-DONE) END-EXEC.

    IF EIBTRNID NOT = LAMU THEN
        EXEC CICS GETMAIN SET(KEYBLL) LENGTH(2000)
            INITIMG(HEX00) END-EXEC
        MOVE '       UPDATE A PROBLEM       ' TO KEYSUBO
        MOVE 'KU'    TO BRAIN
        MOVE -1      TO KEYVALL
        EXEC CICS SEND MAP(KEYMAP) MAPSET(MAPSETNAME)
            FROM(KEYO) ERASE CURSOR END-EXEC
        EXEC CICS RETURN COMMAREA(MYCOMMAREA) LENGTH(2)
            TRANSID(LAMU) END-EXEC.

    MOVE BRAIN2    TO  BRAIN.
    IF FORMATTED-MAP-CODE = 'K' THEN
        EXEC CICS RECEIVE MAP(KEYMAP) MAPSET(MAPSETNAME)
            SET(KEYBLL) END-EXEC
        PERFORM PROCESS-KEY-MAP THRU KEY-MAP-EXIT
    ELSE
        EXEC CICS RECEIVE MAP(DISPLAYMAP)
            MAPSET(MAPSETNAME) SET(DISPBLL) END-EXEC
        PERFORM UPDATE-2 THRU UPDATE-2-EXIT.

    EXEC CICS RETURN COMMAREA(MYCOMMAREA) LENGTH(2)
        TRANSID(LAMU) END-EXEC.
    STOP RUN.

ALL-DONE.
    EXEC CICS SEND FROM(HEX00) LENGTH(0) ERASE END-EXEC.
    EXEC CICS RETURN END-EXEC.

PROCESS-KEY-MAP.
    IF KEYVALI NOT NUMERIC THEN
        MOVE 'PROBLEM NUMBER NOT VALID, REENTER' TO KEYMSGO
        MOVE -1                  TO KEYVALL
```

```
          MOVE ASKIP-BRT-FSET  TO KEYVALA
          EXEC CICS SEND MAP(KEYMAP) MAPSET(MAPSETNAME)
             FROM(KEYO) ERASE CURSOR END-EXEC
       ELSE
          PERFORM UPDATE-RECORD-IN-FILE THRU UPDATE-EXIT.
   KEY-MAP-EXIT.


   UPDATE-RECORD-IN-FILE.
       MOVE KEYVALI    TO    MF-KEY.
       EXEC CICS HANDLE CONDITION NOTFND(UPDT-NOTFND) END-EXEC.
       EXEC CICS READ DATASET(FILENAME) SET(FILEBLL)
          RIDFLD(MF-KEY) END-EXEC.
       EXEC CICS GETMAIN SET(DISPBLL) LENGTH(2000)
          INITIMG(HEX00) END-EXEC.
       PERFORM MOVE-MASTER-DATA-TO-SCREEN.
       PERFORM SET-ATTRIBUTES-FOR-UPDATE.
       MOVE 'DU'             TO BRAIN.
       MOVE -1               TO FIXMML.
       MOVE 'MAKE CHANGES DESIRED, THEN ENTER.   ' TO DISMSGO.
       EXEC CICS SEND MAP(DISPLAYMAP) MAPSET(MAPSETNAME)
          FROM(DISPLAYO) ERASE CURSOR END-EXEC.
       GO TO UPDATE-EXIT.

   UPDT-NOTFND.
       MOVE 'RECORD NOT IN FILE, CANT BE UPDATED' TO KEYMSGO.
       MOVE -1    TO KEYVALL.
       MOVE 'KU'  TO BRAIN.
       EXEC CICS SEND MAP(KEYMAP) MAPSET(MAPSETNAME)
          FROM(KEYO) ERASE CURSOR END-EXEC.
   UPDATE-EXIT.

       EXIT.

   UPDATE-2.
       MOVE 'GOOD'          TO DATA-FLAG.
       PERFORM  EDIT-MASTER-SCREEN-DATA.
       IF DATA-FLAG = 'BAD' THEN
          PERFORM SET-ATTRIBUTES-FOR-UPDATE
          EXEC CICS SEND MAP(DISPLAYMAP) MAPSET(MAPSETNAME)
             FROM(DISPLAYO) ERASE CURSOR END-EXEC
          GO TO UPDATE-2-EXIT.

       MOVE PROBNUMI      TO MF-KEY.
       EXEC CICS HANDLE CONDITION NOTFND(UPDT-2-NOTFND) END-EXEC.
       EXEC CICS READ DATASET(FILENAME) SET(FILEBLL)
          RIDFLD(MF-KEY) UPDATE END-EXEC.
       PERFORM MOVE-SCREEN-DATA-TO-MASTER.
       EXEC CICS HANDLE CONDITION NOSPACE(UPDT-2-NOSPACE) END-EXEC.
```

```
     EXEC CICS REWRITE DATASET(FILENAME) FROM(MASTER-FILE)
        LENGTH(LRECL) END-EXEC.
     EXEC CICS GETMAIN SET(MENUBLL) LENGTH(2000)
        INITIMG(HEX00) END-EXEC.
     MOVE 'RECORD UPDATED, ENTER NEXT REQUEST' TO MENUMSGO.
     MOVE 'M ' TO BRAIN.
     MOVE MENUROUTINE TO LAMU.
     EXEC CICS SEND MAP(MENUMAP) MAPSET(MAPSETNAME)
        FROM(MENUO) ERASE END-EXEC.
     GO TO UPDATE-2-EXIT.

 UPDT-2-NOSPACE.
     EXEC CICS GETMAIN SET(MENUBLL) LENGTH(2000)
        INITIMG(HEX00) END-EXEC.
     MOVE 'NO SPACE IN FILE, CONTACT PROGRAMMER' TO MENUMSGO.
     MOVE 'M ' TO BRAIN.
     MOVE MENUROUTINE TO LAMU.
     EXEC CICS SEND MAP(MENUMAP) MAPSET(MAPSETNAME)
        FROM(MENUO) ERASE END-EXEC.
     GO TO UPDATE-2-EXIT.

 UPDT-2-NOTFND.
     EXEC CICS GETMAIN SET(MENUBLL) LENGTH(2000)
        INITIMG(HEX00) END-EXEC.
     MOVE 'RECORD DELETED FROM UNDERNEATH YOU, SORRY'   TO
        MENUMSGO.
     MOVE 'M ' TO BRAIN.
     MOVE MENUROUTINE TO LAMU.
     EXEC CICS SEND MAP(MENUMAP) MAPSET(MAPSETNAME)
        FROM(MENUO) ERASE CURSOR END-EXEC.
 UPDATE-2-EXIT.

     EXIT.

 MOVE-MASTER-DATA-TO-SCREEN.
     MOVE MF-PROBLEM        TO PROBNUMO.
     MOVE MF-REPORT-MM      TO MMO.
     MOVE MF-REPORT-DD      TO DDO.
     MOVE MF-REPORT-YY      TO YYO.
     MOVE MF-TENNANT        TO TENNANTO.
     MOVE MF-APARTMENT      TO APTNOO.
     MOVE MF-DESCRIPTION-1  TO DESC1O.
     MOVE MF-DESCRIPTION-2  TO DESC2O.
     MOVE MF-FIX-MM         TO FIXMMO.
     MOVE MF-FIX-DD         TO FIXDDO.
     MOVE MF-FIX-YY         TO FIXYYO.
     MOVE MF-STAFF          TO STAFFO.
     MOVE MF-TIME-TO-FIX    TO FIXTIMEO.
     MOVE MF-QUALITY        TO QUALITYO.
```

```
MOVE-SCREEN-DATA-TO-MASTER.
    MOVE PROBNUMI          TO MF-PROBLEM.
    MOVE MMI               TO MF-REPORT-MM.
    MOVE DDI               TO MF-REPORT-DD.
    MOVE YYI               TO MF-REPORT-YY.
    MOVE TENNANTI          TO MF-TENNANT.
    MOVE APTNOI            TO MF-APARTMENT.
    MOVE DESC1I            TO MF-DESCRIPTION-1.
    MOVE DESC2I            TO MF-DESCRIPTION-2.
    MOVE FIXMMI            TO MF-FIX-MM.
    MOVE FIXDDI            TO MF-FIX-DD.
    MOVE FIXYYI            TO MF-FIX-YY.
    MOVE STAFFI            TO MF-STAFF.
    MOVE FIXTIMEI          TO MF-TIME-TO-FIX.
    MOVE QUALITYI          TO MF-QUALITY.
    MOVE SPACES            TO MF-FILLER.

SET-ATTRIBUTES-FOR-UPDATE.
    MOVE ASKIP-BRT-NUM-FSET     TO PROBNUMA.
    MOVE UNPROT-BRT-NUM-FSET    TO MMA.
    MOVE UNPROT-BRT-NUM-FSET    TO DDA.
    MOVE UNPROT-BRT-NUM-FSET    TO YYA.
    MOVE UNPROT-BRT-FSET        TO TENNANTA.
    MOVE UNPROT-BRT-NUM-FSET    TO APTNOA.
    MOVE UNPROT-BRT-FSET        TO DESC1A.
    MOVE UNPROT-BRT-FSET        TO DESC2A.
    MOVE UNPROT-BRT-NUM-FSET    TO FIXMMA.
    MOVE UNPROT-BRT-NUM-FSET    TO FIXDDA.
    MOVE UNPROT-BRT-NUM-FSET    TO FIXYYA.
    MOVE UNPROT-BRT-FSET        TO STAFFA.
    MOVE UNPROT-BRT-NUM-FSET    TO FIXTIMEA.
    MOVE UNPROT-BRT-FSET        TO QUALITYA.

EDIT-MASTER-SCREEN-DATA.
    IF PROBNUMI NOT NUMERIC THEN
        MOVE 'PROBLEM NUMBER IS NOT ALL DIGITS' TO DISMSGO
        MOVE -1 TO PROBNUMA
        MOVE 'BAD'  TO DATA-FLAG
    ELSE
      IF MMI NOT NUMERIC OR MMI < '01' OR MMI > '12' THEN
        MOVE 'MONTH ENTERED IS NOT VALID' TO DISMSGO
        MOVE -1 TO MML
        MOVE 'BAD'  TO DATA-FLAG
      ELSE
        IF DDI NOT NUMERIC OR DDI < '01' OR DDI > '31' THEN
           MOVE 'DAY ENTERED IS NOT VALID' TO DISMSGO
           MOVE -1  TO DDL
           MOVE 'BAD' TO DATA-FLAG
```

```
         ELSE
           IF YYI NOT NUMERIC OR YYI < '01' THEN
             MOVE 'YEAR IS NOT VALID' TO DISMSGO
             MOVE -1  TO DDL
             MOVE 'BAD' TO DATA-FLAG
           ELSE
             IF TENNANTL = +0 OR TENNANTI = LOW-VALUES OR
                TENNANTI = SPACES THEN
               MOVE 'A TENNANT'S NAME MUST BE ENTERED' TO DISMSGO
               MOVE -1  TO TENNANTL
               MOVE 'BAD' TO DATA-FLAG
             ELSE
               IF APTNOI NOT NUMERIC OR APTNOL = +0 THEN
                 MOVE 'PLEASE ENTER AN APARTMENT NUMBER' TO
                         DISMSGO
                 MOVE -1  TO APTNOL
                 MOVE 'BAD' TO DATA-FLAG
               ELSE
                 IF DESC1L = +0 AND DESC2L = +0 THEN
                   MOVE 'A DESCRIPTION MUST BE ENTERED' TO
                           DISMSGO
                   MOVE -1  TO DESC1L
                   MOVE 'BAD' TO DATA-FLAG
                 ELSE
                   NEXT SENTENCE.


IDENTIFICATION DIVISION.
     PROGRAM-ID.  LAMI.
     AUTHOR.      ME.
*------------------------------------------------------------------
*|                   LAMI - INQUIRY ROUTINE
*------------------------------------------------------------------
ENVIRONMENT DIVISION.
DATA DIVISION.
WORKING-STORAGE SECTION.
 01  TIOALEN                      PIC S9(4) COMP VALUE +1920.
 01  LAMI                         PIC X(4)  VALUE 'LAMI'.
 01  MENUMAP                      PIC X(8)  VALUE 'MENU'.
 01  DISPLAYMAP                   PIC X(8)  VALUE 'DISPLAY'.
 01  KEYMAP                       PIC X(8)  VALUE 'KEY'.
 01  MAPSETNAME                   PIC X(8)  VALUE 'LAMSM'.
 01  FILENAME                     PIC X(8)  VALUE 'MASTERF'.
 01  DATA-FLAG                    PIC X(4).
 01  LRECL                        PIC S9(4) COMP VALUE +300.
 01  HEX00                        PIC X     VALUE LOW-VALUES.
 01  MENUROUTINE                  PIC X(8)  VALUE 'LAMS'.
 01  ADDROUTINE                   PIC X(8)  VALUE 'LAMA'.
 01  DELETEROUTINE                PIC X(8)  VALUE 'LAMD'.
```

```
01  UPDATEROUTINE                      PIC X(8)    VALUE 'LAMU'.
01  INQUIREROUTINE                     PIC X(8)    VALUE 'LAMI'.


01  DATE-FROM-SYSTEM.
    02  SYSMM                          PIC X(2).
    02  FILLER                         PIC X.
    02  SYSDD                          PIC X(2).
    02  FILLER                         PIC X.
    02  SYSYY                          PIC X(2).


01  MF-KEY                             PIC 9(5).
01  COPY ATTRBS.
01  COPY DFHAID.


01  MYCOMMAREA.
    02  BRAIN                          PIC X(2).
    02  XXX                            REDEFINES BRAIN.
        03  FORMATTED-MAP-CODE PIC X.
        03  FORMATTED-FUNCTION PIC X.



LINKAGE SECTION.
01  DFHCOMMAREA.
    02  BRAIN2                         PIC X(2).


01  DFHBLLDS.
    02  RESERVED-BLL                   PIC S9(8)  COMP.
    02  MENUBLL                        PIC S9(8)  COMP.
    02  DISPBLL                        PIC S9(8)  COMP.
    02  KEYBLL                         PIC S9(8)  COMP.
    02  FILEBLL                        PIC S9(8)  COMP.

01  COPY LAMSM.

01  MASTER-FILE.
    02  MF-PROBLEM                     PIC 9(5).
    02  MF-REPORTED-ON.
        03  MF-REPORT-MM               PIC X(2).
        03  MF-REPORT-DD               PIC X(2).
        03  MF-REPORT-YY               PIC X(2).
    02  MF-TENNANT                     PIC X(20).
    02  MF-APARTMENT                   PIC X(3).
    02  MF-DESCRIPTION.
        03  MF-DESCRIPTION-1           PIC X(50).
        03  MF-DESCRIPTION-2           PIC X(50).
    02  MF-DATE-FIXED.
        03  MF-FIX-MM                  PIC X(2).
        03  MF-FIX-DD                  PIC X(2).
        03  MF-FIX-YY                  PIC X(2).
```

```
02  MF-STAFF              PIC X(20).
02  MF-TIME-TO-FIX        PIC X(2).
02  MF-QUALITY            PIC X.
02  MF-FILLER             PIC X(138).


PROCEDURE DIVISION.
    EXEC CICS HANDLE AID ANYKEY(ALL-DONE) END-EXEC.

    IF EIBTRNID NOT = LAMI THEN
        EXEC CICS GETMAIN SET(KEYBLL) LENGTH(2000)
            INITIMG(HEX00) END-EXEC
        MOVE '   INQUIRE ON A PROBLEM   ' TO KEYSUBO
        MOVE 'KI' TO BRAIN
        MOVE -1   TO KEYVALL
        EXEC CICS SEND MAP(KEYMAP) MAPSET(MAPSETNAME)
            FROM(KEYO) ERASE CURSOR END-EXEC
        EXEC CICS RETURN COMMAREA(MYCOMMAREA) LENGTH(2)
            TRANSID(LAMI) END-EXEC.

    MOVE BRAIN2     TO  BRAIN.
    IF FORMATTED-MAP-CODE = 'K' THEN
        EXEC CICS RECEIVE MAP(KEYMAP) MAPSET(MAPSETNAME)
            SET(KEYBLL) END-EXEC
        PERFORM PROCESS-KEY-MAP THRU KEY-MAP-EXIT
    ELSE
        MOVE 'M ' TO BRAIN
        EXEC CICS SEND MAP(MENUMAP) MAPSET(MAPSETNAME)
            MAPONLY ERASE END-EXEC
        MOVE MENUROUTINE TO LAMI.

    EXEC CICS RETURN COMMAREA(MYCOMMAREA) LENGTH(2)
        TRANSID(LAMI) END-EXEC.
    STOP RUN.

ALL-DONE.
    EXEC CICS SEND FROM(HEX00) LENGTH(0) ERASE END-EXEC.
    EXEC CICS RETURN END-EXEC.

PROCESS-KEY-MAP.
    IF KEYVALI NOT NUMERIC THEN
        MOVE 'PROBLEM NUMBER NOT VALID, REENTER' TO KEYMSGO
        MOVE -1               TO KEYVALL
        MOVE ASKIP-BRT-FSET   TO KEYVALA
        EXEC CICS SEND MAP(KEYMAP) MAPSET(MAPSETNAME)
            FROM(KEYO) ERASE CURSOR END-EXEC
    ELSE
        PERFORM  DISPLAY-RECORD-TO-SCREEN THRU DISPLAY-EXIT.
KEY-MAP-EXIT.
```

```
DISPLAY-RECORD-TO-SCREEN.
    MOVE KEYVALI   TO    MF-KEY.
    EXEC CICS HANDLE CONDITION NOTFND(INQR-NOTFND) END-EXEC.
    EXEC CICS READ DATASET(FILENAME) SET(FILEBLL)
       RIDFLD(MF-KEY) END-EXEC.
    EXEC CICS GETMAIN SET(DISPBLL) LENGTH(2000)
       INITIMG(HEX00) END-EXEC.
    PERFORM MOVE-MASTER-DATA-TO-SCREEN.
    PERFORM SET-ATTRIBUTES-FOR-INQUIRY.
    MOVE 'DI' TO BRAIN.
    MOVE 'PRESS ENTER TO RETURN TO SYSTEM MENU' TO DISMSGO.
    EXEC CICS SEND MAP(DISPLAYMAP) MAPSET(MAPSETNAME)
       FROM(DISPLAYO) ERASE CURSOR(0) END-EXEC.
    GO TO DISPLAY-EXIT.

INQR-NOTFND.
    MOVE 'SORRY, RECORD NOT IN THE FILE' TO KEYMSGO.
    MOVE -1    TO KEYVALL.
    EXEC CICS SEND MAP(KEYMAP) MAPSET(MAPSETNAME)
       FROM(KEYO) ERASE CURSOR END-EXEC.

DISPLAY-EXIT. EXIT.

MOVE-MASTER-DATA-TO-SCREEN.
    MOVE MF-PROBLEM        TO PROBNUMO.
    MOVE MF-REPORT-MM      TO MMO.
    MOVE MF-REPORT-DD      TO DDO.
    MOVE MF-REPORT-YY      TO YYO.
    MOVE MF-TENNANT        TO TENNANTO.
    MOVE MF-APARTMENT      TO APTNOO.
    MOVE MF-DESCRIPTION-1 TO DESC10.
    MOVE MF-DESCRIPTION-2 TO DESC20.
    MOVE MF-FIX-MM         TO FIXMMO.
    MOVE MF-FIX-DD         TO FIXDDO.
    MOVE MF-FIX-YY         TO FIXYYO.
    MOVE MF-STAFF          TO STAFFO.
    MOVE MF-TIME-TO-FIX    TO FIXTIMEO.
    MOVE MF-QUALITY        TO QUALITYO.


SET-ATTRIBUTES-FOR-INQUIRY.
    MOVE ASKIP-BRT        TO PROBNUMA.
    MOVE ASKIP-BRT        TO MMA.
    MOVE ASKIP-BRT        TO DDA.
    MOVE ASKIP-BRT        TO YYA.
    MOVE ASKIP-BRT        TO TENNANTA.
    MOVE ASKIP-BRT        TO APTNOA.
    MOVE ASKIP-BRT        TO DESC1A.
    MOVE ASKIP-BRT        TO DESC2A.
```

```
MOVE ASKIP-BRT        TO FIXMMA.
MOVE ASKIP-BRT        TO FIXDDA.
MOVE ASKIP-BRT        TO FIXYYA.
MOVE ASKIP-BRT        TO STAFFA.
MOVE ASKIP-BRT        TO FIXTIMEA.
MOVE ASKIP-BRT        TO QUALITYA.
```

BIBLIOGRAPHY

I B M

CUSTOMER INFORMATION CONTROL SYSTEM/VIRTUAL STORAGE
RELEASE 1.5

CICS/VS General Information, pub. SC33-0066.
CICS/VS System/Application Design Guide, pub. SC33-0068.
CICS/VS Systems Programmer's Reference Manual,
   pub. SC33-0069.
CICS/VS CICS Application Programmer's Reference Manual,
   pub. SC33-0077.
CICS/VS Operator's Guide, pub. SC33-0080.
CICS/VS Messages and Codes, pub. SC33-0081.
CICS/VS Program Debugging Reference Summary, pub. SX33-6010.
CICS/VS Application Programmer's Reference Summary,
   pub. GX33-6012.

I B M

CUSTOMER INFORMATION CONTROL SYSTEM/VIRTUAL STORAGE
RELEASE 1.6

CICS/VS General Information, pub. GC33-0155.
CICS/VS Release Guide, pub. GC33-0132.
CICS/VS System/Application Design Guide, pub. SC33-0068.

CICS/VS Resource Definition Guide,
    pub. SC33-0149.
CICS/VS Performance Guide, pub. SC33-0134.
CICS/VS CICS Application Programmer's Reference Manual,
    pub. SC33-0161.
CICS/VS Operator's Guide, pub. SC33-0160.
CICS/VS Messages and Codes, pub. SC33-0156.
CICS/VS Program Debugging Reference Summary, pub. SX33-6038.
CICS/VS Application Programmer's Reference Summary,
    pub. GX33-6037.

INDEX